IPv6 Essentials

Other resources from O'Reilly

Related titles

IPv6 Network Administration	Cisco Cookbook™
TCP/IP Network Administration	BGP
	Essential SNMP
Cisco IOS in a Nutshell	JUNOS Cookbook™

oreilly.com

oreilly.com is more than a complete catalog of O'Reilly books. You'll also find links to news, events, articles, weblogs, sample chapters, and code examples.

oreillynet.com is the essential portal for developers interested in open and emerging technologies, including new platforms, programming languages, and operating systems.

Conferences

O'Reilly brings diverse innovators together to nurture the ideas that spark revolutionary industries. We specialize in documenting the latest tools and systems, translating the innovator's knowledge into useful skills for those in the trenches. Visit *conferences.oreilly.com* for our upcoming events.

Safari Bookshelf (*safari.oreilly.com*) is the premier online reference library for programmers and IT professionals. Conduct searches across more than 1,000 books. Subscribers can zero in on answers to time-critical questions in a matter of seconds. Read the books on your Bookshelf from cover to cover or simply flip to the page you need. Try it today for free.

SECOND EDITION

IPv6 Essentials

Silvia Hagen

O'REILLY®

Beijing · Cambridge · Farnham · Köln · Paris · Sebastopol · Taipei · Tokyo

IPv6 Essentials, Second Edition
by Silvia Hagen

Copyright © 2006, 2002 O'Reilly Media, Inc. All rights reserved.
Printed in the United States of America.

Published by O'Reilly Media, Inc., 1005 Gravenstein Highway North, Sebastopol, CA 95472.

O'Reilly books may be purchased for educational, business, or sales promotional use. Online editions are also available for most titles (*safari.oreilly.com*). For more information, contact our corporate/institutional sales department: (800) 998-9938 or *corporate@oreilly.com*.

Editor: Tatiana Apandi and Mike Loukides	**Indexer:** John Bickelhaupt
Production Editors: Reba Libby and Genevieve d'Entremont	**Cover Designer:** Hanna Dyer
Copyeditor: Reba Libby	**Interior Designer:** David Futato
Proofreader: Genevieve d'Entremont	**Illustrators:** Robert Romano and Jessamyn Read

Printing History:

May 2006:	Second Edition.
July 2002:	First Edition.

Nutshell Handbook, the Nutshell Handbook logo, and the O'Reilly logo are registered trademarks of O'Reilly Media, Inc. *IPv6 Essentials*, the image of a rigatella snail, and related trade dress are trademarks of O'Reilly Media, Inc.

Many of the designations used by manufacturers and sellers to distinguish their products are claimed as trademarks. Where those designations appear in this book, and O'Reilly Media, Inc. was aware of a trademark claim, the designations have been printed in caps or initial caps.

While every precaution has been taken in the preparation of this book, the publisher and author(s) assume no responsibility for errors or omissions, or for damages resulting from the use of the information contained herein.

 This book uses RepKover™, a durable and flexible lay-flat binding.

ISBN: 0-596-10058-2
ISBN13: 978-0-596-10058-2
[M]

Table of Contents

Preface

This book is about the next generation Internet protocol. We have become familiar with the strengths and weaknesses of IPv4; we know how to design and configure it, and we have learned how to troubleshoot it. And now we have to learn a new protocol? Start from scratch? Not really. The designers of IPv6 have learned a lot from over 15 years of experience with IPv4, and they have been working on the new protocol since the early 1990s. They retained the strengths of IPv4, extended the address space from 32 bits to 128 bits, and added functionality that is missing in IPv4. They developed transition mechanisms that make IPv4 and IPv6 coexist peacefully and that guarantee a smooth transition between the protocols. In fact, this was one of the major requirements for the development of the new protocol version.

So you do not need to forget what you know about IPv4; many things will feel familiar with IPv6. When you get started, you will discover new features and functionalities that will make your life a lot easier. IPv6 has features that you will need in tomorrow's networks—features that IPv4 does not provide. The day will come when our Personal Digital Assistants (PDAs) and mobile phones have IP addresses. Aside from the fact that the IPv4 address space could never cover the demand for that number of IP addresses, imagine configuring those devices with the means we have today!

One of the coolest features built into IPv6 is the autoconfiguration capability. Haven't we always struggled with IP address assignment? The advent of DHCP made our lives a little easier, but now we need to maintain and troubleshoot the DHCP servers. And when our refrigerator, our PDA, and our TV each have an IP address, will we need a DHCP server at home? Not with autoconfiguration. If you have an IPv6-enabled host, you can plug it into your network, and it will configure automatically for a valid IPv6 address. Internet Control Message Protocol (ICMP), which is a networker's best friend, has become much more powerful with IPv6. Many of the new features of IPv6, such as autoconfiguration, optimized multicast routing and multicast group management, Neighbor Discovery, path MTU discovery, and Mobile IPv6 are based on ICMPv6.

I hope that this book will help you to become familiar with the protocol and provide an easy-to-understand entry point and guide to exploring this new area.

Audience

This book covers a broad range of information about IPv6 and is an excellent resource for anybody who wants to understand or implement the protocol. Whether you are the owner or manager of a company or an IT department; whether you are a system or network administrator, an engineer, or a network designer; or whether you are just generally interested in learning about the important changes with IPv6, this book discusses economic and strategic aspects as well as technical details. I describe interoperability mechanisms and scenarios that ensure a smooth introduction of IPv6. Quick start guides for different operating systems help with the first hands-on steps. If you are a company owner or manager, you will be most interested in Chapters 1 and 10. If you need to plan your corporate network strategy, you will be most interested in Chapters 1, 4, 8, 9, and 10. If you manage the infrastructure in your company, you will especially be interested in Chapters 4, 7, and 8, which cover ICMPv6, Layer 2 issues and routing, and in Chapter 10, which addresses interoperability. If you are a system or network administrator, all chapters are relevant: this book provides a foundation for IPv6 implementation and integration with IPv4.

About This Book

This book covers IPv6 in detail and explains all the new features and functions. It will show you how to plan for, design, and integrate IPv6 in your current IPv4 infrastructure. It also teaches you what you need to know to get started, to configure IPv6 on your hosts and routers, and to find the right applications that support IPv6.

Now that you know what this book is about, I should explain this this book is not written for developers. This doesn't mean you should not be reading it if you are a developer. If you do read it, you will understand the implications of introducing IPv6 in your network and how important it is to develop cool applications for IPv6. If you need a specific guide to developing for IPv6, look for developer resources.

This book assumes that you have a good understanding of network issues in general and a familiarity with IPv4. It is beyond the scope of this book to discuss IPv4 concepts in detail. I refer to them when necessary, but if you want to learn more about IPv4, there are a lot of good resources on the market. You can find a list of books in Appendix C.

Organization

This book is organized so that a reader familiar with IPv4 can easily learn about the new features in IPv6 by reading Chapters 2 through 6. These chapters cover what you need to know about addressing, the new IPv6 header, ICMPv6, security, and Quality of Service (QoS). Chapters 7 through 11 cover topics such as networking aspects, support of different link-layer services, routing, upper layer protocol support, the transition mechanisms that make IPv6 interoperable with IPv4, and Mobile IPv6. Chapter 12 is a quick-start guide and includes a short description of how different operating systems are configured for IPv6. Here is a chapter-by-chapter breakdown of the book:

- Chapter 1, *Why IPv6?*, briefly explains the history of IPv6 and gives an overview of the new functionality. It draws a bigger picture of Internet and service evolution, showing that the large address space and the advanced functionality of IPv6 are much needed for different reasons. It then discusses the most common misconceptions that prevent people from exploring and integrating the protocol, and provides a summary of the most important steps to undertake today, along with a picture of what is happening around the world.

- Chapter 2, *The Structure of the IPv6 Protocol*, describes the new IPv6 header format with a discussion of each field and trace file examples. It also describes what Extension headers are, what types of Extension headers have been defined, and how they are used.

- Chapter 3, *IPv6 Addressing*, explains everything you need to know about the new address format, address notation, address types, international registry services, and prefix allocation.

- Chapter 4, *ICMPv6*, describes the new ICMPv6 message format, the ICMPv6 Error messages and Informational messages, and the ICMPv6 header in the trace file. This chapter also discusses the extended functionality based on ICMPv6, such as Neighbor Discovery, Autoconfiguration, Path MTU Discovery, and Multicast Listener Discovery (MLD). You will learn how ICMPv6 makes an administrator's life easier.

- Chapter 5, *Security with IPv6*, begins with a short discussion of basic security concepts and requirements. It then covers the IPsec framework, security elements available in IPv6 for authentication and encryption, and how they are used. Our future networks will require new security architectures. This chapter includes a description of a new model.

- Chapter 6, *Quality of Service*, discusses basic requirements and types of QoS. I explain the QoS elements available in IPv6 and how they can be implemented. I also describe different QoS architectures and introduce further work in this area.

- Chapter 7, *Networking Aspects*, discusses Layer 2 support for IPv6 (Ethernet, Token Ring, ATM, frame relay, etc.), the mapping of multicast addresses to Layer 2 addresses, and the Detecting Network Attachment (DNA) working group.

- Chapter 8, *Routing Protocols*, discusses the advanced routing features of IPv6 and covers the available routing protocols such as RIPng, OSPFv3 for IPv6, and BGP extensions for IPv6, IS-IS, and EIGRPv6. (This chapter was written by Stefan Marzohl.)

- Chapter 9, *Upper-Layer Protocols*, discusses what is going on above the IP layer, starting with changes for TCP and UDP, continuing with a detailed discussion of the DHCPv6 specification, DNS extensions for IPv6, SLPv2 in IPv6 networks, FTP, Telnet, and web servers.

- Chapter 10, *Interoperability*, discusses the different transition mechanisms that have been defined, such as dual-stack operation, tunneling, and translation techniques. It also shows how they can be used and combined to ensure peaceful coexistence and smooth transition. A broad variety of case studies show that IPv6 is mature enough to be introduced and that there are many ways to do this. It also provides an overview of what is still missing, security and application aspects, vendor status, and the cost of introduction.

- Chapter 11, *Mobile IPv6*, covers Mobile IPv6. This chapter explains why this technology will become the foundation for a new generation of mobile services.

- Chapter 12, *Get Your Hands Dirty*, explains how to get started with IPv6 on different operating systems, such as Sun Solaris, Linux, BSD, Windows 2003, Windows XP, Mac OS, and a Cisco router. It introduces the most common IPv6 tools available for each operating system. This chapter also explains what I did in my lab and provides examples of trace files.

- Appendix A, *RFCs*, includes a short introduction to the RFC process and authorities, and provides a list of relevant RFCs for IPv6.

- Appendix B, *IPv6 Resources*, reflects the chapter organization of the book and provides summaries of all indexes, protocol numbers, message types, and address allocations.

- Appendix C, *Recommended Reading*, provides a list of books that I recommend.

Some important topics and information appear in multiple places in the book. This is not because I want to bore you, but because I assume that most readers will not read the book from the first page to the last page, but rather will pick and choose chapters and sections depending on interest. So if the information is important with regard to different sections and contexts, I may mention it again.

Conventions Used in This Book

I use the following font conventions in this book:

Italic
> Used to indicate commands, directory paths, filenames, and URLs.

`Constant width`
> Used to indicate IP and MAC addresses, command-line utilities and tools, interfaces, and flags.

Constant width italic
> Used in code examples to show sample text to be replaced with your own values.

Constant width bold
> Used to highlight portions of code, typically new additions to old code.

Using Code Examples

This book is here to help you get your job done. In general, you may use the code in this book in your programs and documentation. You do not need to contact us for permission unless you're reproducing a significant portion of the code. For example, writing a program that uses several chunks of code from this book does not require permission. Selling or distributing a CD-ROM of examples from O'Reilly books *does* require permission. Answering a question by citing this book and quoting example code does not require permission. Incorporating a significant amount of example code from this book into your product's documentation *does* require permission.

We appreciate, but do not require, attribution. An attribution usually includes the title, author, publisher, and ISBN. For example: "*IPv6 Essentials*, Second Edition, by Silvia Hagen. Copyright 2006 O'Reilly Media, Inc., 0-596-10058-2."

Safari® Enabled

 When you see a Safari® enabled icon on the cover of your favorite technology book, that means the book is available online through the O'Reilly Network Safari Bookshelf.

Safari offers a solution that's better than e-Books. It's a virtual library that lets you easily search thousands of top tech books, cut and paste code samples, download chapters, and find quick answers when you need the most accurate, current information. Try it for free at *http://safari.oreilly.com*.

Comments and Questions

Please address comments and questions concerning this book to the publisher:

> O'Reilly Media, Inc.
> 1005 Gravenstein Highway North
> Sebastopol, CA 95472
> (800) 998-9938 (in the United States or Canada)
> (707) 829-0515 (international or local)
> (707) 829-0104 (fax)

This book's web site lists errata, examples, or any additional information. You can access this page at:

http://www.oreilly.com/catalog/ipv6ess2

To comment or ask technical questions about this book, send email to:

bookquestions@oreilly.com

For more information about books, conferences, Resource Centers, and the O'Reilly Network, see the O'Reilly web site at:

http://www.oreilly.com/

Acknowledgments

There are many people all over the world who have contributed to this book. Without their help and input, it would not be what it is. Big thanks go to Stefan Marzohl, who is a Cisco- and Nortel-certified instructor and the author of Chapter 8. He wrote the chapter for the first edition and made all the updates and additions for the second edition. Many thanks go out to Anja Spittler (Maggy). She spent hours, days, and weeks in our lab setting up SuSE Linux, getting BIND and other services to work, and writing parts of Chapters 9 and 12 in the first edition. I also want to thank the technical editors, who have made this book much better with their invaluable comments, corrections, and clarifications. They were great resources when I was struggling with a topic and needed some answers. The technical reviewers of the first edition were Patrick Grossetete, who works as a product manager for the Internet Technology Division (ITD) at Cisco, and Neil Cashell, who is a great TCP/IP guy at Novell. Thanks also to Brian McGehee, who has been working with IPv6 for many years and has written numerous courses for IPv6. He did the final technical edits of the first edition and added a lot of useful information. I'd like to thank Cisco Switzerland, especially René Räber, both for providing an updated router and access to their technical resources as well as for his continuing support of my work for IPv6. Thanks to the guys at SuSE for providing software and supporting us in getting our SuSE host ready for IPv6, Microsoft for providing software and information about their implementations, Network General for providing Sniffer Pro Software for the trace files, Bob Fink for running the 6Bone web site, Cricket Liu for answering my DNS questions, and Peter Bieringer for running a great Internet resource site and for answering my questions with lightning speed.

There were many additional supporters, writers, and reviewers for the second edition. They include: Jim Bound from HP, CTO of the IPv6 Forum and Chair of the NAv6TF; Latif Ladid, President of the IPv6 Forum; Tim Chown, Department of Electronics and Computer Science at the University of Southampton; and Vijayabhaskar from McAfee. Yurie Rich, John Spence, and Mike Owen from Native6 Inc. in Seattle have provided substantial input into Chapters 1, 5, 6, and 10. Gene Cronk from the Robin Shepherd Group has given substantial input into Chapters 5 and 10, and John Jason Brzozowski, North American IPv6 Task Force and Chair of the Mid-Atlantic IPv6 Task Force, contributed great input into Chapters 1 and 9. Thanks to David B. Green from SRI International for the permission to quote his Enterprise Security Model presentation in Chapter 5 and for reviewing different parts of the book. Thanks to Merike Kaeo, Chief Network Security Architect at Double Shot Security, for all her inputs and comments to Chapter 5. And thanks to Chris Engdahl from Microsoft for his review of Chapter 10. Thanks to Jimmy Ott from Sunny Connection for researching and writing all updates for Chapter 12. David Malone, author of the companion book *IPv6 Network Administration*, reviewed the whole book—thank you, David, for your great and clarifying comments. A great thank you goes out to all the people who were ready to share their experience with us and have provided case studies. They are Paolo Vieira from the University of Porto, Pierre David from the University of Strasbourg, Cody Christman from NTT Communications, and Flavio Curti and Ueli Heuer from Cyberlink AG in Zurich. Wolfgang Fritsche from IABG Germany and Karim El-Malki from Ericsson AB in Stockholm reviewed and provided input on Chapter 11 about Mobility. Thanks to the people at Checkpoint for providing information and connections, especially Patrik Honegger and Yoni Appel; and thanks also to Jean-Marc Uzé at Juniper for his information and connections. I also want to thank all the people and developers in the international working groups. Without their visionary power, enthusiasm, and tireless work, we would not have IPv6 ready.

A special thank you goes to Jim Sumser, Mike Loukides, and Tatiana Apandi at O'Reilly. Jim Sumser guided me through the whole writing process of the first edition with a lot of enthusiasm, patience, and experience. Thank you, Jim, for being there, and thank you for never hassling me when I was already struggling. You made a difference! Mike and Tatiana, with whom I worked on the second edition, have also been very supportive throughout the whole process. I also want to thank all the other folks at O'Reilly who contributed to this book, especially Tim O'Reilly for making it possible in the first place.

Another very special thank you goes to Hanspeter Bütler, who was my teacher back in school, for teaching me the beauty of the ancient Greek language. His insightful and sensitive way of guiding me into understanding and feeling the richness of old languages laid the foundation for my understanding of language in general, of different cultures and how the differences in viewing the world are expressed in language. I can probably make him partially responsible for my becoming an author. Language is made to communicate, and the more precisely we use our language, the better we can understand and be understood. Without communication, there can be no understanding. On a different level, TCP/IP is the protocol that enables communication in the network and therefore creates the foundation for Internet communication. And the Internet creates the physical foundation for global communication. It offers a great opportunity to communicate, share, and understand globally across all cultures. That is how we should be using it.

CHAPTER 1

Why IPv6?

The IP version currently used in networks and the Internet is IP Version 4 (IPv4). IPv4 was developed in the early '70s to facilitate communication and information sharing between government researchers and academics in the United States. At the time, the system was closed with a limited number of access points, and consequently the developers didn't envision requirements such as security or quality of service. To its credit, IPv4 has survived for over 30 years and has been an integral part of the Internet revolution. But even the most cleverly designed systems age and eventually become obsolete. This is certainly the case for IPv4. Today's networking requirements extend far beyond support for web pages and email. Explosive growth in network device diversity and mobile communications, along with global adoption of networking technologies, are overwhelming IPv4 and have driven the development of a next-generation Internet Protocol.

IPv6 has been developed based on the rich experience we have from developing and using IPv4. Proven and established mechanisms have been retained, known limitations have been discarded, and scalability and flexibility have been extended. IPv6 is a protocol designed to handle the growth rate of the Internet and to cope with the demanding requirements on services, mobility, and end-to-end security.

When the Internet was switched from using Network Control Protocol (NCP) to Internet Protocol (IP) in one day in 1983, IP was not the mature protocol that we know today. Many of the well-known and commonly used extensions were developed in subsequent years to meet the growing requirements of the Internet. In comparison, hardware vendors and operating system providers have been supporting IPv6 since 1995 when it became a Draft Standard. In the decade since then, those implementations have matured, and IPv6 support has spread beyond the basic network infrastructure and will continue to be extended.

There is certainly a need for caution when considering adoption of IPv6—there is still work to be done to reach parity with the maturity of IPv4 (refer to Chapter 10 for more details). The missing pieces of IPv6 will be developed in the coming years, just the way it happened with IPv4. And many enterprises are not finding enough reasons to adopt it right now. However, it is very important for organizations to pay attention to the introduction of IPv6 because its use is inevitable in the long term. If IPv6 is included in strategic planning; if organizations think about possible integration scenarios ahead of time; and if its introduction is considered when investing in IT capital expenditures, organizations can save considerable cost and can enable IPv6 more efficiently when it is needed.

An interesting and humorous overview of the history of the Internet can be found in RFC 2235, "Hobbes' Internet Timeline." The account starts in 1957 with the launch of Sputnik in Russia and the formation of the Advanced Research Projects Agency (ARPA) by the Department of Defense (DoD) in the United States. The RFC contains a list of yearly growth rate of hosts, networks, and domain registrations in the Internet.

Some excerpts from the RFC:

- 1969: Steve Crocker makes the first Request for Comment (RFC 1): "Host Software."
- 1970: ARPANET hosts start using Network Control Protocol (NCP).
- 1971: 23 hosts connect with ARPANET (UCLA, SRI, UCSB, University of Utah, BBN, MIT, RAND, SDC, Harvard, Lincoln Lab, Stanford, UIU(C), CWRU, CMU, NASA/Ames).
- 1972: InterNetworking Working Group (INWG) is created with Vinton Cerf as Chairman to address the need for establishing agreed-upon protocols. Telnet specification (RFC 318) is published.
- 1973: First international connections to the ARPANET are made at the University College of London (England) and Royal Radar Establishment (Norway). Bob Metcalfe's Harvard Ph.D. thesis outlines the idea for Ethernet. File transfer specification (RFC 454) is published.
- 1976: Queen Elizabeth II sends an email.
- 1981: Minitel (Teletel) is deployed across France by France Telecom.
- 1983: The cutover from NCP to TCP/IP happens on January 1.
- 1984: The number of hosts breaks 1,000.
- 1987: An email link is established between Germany and China using CSNET protocols, with the first message from China sent on September 20. The thousandth RFC is published. The number of hosts breaks 10,000.
- 1988: An Internet worm burrows through the Net, affecting 10 percent of the 60,000 hosts on the Internet.
- 1989: The number of hosts breaks 100,000. Clifford Stoll writes *Cuckoo's Egg*, which tells the real-life tale of a German cracker group that infiltrated numerous U.S. facilities.

- 1991: The World Wide Web (WWW) is developed by Tim Berners-Lee and released by CERN.
- 1992: The number of hosts breaks 1,000,000. The World Bank comes online.
- 1993:The White House comes online during President Bill Clinton's time in office. Worms of a new kind find their way around the Net—WWW Worms (W4) are joined by Spiders, Wanderers, Crawlers, and Snakes.
- 1994: Internet shopping is introduced; the first spam mail is sent; Pizza Hut comes online.
- 1995: The Vatican comes online. Registration of domain names is no longer free.
- 1996: 9,272 organizations find themselves unlisted after the InterNIC drops their name service as a result of their not having paid their domain name fees.
- 1997: The 2,000th RFC is published.

This is as far as the RFC goes. But history goes on. According to *http://www.nua.ie/ surveys/how_many_online/world.html*, the worldwide online population reached 254 million users in 2000 and 580 million users in 2002. According to *http://www. clickz.com/stats/web_worldwide,* the online user population reached 1.08 billion users in 2005. In 2003, the U.S. Department of Defense (DoD) announced that they would be migrating the DoD network to IPv6 by 2008, and the Moonv6 (*http:// www.moonv6.com*) project was started. In 2005, Google registered a /32 IPv6 prefix, and Vint Cerf, known as "Father of the Internet," joined Google. These are just a few selected events and milestones of the Internet's history. Keep watching as more history unfolds.

The History of IPv6

The Internet Engineering Task Force (IETF) began the effort to develop a successor protocol to IPv4 in the early 1990s. Several parallel efforts to solve the foreseen address space limitation and to provide additional functionality began simultaneously. The IETF started the Internet Protocol—Next Generation (IPng) area in 1993 to investigate the different proposals and to make recommendations for further procedures.

The IPng area directors of the IETF recommended the creation of IPv6 at the Toronto IETF meeting in 1994. Their recommendation is specified in RFC 1752, "The Recommendation for the IP Next Generation Protocol." The Directors formed an Address Lifetime Expectation (ALE) working group to determine whether the expected lifetime for IPv4 would allow the development of a protocol with new functionality, or if the remaining time would allow only the development of an address space solution. In 1994, the ALE working group projected that the IPv4 address exhaustion would occur sometime between 2005 and 2011 based on the available statistics.

For those of you who are interested in the different proposals, here's some more information about the process (from RFC 1752). There were four main proposals: CNAT, IP Encaps, Nimrod, and Simple CLNP. Three more proposals followed: the P Internet Protocol (PIP), the Simple Internet Protocol (SIP), and TP/IX. After the March 1992 San Diego IETF meeting, Simple CLNP evolved into TCP and UDP with Bigger Addresses (TUBA), and IP Encaps became IP Address Encapsulation (IPAE). IPAE merged with PIP and SIP and called itself Simple Internet Protocol Plus (SIPP). The TP/IX working group changed its name to Common Architecture for the Internet (CATNIP). The main proposals were now CATNIP, TUBA, and SIPP. For a short discussion of the proposals, refer to RFC 1752.

 CATNIP is specified in RFC 1707; TUBA in RFCs 1347, 1526, and 1561; and SIPP in RFC 1710.

The Internet Engineering Steering Group approved the IPv6 recommendation and drafted a Proposed Standard on November 17, 1994. RFC 1883, "Internet Protocol, Version 6 (IPv6) Specification," was published in 1995. The core set of IPv6 protocols became an IETF Draft Standard on August 10, 1998. This included RFC 2460, which obsoleted RFC 1883.

 Why isn't the new protocol called IPv5? The version number 5 could not be used, because it had been allocated to the experimental stream protocol.

What's New in IPv6?

IPv6 is an evolution of IPv4. The protocol is installed as a software upgrade in most devices and operating systems. If you buy up-to-date hardware and operating systems, IPv6 is usually supported and needs only activation or configuration. Currently available transition mechanisms allow the step-by-step introduction of IPv6 without putting the current IPv4 infrastructure at risk.

Here is an overview of the main changes:

Extended address space
> The address format is extended from 32 bits to 128 bits. This provides an IP address for every grain of sand on the planet. In addition, it also allows for hierarchical structuring of the address space in favor of optimized global routing.

Autoconfiguration
> Perhaps the most intriguing new feature of IPv6 is its *Stateless autoconfiguration* mechanism. When a booting device in the IPv6 world comes up and asks for its network prefix, it can get one or more network prefixes from an IPv6 router on its link. Using this prefix information, it can autoconfigure for one or more valid

global IP addresses by using either its MAC identifier or a private random number to build a unique IP address. In the IPv4 world, we have to assign a unique IP address to every device, either by manual configuration or by using DHCP. Stateless autoconfiguration should make the lives of network managers easier and save substantial cost in maintaining IP networks. Furthermore, if we imagine the number of devices we may have in our homes in the future that will need an IP address, this feature becomes indispensable. Imagine reconfiguring your DHCP server at home when you buy a new television! Stateless autoconfiguration also allows for easy connection of mobile devices, such as a mobile phone or handheld, when moving to foreign networks.

Simplification of header format
    The IPv6 header is much simpler than the IPv4 header and has a fixed length of 40 bytes. This allows for faster processing. It basically accommodates two times 16 bytes for the Source and Destination address and only 8 bytes for general header information.

Improved support for options and extensions
    IPv4 integrates options in the base header, whereas IPv6 carries options in so-called *extension headers*, which are inserted only if they're needed. Again, this allows for faster processing of packets. The base specification describes a set of six extension headers, including headers for routing, Mobile IPv6, and quality of service and security.

Why Do We Need IPv6?

For historic reasons, organizations and government agencies in the United States use approximately 60 percent of the allocatable IPv4 address space. The remaining 40 percent is shared by the rest of the world. Of the 6.4 billion people in the world, approximately 330 million live in North America, 807 million in Europe, and 3.6 billion in Asia. This means that the 5 percent of the world's population living in the United States has 60 percent of the address space allocated. Of the 3.6 billion people living in Asia, approximately 364 million have Internet access, and the growth rate is exponential. This is one explanation of why the deployment of IPv6 in Asia is much more common than in Europe and the United States. (All statistics are based on 2005 numbers.)

 An interesting resource site for statistics can be found at: *http://www.internetworldstats.com/stats.htm.*

The IPv4 address space has a theoretical limit of 4.3 billion addresses. However, early distribution methods allocated addresses inefficiently. Consequently, some organizations obtained address blocks much larger than they needed, and addresses

IPv6 backbone networks and innovative services that leverage many of the beneficial features of IPv6. India, with a growing middle class and a strong presence in the world of IT, has demonstrated substantial interest in the deployment and use of IPv6. In June 2003 and then again in July 2005, the U.S. government mandated the adoption of IPv6. Other countries such as Australia, Taiwan, Singapore, England, and Egypt have all made similar announcements. So IPv6 is on its way, and it happened faster than we expected when we published the first edition of this book.

There still remain some questions about the value of IPv6 to the enterprise, and it is worth conceding that each organization needs to evaluate the benefits of IPv6 carefully for their own internal use and determine the best time for its introduction. In many instances, organizations can find clever ways to use IPv6 to solve "pain" issues without migrating their entire network. Adoption can occur in an incremental fashion with a plan that minimizes integration pain but also ensures that everything is ready when the time comes to "flip the switch." As the case studies in Chapter 10 show, well-planned introduction costs less than you would expect; the step-by-step introduction allows you to learn as you go, thereby saving a lot of money and headaches, and you can do it without putting the current IPv4 infrastructure at risk.

But with all these thoughts and considerations, let's not forget the most essential advantage of IPv6. With its new structure and extensions, IPv6 provides the foundation for a new generation of services. There will be devices and services on the market in the near future that cannot be developed with IPv4. This opens up new markets and business opportunities for vendors and service providers alike. The first-mover opportunities are substantial, as are the opportunities to extend current product lifecycles by refreshing their technology with IPv6. On the other hand, it means that organizations and users will require such services in the mid-term. It is therefore advisable to integrate the new protocol carefully and in a nondisruptive manner, by taking one step at a time to prepare the infrastructure for these new services. This protects you from having to introduce a business-critical application based on IPv6 with no time for thorough planning and unreasonably high cost.

Common Misconceptions

When considering all these advantages, maybe the question should be: "Why not IPv6?" When talking to customers, we often find that they share a similar set of misconceptions preventing them from considering IPv6. Here are the most common ones:

"The introduction of IPv6 puts our current IP infrastructure—our networks and services—at risk."

This concern is unsubstantiated. A major focus in IPv6's development was to create integration mechanisms that allow both protocols to coexist peacefully. You can use IPv6 both in tandem with and independently of IPv4. It is possible to introduce IPv6 and use it for access to new services while retaining IPv4 to access legacy services. This not only ensures undisrupted access to IPv4 services, but it also allows a step-by-step introduction of IPv6. I discuss these mechanisms in Chapter 10.

"The IPv6 protocol is immature and hasn't proven that it stands the test of time or whether it is capable of handling the requirements."

This is only partially true. IPv6 has been implemented in most router and operating systems for almost a decade, and has been tested and optimized extensively. There are substantial international research efforts and test networks for deployment that are further optimizing integration methods. One of the largest tests currently running is Moonv6 (*http://www.moonv6.com*). Moonv6 is a test network where the U.S. Department of Defense (DoD), IPv6 developers and vendors, and various academic and industry bodies conduct extensive interoperability and conformance testing of the IPv6 base features, as well as extended features such as quality of service, mobility, and security. You can find a more detailed description of Moonv6 in Chapter 10.

"The costs of introducing IPv6 are too high."

There will certainly be costs associated with adopting IPv6. In many cases, newer networks will find that the level of IPv6 support in their current infrastructure is actually high. Regardless, the transition will necessitate some hardware and software costs. Organizations will need to train their IT staff, and, depending on the speed at which integration must occur, they may need to seek outside expertise.

However, the cost savings associated with IPv6 are becoming easier to define. Networks based on IPv4 are becoming increasingly more complex. New IT services such as VoIP, instant messaging, video teleconferencing, IPTV, and unified communications are adding layers of middleware and complexity. Merging organizations or those conducting B2B transactions are implementing NAT overlap solutions that have high management costs and are difficult to troubleshoot. And a growing market of mobile devices and network appliances requires robust access models that are expensive and difficult to implement in an IPv4 world. In all of these cases, IPv6 presents a cleaner and more cost-effective model in the long run than IPv4 can provide.

"With Stateless autoconfiguration, we will not be able to control or monitor network access."

While this statement may generally be true for networks that widely utilize Stateless autoconfiguration, administrators will have a choice about their level of control. DHCPv6 as defined in RFC 3315 has been extended to support two general modes of operation, Stateful and Stateless. *Stateful mode* is what those who currently utilize DHCP (for IPv4) are familiar with, in which a node (DHCP client) requests an IP address and configuration options dynamically from a DHCP server. DHCPv6 also offers a *Stateless mode* in which DHCPv6 clients simply request configuration options from a DHCPv6 server and use other means, such as Stateless autoconfiguration, to obtain an IPv6 address. On the other hand, you can configure IPv6 networks to force the use of DHCPv6 for dynamic address assignment and configure DHCPv6 to enhance security, since authentication is available as part of the protocol.

"Our Internet Service Provider (ISP) does not offer IPv6 services, so we can't use it."
You do not have to wait for your ISP to use IPv6 in your corporate or private network. If you want to connect to the global IPv6 Internet, you can use one of the transition mechanisms and tunnel your IPv6 packets over the IPv4 infrastructure of your ISP.

"It would be too expensive and complex to upgrade our backbone."
The transition mechanisms make it possible to use IPv6 where appropriate without dictating an order of upgrade. Usually for the backbone it is advisable to wait for the regular life cycle, when hardware needs to be exchanged anyway. Make sure to choose hardware that supports performance IPv6 routing. In the meantime, you can tunnel your IPv6 packets over the IPv4 backbone. Networks that use MPLS have an easy way to tunnel IPv6 packets over their IPv4 MPLS backbone. Read more about it in Chapter 10.

"It would be too complex and expensive to port all of our applications to IPv6."
The effort necessary to port applications to run over IPv6 is often much lower than expected. If an application is well-written, it may simply run over IPv6 without modification. Instead of assuming that it won't work, test it to find out. For applications that need modifications that are not yet available, or for applications in which porting does not make sense, there are mechanisms available that support IPv4 applications in IPv6 networks and IPv6 applications in IPv4 networks. Alternatively, you can run a *dual-stack network*, in which you use IPv4 to access IPv4 applications and IPv6 to access IPv6 applications.

"We have enough IPv4 addresses; we don't need IPv6."
True—if you have enough IPv4 addresses, there may be no immediate need to integrate IPv6 today. But ignoring IPv6 for this reason is a perspective that assumes that your network stands completely isolated from the rest of the world, including your vendors, partners, and customers. IPv6 adoption is further along in Asia than in the United States, so even though you may have adequate address space for your operations in Denver, interconnecting with a partner organization in Tokyo may eventually become complicated if you do not support IPv6. Plus, the assumption that IPv6 is about address space only doesn't account for the advanced features that IPv6 brings to the table.

When Is It Time for IPv6?

If the rest of the world moves to IPv6 while you insist on continuing to use IPv4, you will exclude yourself from global communication and reachability. This might not be a critical issue today, but times are changing fast these days. The risks if you wait too long include losing potential customers and access to new markets and the inability to use new IPv6-based business applications until you implement it.

There is a golden rule in IT: "Never touch a running system." As long as your IPv4 infrastructure runs well and fulfills your needs, there is no reason to change anything. But from now on, whenever you invest in your infrastructure, you should consider IPv6. An investment in the new technology gives it a much longer lifetime and keeps your network state-of-the-art.

These are the main indicators that it may be time for you to consider switching to or integrating IPv6:

- You need to extend or fix your IPv4 network or NAT implementation.
- You are running out of address space.
- You want to prepare your network for applications that are based on advanced features of IPv6.
- You need end-to-end security for a large number of users and you do not have the address space, or you struggle with a NAT implementation.
- You need to replace your hardware or applications that are at the end of their lifecycles. Make sure you buy products that support IPv6, even if you don't enable it right away.
- You want to introduce IPv6 while there is no time pressure.

The following provisions can be taken in order to prepare for IPv6 adequately:

- Build internal knowledge, educate IT staff, and create a test network.
- Include IPv6 in your IT strategy.
- Create integration scenarios based on your network and requirements.
- Put IPv6 support on all of your hardware and software shopping lists. Be specific about which features (RFCs) must be supported.
- Compel your vendors to add IPv6 support to their products.

If you do this, you can determine the right moment for the introduction of IPv6 in your network. You can also assess whether a further investment in your IPv4 infrastructure makes sense or whether introducing IPv6 would be a better way to go.

There will be no "flag day" for IPv6 like there was for the 1983 move from NCP to IPv4. Probably there will be no killer application either, so don't wait for one. IPv6 will slowly and gradually grow into our networks and the Internet. Taking a step-by-step approach to IPv6 may be the most cost-efficient way to integrate it, depending on your requirements. This method does not put your current infrastructure at risk or force you to exchange hardware or software before you are ready, and it allows you to become familiar with the protocol, to experiment, to learn, and to integrate what you've learned into your strategy.

The Identification, Flags, and Fragment Offset fields handle fragmentation of a packet in the IPv4 header. *Fragmentation* happens if a large packet has to be sent over a network that supports only smaller packet sizes. In that case, the IPv4 router splits the packet into smaller slices and forwards multiple packets. The destination host collects the packets and reassembles them. If only one packet is missing or has an error, the whole transmission has to be redone; this is very inefficient. In IPv6, a host learns the Path Maximum Transmission Unit (MTU) size through a procedure called *Path MTU Discovery*. If a sending IPv6 host wants to fragment a packet, it will use an Extension header to do so. IPv6 routers along the path of a packet do not provide fragmentation as they did with IPv4. So the Identification, Flags, and Fragment Offset fields were removed from the IPv6 header and will be inserted in an Extension header by the source host if needed. I explain Extension headers later in this chapter.

Path MTU Discovery is explained in Chapter 4.

The Header Checksum field was removed to improve processing speed. If routers do not have to check and update checksums, processing becomes much faster. At the time when IPv4 was developed, checksumming at the media access level wasn't common, so the checksum field in the IPv4 header made sense. Today, the risk for undetected errors and misrouted packets is minimal. There is also a checksum field at the transport layer (UDP and TCP). With IPv4, a UDP checksum is optional; with IPv6, a UDP checksum is mandatory. IP is a *best-effort delivery protocol*; it is the responsibility of upper layer protocols to ensure integrity.

The Traffic Class field replaces the "Type of Service" field. IPv6 has a different mechanism to handle preferences. Refer to Chapter 6 for more information.

The Protocol Type and "Time-to-Live" (TTL) fields were renamed and slightly modified. A Flow Label field was added.

The Fields in the IPv6 Header

By becoming familiar with the fields of the IPv6 header, you will better understand how IPv6 works.

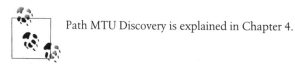

For a detailed description of all the fields in an IPv4 header, refer to *Novell's Guide to Troubleshooting TCP/IP* (Wiley).

Figure 2-1 provides an overview of the IPv6 header. The fields are discussed in detail in the following paragraphs.

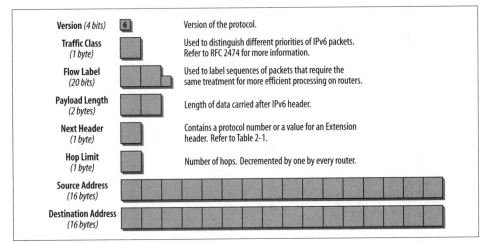

Version *(4 bits)*	Version of the protocol.
Traffic Class *(1 byte)*	Used to distinguish different priorities of IPv6 packets. Refer to RFC 2474 for more information.
Flow Label *(20 bits)*	Used to label sequences of packets that require the same treatment for more efficient processing on routers.
Payload Length *(2 bytes)*	Length of data carried after IPv6 header.
Next Header *(1 byte)*	Contains a protocol number or a value for an Extension header. Refer to Table 2-1.
Hop Limit *(1 byte)*	Number of hops. Decremented by one by every router.
Source Address *(16 bytes)*	
Destination Address *(16 bytes)*	

Figure 2-1. Fields in the IPv6 header

Figure 2-1 shows that even though the header has a total size of 40 bytes, which is twice as long as a default IPv4 header, it has actually been streamlined because most of the header is taken up by the two 16-byte IPv6 addresses. That leaves only 8 bytes for other header information.

Version (4 Bits)

This is a 4-bit field containing the version of the protocol. In the case of IPv6, the number is 6. The version number 5 could not be used because it had already been assigned to the experimental stream protocol.

Traffic Class (1 Byte)

This field replaces the "Type of Service" field in IPv4. It facilitates the handling of real-time data and any other data that requires special handling, and sending nodes and forwarding routers can use it to identify and distinguish between different classes or priorities of IPv6 packets.

RFC 2474, "Definition of the Differentiated Services Field (DS Field) in the IPv4 and IPv6 Headers," explains how the Traffic Class field in IPv6 can be used. RFC 2474 uses the term *DS Field* to refer to the "Type of Service" field in the IPv4 header, as well as to the Traffic Class field in the IPv6 header. Refer to Chapter 6 for more information.

Flow Label (20 Bits)

This field distinguishes packets that require the same treatment in order to facilitate the handling of real-time traffic. A sending host can label sequences of packets with a set of options. Routers keep track of flows and can process packets belonging to the same flow more efficiently because they do not have to reprocess each packet's header. The flow label and address of the source node uniquely identify the flow. Nodes that do not support the functions of the Flow Label field are required to pass the field unchanged when forwarding a packet and to ignore the field when receiving a packet. All packets belonging to the same flow must have the same Source and Destination IP address.

 The use of the Flow Label field is experimental and is currently still under discussion at the IETF at the time of writing. Refer to Chapter 6 for more information.

Payload Length (2 Bytes)

This field specifies the *payload*—i.e., the length of data carried after the IP header. The calculation in IPv6 is different from the one in IPv4. The Length field in IPv4 includes the length of the IPv4 header, whereas the Payload Length field in IPv6 contains only the data following the IPv6 header. Extension headers are considered part of the payload and are therefore included in the calculation.

The fact that the Payload Length field has 2 bytes limits the maximum packet payload size to 64 KB. IPv6 has a *Jumbogram Extension header*, which supports bigger packet sizes if needed. Jumbograms are relevant only when IPv6 nodes are attached to links that have a link MTU greater than 64 KB; they are specified in RFC 2675.

Next Header (1 Byte)

In IPv4, this field is called the Protocol Type field, but it was renamed in IPv6 to reflect the new organization of IP packets. If the next header is UDP or TCP, this field will contain the same protocol numbers as in IPv4—for example, protocol number 6 for TCP or 17 for UDP. But if Extension headers are used with IPv6, this field contains the type of the next Extension header. Extension headers are located between the IP header and the TCP or UDP header. Table 2-1 lists possible values in the Next Header field.

Table 2-1. Values in the Next Header field

Value	Description
0	In an IPv4 header: reserved and not used In an IPv6 header: Hop-by-Hop Option Header following
1	Internet Control Message Protocol (ICMPv4)—IPv4 support
2	Internet Group Management Protocol (IGMPv4)—IPv4 support
4	IPv4
6	TCP
8	Exterior Gateway Protocol (EGP)

Table 2-1. Values in the Next Header field (continued)

Value	Description
9	IGP—any private interior gateway (used by Cisco for their IGRP)
17	UDP
41	IPv6
43	Routing header
44	Fragmentation header
45	Interdomain Routing Protocol (IDRP)
46	Resource Reservation Protocol (RSVP)
47	General Routing Encapsulation (GRE)
50	Encrypted Security Payload header
51	Authentication header
58	ICMPv6
59	No Next Header for IPv6
60	Destination Options header
88	EIGRP
89	OSPF
108	IP Payload Compression Protocol
115	Layer 2 Tunneling Protocol (L2TP)
132	Stream Control Transmission Protocol (SCTP)
135	Mobility Header (Mobile IPv6)
136–254	Unassigned
255	Reserved

Header type numbers derive from the same range of numbers as protocol type numbers, and therefore should not conflict with them.

The complete list of protocol numbers can be found in Appendix B. For the most current list, go to IANA's web site at *http://www.iana.org/assignments/protocol-numbers*.

Hop Limit (1 Byte)

This field is analogous to the TTL field in IPv4. The TTL field contains a number of seconds, indicating how long a packet can remain in the network before being destroyed. In IPv4, most routers simply decrement this value by one at each hop. This field has been renamed Hop Limit in IPv6. The value in this field now expresses a number of hops instead of a number of seconds. Every forwarding node decrements the number by one. If a router receives a packet with a Hop Limit of 1, it decrements it to 0, discards the packet, and sends the ICMPv6 message "Hop Limit exceeded in transit" back to the sender.

Source Address (16 Bytes)

This field contains the IP address of the originator of the packet.

Destination Address (16 Bytes)

This field contains the IP address of the intended recipient of the packet. This can be the ultimate destination or if, for example, a Routing header is present, the address of the next hop router.

Figure 2-2 shows the IPv6 header in the trace file.

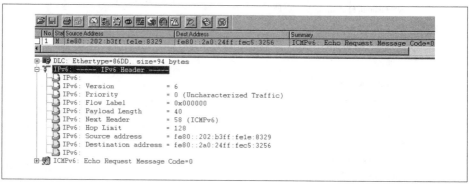

Figure 2-2. The IPv6 header in a trace file

This trace file shows all of the header fields discussed and how they can be presented in a trace file. The Version field is set to 6 for IPv6. The Traffic Class (Priority) and Flow Label fields are not used in this packet and are set to 0. The Payload Length is 40, and the Next Header value is set to 58 for ICMPv6. The Hop Limit is set to 128, and the Source and Destination addresses contain the link local addresses of my IPv6 nodes. The first line in the detail window shows Ethertype 0x86DD. This value indicates that this is an IPv6 packet. For IPv4, the value would be 0x0800. This field can be used to set an analyzer filter for all IPv6 packets.

Analyzer tools can decode packets in different ways. If you use another version or another type of analyzer, your decode may look slightly different. The difference is not in the packet, but in the way the packet is presented in the analyzer.

Extension Headers

The IPv4 header can be extended from a minimum of 20 bytes to a maximum of 60 bytes in order to specify options such as Security Options, Source Routing, or Timestamping. This capacity has rarely been used because it causes a performance hit. For example, IPv4 hardware forwarding implementations have to pass the packet containing options to the main processor (software handling).

The simpler a packet header, the faster the processing is. IPv6 has a new way to deal with options that has substantially improved processing: it handles options in additional headers called *Extension headers*. Extension headers are inserted into a packet only if the options are needed.

The current IPv6 specification (RFC 2460) defines six Extension headers:

- Hop-by-Hop Options header
- Routing header
- Fragment header
- Destination Options header
- Authentication header
- Encrypted Security Payload header

There can be zero, one, or more than one Extension header in an IPv6 packet. Extension headers are placed between the IPv6 header and the upper-layer protocol header. Each Extension header is identified by the Next Header field in the preceding header. The Extension headers are examined or processed only by the node identified in the Destination address field of the IPv6 header. If the address in the Destination address field is a multicast address, the Extension headers are examined and processed by all the nodes belonging to that multicast group. Extension headers must be strictly processed in the order in which they appear in the packet header.

There is one exception to the rule that only the destination node will process an Extension header. If the Extension header is a Hop-by-Hop Options header, the information it carries must be examined and processed by every node along the path of the packet. The Hop-by-Hop Options header, if present, must immediately follow the IPv6 header. It is indicated by the value 0 in the Next Header field of the IPv6 header (see Table 2-1 earlier in this chapter).

 The first four Extension headers are described in RFC 2460. The Authentication header is described in RFC 2402, and the Encrypted Security Payload header in RFC 2406.

This architecture is very flexible for developing additional Extension headers for future uses as needed. New Extension headers can be defined and used without changing the IPv6 header. A good example is the Mobility header defined for Mobile IPv6 (RFC 3775), which is discussed in Chapter 11.

Figure 2-3 shows how Extension headers are used.

Each Extension header's length is a multiple of eight bytes so that subsequent headers can always be aligned. If a node is required to process the next header but cannot

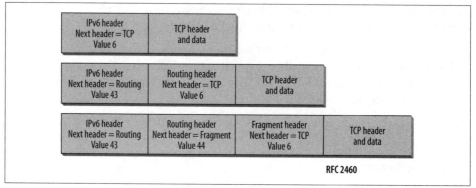

Figure 2-3. The use of Extension headers

identify the value in the Next Header field, it is required to discard the packet and send an ICMPv6 Parameter Problem message back to the source of the packet. (For details on ICMPv6 messages, refer to Chapter 4.)

If more than one Extension header is used in a single packet, the following header order should be used (RFC 2460):

1. IPv6 header
2. Hop-by-Hop Options header
3. Destination Options header (for options to be processed by the first destination that appears in the IPv6 Destination address field, plus subsequent destinations listed in the Routing header)
4. Routing header
5. Fragment header
6. Authentication header
7. Encapsulating Security Payload header
8. Destination Options header (for options to be processed only by the final destination of the packet)
9. Upper-Layer header

In cases when IPv6 is encapsulated in IPv4, the Upper-Layer header can be another IPv6 header and can contain Extension headers that have to follow the same rules.

Hop-by-Hop Options Header

The Hop-by-Hop Options header carries optional information that must be examined by every node along the path of the packet. It must immediately follow the IPv6 header and is indicated by a Next Header value of 0. For example, the Router Alert (RFC 2711) uses the Hop-by-Hop Options header for protocols such as Resource Reservation Protocol (RSVP) or Multicast Listener Discovery (MLD) messages. With

IPv4, the only way for a router to determine whether it needs to examine a datagram is to at least partially parse upper-layer data in all datagrams. This process slows down the routing process substantially. With IPv6, in the absence of a Hop-by-Hop Options header, a router knows that it does not need to process router-specific information and can route the packet immediately to the final destination. If there is a Hop-by-Hop Options header, the router needs only to examine this header and does not have to look further into the packet.

The format of the Hop-by-Hop Options header is shown in Figure 2-4.

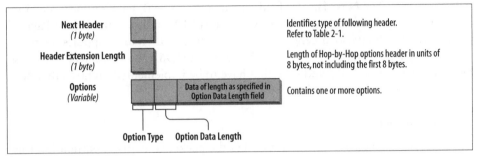

Figure 2-4. Format of the Hop-by-Hop Options header

The following list describes each field:

Next Header (1 byte)
    The Next Header field identifies the type of header that follows the Hop-by-Hop Options header. The Next Header field uses the values listed in Table 2-1, shown earlier in this chapter.

Header Extension Length (1 byte)
    This field identifies the length of the Hop-by-Hop Options header in eight-byte units. The length calculation does not include the first eight bytes. So if the header is shorter than eight bytes, this field contains the value 0.

Options (variable size)
    There can be one or more options. The length of the options is variable and is determined in the Header Extension Length field.

The Option Type Field, the first byte of the Options fields, contains information about how this option must be treated in case the processing node does not recognize the option. The value of the first two bits specifies the actions to be taken:

- 00: Skip and continue processing.
- 01: Discard the packet.
- 10: Discard the packet and send ICMP Parameter Problem, Code 2 message to the packet's Source address pointing to the unrecognized option type.
- 11: Discard the packet and send ICMP Parameter Problem, Code 2 message to the packet's Source address only if the destination is not a multicast address.

The third bit of the Options Type field specifies whether the option information can change en route (value 1) or does not change en route (value 0).

Option Type Jumbogram

This Hop-by-Hop Option Type supports the sending of IPv6 Jumbograms. The IPv6 Payload Length field supports a maximum packet size of 65,535 bytes. The Jumbo Payload Option (RFC 2675) allows for larger packets to be sent.

In the IPv6 header of a packet with the Jumbo Payload option, the Payload Length field is set to 0. The Next Header field contains the value 0, which indicates a Hop-by-Hop Options header. The Option Type value of 194 indicates the Jumbo Payload option. The Jumbo Payload Length field has 32 bits and therefore supports the transmission of packets that are between 65,536 and 4,294,967,295 bytes. RFC 2675 also defines extensions to UDP and TCP that have to be implemented on hosts that need to support the sending of Jumbograms.

Option Router Alert

This option type indicates to the router that the packet contains important information to be processed when forwarding the packet. The option is currently used mostly for MLD (Multicast Listener Discovery) and RSVP (Resource Reservation Protocol). It is specified in RFC 2711.

RSVP uses control packets containing information that needs to be interpreted or updated by routers along the path. These control packets use a Hop-by-Hop Options header, so only routers process the packet. Regular data packets do not have this Extension header and are therefore forwarded immediately without further inspection by the router.

The first 3 bits of the Option Type field are set to 0. A router that doesn't know this option ignores it and forwards the packet. In the remaining 5 bits of the first byte, the option type 5 is specified. The Option Data Length field contains the value 2, which indicates that the following value field has a length of 2 bytes (refer to Figure 2-4). RFC 2711 defines the following values for the value field:

- 0: Packet contains an MLD message
- 1: Packet contains an RSVP message
- 2: Packet contains an Active Networks message
- 3–35: Packet contains an Aggregated Reservation Nesting Level (RFC 3175, RSVP)
- 36–65,535: Reserved by IANA

The list of Router Alert values can be found at *http://www.iana.org/assignments/ipv6-routeralert-values*.

Routing Header

The *Routing header* is used to give a list of one or more intermediate nodes that should be visited on the packet's path to its destination. In the IPv4 world, this is called the "Loose Source and Record Route" option. The Routing header is identified by a Next Header value of 43 in the preceding header. Figure 2-5 shows the format of the Routing header.

Next Header (1 byte)		Identifies type of following header. Refer to Table 2-1.
Header Extension Length (1 byte)		Length of routing header in units of 8 bytes, not including the first 8 bytes.
Routing Type (1 byte)		Identifies type of routing header. Currently type zero defined.
Segments Left (1 byte)		Number of listed nodes until final destination.
Type Specific Data (Variable)		Depends on routing type. For type zero:
	Reserved (4 bytes)	
	Address 1 (16 bytes)	
	Address 2 (16 bytes)	
	Address X (16 bytes)	

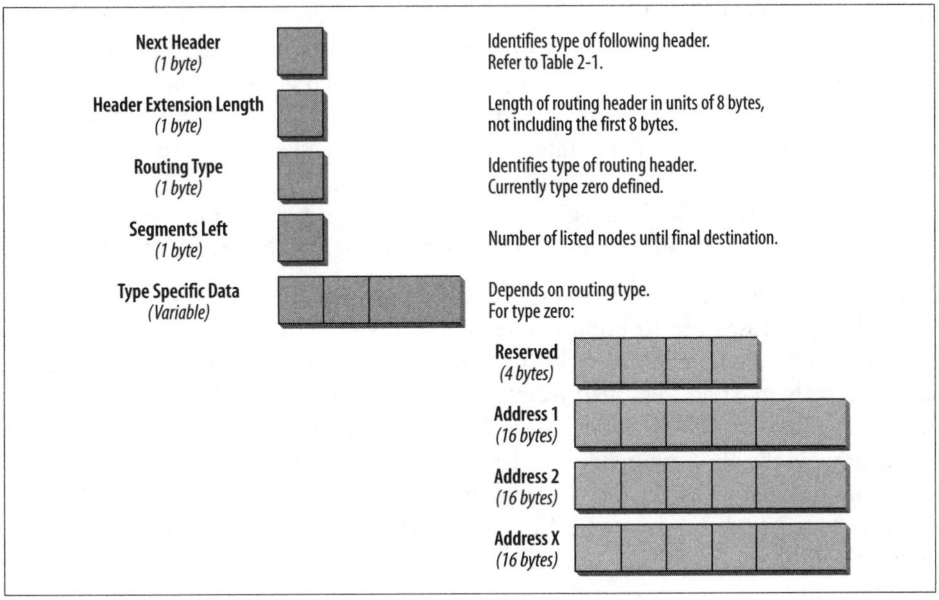

Figure 2-5. Format of the Routing header

The following list describes each field:

Next Header (1 byte)
  The Next Header field identifies the type of header that follows the Routing header. It uses the same values as the IPv4 Protocol Type field (see Table 2-1 earlier in this chapter).

Header Extension Length (1 byte)
  This field identifies the length of the Routing header in 8-byte units. The length calculation does not include the first 8 bytes.

Routing Type (1 byte)

This field identifies the type of Routing header. RFC 2460 describes Routing Type 0. The Mobile IPv6 specification defines a Routing Type 2. (This specification is discussed in Chapter 11.)

Segments Left (1 byte)

This field identifies how many nodes are left to be visited before the packet reaches its final destination.

Type-Specific Data (variable length)

The length of this field depends on the Routing Type. The complete header is always a multiple of 8 bytes.

If a node processing a Routing header cannot identify a Routing Type value, the action taken depends on the content of the Segments Left field. If the Segments Left field does not contain any nodes to be visited, the node must ignore the Routing header and process the next header in the packet, which is determined by the Next Header field's value. If the Segments Left field is not zero, the node must discard the packet and send an ICMP Parameter Problem, Code 0 message to the packet's Source address pointing to the unrecognized Routing Type. If a forwarding node cannot process the packet because the next link MTU size is too small, it discards the packet and sends an ICMP Packet Too Big message back to the source of the packet.

The only Routing Type described in RFC 2460 is a Type 0 Routing header. The first node that processes the Routing header is the node addressed by the Destination address field in the IPv6 header. This node decrements the Segments Left field by one and inserts the next address field from within the Routing header in the IPv6 header Destination address field. Then the packet is forwarded to the next hop that will again process the Routing header as described until the *final destination* is reached. The final destination is the last address in the Routing Header Data field. Refer to Chapter 11 to find out how the Routing header is used for Mobility. Figure 2-6 shows the Routing header in a trace file.

The Next Header field within the IPv6 header shows the value 43 for the Routing header. The Source and Destination addresses have the prefix 2002, which is allocated to 6to4 sites (6to4 is a transition mechanism described in Chapter 10). The Routing header contains the fields discussed earlier in this section. Next Header is ICMPv6, indicated by the value 58. The Header Length contains two 8-byte units, which add up to a total length of 16 bytes (one address). The Segments Left field contains the value 1 because there is one address entry in the Options field. Finally, the Options field lists the addresses to be visited. In this case, there is only one entry. If several hosts are listed here, every *forwarding node* (that is, the destination IP address in the IPv6 header) takes the next entry from this host list, uses it as a new destination IP address in the IPv6 header, decrements the Segments Left field by one, and forwards the packet. This is done until it reaches the last host in the list.

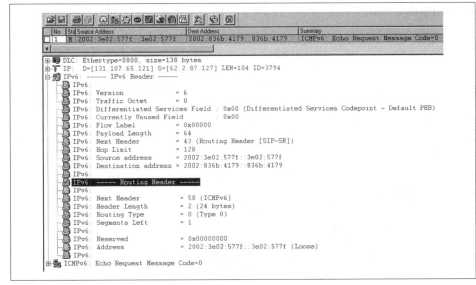

```
        No. St Source Address              Dest Address                Summary
        1   M  2002:3e02:577f::3e02:577f   2002:836b:4179::836b:4179   ICMPv6: Echo Request Message Code=0

      DLC: Ethertype=0800, size=138 bytes
      IP:   D=[131.107.65.121] S=[62.2.87.127] LEN=104 ID=3794
      IPv6: ------ IPv6 Header ------
        IPv6:
        IPv6: Version                  = 6
        IPv6: Traffic Octet            = 0
        IPv6: Differentiated Services Field : 0x00 (Differentiated Services Codepoint - Default PHB)
        IPv6: Currently Unused Field        : 0x00
        IPv6: Flow Label               = 0x00000
        IPv6: Payload Length           = 64
        IPv6: Next Header              = 43 (Routing Header [SIP-SR])
        IPv6: Hop Limit                = 128
        IPv6: Source address           = 2002:3e02:577f::3e02:577f
        IPv6: Destination address      = 2002:836b:4179::836b:4179
        IPv6:
        IPv6: ------ Routing Header ------
        IPv6:
        IPv6: Next Header              = 58 (ICMPv6)
        IPv6: Header Length            = 2 (24 bytes)
        IPv6: Routing Type             = 0 (Type 0)
        IPv6: Segments Left            = 1
        IPv6:
        IPv6: Reserved                 = 0x00000000
        IPv6: Address                  = 2002:3e02:577f::3e02:577f (Loose)
        IPv6:
      ICMPv6: Echo Request Message Code=0
```

Figure 2-6. Routing header in a trace file

A source node S sends a packet to destination node D using a Routing header to send the packet through the intermediate nodes I1, I2, and I3. See the Routing header changes in Table 2-2 (example taken from RFC 2460).

Table 2-2. Processing the Routing header

	IPv6 header	Routing header
Packet from S to I1	Source address S Destination address I1	Segments Left 3 Address (1) = I2 Address (2) = I3 Address (3) = D
Packet from I1 to I2	Source address S Destination address I2	Segments Left 2 Address (1) = I1 Address (2) = I3 Address (3) = D
Packet from I2 to I3	Source address S Destination address I3	Segments Left = 1 Address (1) = I1 Address (2) = I2 Address (3) = D
Packet from I3 to D	Source address S Destination address D	Segments Left = 0 Address (1) = I1 Address (2) = I2 Address (3) = I3

Fragment Header

An IPv6 host that wants to send a packet to an IPv6 destination uses Path MTU discovery to determine the maximum packet size that can be used on the path to that destination. If the packet to be sent is larger than the supported MTU, the source host fragments the packet. Unlike in IPv4, with IPv6 a router along the path does not fragment packets. Fragmentation occurs only at the source host sending the packet. The destination host handles reassembly. A Fragment header is identified by a Next Header value of 44 in the preceding header. The format of the Fragment header is shown in Figure 2-7.

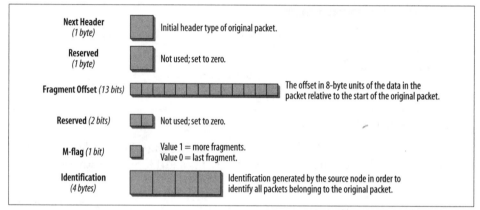

Figure 2-7. Format of the Fragment header

The following list describes each field:

Next Header (1 byte)
> The Next Header field identifies the type of header that follows the Fragment header. It uses the same values as the IPv4 Protocol Type field. (See Table 2-1.)

Reserved (1 byte)
> Not used; set to 0.

Fragment Offset (13 bits)
> The offset in 8-byte units of the data in this packet relative to the start of the data in the original packet.

Reserved (2 bits)
> Not used; set to 0.

M-Flag (1 bit)
> Value 1 indicates more fragments; a value of 0 indicates last fragment.

Identification (4 Bytes)
> Generated by the source host in order to identify all packets belonging to the original packet. This field is usually implemented as a counter, increasing by one for every packet that needs to be fragmented by the source host.

The Fragment header does not contain a Don't Fragment field. It is not necessary, because routers no longer fragment in IPv6. Only the source host can fragment a packet.

The initial unfragmented packet is referred to as the *original packet*. It has an unfragmentable part that consists of the IPv6 header plus any Extension headers that must be processed by nodes along the path to the destination (i.e., Hop-by-Hop Options header). The fragmentable part of the original packet consists of any Extension headers that need only to be processed by the final destination, plus the upper-layer headers and any data. Figure 2-8 (RFC 2460) illustrates the fragmenting process.

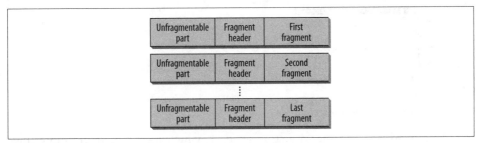

Figure 2-8. Fragmentation with IPv6

The unfragmentable part of the original packet appears in every fragment, followed by the Fragmentation header and then the fragmentable data. The IPv6 header of the original packet has to be slightly modified. The length field reflects the length of the fragment (excluding the IPv6 header) and not the length of the original packet.

The destination node collects all the fragments and reassembles them. The fragments must have identical Source and Destination addresses and the same identification value in order to be reassembled. If all fragments do not arrive at the destination within 60 seconds after the first fragment, the destination will discard all packets. If the destination has received the first fragment (offset = zero), it sends back an ICMPv6 Fragment Reassembly Time Exceeded message to the source.

Figure 2-9 shows a Fragment header.

I created this Fragment header by generating an oversized ping from *Marvin* to *Ford* (Windows to Linux). The whole fragment set consists of two packets, the first of which is shown in Figure 2-9. In the IPv6 header, the Payload Length field has a value of 1456, which is the length of the fragmentation header and this one fragment, not the length of the whole original packet. The Next Header field specifies the value 44, which is the value for the Fragment header. This field is followed by the Hop Limit field and the Source and Destination IP addresses. The first field in the Fragment header is the Next Header field. Because this is a ping, it contains the value 58 for ICMPv6. And because this is the first packet in the fragment set, the value in

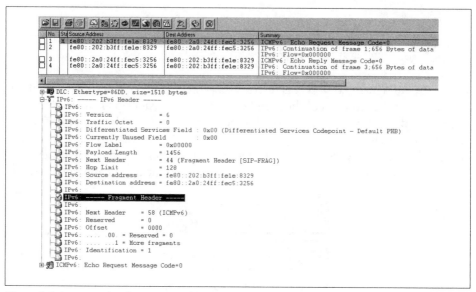

Figure 2-9. Fragment header in a trace file

the Offset field is 0 and the M-Flag is set to 1, which means there are more fragments to come. The Identification field is set to 1 and has to be identical in all packets belonging to this fragment set. Figure 2-10 shows the second packet of the fragment set.

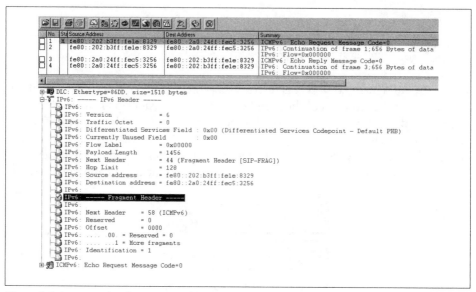

Figure 2-10. The second and last packet in the fragment set

The second and last packet of this fragment set has an Offset value of 0x05A8, which translates to 1448 in decimal notation, the length of the first fragment. The M-Flag is set to 0, which indicates that it is the last packet and tells the receiving host that it is time to reassemble the fragments. The Identification field is set to 1 in both packets.

Destination Options Header

A *Destination Options* header carries optional information that is examined by the destination node only (the Destination address in the IPv6 header). A Next Header value of 60 identifies this type of header. As mentioned previously, the Destination Options header can appear twice in an IPv6 packet. When inserted before a Routing header, it contains information to be processed by the routers listed in the Routing header. When inserted before the upper-layer protocol headers, it contains information for the final destination of the packet. Figure 2-11 shows the format of the Destination Options header.

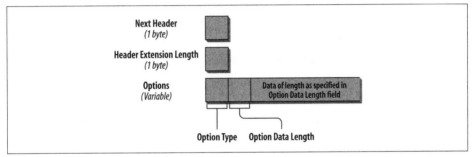

Figure 2-11. Format of the Destination Options header

As you can see, the format is similar to the format of the Hop-by-Hop Options header. The following list describes each field:

Next Header (1 byte)
> The Next Header field identifies the type of header that follows the Destination Options header. It uses the same values listed in Table 2-1, shown earlier in this chapter.

Header Extension Length (1 byte)
> This field identifies the length of the Destination Options header in 8-byte units. The length calculation does not include the first 8 bytes.

Options (variable size)
> There can be one or more options. The length of the options is variable and is determined in the Header Extension Length field.

The Options field is used in the same way as the Hop-by-Hop Options header, which I discussed earlier in this chapter. An example of the use of the Destination Options header is Mobile IPv6. You can find a detailed description of Mobile IPv6 in Chapter 11.

Now that you understand the IPv6 header, read Chapter 3, which describes the IPv6 addressing architecture.

References

The following is a list of the most important RFCs and drafts mentioned in this chapter. Sometimes I include additional subject-related RFCs for your personal further study.

- RFC 791, "Internet Protocol," 1981
- RFC 1812, "Requirements for IP Version 4 Routers," 1995
- RFC 1819, "Internet Stream Protocol Version 2," 1995
- RFC 1981, "Path MTU Discovery for IP version 6," 1996
- RFC 2401, "Security Architecture for the Internet Protocol," 1998
- RFC 2402, "IP Authentication Header," 1998
- RFC 2406, "IP Encapsulating Security Payload (ESP)," 1998
- RFC 2460, "Internet Protocol, Version 6 (IPv6) Specification," 1998
- RFC 2473, "Generic Packet Tunneling in IPv6 Specification," 1998
- RFC 2474, "Definition of the Differentiated Services Field (DS Field)," 1998
- RFC 2475, "An Architecture for Differentiated Services," 1998
- RFC 2507, "IP Header Compression," 1999
- RFC 2675, "IPv6 Jumbograms," 1999
- RFC 2711, "IPv6 Router Alert Option," 1999
- RFC 3175, "Aggregation of RSVP for IPv4 and IPv6 Reservations," 2001
- RFC 3514, "The Security Flag in the IPv4 Header," April 1, 2003

CHAPTER 3

IPv6 Addressing

An IPv4 address has 32 bits and looks familiar. An IPv6 address has 128 bits and looks wild at first glance. Extending the address space was one of the driving reasons to develop IPv6, along with optimization of routing tables, especially on the Internet. This chapter will help you become familiar with the extended address space and will also explain how IPv6 addressing works and why it has been designed to be the way it is. The IPv6 addressing architecture is defined in RFC 4291, which obsoletes RFC 3513 .

The IPv6 Address Space

The 32 bits of the IPv4 address space provide a theoretical maximum of 2^{32} addresses, equal to approximately 4.29 billion addresses. The current world population reaches approximately 6.4 billion people. So even if it were possible to use 100 percent of the IPv4 address space, we would not be able to provide an IP address for everyone on the planet. As a matter of fact, only a small fraction of this address space can be used. In the early days of IP, nobody foresaw the existence of the Internet as we know it today. Therefore, large address blocks were allocated without considerations for global routing and address conservation issues. These address ranges cannot be reclaimed, so consequently there are many unused addresses that are not available for allocation.

 Are you aware that today only about 14 percent of the world's population has Internet access?

If we wanted to provide Internet access to only 20 percent of the world population, the IPv4 address space could never cover the demand. Calculations have shown that this would require around 390 Class A (/8) IPv4 address blocks, but there were only 64 Class A address blocks left in the unallocated IANA pool as of the end of 2005. And the evolution of the Internet and our services shows that in the future, not only are addresses for users and computers needed, but we'll also need more and more addresses for all sorts of devices that need permanent Internet connections, such as cell phones, PDAs, webcams, refrigerators, cars, and many more items. Car manufacturers, as one example, who are designing the networked car of the future, need at least 20 IP addresses per car. These addresses will be used for monitoring and maintenance as well as for access to services such as weather and traffic information. There is a prototype of a Renault car with an integrated Cisco router and a Mobile IPv6 implementation. Most of the big car manufacturers have similar plans and prototypes.

The IPv6 address space uses a 128-bit address, meaning that we have a maximum of 2^{128} addresses available. Do you want to know what this number looks like? It equals 340,282,366,920,938,463,463,374,607,431,768,211,456, or 6.65×10^{23} addresses per square meter on earth. For all of you who, like me, cannot imagine how much this is, it can be compared to providing multiple IP addresses for every grain of sand on the planet.

The IPv4 address space with the originally defined address classes (A, B, C, D, E) allows for 2,113,389 network IDs. With the introduction of Classless Interdomain Routing (CIDR), this number was slightly extended. Let's compare this with IPv6. The address space with the current prefix for global unicast addresses (binary 001) allows for 2^{45} network IDs with a /48 prefix, or 35,184,372,088,832 networks. Each of these networks can further be divided into 65,536 subnets using the remaining 16 bits of the prefix.

Address Types

IPv4 knows unicast, broadcast, and multicast addresses. With IPv6, the broadcast address is not used anymore; multicast addresses are used instead. This is good news because broadcasts are a problem in most networks. The *anycast* address, a new type of address introduced with RFC 1546, has already been used in the IPv4 world but will probably be used on a wider basis with IPv6.

Unicast, Multicast, and Anycast Addresses

An IPv6 address can be classified into one of three categories:

Unicast
> A *unicast* address uniquely identifies an interface of an IPv6 node. A packet sent to a unicast address is delivered to the interface identified by that address.

Multicast
> A *multicast* address identifies a group of IPv6 interfaces. A packet sent to a multicast address is processed by all members of the multicast group.

Anycast
> An *anycast* address is assigned to multiple interfaces (usually on multiple nodes). A packet sent to an anycast address is delivered to only one of these interfaces, usually the nearest one.

Some General Rules

IPv6 addresses are assigned to interfaces as in IPv4, not to nodes as in OSI, so each interface of a node needs at least one unicast address. A single interface can also be assigned multiple IPv6 addresses of any type (unicast, multicast, and anycast). A node can therefore be identified by the address of any of its interfaces. It is also possible to assign one unicast address to multiple interfaces for load-sharing reasons, but if you do this, you need to make sure that the hardware and drivers support it.

 With IPv6, all zeros and ones are legal values for any field in an address.

IPv6 supports addresses of different *scopes*. There are global and non-global (e.g., link-local) scopes. Operationally, the use of non-global addresses has been introduced with IPv4 by using IP addresses from the private range or administratively scoped multicast addresses. The design of IPv6 includes the address scope in the base architecture. Every IPv6 address other than the unspecified address has a specific scope, which is a topological span within which the address may be used as a unique identifier for an interface or set of interfaces. The scope of an address is encoded as part of the address. You can find a description of scopes in the "Multicast Address" section later in this chapter, and refer to RFC 4007, "IPv6 Scoped Address Architecture" for an explanation of scopes.

Address Notation

An IPv6 address has 128 bits, or 16 bytes. The address is divided into eight 16-bit hexadecimal blocks separated by colons. For example:

    2001:DB8:0000:0000:0202:B3FF:FE1E:8329

To make life easier, some abbreviations are possible. For instance, leading zeros in a 16-bit block can be skipped. The example address now looks like this:

    2001:DB8:0:0:202:B3FF:FE1E:8329

A double colon can replace consecutive zeros or leading or trailing zeros within the address. If we apply this rule, our address looks as follows:

    2001:DB8::202:B3FF:FE1E:8329

Note that the double colon can appear only once in an address. The reason for this rule is that the computer always uses a full 128-bit binary representation of the address, even if the displayed address is simplified. When the computer finds a double colon, it expands it with as many zeros as are needed to get 128 bits. If an address had two double colons, the computer would not know how many zeros to add for each colon. So the IPv6 address 2001:DB8:0000:0056:0000:ABCD:EF12:1234 can be represented in the following ways (note the two possible positions for the double colon):

```
2001:DB8:0000:0056:0000:ABCD:EF12:1234
2001:DB8:0:56:0:ABCD:EF12:1234
2001:DB8::56:0:ABCD:EF12:1234
2001:DB8:0:56::ABCD:EF12:1234
```

In environments where IPv4 and IPv6 nodes are mixed, another convenient form of IPv6 address notation is to put the values of an IPv4 address into the four low-order byte pieces of the address. An IPv4 address of 192.168.0.2 can be represented as x:x:x:x:x:x:192.168.0.2, and an address of 0:0:0:0:0:0:192.168.0.2 can be written as ::192.168.0.2. If you prefer, you can also write ::C0A8:2.

Prefix Notation

The notation for prefixes has also been specified in RFC 4291. A *global routing prefix* is the high-order bits of an IP address used to identify the subnet or a specific type of address (refer to Table 3-2). It was called the *format prefix* in earlier RFCs. The prefix notation is very similar to the way IPv4 addresses are written in Classless Interdomain Routing (CIDR) notation, and it is also commonly used for subnetted IPv4 addresses. The notation appends the prefix length, written as a number of bits with a slash, which leads to the following format:

> IPv6 address/prefix length

The prefix length specifies how many left-most bits of the address specify the prefix. This is another way of noting a *subnet mask*. Remember, a subnet mask specifies the bits of the IPv4 address that belong to the network ID. The prefix is used to identify the subnet that an interface belongs to and is used by routers for forwarding. The following example explains how the prefix is interpreted. Consider the IPv6 prefix notation 2E78:DA53:1200::/40. To understand this address, let's convert the hex into binary as shown in Table 3-1.

Table 3-1. Understanding prefix notation

Hex notation	Binary notation		Number of bits
2E 78	0010 1110	0111 1000	16
DA 53	1101 1010	0101 0011	16
12	0001 0010		8
			Total: 40

The *compressed notation* (replacing a sequence of zeros with a double colon) is also applicable to the prefix representation. It should be used carefully, though, because there are often two or more ranges of zeros within an address, and only one can be compressed.

To play with the example in the previous section, check the following prefix notation. The address is 2001:DB8:0000:0056:0000:ABCD:EF12:1234/64, but now we're just interested in the prefix of the address. Lets find out whether the result is correct if we compress it as follows:

2001:DB8::56/64

In order to verify this notation, we'll expand the address again. If we follow the notation rules, we end up with an address of 2001:DB8:0000:0000:0000:0000:0000:0056, with 2001:DB8:0000:0000 for the 64-bit prefix. So the compression leads to a wrong interpretation. It is not identical to the original address and prefix. To make sure the address interpretation is unambiguous, we have to note it as follows:

2001:DB8:0:56::/64

Global Routing Prefixes

Table 3-2 outlines the current assignment of reserved prefixes and special addresses, such as link-local addresses or multicast addresses. The major part of the address space (over 80 percent) is unassigned, which leaves room for future assignments.

Table 3-2. List of assigned prefixes

Allocation	Prefix binary	Prefix hex	Fraction of address space
Unassigned	0000 0000	::0/8	1/256
Reserved	0000 001		1/128
Global unicast	001	2000::/3	1/8
Link-local unicast	1111 1110 10	FE80::/10	1/1024
Reserved (formely Site-local unicast)	1111 1110 11	FEC0::/10* * deprecated	1/1024
Local IPv6 address	1111 110	FC00::/7	
Private administration	1111 1101	FD00::/8	
Multicast	1111 1111	FF00::/8	1/256

All address ranges not listed in Table 3-2 are currently reserved or unassigned. The Internet Assigned Numbers Authority (IANA) currently assigns only out of the binary range starting with 001.

 The updated list of address allocations can be found at: *http://www.iana.org/assignments/ipv6-address-space*.

Some special addresses are assigned out of the reserved address space with the binary prefix 0000 0000. These include the *unspecified address*, the *loopback address*, and

IPv6 addresses with embedded IPv4 addresses, which I discuss in detail later in this chapter.

Unicast addresses can be distinguished from multicast addresses by their prefixes. Globally unique unicast addresses have a high-order byte starting with 001. An IPv6 address with a high-order byte of 1111 1111 (FF in hex) is always a multicast address. For more information about multicast addresses, refer to the "Multicast Address" section later in this chapter.

Anycast addresses are taken from the unicast address space, so they can't be identified as anycast just by looking at the prefix. If you assign a unicast address to multiple interfaces, thereby making it an anycast address, you have to configure the interfaces so they all know that this address is an anycast address. For more information about anycast addresses, refer to the "Anycast Address" section later in this chapter.

Global Unicast Address

Global unicast addresses are identified by the binary prefix 001, as shown earlier in Table 3-2. RFC 4291 defines the global unicast address format as shown in Figure 3-1.

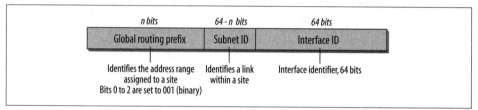

Figure 3-1. Format of the global unicast address

The *global routing prefix* identifies the address range allocated to a site. This part of the address is assigned by the international registry services and the Internet service providers (ISP) and has a hierarchical structure. The *subnet ID* identifies a link within a site. A link can be assigned multiple subnet IDs. A local administrator of a site assigns this part of the address. The *interface ID* identifies an interface on a subnet and must be unique within that subnet.

You may find the terms top-level aggregation identifier (TLA), next-level aggregation identifier (NLA), and site-level aggregation identifier (SLA) in certain IPv6 documents. They originate in an earlier specification (RFC 2374) and are not used anymore. The current specification has a much simpler address format and is more flexible for hierarchical allocation.

International Registry Services and Current Address Allocations

The international allocation of IPv6 addresses has been delegated to several regional registry services: ARIN (American Registry for Internet Numbers) for North America and sub-Saharan Africa; RIPE NCC (Réseau IP Européens Network Coordination Center) for Europe, the Middle East, Central Asia, and North Africa; APNIC (Asia Pacific Network Information Center) for the Asia/Pacific region; and LACNIC (Latin American and Caribbean Internet Addresses Registry) for Latin America. AfriNIC (African Network Information Center) went into operation in 2005 to cover Africa in the future.

Each of these registries has information on their site about address allocation issues, current practices, and procedures.

Several allocations have been made, as listed in Table 3-3.

Table 3-3. Current allocations

Prefix	Allocation	RFC
2000::/3	Assignable Global Unicast Address space Allocations made out of the 2000::/3 space can be viewed at *http://www.iana.org/assignments/ipv6-unicast-address-assignments*	RFC 3513
2001:0000::/32	Teredo	RFC 4380
2001:DB8::/32	For documentation purposes only, nonroutable	RFC 3849
2002::/16	6to4	RFC 3056
3FFE::/16	6Bone Testing (to be phased out by June 2006)	RFC 2471

http://www.iana.org/ipaddress/ip-addresses.htm is a great entry point for global IP address services, current address allocations for both IPv4 and IPv6, and information about how to request IPv6 address services.

The address space for 6Bone operation (3FFE) will be phased out by June 2006 and the prefix returned to the unassigned address pool. It was created in order to allow for global testing of IPv6 while address allocation was not standardized. Now that it is, 6Bone hosts will all be moved to the official IPv6 address space. For more information, visit the 6Bone web site at *http://www.6bone.net*.

Organizations and end users get their address allocations from their ISP. ISPs find information about their regional registries at the following web sites:

ARIN Registration Services
    http://www.arin.net/registration/ipv6/index.html

RIPE-NCC Registration Services
    http://www.ripe.net/rs/index.html

APNIC Registration Services
   http://www.apnic.net/services/ipv6_guide.html

LACNIC Registration Services
   http://www.lacnic.net/en/bt-IPv6.html

AFRINIC Registration Services
   http://www.afrinic.net/registrationServices.htm

Address allocation is a work in progress. Information about the latest status, clarifications, and current practices can be found at *http://www.arin.net*. There is also an informational RFC called "IAB/IESG Recommendations on IPv6 Address Allocations to Sites," numbered RFC 3177. It contains recommendations how the address space should be further divided.

Prefixes

The main rules for address allocation according to RFC 3177 are:

- Home network subscribers should receive a /48 prefix.
- Small and large enterprises should receive a /48 prefix.
- Very large subscribers can receive a /47 prefix or multiple /48 prefixes.
- Mobile networks, such as vehicles or mobile phones with an additional network interface (such as Bluetooth or 802.11b) should receive a static /64 prefix, to allow the connection of multiple devices through one subnet.
- A single PC with no additional need to subnet, such as one dialing up from a hotel room, may receive its /128 IPv6 address for a PPP style connection as part of a /64 prefix.
- A /64 prefix can be allocated when it is known that one and only one subnet is needed by design.
- A /128 prefix can be allocated when it is absolutely known that one and only one device is connecting.

There are several reasons why it is recommended to adhere to the /48 prefix:

- Changing ISPs is much easier if the /48 boundary is used by all providers. Otherwise, corporate subnets may have to be restructured when switching ISPs.
- The process for renumbering a site, which may include parallel operation of the old and the new prefix for a certain time, is much easier to handle.
- There are several approaches for *multihoming* solutions with IPv6 in discussion. Multihoming is when a host is connected to more than one network. No matter which approach is used, complexity will be reduced if subnet boundaries are equal.
- A site can manage all prefixes with one single DNS reverse zone.
- For sites that started out using the 6to4 transition mechanism, the transition to the official IPv6 address space will be easier, as the 6to4 prefix is a /48 prefix.

So a site usually will receive a /48 prefix, which provides 16 bits for subnetting, allowing for 65,536 subnets. In special cases, a very large enterprise can request a shorter prefix.

The Interface ID

Addresses in the prefix range 001 to 111 should use a 64-bit interface identifier that follows the EUI-64 (Extended Unique Identifier) format (except for multicast addresses with the prefix 1111 1111). The EUI-64 is a unique identifier defined by the Institute of Electrical and Electronics Engineers (IEEE); for more information, refer to *http:// standards.ieee.org/regauth/oui/tutorials/EUI64.html*. Appendix A of RFC 4291 explains how to create EUI-64 identifiers, and more details can be found in the link-specific RFCs, such as "IPv6 over Ethernet" or "IPv6 over FDDI." Chapter 7 and Appendix A of this book contain a short discussion and a complete list of these RFCs, respectively.

A host uses an identifier following the EUI-64 format during autoconfiguration. For example, when our host Marvin autoconfigures for a link-local address on an Ethernet interface using its MAC address, the 64-bit interface identifier has to be created from the 48-bit (6-byte) Ethernet MAC address. First, the hex digits 0xff-fe are inserted between the third and fourth bytes of the MAC address. Then the universal/local bit, the second low-order bit of 0x00 (the first byte) of the MAC address, is complemented. The second low-order bit of 0x00 is 0, which, when complemented, becomes 1; as a result, the first byte of the MAC address becomes 0x02. Therefore, the IPv6 interface identifier corresponding to the Ethernet MAC address 00-02-b3-1e-83-29 is 02-02-b3-ff-fe-1e-83-29. This example discusses only the EUI-64 creation process. Many other steps occur during autoconfiguration.

The link-local address of a node is the combination of the prefix fe80::/64 and a 64-bit interface identifier expressed in IPv6 colon-hexadecimal notation. Therefore, the MAC-based link-local address of the previous example node, with prefix fe80::/64 and interface identifier 02-02-b3-ff-fe-1e-83-29, is fe80::202:b3ff:fe1e:8329. This process is described in RFC 2464, "Transmission of IPv6 Packets over Ethernet Networks."

 To learn how IPv6 autoconfiguration works, refer to Chapter 4.

Address Privacy

The privacy of autoconfigured IPv6 addresses using the interface identifier was a major issue in the IETF. If an IPv6 address is built using the MAC identifier, your Internet access could be traced because this identifier is unique to your interface. Part of the concern is the result of a misunderstanding. An IPv6 node *can* have an address based on the interface identifier, but this is not a requirement. As an alternative, the IPv6 device can have an address like the ones currently used with IPv4, either static and manually configured or dynamically assigned by a DHCP server. In early 2001, RFC 3041, "Privacy Extensions for Stateless Address Autoconfiguration in IPv6," was published, introducing a new kind of address available only in IPv6 that contains a random number in place of the factory-assigned serial number. This address can also change over time. An Internet device that is a target for IP communication—for instance, a web or FTP server—needs a unique and stable IP address. But a host running a browser or an FTP client does not need to have the same address every time it connects to the Internet. Some organizations have modified their DHCPv6 server to generate random interface identifiers according to RFC 3041, rotate those identifiers regularly, and maintain audit tables of the address assignments. This way, they use DHCPv6 to manage their address space but prevent anyone from topology mapping their network or tracking their nodes.

With the address architecture in IPv6, you can choose between two types of addresses:

Unique stable IP addresses
Assigned through manual configuration, a DHCP server, or autoconfiguration using the interface identifier

Temporary transient IP addresses
Assigned using a random number in place of the interface identifier

Special Addresses

There are a number of special addresses that we need to discuss. The first part of the IPv6 address space with the prefix of 0000 0000 is reserved. Out of this prefix, special addresses have been defined as follows:

The unspecified address
The unspecified address has a value of 0:0:0:0:0:0:0:0 and is therefore also called the *all-zeros address*. It is comparable to 0.0.0.0 in IPv4. It indicates the absence of a valid address, and it can, for example, be used as a Source address by a host during the boot process when it sends out a request for address configuration information. If you apply the notation conventions discussed earlier in this chapter, the unspecified address can also be abbreviated as ::. It should never be statically or dynamically assigned to an interface, and it should not appear as a destination IP address or within an IPv6 routing header.

The loopback address
The IPv4 loopback address, 127.0.0.1, is probably familiar to you. It is helpful in troubleshooting and testing the IP stack because it can be used to send a packet to the protocol stack without sending it out on the subnet. With IPv6, the loopback address works the same way and is represented as 0:0:0:0:0:0:0:1, abbreviated as ::1. It should never be statically or dynamically assigned to an interface.

The next sections describe different types of addresses that have been specified to be used with different transition mechanisms. These virtual interfaces are called *pseudo-interfaces*. A description of the transition mechanisms can be found in Chapter 10.

IPv6 Addresses with Embedded IPv4 Addresses

Because the transition to IPv6 will be gradual, two special types of addresses have been defined for backward compatibility with IPv4. Both are described in RFC 4291:

IPv4-compatible IPv6 address
> This type of address is used to tunnel IPv6 packets dynamically over an IPv4 routing infrastructure. IPv6 nodes that use this technique are assigned a special IPv6 unicast address that carries an IPv4 address in the low-order 32 bits. This address type has so far rarely been used and is deprecated in RFC 4291. New or updated implementations will no longer need to support this type of address.

IPv4-mapped IPv6 address
> This type of address is used to represent the addresses of IPv4-only nodes as IPv6 addresses. An IPv6 node can use this address to send a packet to an IPv4-only node. The address also carries the IPv4 address in the low-order 32 bits of the address.

Figure 3-2 shows the format of both these addresses.

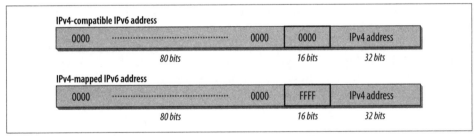

Figure 3-2. Format of IPv6 addresses with an embedded IPv4 address

The two addresses are pretty much the same. The only difference is the 16 bits in the middle. When they are set to 0, the address is an IPv4-compatible IPv6 address; if these bits are set to 1, it is an IPv4-mapped IPv6 address.

6to4 Addresses

The IANA has permanently assigned a 13-bit TLA identifier for 6to4 operations within the global unicast address range (001). 6to4 is one of the mechanisms defined to let IPv6 hosts or networks communicate over an IPv4-only infrastructure. I describe 6to4 in Chapter 10, and is specified in RFC 3056. The 6to4 TLA identifier is 0x0002. The address format is shown in Figure 3-3.

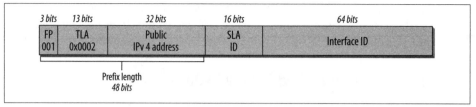

Figure 3-3. Format of the 6to4 address

The prefix has a total length of 48 bits. The IPv4 address in the prefix must be a public IPv4 address and is represented in hexadecimal notation. For instance, if you configure an interface for 6to4 with an IPv4 address of 62.2.84.115, the 6to4 address is 2002:3e02:5473::/48. Through this interface, all IPv6 hosts on this link can tunnel their packets over the IPv4 infrastructure.

 The 6to4 specification was written when RFC 2374 was current, so it uses the old terms and formats (format prefix, TLA, SLA).

ISATAP addresses

The *Intra-Site Automatic Tunnel Addressing Protocol* (ISATAP) is an automatic tunneling mechanism specified in RFC 4214. It is designed for dual stack nodes that are separated by an IPv4-only infrastructure. It treats the IPv4 network as one large link-layer network and allows those dual stack nodes to automatically tunnel between themselves using any format of IPv4 address. Windows XP includes an implementation of ISATAP. ISATAP uses a type identifier of 0xFE for specifying an IPv6 address with an embedded IPv4 address. The format of an ISATAP address is shown in Figure 3-4.

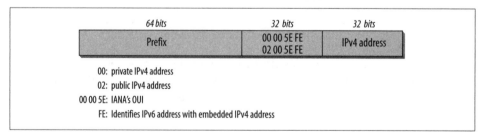

Figure 3-4. Format of the ISATAP address

The first 64 bits follow the format of the global unicast address. IANA owns the IEEE Organizationally Unique Identifier (OUI) 00-00-5E and specifies the EUI-48 format interface identifier assignments within that OUI. Within the first 16 bits, a type identifier shows whether the IPv4 address is from the private range (0000) or a globally unique address (0200). The next eight bits contain a type identifier to indicate that this is an IPv6 address with an embedded IPv4 address. The type identifier is 0xFE. The last 32 bits contain the embedded IPv4 address, which can be written in dotted decimal notation or in hexadecimal representation.

Assume we have a host with an IPv4 address of 192.168.0.1 and the host is assigned a 64-bit prefix of 2001:DB8:510:200::/64. The ISATAP address for this host is 2001: DB8:510:200:0:5EFE:192.168.0.1. Alternatively, you can use the hexadecimal representation for the IPv4 address, in which case the address is written 2001:DB8:510: 200:0:5EFE:C0A8:1. The link-local address for this host is FE80::5EFE:192.168.0.1.

 To learn how IPv6 and IPv4 can coexist using these addresses, refer to Chapter 10.

Teredo Addresses

Teredo is a mechanism designed to provide IPv6 connectivity to hosts that sit behind one or more NATs. This is done by tunneling the IPv6 packet within UDP. The mechanism consists of Teredo clients, servers, and relays. The Teredo relays are IPv6 routers sitting between the Teredo service and the native IPv6 network. Teredo is specified in RFC 4380. As many private Internet users are sitting behind NATs, it is expected that this service will be common until ISPs have upgraded to native IPv6 services.

A Teredo address has the format shown in Figure 3-5.

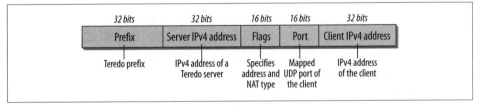

Figure 3-5. Format of the Teredo address

The prefix has a length of 32 bits. The global Teredo IPv6 Service Prefix is 2001:0000: /32. The server IPv4 address field has a length of 32 bits and contains the IPv4 address of a Teredo server. The flags field has 16 bits and specifies the type of address and NAT in use. The 16-bit port field contains the mapped UDP port of the Teredo service on the client and the client IPv4 address field contains the mapped IPv4 address of the client. In this format, both the mapped UDP port and the mapped IPv4 address of the client are obfuscated: each bit in the address and port number is reversed.

 To learn how IPv6 and IPv4 can coexist using these addresses, refer to Chapter 10.

Link- and Site-Local Addresses

With IPv4, organizations often use IP addresses from the private range as defined in RFC 1918. The addresses reserved for private use should never be forwarded over Internet routers but should instead be confined to the organization's network. For connection to the Internet, Network Address Translation (NAT) maps internal private addresses to publicly registered IPv4 addresses.

The original IPv6 specification allocated two separate address spaces (scopes) for link- and site-local use, both identified by their prefixes. In the meantime, the site-local address has been deprecated. Too many problems arose in the application of this address. A *link-local* address is for use on a single link and should never be routed. It doesn't need a global prefix and can be used for autoconfiguration mechanisms, for neighbor discovery, and on networks with no routers, so it is useful for creating temporary networks. Let's say you meet your friend in a conference room and you want to share files on your computers. You can connect your computers using a wireless network or a cross-cable between your Ethernet interfaces, and you can share files without any special configuration by using the link-local address.

The replacement for site-local addresses is called *unique local IPv6 unicast address*, or *local IPv6 address* for short. It is specified in RFC 4193. These addresses are globally unique but should not be routed to the global Internet. They are designed to be used within corporate sites or confined sets of networks.

The characteristics of unique local IPv6 unicast adresses are the following:

- Have a unique, global prefix, which allows for filtering at network boundaries
- Allow for private connection of networks without the risk of address conflicts and the consequence of having to renumber one of the sites
- Are independent of ISP
- Can be used for internal communication without an Internet connection
- If accidentally routed to the global Internet, no address conflicts arise
- Can be used by applications just like regular Global unicast addresses

The format of these addresses is shown in Figure 3-6.

In hexadecimal notation, a link-local address is identified by the prefix FE80. For the local IPv6 address, RFC 4193 specifies a prefix of FC00::/7. The eights bit is currently set to 1 and specifies local administration of the prefix. Setting the eighth bit to 0 may be used in the future for centrally administrated addresses. For the moment, it was decided to standardize only a locally assigned version. The centrally assigned form may be defined in the future if a strong need is identified.

So for locally administered addresses, we currently have a hexadecimal prefix of FD00::/8. It is followed by the 40 bits for the global ID, which is randomly created to

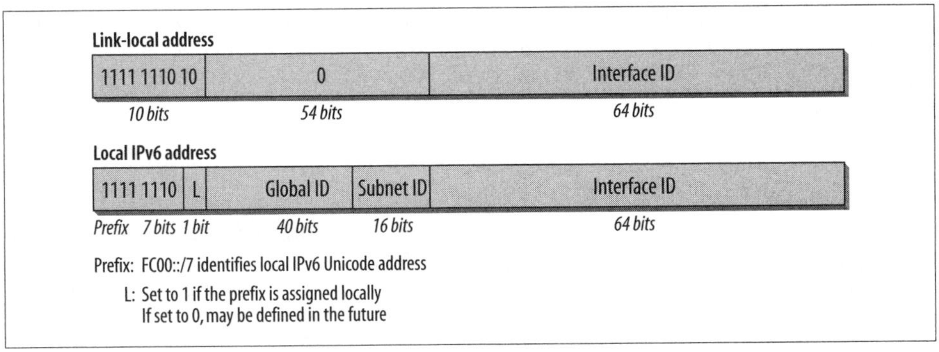

Figure 3-6. Address formats for link- and site-local use

ensure a high probability of uniqueness; 16 bits used for subnet IDs; and 64 bits for the interface identifier. You may still find the site-local address with the prefix FEC0 if you use older implementations, but it should not be used for new implementations anymore.

As mentioned previously, these local addresses should not be routed to the Internet. Border routers should be configured to filter these prefixes. Local addresses should not appear in global DNS servers. They can be used on your internal, private DNS server.

Link-local addresses (FE80) are by default assigned through autoconfiguration. Local IPv6 addresses have to be configured by configuring the local prefix on your routers (*Router Advertisement*) or through DHCPv6.

If you are interested in the reasons for deprecating the site-local address, refer to RFC 3879.

Anycast Address

Anycast addresses are designed to provide redundancy and load balancing in situations where multiple hosts or routers provide the same service. Anycast was not created for IPv6; it was defined in RFC 1546 in 1993 as an experimental specification to be used with IPv4. The RFC allots a special prefix for anycast, which would make an anycast address recognizable as such based on the prefix. Anycast was meant to be used for services such as DNS and HTTP. The RFC discusses possible modifications to TCP to deal with these addresses that are not globally unique.

In practice, anycast has not been implemented as it was designed to be. Often a method called *shared unicast address* is chosen. This method is implemented by assigning a regular unicast address to multiple interfaces and creating multiple entries in the routing table. In this case, the network and transport layer assume that it is a globally unique IP address. If it is not, the mechanism to deal with ambiguous addresses needs to be built into the application. An exception to this rule is if the application uses independent stateless request/reply transactions—for instance, DNS over UDP. The root DNS servers in the Internet are set up using shared unicast addresses. As this procedure does not require any support from the network layer, it can also be used with IPv6.

From the beginning, the IPv6 developers considered anycast to be incorporated in the network layer according to RFC 1546. No special prefix was assigned. IPv6 anycast addresses are in the same address range as global unicast addresses, and each participating interface must be configured to have an anycast address. Within the region where the interfaces containing the same anycast addresses are, each host must be advertised as a separate entry in the routing tables. If the anycast interfaces have no definable region, each anycast entry (in the worst case) has to be propagated throughout the Internet, which obviously does not scale. It is expected, therefore, that support for such global anycast addresses will be either unavailable or very restricted.

Within one network where a group of routers can provide access to a common routing domain, they can be assigned a single address. When a client sends a packet to this address, it will be forwarded to the next available router. One example is the 6to4 relay anycast address that is specified in RFC 3068 and described in Chapter 10. The Mobile IPv6 specification also uses anycast addresses.

When using anycast addresses, we have to be aware of the fact that the sender has no control over which interface the packet will be delivered. This decision is taken on the level of the routing protocol. When a sender sends multiple packets to an anycast address, the packets may arrive at different destinations. If there is a series of requests and replies or if the packet has to be fragmented, this may cause problems.

The *subnet-router anycast address*, which is defined in RFC 4291 and shown in Figure 3-7, is a required anycast address.

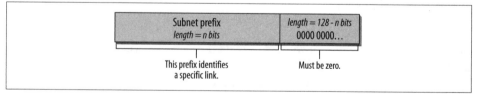

Figure 3-7. Format of the subnet-router anycast address

Basically, the address looks like a regular unicast address with a prefix specifying the subnet and an identifier set to all zeros. A packet sent to this address will be delivered to one router on that subnet. All routers are required to support the subnet-router anycast address for subnets to which they have interfaces.

RFC 2526 provides more information about anycast address formats and specifies other reserved subnet anycast addresses and IDs. A reserved subnet anycast address can have one of two formats, as shown in Figure 3-8.

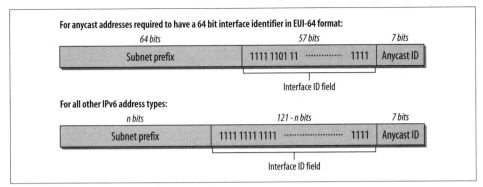

Figure 3-8. General format of anycast addresses

RFC 2526 specifies that within each subnet, the highest 128 interface identifier values are reserved for assignment as subnet anycast addresses. Currently, the anycast IDs listed in Table 3-4 have been reserved.

Table 3-4. Reserved anycast IDs

Decimal	Hexadecimal	Description
127	7F	Reserved
126	7E	Mobile IPv6 Home-Agents anycast
0–125	00-7D	Reserved

The main difference between this form of using anycast and the shared unicast address is that in the latter, the application needs to support anycast, while in the former, this support is avoided if possible. Guidelines of how to use this and modifications to existing stateful transport protocols are needed. *Draft-doi-ipv6-anycast-func-term-05.txt* clarifies the usage of terms for IPv6 anycast and its outline.

Multicast Address

This section covers the multicast address format. For a more general description of multicast and Multicast Listener Discovery (MLD), also known as Multicast Group Management, refer to Chapter 4.

A multicast address is an identifier for a group of nodes identified by the high-order byte FF, or 1111 1111 in binary notation (refer to Table 3-2, earlier in the chapter). A node can belong to more than one multicast group. When a packet is sent to a multicast address, all members of the multicast group process the packet. Multicast exists in IPv4, but it has been redefined and improved for IPv6. The multicast address format is shown in Figure 3-9.

The first byte identifies the address as a multicast address. The next four bits are used for Flags, defined as follows: the first bit of the Flag field must be zero; it is

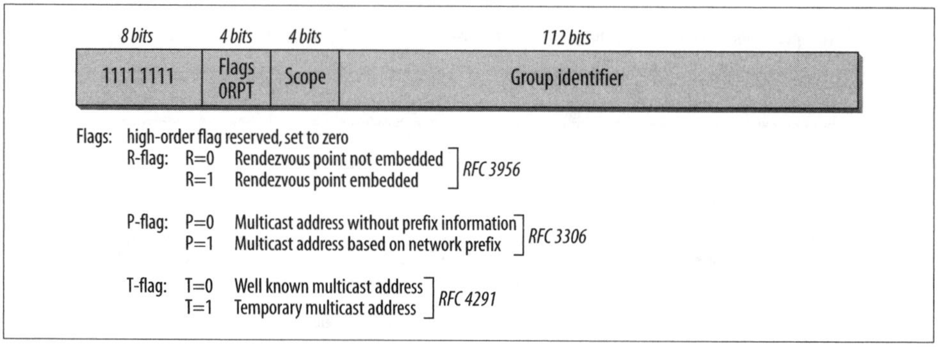

Figure 3-9. Format of the multicast address

reserved for future use. The second bit indicates whether this multicast address embeds the *Rendezvous Point*. A Rendezvous Point is a point of distribution for a specific multicast stream in a multicast network (RFC 3956). The third bit indicates whether this multicast address embeds prefix information (discussed later in this chapter, RFC 3306). The last bit of the Flag field indicates whether this address is permanently assigned—i.e., one of the well-known multicast addresses assigned by the IANA—or a temporary multicast address. A value of zero for the last bit defines a well-known address; a value of one indicates a temporary address. The Scope field is used to limit the scope of a multicast address. The possible values are shown in Table 3-5.

Table 3-5. Values for the Scope field

Value	Description
0	Reserved
1	Interface-local scope (used to be called Node-local scope in earlier specs)
2	Link-local scope
3	Reserved
4	Admin-local scope
5	Site-local scope
6, 7	Unassigned
8	Organization-local scope
9, A, B, C, D	Unassigned
E	Global scope
F	Reserved

The boundaries of zones of a scope other than interface-local, link-local, and global must be defined and configured by network administrators. The reserved scopes should not be used. RFC 4007, "IPv6 Scoped Address Architecture," specifies the architectural characteristics, expected behavior, textual representation, and usage of IPv6 addresses of different scopes.

Well-Known Multicast Addresses

According to RFC 4291, the last 112 bits of the address carry the multicast group ID. In a previous version of the specification, the group ID was limited to 32 bits to make it easier to map the group address to MAC addresses. RFC 3307 "Allocation Guidelines for IPv6 Multicast Addresses," refers to a 32-bit group ID. In practice, the group IDs are usually limited to 32 bits.

RFC 2375 defines the initial assignment of IPv6 multicast addresses that are permanently assigned. Some assignments are made for fixed scopes, and some assignments are valid over all scopes. Table 3-6 gives an overview of the addresses that have been assigned for fixed scopes. Note the scope values that are listed in Table 3-5 in the byte just following the multicast identifier of FF (first byte).

Table 3-6. Well-known multicast addresses

Address	Description
Interface-local scope	
FF01:0:0:0:0:0:0:1	All-nodes address
FF01:0:0:0:0:0:0:2	All-routers address
Link-local scope	
FF02:0:0:0:0:0:0:1	All-nodes address
FF02:0:0:0:0:0:0:2	All-routers address
FF02:0:0:0:0:0:0:3	Unassigned
FF02:0:0:0:0:0:0:4	DVMRP routers
FF02:0:0:0:0:0:0:5	OSPFIGP
FF02:0:0:0:0:0:0:6	OSPFIGP designated routers
FF02:0:0:0:0:0:0:7	ST routers
FF02:0:0:0:0:0:0:8	ST hosts
FF02:0:0:0:0:0:0:9	RIP routers
FF02:0:0:0:0:0:0:A	EIGRP routers
FF02:0:0:0:0:0:0:B	Mobile agents
FF02:0:0:0:0:0:0:D	All PIM routers
FF02:0:0:0:0:0:0:E	RSVP encapsulation
FF02:0:0:0:0:0:0:16	All MLDv2-capable routers
FF02:0:0:0:0:0:0:6A	All snoopers
FF02:0:0:0:0:0:1:1	Link name
FF02:0:0:0:0:0:1:2	All DHCP agents
FF02:0:0:0:0:0:1:3	Link-local Multicast Name Resolution
FF02:0:0:0:0:0:1:4	DTCP Announcement
FF02:0:0:0:0:1:FFXX:XXXX	Solicited-node address

Table 3-6. Well-known multicast addresses (continued)

Address	Description
Site-local scope	
FF05:0:0:0:0:0:0:2	All-routers address
FF05:0:0:0:0:0:1:3	All DHCP servers
FF05:0:0:0:0:0:1:4	Deprecated
FF05:0:0:0:0:0:1:1000 to FF05:0:0:0:0:01:13FF	Service location (SLP) Version 2

The term "node-local" scope from RFC 2375 has been changed to "interface-local scope," so you may encounter both terms. The list for the permanently assigned multicast addresses that are independent of scopes is long, and it is available in the Appendix and in RFC 2375. All those addresses are noted beginning with FF0X; X is the placeholder for a variable scope value.

The IPv4 broadcast address is replaced by the link-local all-nodes multicast address FF02::1. There is no equivalent to the subnet broadcast address used with IPv4.

> Find the most updated list of multicast address assignments at *http://www.iana.org/assignments/ipv6-multicast-addresses*.

As an example, let's look at the one described in RFC 2373. There is a multicast group ID defined for all NTP servers. The multicast group ID is 0x101. This group ID can be used with different scope values as follows:

FF01:0:0:0:0:0:0:101
  All NTP servers on the same node as the sender

FF02:0:0:0:0:0:0:101
  All NTP servers on the same link as the sender

FF05:0:0:0:0:0:0:101
  All NTP servers on the same site as the sender

FF0E:0:0:0:0:0:0:101
  All NTP servers in the Internet

Temporarily assigned multicast addresses are meaningful only within a defined scope.

> Multicast addresses should not be used as a Source address in IPv6 packets or appear in any routing header.

For the management of multicast, IPv6 uses Multicast Listener Discovery (MLD) based on ICMPv6. To learn how multicast addresses are managed, refer to the section "Multicast Listener Discovery" in Chapter 4.

Solicited-Node Multicast Address

The *solicited-node multicast address* is a multicast address that every node must join for every unicast and anycast address it is assigned. It is used in Neighbor Discovery, which is described in Chapter 4. RFC 4291 specifies the solicited-node multicast address.

In the IPv4 world, an ARP request (used to determine the MAC address of an interface) is sent to the MAC-layer broadcast address and therefore examined by every interface on the link. In the IPv6 world, resolving the MAC address of an interface is done by sending a Neighbor Solicitation message (discussed in Chapter 4) to the solicited-node multicast address, and not to the link-local all-nodes multicast address. This way, only the node registered to this multicast address will examine the packet.

This address is formed by taking the low-order 24 bits of an IPv6 address (the last part of the host ID) and appending those bits to the well-known prefix FF02:0:0:0:0:1:FF00::/104. Thus, the range for solicited-node multicast addresses goes from FF02:0:0:0:0:1:FF00:0000 to FF02:0:0:0:0:1:FFFF:FFFF.

For example, our host Marvin has the MAC address 00-02-B3-1E-83-29 and the IPv6 address fe80::202:b3ff:fe1e:8329. The corresponding solicited-node multicast address is FF02::1:ff1e:8329. If this host has other IPv6 unicast or anycast addresses, each one will have a corresponding solicited-node multicast address.

Dynamic Allocation of Multicast Addresses

The multicast address architecture has been extended in RFC 3306. It contains definitions that allow the allocation of unicast prefix–based addresses and of source-specific multicast addresses. It is based on a modified multicast address format that contains prefix information. The goal of this specification is to reduce the number of protocols needed for the allocation of multicast addresses.

Figure 3-10 shows the format of the extended multicast address.

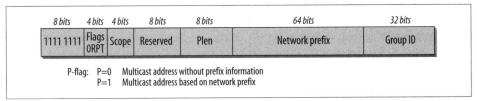

Figure 3-10. Format of the extended multicast address

In the original specification, the flags field only uses the last bit (T) to specify whether the multicast address is a well-known or temporary one. The extended format shown here uses the second last bit (P) to indicate whether the multicast address assignment is based on the network prefix (value 1) or not (value 0). A P setting of 1 indicates that it is a multicast address following the extended format. The use of the scope field has not changed. If the P flag is set to 1, the eight bits following the scope field are reserved and set to 0. The next eight bits (PLen) specify the length of the prefix in the prefix field. If the prefix length is smaller than 64 bits, the unused bits in the prefix field should be set to 0. The group ID uses 32 bits. Note that when P is set to 1 (extended multicast address), the T flag should also be set to 1 (temporary multicast address).

For an overview of source specific multicast, refer to RFC 3569. In the traditional multicast model called any-source multicast (ASM), a multicast listener cannot control the source of the data it wants to receive. With source-specific multicast (SSM), an interface can register for a multicast group and specify the source(s) for the data. SSM can be implemented using MLDv2 and the extended multicast address format.

> Refer to Chapter 4 for more general information on Multicast and Multicast Listener Discovery (MLD).

For a source-specific multicast address, the T and the P flag are set to 1. Prefix length and network prefix are both set to 0. This leads to a multicast prefix of FF3x:/32, where x is a scope value. The Source address in the IPv6 header identifies the owner of the multicast address. All SSM addresses have the format FF3X::/96.

> Refer to RFC 3307, "Allocation Guidelines for IPv6 Multicast Addresses," for more information.

There is a draft in the works defining an extension to the multicast addressing architecture of the IPv6 protocol. The extension allows for the use of interface identifiers to allocate link-local scoped multicast addresses. The draft is *draft-ietf-ipv6-link-scoped-mcast-09.txt* and will become an RFC before this book is printed. In this multicast address, the flags field is set to binary 0011; the scope field is set to 2 for link-local scope; the PLen field is set to FF (all ones in binary); and the 64 bits of the network ID field are used for the interface identifier. The group ID is generated to indicate a multicast application and needs to be unique only on this host.

Required Addresses

The standard specifies that each host must assign the following addresses to identify itself:

- Its link-local address for each interface
- Any assigned unicast and anycast addresses
- The loopback address

- The all-nodes multicast address
- Solicited-node multicast address for each of its assigned unicast and anycast addresses
- Multicast addresses of all other groups to which the host belongs

A router needs to recognize all of the previous address, plus the following:

- The subnet-router anycast address for the interfaces for which it is configured to act as a router on each link
- All anycast addresses with which the router has been configured
- The all-routers multicast address
- Multicast addresses of all other groups to which the router belongs

Default Address Selection

The architecture of IPv6 allows an interface to have multiple addresses. The addresses may differ in scope (link-local, global) or state (preferred, deprecated); they may be part of mobility (home-address, care-of-address) or multihoming situation; or they may be permanent public addresses or virtual tunnel interfaces. Dual-stack hosts have IPv6 and IPv4 addresses. The result is that IPv6 implementations that need to initiate a connection are often faced with a choice between multiple Source and Destination addresses.

Imagine a situation where a client issues a DNS request for an external service and receives a global IPv6 and a public IPv4 address back. If this client has a private IPv4 address and a global IPv6 address, it might make sense to use IPv6 to access this external service. But if the client has a link-local IPv6 address and a public IPv4 address, choose the IPv4 address for connecting to the service. These are types of situations and choices that will have to be dealt with in the future world of mixed networks, some IPv4-only, some IPv6-only, and some dual-stack. The way this is dealt with depends on the implementations. Application developers have to be aware of this and try to provide mechanisms that will make their applications behave optimally in every possible environment.

RFC 3484, "Default Address Selection for IPv6," defines two general algorithms, one for Source address selection and the other for Destination address selection. All IPv6 nodes (host and router) have to implement RFC 3484. The algorithms specify default behavior for IPv6 nodes. The algorithms do not override choices made by applications or upper-layer protocols.

Here's a summary of the most important rules:

- Address pairs of the same scope or type (link-local, global) are preferred.
- A smaller scope for the Destination address is preferred (use the smallest scope possible).

- A preferred (non-deprecated) address is preferred.
- Transitional addresses (e.g., ISATAP or 6to4 addresses) are not used if native IPv6 addresses are available.
- If all criteria are similar, address pairs with the longest common prefix are preferred.
- For the Source address, global addresses are preferred over temporary addresses.
- In Mobile IP situations, home addresses are preferred over care-of addresses.

The rules in RFC 3484 are to be used in all situations when nothing else is specified. The specification also allows the configuration of a policy that can override these defaults with preferred combinations of Source and Destination addresses.

Now that we are familiar with the extended address space and the IPv6 address types, the next chapter introduces the advanced features of ICMPv6, which offer management functionality not known with ICMPv4.

References

The following are lists of the most important RFCs and drafts mentioned in this chapter. Sometimes I include additional subject-related RFCs for your personal further study.

RFCs

- RFC 1546, "Host Anycasting Service," 1993
- RFC 1918, "Address Allocation for Private Internets," 1996
- RFC 2101, "IPv4 Address Behaviour Today," 1997
- RFC 2365, "Administratively Scoped IP Multicast," 1998
- RFC 2464, "Transmission of IPv6 Packets over Ethernet Networks," 1998
- RFC 2471, "IPv6 Testing Address Allocation" (6Bone), 1998
- RFC 2526, "Reserved IPv6 Subnet Anycast Addresses," 1999
- RFC 2710, "Multicast Listener Discovery (MLD) for IPv6," 1999
- RFC 2908, "The Internet Multicast Address Allocation Architecture," 2000
- RFC 3041, "Privacy Extensions for Stateless Address Autoconfiguration in IPv6," 2001
- RFC 3056, "Connection of IPv6 Domains via IPv4 Clouds" (6to4), 2001
- RFC 3068, "An Anycast Prefix for 6to4 Relay Routers," 2001
- RFC 3177, "IAB/IESG Recommendations on IPv6 Address Allocations to Sites," 2001
- RFC 3306, "Unicast-Prefix-based IPv6 Multicast," 2002
- RFC 3307, "Allocation Guidelines for IPv6 Multicast Addresses," 2002

- RFC 3484, "Default Address Selection for Internet Protocol version 6 (IPv6)," 2003
- RFC 3513, "Internet Protocol Version 6 (IPv6) Addressing Architecture," 2003
- RFC 3569, "An Overview of Source-Specific Multicast (SSM)," 2003
- RFC 3587, "IPv6 Global Unicast Address Format," 2003
- RFC 3810, "Multicast Listener Discovery Version 2 (MLDv2) for IPv6," 2004
- RFC 3849, "IPv6 Documentation Address," 2004
- RFC 3879, "Deprecating Site Local Addresses," 2004
- RFC 3956, "Embedding the Rendezvous Point (RP) Address in an IPv6 Multicast Address," 2004
- RFC 4007, "IPv6 Scoped Address Architecture," 2005
- RFC 4192, "Procedures for Renumbering an IPv6 Network without a Flag Day," 2005
- RFC 4193, "Unique Local IPv6 Unicast Addresses," 2005
- RFC 4214, "Intra-Site Automatic Tunnel Addressing Protocol (ISATAP)," 2005
- RFC 4291, "IPv6 Addressing Architecture," 2006
- RFC 4380, "Teredo: Tunneling IPv6 over UDP through Network Address Translations (NATs)," 2006

Drafts

Drafts can be found at *http://www.ietf.org/ID.html*. To locate the latest version of a draft, refer to *https://datatracker.ietf.org/public/pidtracker.cgi*. You can enter the draft name without a version number, and the most current version will come up. If a draft does not show up, it was either deleted or published as an RFC. Alternatively, you can go to the new Internet drafts database interface at *https://datatracker.ietf.org/ public/idindex.cgi*. *http://tools.ietf.org/wg* is also a very useful site. More information on the process of standardization, RFCs, and drafts can be found in the Appendix.

Here's a list of the drafts referred to in this chapter, as well as interesting drafts related to the topics in this chapter.

- *draft-ietf-ipv6-link-scoped-mcast-09.txt* (RFC queue), A Method for Generating Link Scoped IPv6 Multicast Addresses
- *draft-doi-ipv6-anycast-func-term-05.txt*, IPv6 Anycast Terminology Definition
- *draft-jabley-v6-anycast-clarify-00.txt*, Anycast Addressing in IPv6
- *draft-ietf-grow-anycast-03.txt*, Operation of Anycast Services
- *draft-vandevelde-vbops-addcon-00.txt*, IPv6 Unicast Address Assignment Considerations

CHAPTER 4

ICMPv6

If you are familiar with IPv4, the Internet Control Message Protocol (ICMP) for IPv4 is probably a good friend of yours: it gives important information about the health of the network. ICMPv6 is the version that works with IPv6. It reports errors if packets cannot be processed properly and sends informational messages about the status of the network. For example, if a router cannot forward a packet because it is too large to be sent out on another network, it sends an ICMP message back to the originating host. The source host can use this ICMP message to determine a better packet size and then resend the data. ICMP also performs diagnostic functions, such as the well-known *ping*, which uses ICMP Echo Request and Echo Reply messages to test availability of a node.

ICMPv6 is much more powerful than ICMPv4 and contains new functionality, as described in this chapter. For instance, the Internet Group Management Protocol (IGMP) function that manages multicast group memberships with IPv4 has been incorporated into ICMPv6. The same is true for the Address Resolution Protocol/Reverse Address Resolution Protocol (ARP/RARP) function used in IPv4 to map layer two addresses to IP addresses (and vice versa). Neighbor Discovery (ND) is introduced; it uses ICMPv6 messages to determine link-layer addresses for neighbors attached to the same link, find routers, keep track of which neighbors are reachable, and detect changed link-layer addresses. New message types have been defined to allow for simpler renumbering of networks and updating of address information between hosts and routers. ICMPv6 also supports Mobile IPv6, which is described in Chapter 11. ICMPv6 is part of IPv6, and it must be implemented fully by every IPv6 node. The protocol is defined in RFC 4443. Neighbor Discovery is defined in RFC 2461.

General Message Format

There are two classes of ICMP messages:

ICMP error messages
> *Error messages* have a 0 in the high-order bit of their message Type field. ICMP error message types are, therefore, in the range from 0 to 127.

ICMP informational messages
> *Informational messages* have a 1 in the high-order bit of their message Type field. ICMP informational message types are, therefore, in the range from 128 to 255.

An IPv6 header and zero or more Extension headers precede every ICMPv6 message. The header just preceding the ICMP header has a next header value of 58. This value is different from the value for ICMPv4 (which has the value 1).

> The values for the Next Header field are discussed in Chapter 2.

The following message types are described in RFC 4443:

- ICMPv6 error messages
  - Destination Unreachable (message type 1)
  - Packet Too Big (message type 2)
  - Time Exceeded (message type 3)
  - Parameter Problem (message type 4)
- ICMPv6 informational messages
  - Echo Request (message type 128)
  - Echo Reply (message type 129)

> For the most current list of ICMPv6 message types, refer to the Internet Assigned Number Authority (IANA) at *http://www.iana.org/assignments/icmpv6-parameters*. All IPv4 ICMP parameters can be found at *http://www.iana.org/assignments/icmp-parameters*.

All ICMPv6 messages have the same general header structure, as shown in Figure 4-1. Notice that the first three fields for type, code, and checksum have not changed from ICMPv4.

Type (1 Byte)

This field specifies the type of message, which determines the format of the remainder of the message. Tables 4-1 and 4-2 list ICMPv6 message types and numbers.

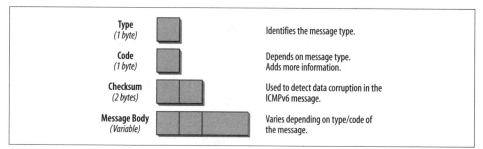

Figure 4-1. General ICMPv6 header format

Code (1 Byte)

The Code field depends on the message type and allows for more granular information in certain cases. Refer to Tables 4-1 and 4-2 for a detailed list.

Checksum (2 Bytes)

The Checksum field is used to detect data corruption in the ICMPv6 header and in parts of the IPv6 header. In order to calculate the checksum, a node must determine the Source and Destination address in the IPv6 header. If the node has more than one unicast address, there are rules for choosing the address (refer to RFC 4443 for details). There is also a pseudoheader included in the checksum calculation, which is new with ICMPv6.

Message Body (Variable Size)

Depending on the type and code, the message body will hold different data. In the case of an error message, it will contain as much as possible of the packet that invoked the message to assist in troubleshooting. The total size of the ICMPv6 packet should not exceed the minimum IPv6 MTU, which is 1,280 bytes. Tables 4-1 and 4-2 provide an overview of the different message types, along with the additional code information, which depends on the message type.

Table 4-1. ICMPv6 error messages and code type

Message number	Message type	Code field
1	Destination Unreachable	0 = no route to destination 1 = communication with destination administratively prohibited 2 = beyond scope of Source address 3 = address unreachable 4 = port unreachable 5 = Source address failed ingress/egress policy 6 = reject route to destination
2	Packet Too Big	Code field set to 0 by the sender and ignored by the receiver
3	Time Exceeded	0 = hop limit exceeded in transit 1 = fragment reassembly time exceeded

Table 4-1. ICMPv6 error messages and code type (continued)

Message number	Message type	Code field
4	Parameter Problem	0 = erroneous header field encountered 1 = unrecognized next header type encountered 2 = unrecognized IPv6 option encountered
		The pointer field identifies the octet offset within the invoking packet where the error was detected. The pointer points beyond the end of the ICMPv6 packet if the field in error is beyond what can fit in the maximum size of an ICMPv6 error message.
100 and 101	Private experimentation	RFC 4443
127	Reserved for expansion of ICMPv6 error messages	RFC 4443

Note that the message numbers and types have substantially changed compared to ICMPv4. ICMP for IPv6 is a different protocol, and the two versions of ICMP are not compatible. Your analyzer should properly decode all this information, so you do not have to worry about memorizing it.

Table 4-2. ICMPv6 informational messages

Message number	Message type	Description
128	Echo Request	RFC 4443. Used for the ping command.
129	Echo Reply	
130	Multicast Listener Query	RFC 2710. Used for multicast goup management.
131	Multicast Listener Report	
132	Multicast Listener Done	
133	Router Solicitation	RFC 2461. Used for neighbor discovery and autoconfiguration.
134	Router Advertisement	
135	Neighbor Solicitation	
136	Neighbor Advertisement	
137	Redirect Message	
138	Router Renumbering	RFC 2894 Codes: 0 = Router renumbering command 1 = Router renumbering result 255 = Sequence number reset
139	ICMP Node Information Query	*draft-ietf-ipngwg-icmp-name-lookups-15.txt*
140	ICMP Node Information Response	
141	Inverse ND Solicitation	RFC 3122
142	Inverse ND Adv Message	RFC 3122
143	Version 2 Multicast Listener Report	RFC 3810

Table 4-2. ICMPv6 informational messages (continued)

Message number	Message type	Description
144	ICMP Home Agent Address Discovery Request Message	RFC 3775 ICMPv6 Messages for Mobile IPv6
145	ICMP Home Agent Address Discovery Reply Message	
146	ICMP Mobile Prefix Solicitation Message	
147	ICMP Mobile Prefix Advertisement Message	
148	Certification Path Solicitation Message	RFC 3971 ICMPv6 Messages for SEcure Neighbor Discovery
149	Certification Path Advertisement Message	
151	Multicast Router Advertisement	RFC 4286
152	Multicast Router Solicitation	
153	Multicast Router Termination	
200	Private experimentation	RFC 4443
201		
255	Reserved for expansion of ICMPv6 informational messages	RFC 4443

With the exception of the router renumbering message (138), the ICMPv6 informational messages do not use the Code field. It is, therefore, set to zero.

ICMP Error Messages

Every ICMP message can have a slightly different header depending on the kind of error report or information it carries. The following sections outline the structure of each type of ICMPv6 message.

Destination Unreachable

A *Destination Unreachable* message is generated if an IP datagram cannot be delivered. A Type field with the value 1 identifies this message. The ICMP message is sent to the Source address of the invoking packet. The format of the Destination Unreachable message is shown in Figure 4-2.

The Type field is set to 1, which is the value for the Destination Unreachable message. The Code field supplies more information about the reason why the datagram was not delivered. The possible codes are listed in Table 4-3. The data portion of the ICMP message contains as much of the original message as will fit into the ICMP message.

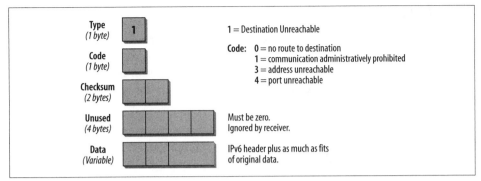

Figure 4-2. Format of the Destination Unreachable message

Table 4-3. Code values of the Destination Unreachable message (type 1)

Code	Description
0	"No route to destination." This code is used if a router cannot forward a packet because it does not have a route in its table for a destination network. This can happen only if the router does not have an entry for a default route.
1	"Communication with destination administratively prohibited." This type of message can, for example, be sent by a firewall that cannot forward a packet to a host inside the firewall because of a packet filter. It might also be sent if a node is configured not to accept unauthenticated Echo Requests.
2	"Beyond scope of Source address." This code is used if the Destination address is beyond the scope of the Source address, e.g., if a packet has a link-local Source address and a global Destination address.
3	"Address unreachable." This code is used if a Destination address cannot be resolved into a corresponding network address or if there is a data-link layer problem preventing the node from reaching the destination network.
4	"Port unreachable." This code is used if the transport protocol (e.g., UDP) has no listener and there is no other means to inform the sender. For example, if a Domain Name System (DNS) query is sent to a host and the DNS server is not running, this type of message is generated.
5	"Source address failed ingress/egress policy." This code is used if a packet with this Source address is not allowed due to ingress or egress filtering policies.
6	"Reject route to destination." This code is used if the route to the destination is a reject route.

If the destination is unreachable due to congestion, no ICMP message is generated. A host that receives a Destination Unreachable message must inform the upper-layer process.

Packet Too Big

If a router cannot forward a packet because it is larger than the MTU of the outgoing link, it will generate a Packet Too Big message (shown in Figure 4-3). This ICMPv6 message type is used as part of the Path MTU discovery process that I discuss later in this chapter. The ICMP message is sent to the Source address of the invoking packet.

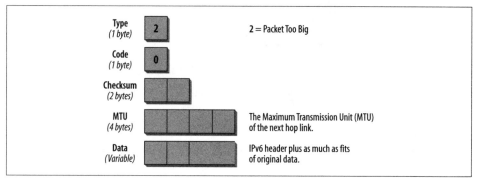

Figure 4-3. Format of the Packet Too Big message

The Type field has the value 2, which identifies the Packet Too Big message. In this case, the Code field is not used and is set to 0. The important information for this type of message is the MTU field, which contains the MTU size of the next hop link.

RFC 4443 states that an ICMPv6 message should not be generated as a response to a packet with an IPv6 multicast Destination address, a link-layer multicast address, or a link-layer broadcast address. The Packet Too Big message is an exception to this rule. Because the ICMP message contains the supported MTU of the next hop link, the source host can determine the MTU that it should use for further communication. A host that receives a Packet Too Big message must inform the upper-layer process.

Time Exceeded

When a router forwards a packet, it always decrements the hop limit by one. The hop limit makes sure that a packet does not endlessly travel through a network. If a router receives a packet with a hop limit of 1 and decrements the limit to 0, it discards the packet, generates a Time Exceeded message with a code value of 0, and sends this message back to the source host. This error can indicate a routing loop or the fact that the sender's initial hop limit is too low. It can also tell you that someone used the *traceroute* utility, which is described later in this chapter. Figure 4-4 shows the format of the Time Exceeded message.

The Type field carries the value 3, specifying the Time Exceeded message. The Code field can be set to 0, which means the hop limit was exceeded in transit, or to 1,

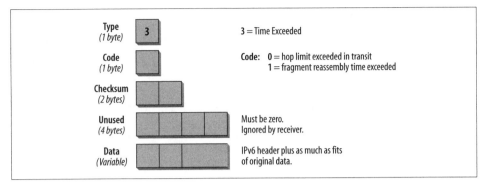

Figure 4-4. Format of the Time Exceeded message

which means that the fragment reassembly time is exceeded. The data portion of the ICMP message contains as much of the original message as will fit into the ICMP message, depending on the MTU used.

An incoming Time Exceeded message must be passed to the upper-layer process. Table 4-4 shows the Code fields for the Time Exceeded message.

Table 4-4. Code values for Time Exceeded message (type 3)

Code	Description
0	"Hop limit exceeded in transit."
	Possible causes: the initial hop limit value is too low; there are routing loops; or use of the *traceroute* utility.
1	"Fragment reassembly time exceeded."
	If a fragmented packet is sent by using a fragment header (refer to Chapter 2 for more details) and the receiving host cannot reassemble all packets within a certain time, it notifies the sender by issuing this ICMP message.

The "Hop limit exceeded in transit" message type is commonly used to do the *traceroute* function. *Traceroute* is helpful in determining the path that a packet takes when traveling through the network. In order to do this, a first packet is sent out with a hop limit of 1. The first router in the path decrements the hop limit to 0, discards the packet, and sends back an ICMP message type 3, code 0. The source host now knows the address of the first hop router. Next, it sends out a second packet with a hop limit of 2. This packet is forwarded by the first router, which decrements the hop limit to 1. The second router in the path decrements the hop limit to 0, discards the packet, and sends back an ICMP message type 3, code 0. Now the source knows about the second router in the path. Raising the hop limit by one (with every packet sent until the packet reaches the final destination) continues this process. Every router in the path to the final destination sends an ICMP message back to the source host, thereby providing its IP address. It is important to know that if there are redundant paths to the destination, *traceroute* does not necessarily show the same route for all tests because it might choose different paths.

Parameter Problem

If an IPv6 node cannot complete the processing of a packet because it has a problem identifying a field in the IPv6 header or in an Extension header, it must discard the packet, and it should send an ICMP Parameter Problem message back to the source of the problem packet. This type of message is often used when an error that does not fit into any of the other categories is encountered. The format of this ICMP message is shown in Figure 4-5.

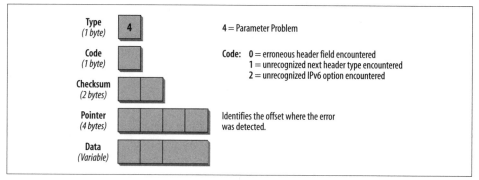

Figure 4-5. Format of the Parameter Problem message

The Type field has the value 4, which specifies the Parameter Problem message. The Code field can contain any of the three values described in Table 4-5. The Pointer field identifies at which byte in the original packet the error was detected. The ICMP message includes as much of the original data as fits, up to the minimum IPv6 MTU. It is possible that the pointer points beyond the ICMPv6 message. This would be the case if the field in error was beyond what can fit in the maximum size of an ICMPv6 error message.

Table 4-5 shows the Code fields for the Parameter Problem message.

Table 4-5. Code values for Parameter Problem (type 4)

Code	Description
0	Erroneous header field encountered
1	Unrecognized next header type encountered
2	Unrecognized IPv6 option encountered

For example, an ICMPv6 message of type 4 with a code value of 1 and a pointer set to 40 indicates that the next header type in the header following the IPv6 header was unrecognized.

An incoming Parameter Problem message must be passed to the upper-layer process.

ICMP Informational Messages

In RFC 4443, two types of informational messages are defined: the Echo Request and the Echo Reply messages. Other ICMP informational messages are used for Path MTU Discovery and Neighbor Discovery. These messages are discussed at the end of this chapter and defined in RFC 2461, "Neighbor Discovery for IP Version 6," and RFC 1981, "Path MTU Discovery for IP Version 6."

The Echo Request and Echo Reply messages are used for one of the most common TCP/IP utilities: Packet INternet Groper (ping). Ping is used to determine whether a specified host is available on the network and ready to communicate. The source host issues an Echo Request message to the specified destination. The destination host, if available, responds with an Echo Reply message. Figures 4-8 and 4-9 (later in the chapter) show what a ping looks like in the trace file.

Echo Request Message

The format of the Echo Request message is shown in Figure 4-6.

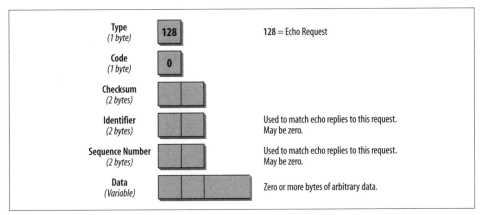

Figure 4-6. Format of the Echo Request message

The Type Field is set to 128, the value for the Echo Request. The Code Field is not used for this message and is therefore set to 0. The Identifier and Sequence Number fields are used to match requests with replies. The reply must always contain the same numbers as the request. Whether an identifier and a sequence number are used and what kind of arbitrary data is included in the Echo Request depends on the TCP/IP stack you are using. When you analyze trace files with Echo Request and Echo Reply messages and you are familiar with some stacks, you can determine the TCP/IP stack of the sender by looking at the arbitrary data. You can see an example of this in Figures 4-8 and 4-9, later in this chapter.

Echo Reply

The format of the Echo Reply message is very similar to that of the Echo Request, as shown in Figure 4-7.

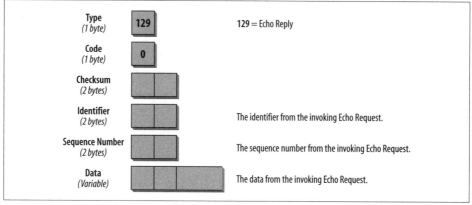

Figure 4-7. Format of the Echo Reply message

The Type field contains the value 129 for Echo Reply. The Code field is unused and set to 0. The Identifier and Sequence Number fields must match the fields in the request. The data of the Echo Request message must be copied into the reply entirely and unmodified. If an upper-layer process initiated the Echo Request, the reply must be passed to that process. If the Echo Request message was sent to a unicast address, the Source address of the Echo Reply message must be the same as the Destination address of the Echo Request message. If the Echo Request was sent to an IPv6 multicast address, the Source address of the Echo Reply must be a unicast address of the interface on which the multicast Echo Request was received.

ICMPv6 Echo Request and Reply messages can be authenticated, using an IPv6 authentication header. This means that a node can be configured to ignore nonauthenticated ICMPv6 pings and provide protection against different ICMPv6 attacks.

Processing Rules

There are several rules that govern processing of ICMP packets. They can be found in RFC 4443 and are summarized as follows:

- If a node receives an ICMPv6 error message of unknown type, it must pass it to the upper layer.
- If a node receives an ICMPv6 informational message of unknown type, it must be silently discarded.

- As much as possible of the packet that caused the ICMP error message will be included in the ICMP message body. The ICMP packet should not exceed the minimum IPv6 MTU.
- If the error message has to be passed to the upper-layer protocol, the protocol type is determined by extracting it from the original packet (present in the body of the ICMPv6 error message). In case the protocol type cannot be found in the body of the ICMPv6 message (because there were too many extension headers present in the original packet, and the part of the header that contained the upper-layer protocol type was truncated), the ICMPv6 message is silently discarded.

An ICMPv6 error message must not be sent in the following cases:

- As a result of an ICMPv6 error message.
- As a result of an ICMPv6 redirect message.
- As a result of a packet sent to an IPv6 multicast address. There are two exceptions to this rule: the Packet Too Big message that is used for Path MTU discovery, and the Parameter Problem with the code value 2 for an unrecognized IPv6 option.
- As a result of a packet sent as a link-layer multicast (exceptions just described apply).
- As a result of a packet sent as a link-layer broadcast (exceptions just described apply).
- As a result of a packet whose Source address does not uniquely identify a single node. This could be an IPv6 unspecified address, an IPv6 multicast address, or an IPv6 address known to be an anycast address.

Every IPv6 node must implement a rate-limiting function that limits the rate of ICMPv6 messages it sends, and it should be configurable. If this function is implemented properly, it protects against Denial of Service attacks.

The ICMPv6 Header in a Trace File

After reading through all that dry information, you deserve something different. The following screenshot (Figure 4-8) shows what a ping looks like in the trace file and provides details of many of the fields discussed so far.

The two frames in this trace file were captured when my Windows host issued a ping command to a Linux host. Note that the Source address of the second frame, the Echo Reply, is the same as the Destination address in the first frame, the Echo Request. The IPv6 header provides more information. The Version field indicates that this is an IPv6 packet. The Next Header field has the value 58, which is the value for ICMPv6. We can also see source and destination IP address. The prefix fe80: indicates that these two addresses are link-local addresses.

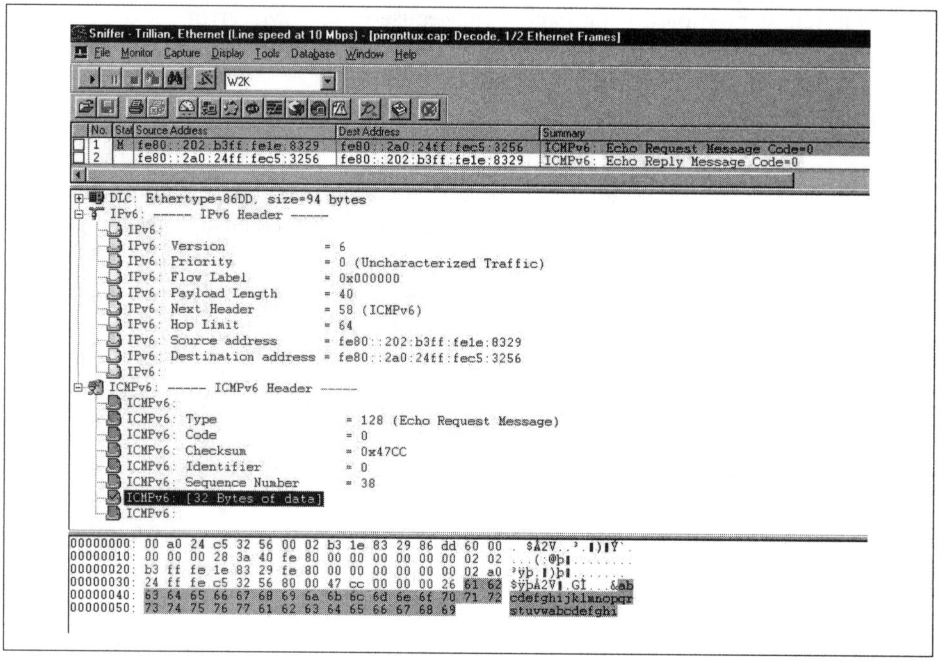

Figure 4-8. Echo Request in a trace file

Note the first three fields of the ICMPv6 header. They are the fields that are common for every ICMPv6 message: the Type, Code, and Checksum fields. The Type field contains the value 128, which is the value for an Echo Request. The Identifier and Sequence Number fields are unique to the Echo Request and Echo Reply message. The Identifier is not used in this case, and the sender has set the sequence to 38. It has to be identical in the matching reply shown in the following screenshot. The Data field contains arbitrary data that doesn't need to make sense to anyone.

Oh, I almost forgot that earlier I had promised to show vendor stack–related data in the Echo Request message. What you see here—the alphabet up to the letter "w"—is what Microsoft uses. Whenever you see this in a trace file, a Microsoft stack is sending the request. Figure 4-9 shows the Echo Reply in detail.

Again, the IPv6 header shows a value of 6 for the IP version and a Next Header value of 58 for ICMPv6. The Destination address of the previous frame is now the Source address, and the previous Source address is now the Destination address. The Type field in the ICMPv6 header shows a value of 129, which is the value for an Echo Reply. The Identifier and Sequence Number fields, as well as the Data field, match the ones in the Echo Request.

```
Sniffer - Trillian, Ethernet (Line speed at 10 Mbps) - [pingnttux.cap: Decode, 2/2 Ethernet Frames]
File  Monitor  Capture  Display  Tools  Database  Window  Help

                                    W2K

No. Stat Source Address          Dest Address           Summary
  1  M  fe80::202:b3ff:fe1e:8329  fe80::2a0:24ff:fec5:3256  ICMPv6: Echo Request Message Code=0
  2     fe80::2a0:24ff:fec5:3256  fe80::202:b3ff:fe1e:8329  ICMPv6: Echo Reply Message Code=0

DLC: Ethertype=86DD, size=94 bytes
IPv6: ------ IPv6 Header ------
    IPv6:
    IPv6: Version            = 6
    IPv6: Priority           = 0 (Uncharacterized Traffic)
    IPv6: Flow Label         = 0x000000
    IPv6: Payload Length     = 40
    IPv6: Next Header         = 58 (ICMPv6)
    IPv6: Hop Limit          = 64
    IPv6: Source address     = fe80::2a0:24ff:fec5:3256
    IPv6: Destination address = fe80::202:b3ff:fe1e:8329
    IPv6:
ICMPv6: ------ ICMPv6 Header ------
    ICMPv6:
    ICMPv6: Type             = 129 (Echo Reply Message)
    ICMPv6: Code             = 0
    ICMPv6: Checksum         = 0x46CC
    ICMPv6: Identifier       = 0
    ICMPv6: Sequence Number  = 38
    ICMPv6: [32 Bytes of data]
    ICMPv6:

00000000: 00 02 b3 1e 83 29 00 a0 24 c5 32 56 86 dd 60 00  ...³..)..$.2V..`.
00000010: 00 00 00 28 3a 40 fe 80 00 00 00 00 00 00 02 a0  ...(:@þ.........
00000020: 24 ff fe c5 32 56 fe 80 00 00 00 00 00 00 02 02  $ÿþÅ2Vþ.........
00000030: b3 ff fe 1e 83 29 81 00 46 cc 00 00 00 26 61 62  ³ÿþ..)..FÌ...&ab
00000040: 63 64 65 66 67 68 69 6a 6b 6c 6d 6e 6f 70 71 72  cdefghijklmnopqr
00000050: 73 74 75 76 77 61 62 63 64 65 66 67 68 69        stuvwabcdefghi
```

Figure 4-9. Echo Reply in a trace file

Neighbor Discovery (ND)

Neighbor Discovery (ND) is specified in RFC 2461. The specifications in this RFC relate to different protocols and processes known from IPv4 that have been modified and improved. New functionality has also been added. It combines Address Resolution Protocol (ARP) and ICMP Router Discovery and Redirect. With IPv4, we have no means to detect whether a neighbor is reachable. With the Neighbor Discovery protocol, a Neighbor Unreachability Detection (NUD) mechanism has been defined. Duplicate IP address detection (DAD) has also been implemented. IPv6 nodes use Neighbor Discovery for the following purposes:

- For autoconfiguration of IPv6 addresses
- To determine network prefixes, routes and other configuration information
- For Duplicate IP address detection (DAD)
- To determine layer two addresses of nodes on the same link
- To find neighboring routers that can forward their packets
- To keep track of which neighbors are reachable and which are not (NUD)
- To detect changed link-layer addresses

The following improvements over the IPv4 set of protocols can be noted:

- Router Discovery is now part of the base protocol set. With IPv4, the mechanism needs to get the information from the routing table.

- Router Advertisement packets contain link-layer addresses for the router. There is no need for the node receiving a Router Advertisement to send out an additional ARP request (as an IPv4 node would have to do) to get the link-layer address for the router interface. The same is true for ICMPv6 Redirect messages; they contain the link-layer address of the new next-hop router interface.

- Router Advertisement packets contain the prefix for a link (subnet information). There is no longer a need to configure subnet masks; they can be learned from the Router Advertisement.

- Neighbor Discovery (ND) provides mechanisms to renumber networks more easily. New prefixes and addresses can be introduced while the old ones are still in use, and the old ones can be deprecated and removed gradually.

- Router Advertisements enable stateless address autoconfiguration and can tell hosts when to use stateful address configuration (e.g., DHCP).

- Routers can advertise an MTU to be used on a link.

- Multiple prefixes can be assigned to one link. By default, hosts learn all prefixes from the router, but the router can be configured not to advertise some or all of the prefixes. In that case, hosts assume that a non-advertised prefix destination is remote and send the packets to the router. The router can then issue ICMP Redirect messages as needed.

- Neighbor Unreachability Detection is part of the base protocol. It substantially improves packet delivery in case of failed routers or link interfaces that changed their link-layer address. It solves the issues with outdated ARP caches. ND detects failed connectivity, and traffic is not sent to unreachable neighbors. The Neighbor Unreachability Detection also detects failed routers and switches to live ones.

- Router Advertisements and ICMP redirects use link-local addresses to identify routers. This allows hosts to maintain their router associations even in the case of renumbering or use of new global prefixes.

- Neighbor Discovery messages have a hop limit value of 255, and requests with a lower hop limit are not answered. This makes Neighbor Discovery immune to remote hosts that try to sneak into your link, because their packets have a decremented hop limit and are thus ignored.

- Standard IP authentication and security mechanisms can be applied to neighbor discovery.

This summary gives an idea of what can be expected from this part of the specification. Now let's discuss the different processes in detail. The Neighbor Discovery protocol consists of five ICMP messages: a pair of Router Solicitation/Router Advertisement messages, a pair of Neighbor Solicitation/Neighbor Advertisement messages, and an ICMP Redirect message (refer to Table 4-2 earlier in this chapter for a summary of ICMP informational message types).

To summarize, the Neighbor Discovery Protocol (NDP) specification is used by both hosts and routers. Its functions include Neighbor Discovery (ND), Router Discovery (RD), Address Autoconfiguration, Address Resolution, Neighbor Unreachability Detection (NUD), Duplicate Address Detection (DAD), and Redirection.

Router Solicitation and Router Advertisement

Routers send out Router Advertisement messages at regular intervals. Hosts can request Router Advertisements by issuing a Router Solicitation message. This will trigger routers to issue Router Advertisements immediately, outside of the regular interval. The format is shown in Figure 4-10.

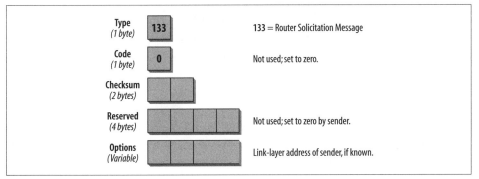

Figure 4-10. Router Solicitation message

In the IP header of a Router Solicitation message, you will usually see the all-routers multicast address of FF02::2 as a Destination address. The hop limit is set to 255. The ICMP Type field is set to 133, which is the value for the Router Solicitation message. The Code field is unused and set to 0. The following two bytes are used for the Checksum. The next four bytes are unused and reserved for future use. The sender sets them to 0, and the receiver ignores those fields. For a Router Solicitation message, a valid option is the link-layer address of the sending host, if the address of the sending host is known. If the Source address on the IP layer is the unspecified (all-zeros) address, this field is not used. More options may be defined in future versions of ND. If a host cannot recognize an option, it should ignore the option and process the packet.

Routers that receive this Solicitation message reply with a Router Advertisement message. Routers also issue those messages periodically. The format of the Router Advertisement message is shown in Figure 4-11.

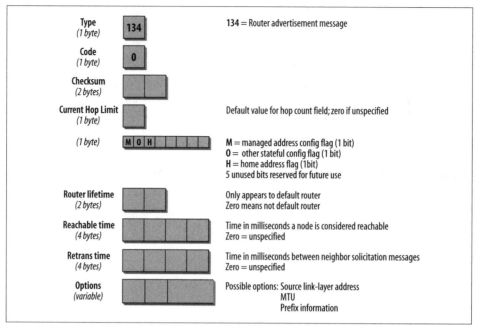

Figure 4-11. Router Advertisement message

By inspecting the IP header of the Router Advertisement message, you can determine whether this Router Advertisement is periodic or was sent in reply to a Solicitation message. A periodic advertisement's Destination address will be the all-nodes multicast address FF02::1. A solicited advertisement's Destination address will be the address of the interface that originated the solicitation message. Again, the hop limit is set to 255.

The ICMP Type field is set to 134, the value for a Router Advertisement message; the Code field is unused and set to 0. The Current Hop Limit field can be used to configure all nodes on a link for a default hop limit. The value entered in this field will be used as a default hop limit value in outgoing packets by all nodes on the link. A value of 0 in this field means that this option is unspecified by this router—in which case the default hop limit values of the source hosts are used.

The next 1-bit field, the M flag, specifies whether *Stateful configuration* is to be used. Stateful configuration refers to what we know as DHCP with IPv4. If this bit is 0, the nodes on this link use Stateless autoconfiguration. If the bit is set to 1, it specifies Stateful autoconfiguration. The O-flag configures whether nodes on this link use Stateful configuration other than IP address information. A value of 1 means the nodes on this link use Stateful configuration for non-address-related information. The Mobile IPv6 specification (RFC 3775) defines the third bit, the home address flag (H-flag). When a router sets the H-flag to 1, it means that it is a home agent for this link. For a discussion of Mobile IPv6, refer to Chapter 11. The remaining five bits of this byte are reserved for future use and must be 0.

The Router Lifetime field is important only if this router is to be used as a default router by the nodes on the link. A value of 0 indicates that this router is not a default router and will therefore not appear on the default router list of receiving nodes. Any other value in this field specifies the lifetime, in seconds, associated with this router as a default router. The maximum value is 18.2 hours.

There is an optional extension to the Router Advertisement message, which allows routers to advertise preferences and more specific routes. This makes it possible for hosts to choose the best router in situations where they receive more than one router advertisement. It is also important for multihomed routers, which will be an increasingly important scenario in the IPv6 network. This extension uses the two bits after the H-flag in the router advertisement as a *Preference flag* and defines a *Route Information option*. It is specified in RFC 4191.

The Reachable Time field indicates the time in which a host assumes that neighbors are reachable after having received a reachability confirmation. A value of 0 means that it is unspecified. The Neighbor Unreachability Detection algorithm uses this field.

The Retrans Timer field is used by the address resolution and Neighbor Unreachability Detection mechanisms; it states the time in milliseconds between retransmitted Neighbor Solicitation messages. A value of 0 indicates that this router is not configured with a retransmission timer.

For the Options field, there are currently three possible values:

- Source link-layer address.
- MTU size to be used on links with variable MTU sizes (Token Ring, for example).
- Prefix information, important for Stateless autoconfiguration. The router inserts all its prefixes for the link that the nodes on the link need to know.

More options may be defined in future versions of ND. A trace file later in this chapter shows what the options look like.

Neighbor Solicitation and Neighbor Advertisement

This pair of messages fulfills two functions: the link-layer address resolution that is handled by ARP in IPv4, and the Neighbor Unreachability Detection mechanism. If the Destination address is a multicast address (usually the solicited node multicast address), the source is resolving a link-layer address. If the source is verifying the reachability of a neighbor, the Destination address is a unicast address. This message type is also used for Duplicate IP Address Detection (DAD).

The format of the Neighbor Solicitation message is shown in Figure 4-12.

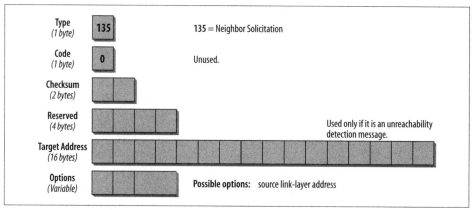

Figure 4-12. Format of the Neighbor Solicitation message

In the IP header of this message type, the Source address can be either the interface address of the originating host or, in the case of Stateless autoconfiguration and DAD, the unspecified (all-zeros) address. The hop limit is set to 255. The Type field in the ICMP header is set to 135, and the Code field is unused and set to 0. After the two checksum bytes, four unused bytes are reserved and must be set to 0. The target address is used in Neighbor Advertisement and Redirect messages. It must not be a multicast address.

The Options field can contain the link-layer Source address, but only if it is not sent from the all-zeros address. During Stateless autoconfiguration, in a message that uses the unspecified address as a Source address, the Options field is set to 0. The link-layer option must be used in multicast solicitations (link layer address detection) and can be used in unicast solicitations (Unreachability Detection).

Neighbor Advertisement messages are sent as a reply to Neighbor Solicitation messages or to propagate new information quickly. The format of the message is shown in Figure 4-13.

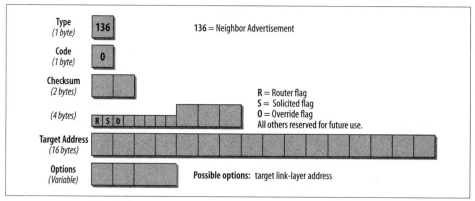

Figure 4-13. Format of the Neighbor Advertisement message

The type of address in the IP header indicates whether the message is the answer to a solicitation or an unsolicited message. In the case of a solicited advertisement, the destination IP address is the Source address of the interface that sent the solicitation. If the message is the reply to a DAD message that originated from an unspecified Source address, the reply will go to the all-nodes multicast address of FF02::1. The same is true for all unsolicited periodic advertisements.

The Type field in the ICMP header is set to 136, the value for Neighbor Advertisement messages. The Code field is unused and set to 0. When the Router flag is set, the sender is a router.

When the Solicited flag is set, the message is sent in response to a Neighbor Solicitation. For instance, if a host confirms its reachability in answer to an unreachability detection message, the S bit is set. The S bit is not set in multicast advertisements. The Override flag indicates that the information in the Advertisement message should override existing Neighbor Cache entries and update any cached link-layer addresses. If the O bit is not set, the advertisement will not update a cached link-layer address, but it will update an existing Neighbor Cache entry for which no link-layer address exists. The O bit should not be set in an advertisement for an anycast address. I discuss the cache entries later in this chapter. The remaining 29 bits are reserved for future use and set to 0.

In solicited advertisements, the Target Address contains the address of the interface that sent the solicitation. In unsolicited advertisements, this field contains the address of the interface whose link-layer address has changed. A possible option for the Options field is the target link-layer address.

Table 4-6 helps you to identify what you are looking at and summarizes the different processes.

Table 4-6. Identification of ND messages

Source address	Destination address	Message type
All-zero (::0)	All-routers multicast Solicited node multicast	Stateless autoconfiguration DAD
Unicast	Solicited node multicast Unicast	Resolve link-layer address Unreachability detection

The ICMP Redirect Message

Routers issue ICMP Redirect messages to inform a node of a better first-hop node on the path to a given destination. A Redirect message can also inform a node that the destination used is in fact a neighbor on the same link and not a node on a remote subnet. The format of the ICMPv6 Redirect message is shown in Figure 4-14.

The Source address in the IP header must be the link-local address of the interface from which the message is sent. The Destination address in the IP header is the

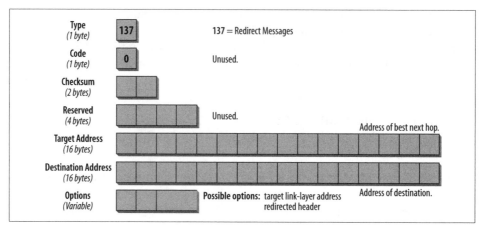

Figure 4-14. Format of the ICMP Redirect message

Source address from the packet that triggered the redirect message. The hop limit is set to 255.

The Target Address field contains the link-local address of the interface that is a better next-hop to use for the given Destination address. The Destination Address field contains the address of the destination that is redirected. If the address in the Target Address field is the same as the address in the Destination Address field, the destination is a neighbor and not a remote node. The Options field contains the link-layer address for the target (the best next-hop router) if it is known. This is an improvement on the IPv4 version, in which the host needed to issue a separate ARP request to determine the link-layer address of the next-hop router. The remaining bits in the options field contain as much of the redirected header as fits into the minimum IPv6 MTU of 1,280 bytes.

Inverse Neighbor Discovery

Inverse Neighbor Discovery (IND) is an extension to ND. It was originally designed for Frame Relay networks, but it can be used in other networks with similar requirements. IND is specified in RFC 3122. It consists of two messages: the IND Solicitation and the IND Advertisement message. The messages are used to determine the IPv6 address of hosts for which the link layer address is known. IND corresponds to the Reverse Address Resolution Protocol (RARP) used with IPv4. The messages have the same format as the ND messages. The IND Solicitation has a message type of 141 and the IND Advertisement of 142. The code field is always set to 0.

The Options field has the same format as in the ND messages and contains the same options. Two new IND-specific options have been defined. Option Type 9 defines the Source Address list; option Type 10 the Target Address list (see the overview in Table 4-7).

Source Address list—option Type 9
> List of one or more IPv6 addresses of the interface, which is specified in the Source Link Layer address option.

Target Address list—option Type 10
> List of all IPv6 addresses of the interface, which is specified in the Target Link Layer address list.

When a host wants to determine the IPv6 address of an interface for which it knows the link-layer address, it sends an IND solicitation to the all-nodes multicast address. On the link layer, the message is sent directly to the interface in question. The destination replies with an IND advertisement containing the Target Address list. If the interface has more IPv6 addresses than fit into a single advertisement message, it must send multiple IND advertisements. Like in all other ND messages, the hop limit is set to 255, and messages with a hop limit lower than 255 must be ignored.

Neighbor Discovery Options

Neighbor Discovery messages contain a variable-size Options field that has the format shown in Figure 4-15.

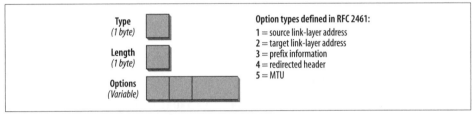

Figure 4-15. Format of the Option field

The Type field indicates what type of option follows. The following types are defined in RFC 2461:

- Type 1: source link-layer address
- Type 2: target link-layer address
- Type 3: prefix information
- Type 4: redirected header
- Type 5: MTU

The Length field indicates the length of the option. Value 0 is invalid for this field, and packets with this value must be discarded. The calculation of the length includes the Type and Length fields.

Table 4-7 shows an overview of the different options and the message types in which they are used.

Table 4-7. *Overview of ND options*

Option type	Used in
Type 1 Source link-layer address	Neighbor solicitation Router solicitation Router advertisement IND solicitation/advertisement
Type 2 Target link layer address	Neighbor advertisement Redirect IND solicitation/advertisement
Type 3 Prefix	Router advertisement
Type 4 Redirected header	Redirect
Type 5 MTU	Router advertisement IND solicitation/advertisement
Type 7 Advertisement interval	Router advertisement (defined in Mobile IPv6 specification)
Type 8 Home Agent information	Router advertisement (defined in Mobile IPv6 specification)
Type 9 Source address list	IND Solicitation
Type 10 Target address list	IND Advertisement

Secure Neighbor Discovery

ND can be used for a number of attacks and should therefore be protected. An example of a Denial of Service attack is when a node on the link can both advertise itself as a default router and also send "forged" Router Advertisement messages that immediately time out all other default routers as well as all on-link prefixes.

The first protection is that packets coming from off-link (with a hop limit lower than 255) must be ignored. Further, the original ND specification suggests using IPsec to secure ND messages. However, this requires manual setup of security associations or the use of a key management protocol. The number of security associations to be configured for protecting ND can be very large, so this approach may be impractical.

The Secure Neighbor Discovery (SEND) working group was chartered with the goal to define the protocol support needed to secure ND. Three different trust models were outlined, roughly corresponding to secured corporate intranets, public wireless access networks, and pure ad hoc networks. A number of possible threats are discussed relating to these trust models. Refer to RFC 3756 for more details.

The SEND protocol, defined in RFC 3971, is designed to counter the threats to ND. SEND can be used in environments where physical security on the link is not assured (such as over wireless) and attacks on ND are a concern. The following components are specified in RFC 3971:

- Certification paths anchored on trusted parties certify the authority of routers. A host must be configured with a trust anchor to which the router has a certification path before the host can adopt the router as its default router. *Certification Path Solicitation and Advertisement* messages are used to discover a certification path to the trust anchor.

- *Cryptographically Generated Addresses* (CGA) are used to make sure that the sender of a Neighbor Discovery message is the owner of the claimed address. A public-private key pair is generated by all nodes before they can claim an address. A new ND option, the CGA option, is used to carry the public key and associated parameters.

- Another new ND option, the *RSA Signature* option, is used to protect all messages relating to Neighbor and Router discovery.

- Two new ND options, the *Timestamp* and *Nonce* options, have been introduced to prevent replay attacks.

The SEND protocol uses Cryptographically Generated Addresses. SEND currently does not support the protection of ND messages for nodes configured with a static address or with addresses configured through IPv6 Stateless autoconfiguration mechanisms. All new option types and messages are specified in RFC 3971.

Cryptographically Generated Addresses (CGA) are specified in RFC 3972, which defines a method for binding a public signature key to an IPv6 address in the SEND protocol. CGA are IPv6 addresses for which the interface identifier is generated by computing a cryptographic one-way hash function from a public key and auxiliary parameters.

ND in the Trace File

At this point, you all deserve a refreshment. The following trace file shows what ND looks like in the real world and illustrates what we have been talking about.

The screenshot in Figure 4-16 shows the details of a Router Advertisement with two Option fields. This trace file was taken when we had just set up our router. Besides initializing the IPv6 stack and configuring it for the prefix, we have not changed any of the configuration parameters. The options used in this case are options 1 (source link-layer address) and 3 (prefix information). Note the format of the Option fields.

The Type field is set to 134, the value for a Router Advertisement. The Current Hop Limit has a value of 64. All nodes on this link will use this value for their Hop Count field. The M and O flags are not set by default. The Router Lifetime is set to 1800, which indicates that this is a default router. The first Option listed is type 1. The link-layer address in the detail screen contains the link-layer address of the router

```
No. St Source Address                    Dest Address          Summary
11    fe80::210:7bff:fe0b:75a0           ff02::1               ICMPv6: Router Advertisement Code=0
```

```
DLC: Ethertype=86DD, size=110 bytes
IPv6: Flow=0x000000
ICMPv6: ----- ICMPv6 Header -----
    ICMPv6:
    ICMPv6: Type                      = 134 (Router Advertisement)
    ICMPv6: Code                      = 0
    ICMPv6: Checksum                  = 786B (correct)
    ICMPv6: Current Hop Limit         = 64
    ICMPv6: M/O/H/Reserved bits       = 00
    ICMPv6:              0... ....    = administered protocol not used (address)
    ICMPv6:              .0.. ....    = administered protocol not used (non-address)
    ICMPv6:              ..0. ....    = Home Agent bit
    ICMPv6:              ...0 0000    = Reserved            = 0x00
    ICMPv6: Router Lifetime           = 1800 s
    ICMPv6: Reachable Time            = 0 ms (unspecified)
    ICMPv6: Retrans Timer             = 0 ms (unspecified)
    ICMPv6:
    ICMPv6: Options follow
    ICMPv6: Type                      = 1 (Source Link-Layer Address)
    ICMPv6: Length                    = 1 (units of 8 octets)
    ICMPv6: Link Layer Address        = Station Cisco 0B75A0
    ICMPv6: Type                      = 3 (Prefix Information)
    ICMPv6: Length                    = 4 (units of 8 octets)
    ICMPv6: Prefix Length             = 64
    ICMPv6: L/A/R bits                = C0
    ICMPv6:              1... ....    = on-link determination
    ICMPv6:              .1.. ....    = autonomous address configuration
    ICMPv6:              ..0. ....    = Router Address bit
    ICMPv6:              ...0 0000    = Reserved            = 0x00
    ICMPv6: Valid Lifetime            = 4294967295 s (infinity)
    ICMPv6: Preferred Lifetime        = 4294967295 s (infinity)
    ICMPv6: Reserved                  = 0x00000000
    ICMPv6: Prefix                    = caff:ca01:0:56::
    ICMPv6:
```

Figure 4-16. The Router Advertisement in a trace file

interface. The second Option is of type 3 for prefix information. Note all the additional information that can be given with a prefix. The Prefix Length field specifies the number of bits valid for the prefix (i.e., the length of the subnet mask). The L bit is the on-link flag. If set, it indicates that this prefix can be used for on-link determination. If it is not set, the advertisement does not make a statement, and the prefix can be used for on- and off-link configuration. The A bit is the autonomous address configuration flag. If set, it indicates that the prefix can be used for autonomous address configuration. In this case, the host will generate an address by adding the interface identifier to the prefix or, if the privacy options are used, by adding a random number. The Valid Lifetime field specifies how long this prefix is valid. A value of all Fs means infinity. The Preferred Lifetime specifies how long the address being configured with this prefix can remain in the preferred state. Here as well, a value of all Fs means infinity. The last field shows the prefix of `caff:ca01:0:56::` advertised by this router.

Link-Layer Address Resolution

Link Layer Address Resolution is the process that happens when a node wants to determine the link-layer address of an interface for which it knows the IP address.

With IPv4, this is the functionality of ARP. Link Layer Address Resolution is performed only for nodes that are known to be on the same link (neighbors) and is never performed for multicast addresses.

With IPv6, this is a functionality accomplished with ND messages. A node wanting to resolve a link layer address sends a Neighbor Solicitation message to the solicited node multicast address of the neighbor. This solicitation message contains the link-layer address of the sender in the ND option field. If the destination is reachable, it replies with a Neighbor Advertisement message containing its link-layer address. If the resolving node does not receive an answer within a preconfigured number of attempts, the address resolution has failed.

Neighbor Unreachability Detection (NUD)

A neighbor is considered reachable if the node has recently received a confirmation that packets sent to the neighbor have been received by its IP layer. This confirmation can come in one of two ways: it can be a Neighbor Advertisement in response to a Neighbor Solicitation, or it can be an upper-layer process that indicates the successful connection (e.g., an active TCP connection). In this case, the receipt of TCP acknowledgements implies the reachability of the neighbor.

To keep track of active and reachable connections, IPv6 nodes use different tables. Two important tables relating to ND are the Neighbor and Destination Caches, which I discuss in the next section.

Neighbor Cache and Destination Cache

IPv6 nodes need to maintain different tables of information. Among these tables, the Neighbor Cache and Destination Cache are particularly important. Depending on the IPv6 stack you are working with, the implementation and the troubleshooting utilities will be different. But the information must be available on every IPv6 node.

Neighbor Cache

The *Neighbor Cache* maintains a list of neighbors to which traffic has been sent recently. They are listed by their unicast IP addresses, and each entry contains information about the neighbor's link-layer address and a flag that indicates whether the neighbor is a router or host. This can be compared to the ARP cache in an IPv4 node. The entry also contains information about whether there are packets queued to be sent to that destination, information about the neighbor's reachability, and the time the next neighbor unreachability detection event is scheduled to take place.

Destination Cache

This table maintains information about destinations to which traffic has been sent recently, including local and remote destinations. The Neighbor Cache can be seen as a subset of Destination Cache information. In case of remote destinations, the entry lists the link-layer address of the next-hop router. The Destination Cache is updated with information received by ICMP Redirect messages. It can also contain additional information about MTU sizes and roundtrip timers.

The Neighbor and Destination Caches have been mentioned in regard to the Override flag that can be set in a Neighbor Advertisement message. If the Override flag is set, the information in the Advertisement message should override existing Neighbor Cache entries and update any cached link-layer addresses in the cache of the host that receives the advertisement. If the O bit is not set, the advertisement will not update a cached link-layer address, but it will update an existing Neighbor Cache entry for which no link-layer address exists.

The screenshot in Figure 4-17 shows the Neighbor Cache entries of our Cisco router. There were two hosts on the link at the time the screenshot was taken.

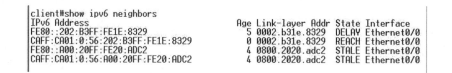

```
client#show ipv6 neighbors
IPv6 Address                            Age Link-layer Addr State Interface
FE80::202:B3FF:FE1E:8329                  5 0002.b31e.8329  DELAY Ethernet0/0
CAFF:CA01:0:56:202:B3FF:FE1E:8329         0 0002.b31e.8329  REACH Ethernet0/0
FE80::A00:20FF:FE20:ADC2                  4 0800.2020.adc2  STALE Ethernet0/0
CAFF:CA01:0:56:A00:20FF:FE20:ADC2         4 0800.2020.adc2  STALE Ethernet0/0
```

Figure 4-17. Neighbor Cache entries on a router

According to RFC 2461, a Neighbor Cache entry can be in one of five states. The five states are explained in Table 4-8.

Table 4-8. States of Neighbor Cache entries

State	Description
Incomplete	Address resolution is currently being performed and awaiting either a response or a timeout. Specifically, a Neighbor Solicitation has been sent to the solicited-node multicast address of the target, but the corresponding Neighbor Advertisement has not yet been received.
Reachable	This neighbor is currently reachable, which means positive confirmation was received within the last ReachableTime milliseconds that the neighbor was functioning properly.
Stale	More than ReachableTime milliseconds have elapsed since the last positive confirmation that the forward path was functioning properly was received. No action will take place regarding this neighbor until a packet is sent.
Delay	This neighbor's Reachable Time has expired, and a packet was sent within the last DelayFirstProbeTime seconds. If no confirmation is received within the DelayFirstProbeTime seconds, send a Neighbor Solicitation and change the neighbor state to Probe state. The use of Delay allows upper-layer protocols additional time to provide reachability confirmation. Without this extra time, possible redundant traffic would be generated.
Probe	A reachability confirmation is being actively attempted by sending Neighbor Solicitations every RetransTimer milliseconds until reachability is confirmed.

If you are interested in the details about the timers, default values, and configuration options, refer to RFC 2461.

Autoconfiguration

The autoconfiguration capability of IPv6 saves network administrators a lot of work. It has been designed to ensure that manually configuring hosts before connecting them to the network is not required. Even larger sites with multiple networks and routers should not need a DHCP server to configure hosts. The autoconfiguration features of IPv6 will be a key feature of the protocol when all sorts of devices—such as televisions, refrigerators, DVD players, and mobile phones—use IP addresses. You don't want to depend on a DHCP server to use your home devices.

IPv6 knows both Stateless and Stateful autoconfiguration. Stateful autoconfiguration is what we call DHCP in the IPv4 world; it is discussed in Chapter 9. What's really new with IPv6 is that hosts can autoconfigure their IPv6 addresses without any manual configuration of the host. Some configuration might be done on the routers, but no DHCP servers are required for this configuration mechanism. To generate its IP address, a host uses a combination of local information, such as its MAC address or a randomly chosen ID, and information received from routers. Routers can advertise multiple prefixes, and hosts determine prefix information from these advertisements. This allows for simple renumbering of a site: only the prefix information on the router has to be changed. For instance, if you change your ISP and the new ISP assigns a new IPv6 prefix, you can configure your routers to advertise this new prefix, keeping the subnet IDs that you used with the old prefix. All hosts attached to those routers will renumber themselves through the autoconfiguration mechanism. You can find more on renumbering networks later in this chapter. If there is no router present, a host can generate only a link-local address with the prefix FE80, but this address is sufficient for communication of nodes attached to the same link.

Stateless and Stateful autoconfiguration can also be combined. For instance, a host can use Stateless autoconfiguration to generate an IPv6 address but then use Stateful autoconfiguration for additional parameters.

An IPv6 address is leased to a node for a certain lifetime. When the lifetime expires, the address becomes invalid. To make sure an address is unique on a link, a node runs the Duplicate Address Detection (DAD) process. The DAD algorithm is defined in RFC 2462. An IPv6 address can have different states:

Tentative address
> This is an address that has not yet been assigned. It is the state prior to the assignment, when uniqueness is being verified (during DAD). A node cannot communicate in the network using a tentative address. The only messages that can be processed with a tentative address are ND messages relating to the autoconfiguration process.

Preferred address
> This is the address that has been assigned to an interface and can be used without any restrictions for the lifetime assigned.

Deprecated address

The use of this address is discouraged but not forbidden. A deprecated address might be one whose lifetime is about to expire. It can still be used to continue a communication that would disrupt a service if the address changed. It is no longer used as a Source address for newly established communications.

Valid address

This term is used for both the Preferred and Deprecated address.

Invalid address

An invalid address is not assigned to an interface. A valid address becomes invalid when its lifetime expires.

 Autoconfiguration as defined in RFC 2462 only applies to hosts, not to routers. Routers should be configured in a different way. A router can use Stateless autoconfiguration for the generation of its link-local addresses, and it must use the DAD process for each of its addresses.

When a node is autoconfigured, the following steps are performed:

1. A link-local address is generated by using the link-local prefix of FE80 and appending the interface identifier. This address is a tentative address.

2. The node joins the following multicast groups: the all-nodes multicast group (FF02::1) and the solicited-node multicast group for the tentative address (from step 1).

3. A Neighbor Solicitation message is sent out with the tentative address as the target address. The IP Source address of this message is the all-zeros address; the IP Destination address is the solicited-node multicast address. This detects whether another node on the link already uses this address; i.e., this is DAD. If there is such a node, it replies with a Neighbor Advertisement message, and the autoconfiguration mechanism stops. In this case, manual reconfiguration of the host is required. If there is no answer to the Neighbor Solicitation, it is safe to use the address; the address is assigned to the interface and the state of the address changes to "preferred." IP connectivity on the local link is now established. So far, the process is the same for hosts and routers, but only hosts perform the next step.

4. In order to determine which routers are out there and what the prefix is, the host sends a Router Solicitation message to the all-routers multicast group of FF02::2.

5. All routers on the link reply with a Router Advertisement. For each prefix in Router Advertisements with the Autonomous Configuration flag set, an address is generated, combining the prefix with the interface identifier. These addresses are added to the list of assigned addresses for the interface.

All addresses must be verified with a Neighbor Solicitation message (DAD) before they are assigned. If the link-local address was generated through the autoconfiguration mechanism using the interface identifier, uniqueness has been verified in step 3 and may not need to be repeated for additional addresses that use the same interface identifier. All other addresses configured manually or through Stateful configuration need to be verified individually. Multihomed hosts perform autoconfiguration for each interface.

The trace shown in the screenshot in Figure 4-18 was taken during the autoconfiguration process of Marvin, our Windows host. Figure 4-18 shows some of the processes and message types discussed earlier, and the discussion of the trace summarizes the concepts in this section.

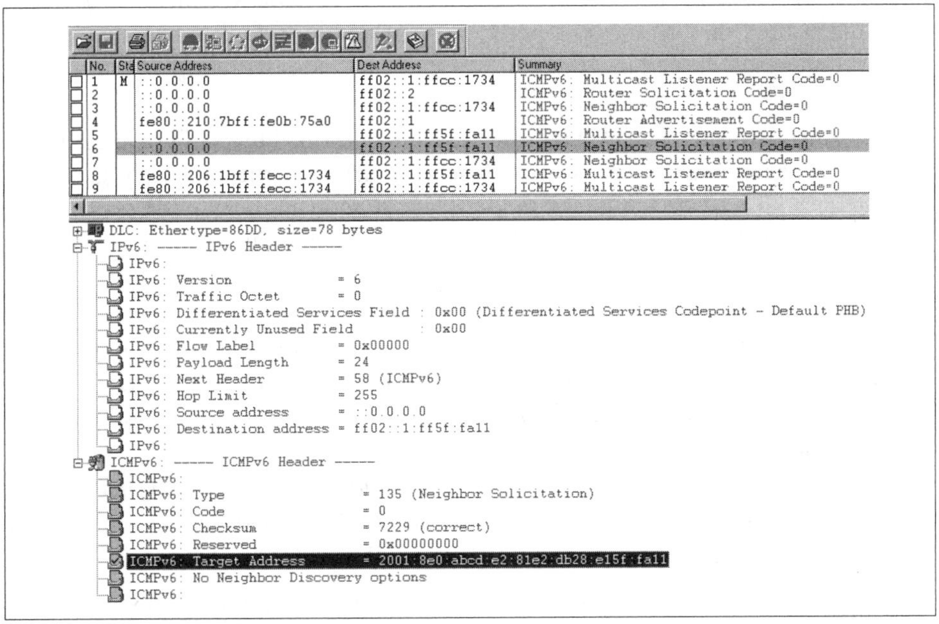

Figure 4-18. Autoconfiguration in the trace file

As long as the booting host does not have a valid IPv6 address it sends all packets from its unspecified all-zeros address, represented as ::0.0.0.0 in the trace file.

First packet

> With the first packet, the booting host registers for its solicited node multicast address based on its MAC identifier. The packet contains a Hop-by-Hop Options header with option type 5 for MLD messages. The hop limit is set to 1.

Second packet

> With the second packet, it sends a Router Solicitation message to the all-routers multicast address FF02::2.

Third packet

> In packet three, it sends a Neighbor Solicitation to the solicited node address in order to perform DAD. The Target Address field of the ICMPv6 header contains

the link local address of FE80::206:1BFF:FECC:1734. If another node on the link already used this address, it would reply with a Neighbor Advertisement message.

Fourth packet

The router sends a Router Advertisement to the all-nodes multicast address of FF02::1, because the host does not have a valid IPv6 address yet. This Router Advertisement has the Autonomous Address Configuration flag set to one and contains the prefix 2001:8E0:ABCD:E2::/64.

Fifth packet

With this packet, the host registers for the solicited node multicast address of FF02::1:FF5F:FA11. This is not the interface ID used in packet one. Microsoft has implemented the privacy option and it is enabled by default, so this is the randomly generated interface ID.

Sixth packet

The host performs the DAD test for the address formed by combining the prefix sent in the Router Advertisement (packet four) with the randomly generated interface ID. The packet is sent to the solicited node multicast address. The IPv6 address can be seen in the highlighted line in the detail window opened for packet six.

Seventh packet

The host performs the DAD test for the IPv6 address formed by combining the prefix learned from the Router Advertisement and the MAC identifier. The Target Address field contains the IPv6 address 2001:8E0:ABCD:E2:206:1BFF:FECC:1734.

Eighth and ninth packets

The host uses its MAC identifier based IPv6 address that is in preferred state to register for its two solicited node multicast addresses. Both packets contain the Hop-by-Hop Options header with option type 5 for MLD messages.

When you take your own traces to analyze a boot process and use different operating systems, you will also find differences in the process shown in the trace file. Figure 4-18 is what the boot process looks like with a Windows XP host with SP1 and the advanced networking pack. The differences come from the fact that the RFCs leave room for interpretation of the standard, which can be implemented slightly differently by different vendors. As long as the "must-use" rules in the RFCs are followed, compliance should not be an issue. Note the "should"; this is where your trace file analysis expertise will be helpful in case of failures. Another reason for differences is that the implementation behavior depends on what level and state of the standardization has been implemented. If Microsoft implements the privacy option, this stack will obviously behave differently from a stack that has not implemented the privacy option. So when you analyze processes of a specific operating system, get enough information from the vendor about which RFCs (and sometimes drafts) have been implemented. And if the vendor states that it implemented something, you can use your trace files to verify whether the stack works as it should.

To configure hosts that use Stateless autoconfiguration for additional information (e.g., DNS servers), a Stateless DHCP server has been specified. See the description in Chapter 9 of upper-layer protocols.

Network Renumbering

With the mechanisms given by ICMPv6, renumbering a network in an IPv6 world may become a lot easier in the future. Currently there is not much operational experience.

Renumbering a network means replacing an old prefix with a new prefix. This can become necessary for a number of reasons, a common one being a change of provider, which usually implies a change of prefix.

Renumbering a network may encompass the following steps:

1. Each link in the network must be assigned a subprefix from the new prefix before beginning the procedure. This is important for the overall process, in order to ensure proper configuration of all relevant devices and services such as routers, switches, interfaces, DNS, DHCP, etc.

2. The DNS database must be updated with the addresses for interfaces from the new prefix, and addresses for interfaces from the old prefix must be removed. Obviously the changes to DNS must be coordinated with the changes to addresses assigned to interfaces. The propagation of this new information can be controlled by parameters such as the "Time to Live" (TTL) for DNS records and the update interval between primary and secondary DNS servers.

3. Switches and routers are prepared for the new prefix. All necessary changes in the routing infrastructure for the new prefix are added in parallel to the old prefix, while the old prefix is still used for datagram services. This includes not only routers and switches, but also firewalls, ingress and egress filters, and all other filtering functions. For propagating subnet prefix information to routers, the IPv6 Prefix option for DHCPv6 (RFC 3633) may be used. In the case where hosts use Stateless autoconfiguration, the routers are not configured to advertise the prefix for autoconfiguration yet (meaning that the Autonomous Address Configuration flag is not set). This will be done once stable routing for the new prefix has been verified.

4. All access lists, route maps, and other network configuration options (e.g., name services other than DNS) that use IP addresses should be checked to ensure that hosts and services that use the new prefix will behave as they did with the old one.

5. Test and verify network infrastructure and routing for the new prefix.

6. Advertise the new prefix outside of the corporate network. Configure all border defense systems accordingly to protect the new prefix from outside attacks.

7. Assign addresses from the new prefix to interfaces on hosts while still retaining the addresses from the old prefix. If Stateless autoconfiguration is used, the "autonomous address-config" flag is set for the new prefix, so hosts configure addresses for the new prefix in addition to the old addresses. DHCP now assigns addresses from both prefixes if it is used. The new information can be propagated by using the DHCP Reconfigure message, which will cause every DHCP client to contact the DHCP server. The addresses from the new prefix will not be used until they are inserted into DNS.

8. When the new prefix has been fully integrated into the network infrastructure and tested for stable operation, hosts, switches, and routers can begin using the new prefix. Once the transition has completed, the old prefix will not be in use in the network and can be removed step by step from DNS.

Special attention has to be given to applications and devices that do not get their IP addresses from DHCP or DNS, or that cache or store IP address information locally.

This is a high-level view of a renumbering process and obviously—as all network administrators know well—there are many details and possible pitfalls to be considered. Thorough and careful planning of this process is a must. RFC 4192 describes this process.

Path MTU Discovery

With IPv4, every router can fragment packets if needed. If a router cannot forward a packet because the MTU of the next link is smaller than the packet it has to send, the router fragments the packet. It cuts it into slices that fit the smaller MTU and sends it out as a set of fragments. The packet is then reassembled at the final destination. Depending on the network design, an IPv4 packet may be fragmented more than once during its travel through the network.

With IPv6, routers do not fragment packets anymore; the sender takes care of it. Path MTU discovery tries to ensure that a packet is sent using the largest possible size that is supported on a certain route. The Path MTU is the smallest link MTU of all links from a source to a destination. The discovery of the Path MTU is described in RFC 1981.

The discovery process works like this. First, a host assumes that the Path MTU is the same as the MTU of the first hop link and it uses that size. If the packet is too big for a certain router along the path to deliver the packet to the next link, the router discards the packet and sends back an ICMPv6 Packet Too Big message. Recall that this message type includes the MTU size of the next hop link. The host now uses this MTU for sending further packets to the same destination. The host will never go below the IPv6 minimum MTU size of 1280 bytes, however. The process of receiving a Packet Too Big message and reducing the size of the packets can happen more than once before the packet reaches its destination. The discovery process ends when the packets arrive at the final destination.

The path from a given source to a given destination can change, and so can the Path MTU. Smaller MTU sizes are discovered by getting Packet Too Big messages. An IPv6 host will try to increase the MTU size from time to time in order to be able to detect a larger Path MTU. Path MTU discovery also supports multicast destinations. If the destination is multicast, there are many paths that copies of the packets may travel, and each path can have a different Path MTU. Packet Too Big messages will be generated just as with a unicast destination, and the packet size used by the sender is the smallest Path MTU of the whole set of destinations.

Multicast Listener Discovery (MLD)

Multicast has been available in IPv4 since 1988 and is used to address a certain group of hosts at the same time. Instead of sending out a broadcast, which is not routable and has to be processed by every node on the subnet, the multicast packet is addressed to a multicast group address out of the Class D address range. Only the hosts that are members of that multicast group will process the packet. Multicast messages can be forwarded over routers. In order to make this routing efficient, a multicast group management protocol ensures that routers only forward multicast packets over interfaces to links with members of the multicast group.

In IPv6, multicast is an integral part of the protocol and is available on all IPv6 nodes. A new multicast address format has been defined with a prefix of FF and with added functionality by using scopes in addition to the group address. For example, a multicast group address can be in a link-local scope (FF02), a site-local scope (FF05), or a global scope (FF0E). For an explanation of the multicast address format and a list of scope identifiers, refer to Chapter 3.

Multicast group management in IPv4 is done through Internet Group Management Protocol (IGMP). Version 2 of IGMP is defined in RFC 2236. IPv6 uses ICMPv6 messages for the same functionality; initial development was based on the IGMPv2 specification. It is now called *Multicast Listener Discovery* (MLD). Version 1 of MLD is defined in RFC 2710. In 2004, MLD Version 2 was defined. It extends MLD Version 1 to support the use of Source Specific Multicast (SSM). It is based on IGMPv3 (RFC 3376) and is specified in RFC 3810. MLDv2 is compatible with MLD Version 1.

MLD is the protocol that allows multicast listeners to register for multicast addresses they want to use, to ensure efficient routing. Therefore, a routing mechanism is needed to manage the forwarding of multicast messages. PIM (Protocol Independent Multicast, RFC 2362) can be used with IPv6 with minimal changes. To find information about the status of PIM, go to the IETF working group at *http://www.ietf.org/ html.charters/pim-charter.html*.

MLD is an asymmetric protocol. The behavior of *listeners*, i.e., nodes that want to receive messages destined for a specific multicast group, differs from the behavior of routers. For multicast addresses where a router is a listener, it uses both parts of the protocol. Routers use MLD to discover which multicast addresses have listeners on each of their links. For each attached link, the router keeps a list of listener addresses. It does not keep track of how many members are listening to an address. A multicast address is listed as long as there is at least one member on the link. A listener sends member reports for its multicast addresses. With these messages, it registers with routers on the link to receive the messages addressed to the respective multicast group. If the multicast address is not in the routers list for this link, the router adds the address to its list of multicast addresses to be forwarded over this interface. With a Done message, a listener deregisters for a multicast address. When the last member of a group deregisters for a multicast address, the router removes the address from its list for this link.

All MLD messages are sent with a link-local IPv6 Source address and a hop limit of one to make sure they remain on the local link. The packet has a Hop-by-Hop Options header with the Router Alert flag set. Thus, routers will not ignore the packet, even if they are not listening to the multicast group address in question. Refer to Chapter 2 for more information on Extension headers.

MLDv1

The following message types have been specified for MLDv1 (RFC 2710):

Multicast Listener Query—type 130
> Used by an IPv6 router to query the multicast addresses on a link. There are two types of queries: the general query used to determine the multicast addresses that have listeners on the link (in the general query, the multicast address field is set to zero) and the address specific query used to find out whether there are members for a specific multicast address on a link (the multicast address field is set to the multicast address for which the query is done).

Multicast Listener Report—type 131
> Used by a listener to register for a multicast group. This can be an unsolicited registration or the answer to a multicast listener query from the router.

Multicast Listener Done—type 132
> Sent by a listener to deregister for a multicast address. When a router receives a Multicast Listener Done message from the last member of the multicast address on a link, it will delete the multicast address from its list of multicast addresses to be forwarded over this interface.

All three message types of MLDv1 have the same format, which is shown in Figure 4-19.

The Type field is 130 for Multicast Listener Queries, 131 for Multicast Listener Reports, or 132 for Multicast Listener Done messages. The Code field is set to 0 by

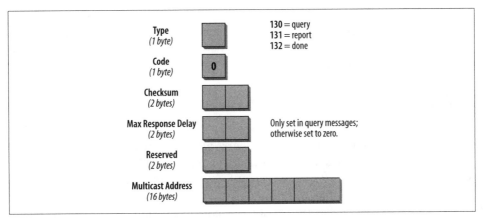

Figure 4-19. MLD message format

the sender and ignored by the receiver. The Maximum Response Delay field is used only in query messages. This is the maximum allowed delay (in milliseconds) in which a node has to send a report if it has a listener. In all other messages, this field is set to 0. The Multicast Address field is set to 0 in a general query. In an address-specific query, it contains the multicast group address to be queried. In report and done messages, this field contains either the multicast group to which a member listens (report message) or the group it is leaving (done message).

Routers send general queries to the link-local scope all-nodes multicast address FF02::1. Any station that wants to send a report in answer to a query starts a timer when it receives the query and is supposed to wait some random delay before sending the report. The maximum delay is the one specified in the Maximum Response Delay field in the query. If the station sees another station sending a report within that delay, it stops the process. Thus, multiple reports for the same address can be avoided. Group membership join reports and terminations are sent to the address in question.

The link-local scope all-nodes address (FF02::1) is a special address. It never sends a membership report or a done message. If an address has a scope of 1 (interface-local), MLD messages are never sent. Table 4-9 summarizes the message types and their Destination address.

Table 4-9. Message types and their destinations

Message type	IPv6 Destination address
General Query	Link-local scope all-nodes (FF02::1)
Multicast Address–Specific Query	The multicast address being queried
Report	The multicast address being reported
Done	Link-local scope all-routers (FF02::2)

RFC 2710 contains a lot of interesting and detailed information. It discusses various states that nodes can go through and includes state transition diagrams. There is also much detailed information on timers: how they are used, their default values, and how they can be configured.

MLDv2

MLD Version 2 has been specified in RFC 3810. It is based on IGMPv3 (RFC 3376). MLDv2 adds the ability for a node to do *source filtering*, which means to report interest in listening to packets with a particular multicast address from only specific Source addresses or from all sources except for specific Source addresses. This is also referred to as Source Specific Multicast (SSM) as opposed to Any Source Multicast (ASM), which is the name for the previous version, based on IGMPv2 (MLDv1).

There are two message types for MLDv2:

- Multicast Listener Query—Type 130
- Version 2 Multicast Listener Report—Type 143 (RFC 3810)

To be interoperable with MLDv1, MLDv2 implementations also need to support Version 1 Multicast Listener Report (Type 131) and Version 1 Multicast Listener Done (Type 132) messages.

For MLDv2 query messages, the MLD header shown in Figure 4-19 is extended with the following fields, which are appended after the Multicast Address field shown in Figure 4-19:

Reserved—4 bits
Must be set to zero.

S-Flag (Suppress Router-Side Processing)—1 bit
When set to one, the S-Flag indicates to any receiving multicast routers that they have to suppress the normal timer updates they perform upon hearing a Query.

QRV (Querier's Robustness Variable)—3 bits
If non-zero, the QRV field contains the Robustness Variable value used by the Querier. This value affects timers and the number of retries. Included in queries in order to synchronize all MLDv2 routers connected to the same link.

QQIC (Querier's Query Interval Code)—8 bits
The Querier's Query Interval Code field specifies the Query Interval used by the Querier. Included in queries in order to synchronize all MLDv2 routers connected to the same link.

Number of Sources—16 bits
The Number of Sources (N) field specifies how many Source addresses are present in the Query. This number is zero in a General Query or a Multicast Address Specific Query, and nonzero in a Multicast Address and Source Specific Query.

Source Address—variable length
> Contains the Source addresses. Length is defined by the number of addresses specified in the N-Field.

MLDv2 Listener Done messages have the following format:

- Type Field—1 byte, set to 143
- Reserved—1 byte
- Checksum—2 bytes
- Reserved—2 bytes
- M-Field (Number of Multicast Address Records) —2 bytes
- Multicast Address Records—variable length

Each Multicast Address Record is a block of fields that contain information on the sender listening to a single multicast address on the interface from which the Report is sent. It includes a field specifying the number of sources and the list of sources for a particular multicast address.

There are different types of multicast address records that can be included in a Report message (RFC 3810; description follows).

A node that receives a Query on an interface responds with a *Current State Record* to report the state of the interface regarding the multicast address in question. The Current State Record can have one of two values:

Value 1—MODE_IS_INCLUDE
> Indicates that the interface has a filter mode of INCLUDE for the specified multicast address

Value 2—MODE_IS_EXCLUDE
> Indicates that the interface has a filter mode of EXCLUDE for the specified multicast address

If there is a change of the filter mode, a node sends a *Filter Mode Change Record*. This record is included in a report sent from the interface where the change occurred. The Filter Mode Change Record can have one of two values:

Value 3—CHANGE_TO_INCLUDE_MODE
> Indicates that the interface has changed to INCLUDE filter mode for the specified multicast address. The Source Address fields in this Multicast Address Record contain the interface's new source list for the specified multicast address, if it is nonempty.

Value 4—CHANGE_TO_EXCLUDE_MODE
> Indicates that the interface has changed to EXCLUDE filter mode for the specified multicast address. The Source Address fields in this Multicast Address Record contain the interface's new source list for the specified multicast address, if it is nonempty.

If there is a change of source list, a node includes a *Source List Change Record* in a report sent from the interface where the change occurred. The Source List Change Record can have one of two values:

Value 5—ALLOW_NEW_SOURCES
> Indicates that the Source Address fields in this Multicast Address Record contain a list of the additional sources that the node wishes to listen to, for packets sent to the specified multicast address. If the change was to an INCLUDE source list, these are the addresses that were added to the list; if the change was to an EXCLUDE source list, these are the addresses that were deleted from the list.

Value 6—BLOCK_OLD_SOURCES
> Indicates that the Source Address fields in this Multicast Address Record contain a list of the sources that the node no longer wishes to listen to for packets sent to the specified multicast address. If the change was to an INCLUDE source list, these are the addresses that were deleted from the list; if the change was to an EXCLUDE source list, these are the addresses that were added to the list.

Version 2 Multicast Listener Reports are sent with an IP Destination address of FF02:0:0:0:0:0:0:16. All MLDv2-capable multicast routers listen to this address.

> For more information about Multicast and Anycast Group Membership, refer to the IETF Magma Group at *http://www.ietf.org/html.charters/ magma-charter.html*.

Multicast Router Discovery (MRD)

Multicast Router discovery is a general mechanism that allows for the discovery of multicast routers. It does not depend on a specific multicast routing protocol. It is specified in RFC 4286 and introduces three new message types:

Multicast Router Advertisement (message type 151)
> This message is sent by routers to advertise that IP multicast forwarding is enabled. It is sent from a link-local Source address to the All-Snoopers multicast address (FF02:0:0:0:0:0:0:6A).

Multicast Router Solicitation (message type 152)
> This message is sent by devices in order to solicit Advertisement messages from multicast routers. It is sent from a link-local Source address to the all-routers multicast address (FF02:0:0:0:0:0:0:2).

Multicast Router Termination (message type 153)
> This message is sent by routers to advertise that it stops IP multicast routing functions on an interface. It is sent from a link-local Source address to the All-Snoopers multicast address (FF02:0:0:0:0:0:0:6A).

All MRD messages are sent with an IPv6 Hop Limit of 1 and contain the Router Alert Option.

Now that you know how all the cool functionality of IPv6 works, the next chapter discusses what you need to know about security with IPv6.

References

Here's a list of the most important RFCs and drafts mentioned in this chapter. Sometimes I include additional subject-related RFCs for your personal further study.

RFCs

- RFC 1191, "Path MTU Discovery," 1991
- RFC 1981, "Path MTU Discovery for IP version 6," 1996
- RFC 2236, "Internet Group Management Protocol, Version 2," 1997
- RFC 2362, "Protocol Independent Multicast-Sparse Mode (PIM-SM): Protocol Specification," 1998
- RFC 2365, "Administratively Scoped IP Multicast," 1998
- RFC 2461, "Neighbor Discovery for IP Version 6," 1998
- RFC 2462, "IPv6 Stateless Address Autoconfiguration," 1998
- RFC 2463, "Internet Control Message Protocol (ICMPv6)," 1998
- RFC 2710, "Multicast Listener Discovery (MLD) for IPv6," 1999
- RFC 2715, "Interoperability Rules for Multicast Routing Protocols," 1999
- RFC 2894, "Router Renumbering for IPv6," 2000
- RFC 3041, "Privacy Extensions for Stateless Address Autoconfiguration in IPv6," 2001
- RFC 3122, "Extensions to IPv6 Neighbor Discovery for Inverse Discovery Specification," 2001
- RFC 3306, "Unicast-Prefix-based IPv6 Multicast Addresses," 2002
- RFC 3353, "Overview of IP Multicast in a Multi-Protocol Label Switching (MPLS) Environment," 2002
- RFC 3376, "Internet Group Management Protocol, Version 3," 2002
- RFC 3484, "Default Address Selection for Internet Protocol version 6 (IPv6)," 2003
- RFC 3569, "An Overview of Source-Specific Multicast (SSM)," 2003
- RFC 3590, "Source Address Selection for the Multicast Listener Discovery (MLD) Protocol," 2003
- RFC 3756, "IPv6 Neighbor Discovery (ND) Trust Models and Threats," 2004
- RFC 3810, "Multicast Listener Discovery Version 2 (MLDv2) for IPv6," 2004
- RFC 3971, "SEcure Neighbor Discovery (SEND)," 2005

- RFC 3972, "Cryptographically Generated Addresses (CGA)," 2005
- RFC 3973, "Protocol Independent Multicast—Dense Mode (PIM-DM): Protocol Specification (Revised)," 2005
- RFC 4065, "Instructions for Seamoby and Experimental Mobility Protocol IANA Allocations," 2005
- RFC 4191, "Default Router Preferences and More-Specific Routes," 2005
- RFC 4192, "Procedures for Renumbering an IPv6 Network without a Flag Day," 2005
- RFC 4213, "Basic Transition Mechanisms for IPv6 Hosts and Routers," 2005
- RFC 4286, "Multicast Router Discovery," 2005
- RFC 4443, "Internet Control Message Protocol (ICMPv6) for the Internet Protocol Version 6 (IPv6) Specification," 2006

Drafts

Drafts can be found at *http://www.ietf.org/ID.html*. To locate the latest version of a draft, refer to *https://datatracker.ietf.org/public/pidtracker.cgi*. You can enter the draft name without a version number and the most current version will come up. If a draft does not show up, it was either deleted or published as an RFC. Alternatively, you can go to the new Internet drafts database interface at *https://datatracker.ietf.org/public/ididindex.cgi*. *http://tools.ietf.org/wg* is also a very useful site. More information on the process of standardization, RFCs, and drafts can be found in the Appendix.

Here's a list of drafts that I refer to in this chapter, along with interesting drafts that relate to the topics in this chapter:

- *draft-ietf-ipv6-2461bis-06.txt* (obsoletes RFC 2461), Neighbor Discovery for IP Version 6 (IPv6)
- *draft-ietf-v6ops-onlinkassumption-04.txt*, IPv6 Neighbor Discovery On-Link Assumption Considered Harmful
- *draft-ietf-ipngwg-icmp-name-lookups-15*.txt, IPv6 Node Information Queries
- *draft-ietf-pim-sm-v2-new-12.txt*, Protocol Independent Multicast—Sparse Mode (PIM-SM): Protocol Specification (Revised)
- *draft-ietf-pim-anycast-rp-07.txt*, Anycast-RP Using PIM
- *draft-ietf-ssm-arch-07.txt*, Source-Specific Multicast for IP
- *draft-holbrook-idmr-igmpv3-ssm-08.txt*, Using IGMPv3 and MLDv2 for Source-Specific Multicast
- *draft-ietf-magma-igmpv3-and-routing-05.txt*, IGMPv3/MLDv2 and Multicast Routing Protocol Interaction
- *draft-ietf-v6ops-icmpv6-filtering-bcp-01.txt*, Best Current Practice for Filtering ICMPv6 Messages in Firewalls

CHAPTER 5

Security with IPv6

The developers of IPv4 did not rack their brains about security. The "Internet" in those early days connected a few trusted networks of some visionary researchers. The individuals who controlled these networks, as well as those who were allowed to use the networked resources, were implicitly trusted to not cause any malicious or destructive behavior. This is the reason why the original IP architecture does not include a security framework that can be used by all applications. If security was needed, it was usually rudimentary authentication/authorization and was included in the application code (e.g., the password for Telnet and FTP). Many years later, IPsec was introduced when IPv4 had already been widely deployed. Therefore, it needed to be retrofitted into existing deployments. Due to many interoperability and performance issues, IPsec is not widely deployed in many IPv4 scenarios. This is in contrast to IPv6, which from the beginning had the notion that fundamental security functionality had to be included in the base protocol in order to be used on any Internet platform. A standards-conforming IPv6 implementation must include IPsec to allow more secured communication once it is appropriately configured. Before we dive into the technical details, I want to talk about some general security concepts and practices.

General Security Concepts

In order to protect data, one has to be aware of the possible threats. People often focus solely on malicious attacks from foreign networks. A comprehensive security concept needs to consider many other aspects. Following is a list of possible points of weakness:

- Insufficient or nonexistent IT security concepts and corresponding provisions
- Nonobservance or insufficient control of IT security provisions
- Usurping of rights (password theft)
- Incorrect use or faulty administration of IT systems
- Abuse of rights

- Weaknesses in software (buffer/heap overflows in conjunction with applications running with superuser rights)
- Manipulation, theft, or destruction of IT devices, software, or data (physical security)
- Network eavesdropping (sniffing wired or wireless networks) or replaying of messages
- Trojan horses, viruses, and worms
- Security attacks such as masquerading, IP spoofing, Denial of Service (DoS) attacks, or man-in-the-middle attacks
- Routing misuse

There are many statistics showing that malicious attacks from the outside are only a smaller fraction of all the possible risks. Many threats come from within the internal network and can in many cases be related to human misconduct or faulty administration. Many of these risks cannot be controlled by technical mechanisms. This chapter is not a guide to an overall security concept; it discusses the technology aspects of security with IPv6.

General Security Practices

Standard security practices involve two "triads" of thought, CIA and AAA. The CIA triad includes:

Confidentiality
  Stored or transmitted information cannot be read or altered by an unauthorized party.

Integrity
  Any alteration of transmitted or stored information can be detected.

Availability
  The information in question is readily accessible to authorized users at all times.

The AAA triad includes:

Authentication
  Ensuring an individual or group is who they say they are. The act of clarifying a claimed identity. Common forms of authentication include usernames and passwords or ATM card/PIN combinations.

Authorization
  Ensuring that the authenticated user or group has the proper rights to access the information they are attempting to access. Common implementations include access control lists (ACLs).

Accounting
  The act of collecting information on resource usage. The log of an HTTP server would be a common form of accounting.

Nonrepudiation is not included in the CIA/AAA Triads. Nonrepudiation means a specified action such as sending, receiving, or deleting of information cannot be denied by any of the parties involved.

These security requirements need to be provided by two basic security elements: encryption (to provide confidentiality) and secure checksums (to provide integrity). Suitable combinations of these two elements may then be used to provide more complex services, such as authenticity and nonrepudiation.

There are two forms of encryption that are commonly used. The first is called "Secret Key Cryptography," also termed *symmetric key encryption*, which requires the sender and recipient to agree on a shared secret (i.e., a key or password) that is then used to encrypt and decrypt the information exchanged. Common symmetric key algorithms are DES, 3DES, IDEA, RC-4, and AES.

The second is called "Public Key Cryptography," also termed *asymmetric encryption*. An asymmetric encryption algorithm uses a key pair consisting of a known and distributed public key and an individual private key. When a message is encrypted using the public key and decrypted by the receiver with the corresponding private key, only the intended recipient is capable of seeing the encrypted message. This form of encryption can be used to establish a confidential data exchange. If in addition, the message was also encrypted with the sender's private key and then decrypted by the recipient with a corresponding public key, the security services of data origin authentication and nonrepudiation are added. Common asymmetric key algorithms are RSA and ElGamal.

Secure checksums or hash functions often provide data integrity. A hash function takes input of an arbitrary length and outputs fixed-length code. The fixed-length output is called the *message digest*, or the *hash*, of the original input message. These hashes are unique and thereby provide the integrity and authenticity of the message. Common one-way hash functions are MD-5 and SHA-1.

The IPsec standard uses a combination of algorithmic choices based on symmetric and asymmetric cryptography, as well as one-way hash functions. This chapter describes the IPsec framework and the security elements in IPv6 and includes a discussion about special issues to be aware of when securing an IPv6 network.

IPsec Basics

IPsec, originally defined in RFC 2401 and updated in RFC 4301, describes a security architecture for both versions of IP for IPv4 and IPv6.

The following elements are part of the IPsec framework:

- A general description of security requirements and mechanisms at the network layer
- A protocol for encryption (Encapsulating Security Payload, ESP)

- A protocol for authentication (Authentication Header, AH)
- A definition for the use of cryptographic algorithms for encryption and authentication
- A definition of security policies and security associations between communication peers
- Key management

The configuration of IPsec creates a boundary between a protected and an unprotected area. The boundary can be around a single host or a network. The access control rules specified by the administrator determine what happens to packets traversing the boundary. The security requirements are defined by a Security Policy Database (SPD). Generally, each packet is either protected using IPsec security services, discarded, or allowed to bypass IPsec protection, based on the applicable SPD policies identified by the *selectors*. The selectors are the specific traffic match criteria defined by an administrator—for example, a specific application being transmitted from a subnet to a specific end-host.

RFC 4301 contains a section listing all the changes since RFC 2401. The basic IPsec concepts remain the same. Changes have been made to address new IPsec scenarios, improve performance, and simplify implementation. A new database, the Peer Authorization Database (PAD), has been added and is described later in this chapter.

Security Associations

Security Associations (SA) are agreements between communication peers. Three elements are part of the agreement: a key, an encryption or authentication mechanism, and additional parameters for the algorithm. SAs are unidirectional, and each separate security service requires an SA. This means that two communication peers who want to encrypt and authenticate a two-way communication need four SAs (one pair for encryption and one pair for authentication). Bidirectional application traffic—for example, a bidirectional Telnet connection—also requires four SAs at each communication peer. Peer A must protect the traffic it initiates and the return traffic from Peer B. It also requires two additional SAs to ensure that if Peer B initiates a Telnet session, both it and the return traffic for this scenario are protected.

IPsec differentiates two modes of transport:

Transport mode
> The SA is made between two end nodes and defines the encryption or authentication for the payload of all IP packets for that connection. The IP header is not encrypted.

Tunnel mode
> The SA is usually made between two security gateways. The whole packet including the original IP header is encrypted or authenticated by encapsulating it in a new header. This is the foundation for a virtual private network (VPN).

Key Management

Most of the security mechanisms provided by IPsec require the use of cryptographic keys. A separate set of mechanisms has been defined for putting the keys in place. Support for both manual and automated distribution of keys is a requirement. RFC 4301 specifies IKEv2 (described later in this section) as an automated key distribution mechanism. Other mechanisms may be used.

In order to establish a Security Association (SA), the communication peers have to agree on a cryptographic algorithm and negotiate keys. The negotiation of an SA often happens over insecure paths. Internet Key Exchange (IKE) specifies a protocol that allows for the exchange and negotiation of parameters for an SA.

IKEv1

IKEv1 is specified in RFC 2409 and updated in RFC 4109. It consists of selected functions from three different protocols:

ISAKMP (Internet Security Association and Key Management Protocol)
ISAKMP specifies a framework for the management of SAs and key exchange without describing the process in detail. It therefore supports different key exchange mechanisms. It is specified in RFC 2408, which was obsoleted by RFC 4206.

Oakley Key Determination Protocol
The Oakley Key Determination protocol is used for the exchange of keys and is specified in RFC 2412. It is an extension of the Diffie/Hellman algorithm. It uses only a subset of the functions of the Oakley protocol.

SKEME (Versatile Secure Key Exchange Mechanism for the Internet)
SKEME is a fast key exchange technique described in "SKEME: A Versatile Secure Key Exchange Mechanism for Internet," from *IEEE Proceedings of the 1996 Symposium on Network and Distributed Systems Security* by H. Krawczyk. IKE uses only a subset of the functions defined for the SKEME protocol.

IKEv1 uses UDP on port 500 and goes through two phases:

In phase one, the ISAKMP communication peers negotiate a secure, authenticated communication channel called ISAKMP Security Association. Note that some implementations use the term "IKE SA," which is synonymous with the ISAKMP SA. The phase one exchange is based on the Diffie/Hellman algorithm and encrypted identification tokens. The authentication can be secured by either preshared keys, an RSA checksum encrypted with the private key of the sender, or the public key of the receiver.

In phase two, the cryptographic algorithms and the keys for other protocols (e.g., ESP and/or AH) can be exchanged over the secure communication channel established in phase one. The outcome of IKE phase two results in an IPsec SA. These IPsec SAs define the security services to be used for protecting the traffic in transit. Multiple IPsec SAs can be negotiated via the secure channel set up in phase one. This allows for more granular and more flexible security services to be negotiated. Both the IPsec SAs and ISAKMP SAs generate new cryptographic keys on a periodic basis to provide greater security. Typically, the IPsec SAs are rekeyed at a faster rate than the ISAKMP SAs.

RFC 4109 updates the original specification. The changes are made to ensure that the suggested and required algorithms reflect the current market situation. The changes are intended to be deployed for all IKEv1 implementations.

Table 5-1 lists the changes as presented in the RFC.

Table 5-1. Changes in RFC 4109

Algorithm	RFC 2409	RFC 4109
DES for encryption	MUST	MAY (crypto weakness)
TripleDES for encryption	SHOULD	MUST
AES-128 for encryption	N/A	SHOULD
MD5 for hashing and HMAC	MUST	MAY (crypto weakness)
SHA1 for hashing and HMAC	MUST	MUST
Tiger for hashing	SHOULD	MAY (lack of deployment)
AES-XCBC-MAC-96 for PRF	N/A	SHOULD
Preshared secrets	MUST	MUST
RSA with signatures	SHOULD	SHOULD
DSA with signatures	SHOULD	MAY (lack of deployment)
RSA with encryption	SHOULD	MAY (lack of deployment)
D-H Group 1 (768)	MUST	MAY (crypto weakness)
D-H Group 2 (1024)	SHOULD	MUST
D-H Group 14 (2048)	N/A	SHOULD
D-H elliptic curves	SHOULD	MAY (lack of deployment)

All algorithms with a "should" or "must" level in the new recommendation are seen to be secure and robust at the time of writing.

 You can find all IKEv1 relevant and updated numbers and codes at *http://www.iana.org/assignments/ipsec-registry*.

IKEv2

IKEv2 is specified in RFC 4306, which combines and therefore obsoletes RFC 2407, "The Internet IP Security Domain of Interpretation for ISAKMP," RFC 2408, "Internet Security Association and Key Management Protocol (ISAKMP)," and RFC 2409, "The Internet Key Exchange (IKE)." IKEv2 brings, among other things, enhancements for the use of IPsec in combination with NAT traversal, for Extensible Authentication, and for Remote Address acquisition.

IKEv2 runs over UDP ports 500 and 4500, and must accept packets from any ports and respond to those same ports.

The initial exchange (called *phase one* in IKEv1 terminology) normally consists of two pairs of messages. The first message pair negotiates cryptographic algorithms, exchanges nonces, and does a Diffie-Hellman exchange. The second message pair authenticates the previous messages, exchanges identities and certificates, and establishes the first `CHILD_SA`.

In IKEv1, SA lifetimes were negotiated. In IKEv2, each end of the SA is responsible for enforcing its own lifetime policy on the SA and rekeying the SA when necessary. The end with the shorter lifetime will have to request the rekeying if the lifetime policies are different. Another difference between the two IKE versions is that IKEv2 allows parallel SAs with the same traffic selectors between common endpoints. This difference, among other things, supports traffic with different Quality of Service (QoS) requirements among the SAs. Hence, unlike IKEv1, the combination of the endpoints and the traffic selectors may not uniquely identify an SA between those endpoints. Therefore, with IKEv2, SAs can no longer be deleted based on duplicate traffic selectors.

Opening an IPsec connection through a NAT creates some special problems. The changing of IP addresses changes the checksums, so they will fail and cannot be corrected by the NAT, because they are cryptographically protected. IKEv2 has improved support for such situations by negotiating UDP encapsulation of IKE and ESP packets. Port 4500 is reserved for UDP-encapsulated ESP and IKE. Because NATs often translate TCP and UDP port numbers, IPsec packets must be accepted from any port and sent back to that same port.

 You can find all relevant and updated IKEv2 numbers and codes at *http://www.iana.org/assignments/ikev2-parameters*.

A summary of the changes and goals for RFC 4306 can be taken from the RFC. Here are some of the main points (refer to the RFC for the whole list):

- To define the entire IKE protocol in a single document, replacing RFCs 2407, 2408, and 2409, and incorporating subsequent changes to support NAT Traversal, Extensible Authentication, and Remote Address acquisition.

- To simplify IKE by replacing the eight different initial exchanges with a single four-message exchange.

- To decrease IKE's latency in the common case by making the initial exchange two round trips (four messages) and allowing the ability to piggyback setup of a `CHILD_SA` on that exchange.

- To reduce the number of possible error states by making the protocol reliable. This is done by requiring all messages to be acknowledged and sequenced. This allows shortening `CREATE_CHILD_SA` exchanges from three messages to two.

- To maintain existing syntax and magic numbers to the extent possible to make it likely that implementations of IKEv1 can be enhanced to support IKEv2 with minimum effort.

A list of algorithms to be used with IKEv2 is specified as mandatory to implement in RFC 4307 "Cryptographic Algorithms for Use in the Internet Key Exchange Version 2 (IKEv2)." This is in order to ensure interoperability between different implementations.

IPsec Databases

There are three important databases in the IPsec model:

Security Policy Database (SPD)
Specifies the policies that determine the disposition of all IP traffic (inbound or outbound) from a host or security gateway. There are three possible processing rules after application of the SPD policies: discard, bypass, or protect.

Security Association Database (SAD)
Contains an entry for each SA and the parameters associated with it.

Peer Authorization Database (PAD)
Provides a link between an SA management protocol (such as IKE) and the SPD.

The Peer Authorization Database is new with the specification in RFC 4301. Its main functions are to identify the peers or groups of peers authorized to communicate with the IPsec entity, to specify the protocol and method used to authenticate each peer, and to contain the authentication data for each peer.

For a good overview of the relevant security RFCs and drafts, go to the IETF Security working group at *http://www.ietf.org/html.charters/ wg-dir.html* and at *http://sec.ietf.org*.

IPsec Performance

There is work in progress to ensure that IPsec performance concerns are addressed so that vendors can create sound implementations. This work is part of the Bench-marking Methodology Working Group (BMWG). If you are interested in this work, go to the BMWG at *http://www.ietf.org/html.charters/bmwg-charter.html* or refer to the drafts: *draft-ietf-bmwg-ipsec-term-08.txt* and *draft-ietf-bmwg-ipsec-meth-01.txt*.

IPv6 Security Elements

IPsec describes general security mechanisms that can be used with both protocols, IPv6 and IPv4. This means that IPv6 is not more secure than IPv4. The difference in security is that IPsec may be installed separately for IPv4, whereas it is a mandatory and integral part of the IPv6 stack, and therefore available with any implementation.

The IPsec specification defines protocols for the Authentication header (AH) and the Encapsulating Security Payload header (ESP). With IPv6, these headers are included as Extension headers. An IPsec implementation must support ESP and may support AH. With the older specification, support for both protocols was required. The requirement for AH support has been removed because ESP can be used to provide integrity, which in most cases has proven to be sufficient.

Authentication Header

The Authentication Header (AH) provides integrity and authentication (no confidentiality) for all end-to-end data transported in an IP packet. It supports different authentication mechanisms. It is specified in RFC 4302 (which obsoletes RFC 2402) and is indicated by the protocol value 51 in the preceding header.

The AH is located between the IPv6 header and upper-layer headers (e.g., TCP, UDP, ICMP). If extension headers are present, it has to be placed after the Hop-by-Hop, Routing, and Fragment Extension headers.

The format of the AH is shown in Figure 5-1.

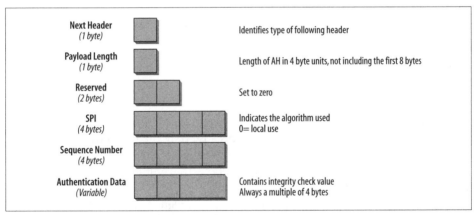

Figure 5-1. The format of the Authentication Header

Each field is discussed in the following list:

Next Header (1 byte)
> The Next Header field identifies the type of header that follows the Authentication header. It uses the values listed in Table 2-1.

Payload Length (1 byte)
> Describes the length of the header in four-byte units, not including the first eight bytes in the calculation. This length indication is necessary because the authentication data in the AH may differ in length depending on the algorithm used.

Reserved (2 bytes)
> Not used; set to 0.

Security Parameter Index (SPI) (4 bytes)

Arbitrary 32-bit value. Used by the receiver to identify the SA to which an incoming packet belongs. The SPI field is mandatory, and this mechanism for mapping inbound traffic to unicast SAs must be supported by all AH implementations. If an IPsec implementation supports multicast, it must additionally support multicast SAs using the de-multiplex algorithm specified for this purpose for mapping inbound IPsec datagrams to SAs. SPI values in the range of 1 through 255 are reserved by the Internet Assigned Numbers Authority (IANA) for future use. The SPI value of 0 is reserved for local, implementation-specific use and must not be sent on the wire.

Sequence Number (4 bytes)

This 32-bit sequence number is a monotonically increasing counter value. It has to be set by the sender, but it is the choice of the receiver whether to act on it. It ensures that packets with identical data are not resent repeatedly. This prevents replay attacks in a unicast or single-sender SA. For a multi-sender SA, the anti-reply features of AH are not available, because the AH does not have a means to synchronize packet counters among multiple senders. On establishment of an SA, the value is set to 0 at the sender and at the receiver. The first packet always has the value 1, which is increased by one for every consecutive packet. When the value 2^{32} is reached, the counter is reinitialized to 0.

Integrity Check Value (variable length)

This field contains the checksum (Integrity Check Value, ICV) for the packet. The length depends on the algorithm chosen on establishing the SA. It is always a multiple of four bytes.

The AH Specification in RFC 4302 defines a new Extended (64-bit) Sequence Number (ESN). It cannot be seen in Figure 5-1 because only the low-order 32 bits of the Extended Sequence Number are transmitted. The high-order 32 bits are maintained as part of the sequence number counter by both transmitter and receiver, and are included in the computation of the ICV. The 64-bit sequence number is a new option designed to support high-speed IPsec implementations. The use of an Extended Sequence Number is negotiated on setup of the SA. The default with IKEv2 is ESN, unless 32-bit is explicitly negotiated.

The checksum is calculated over the following fields:

- All fields of the IP header or Extension header fields before the AH that do not change in transit or whose value when arriving at the destination can be predicted. For example, if a Routing Extension header is present, the last address in the Routing Extension header is used for the calculation. The Class field, the Flow Label, and the Hop Limit are not included in the calculation.
- All fields of the Authentication header.
- Other Extension headers present and the payload.

- The high-order bits of the ESN (if employed) and any implicit padding required by the integrity algorithm.

The following algorithms are considered suitable for IPsec:

- Keyed Message Authentication Codes (MACs) based on symmetric encryption algorithms
- One-way hash functions (e.g., MD5, SHA-1, SHA-256, etc.)

Other algorithms can be negotiated. RFC 4305, "Cryptographic Algorithm Implementation Requirements for Encapsulating Security Payload (ESP) and Authentication Header (AH)," lists the following implementation rules for AH:

- MUST, HMAC-SHA1-96 (RFC 2404)
- SHOULD, AES-XCBC-MAC-96 (RFC 3566)
- MAY, HMAC-MD5-96 (RFC 2403)

Weaknesses have become apparent in MD5; however, they should not affect the use of MD5 with HMAC.

The Authentication header can be used in both transport and tunnel modes, as shown in Figure 5-2.

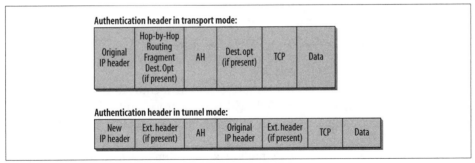

Figure 5-2. Authentication header in transport and tunnel mode

In transport mode, the whole payload, including the fields of the IPv6 header, which do not change in transit, is secured. In tunnel mode, the inner packet contains the IP address of sender and receiver. The outer IP header contains the IP address of the tunnel endpoints. In this case, the complete original packet, including the fields of the outer header that do not change in transit, is secured.

Encapsulating Security Payload Header

The Encapsulating Security Payload Header (ESP) provides Integrity, Confidentiality, Data Origin Authentication, Anti-Replay Service, and limited Traffic Flow Confidentiality for all end-to-end data transported in an IP packet. The set of services provided is negotiated on establishment of the SA. The ESP is defined in RFC 4303 (which obsoletes RFC 2406) and indicated by a protocol value of 50 in the preceding header.

The ESP is located in front of the transport (e.g., UDP or TCP), network control (e.g, ICMP), or routing (e.g., OSPF) protocol header.

The format of the ESP is shown in Figure 5-3.

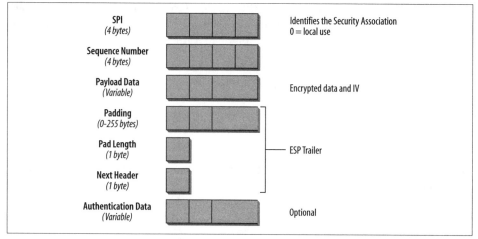

Figure 5-3. Format of the Encapsulating Security Payload header

Security Parameter Index (SPI, 4 bytes)
> Arbitrary 32-bit value. Used by the receiver to identify the SA to which an incoming packet belongs. The SPI field is mandatory, and this mechanism for mapping inbound traffic to unicast SAs must be supported by all ESP implementations. If an IPsec implementation supports multicast, it must additionally support multicast SAs using the de-multiplex algorithm specified for this purpose for mapping inbound IPsec datagrams to SAs. SPI values in the range of 1 through 255 are reserved by the Internet Assigned Numbers Authority (IANA) for future use. The SPI value of 0 is reserved for local, implementation-specific use and must not be sent on the wire.

Sequence Number (4 bytes)
> This 32-bit sequence number is a monotonically increasing counter value. It has to be set by the sender, but it is the choice of the receiver whether to act on it. It ensures that packets with identical data are not resent repeatedly. This prevents replay attacks in a unicast or single-sender SA. For a multi-sender SA, the anti-reply features of ESP are not available, because the ESP does not have a means to synchronize packet counters among multiple senders. On establishment of an

SA, the value is set to 0 at the sender and at the receiver. The first packet always has the value 1, which is increased by one for every consecutive packet. When the value 2^{32} is reached, the counter is reinitialized to 0.

Payload Data (variable length)
Contains the encrypted data as well as the encryption initialization vector (IV) if required by the encryption mechanism.

Padding (0 to 255 bytes)
Used to align the packet to a multiple of 4 bytes and to reach a minimum packet size if the encryption mechanism requires one.

Pad Length (1 byte)
Indicates the number of preceding padding bytes.

Next Header (1 byte)
Identifies the type of header that follows the ESP header. It uses the values listed in Table 2-1. To facilitate the rapid generation and discarding of the padding traffic in support of traffic flow confidentiality, the protocol value 59 (no next header) designates a "dummy" packet. The receiver of a dummy packet must discard it without creating an error message.

Integrity Check Value (variable length)
The Integrity Check Value (ICV) is a variable-length field containing a checksum computed over the ESP header, Payload, and ESP trailer fields. The ICV field is optional. It is present only if the integrity service is selected, and it is provided by either a separate integrity algorithm or a combined mode algorithm that uses an ICV. The length of the field is specified by the integrity algorithm selected and associated with the SA.

The Padding, Pad Length, and Next Header fields are part of the ESP Trailer. The encryption algorithm is either specified manually and included in the SA for the packet stream or negotiated dynamically by the key exchange protocol.

The new ESP Specification in RFC 4303 defines a new Extended (64-bit) Sequence Number (ESN). It cannot be seen in Figure 5-3, because only the low order 32 bits of the Extended Sequence Number are transmitted. The high-order 32 bits are maintained as part of the sequence number counter by both transmitter and receiver and are included in the computation of the ICV. The 64-bit sequence number is a new option designed to support high-speed IPsec implementations. The use of an Extended Sequence Number is negotiated on setup of the SA. The default with IKEv2 is ESN unless 32-bit is explicitly negotiated.

RFC 4305, "Cryptographic Algorithm Implementation Requirements for Encapsulating Security Payload (ESP) and Authentication Header (AH)," lists the implementation rules for ESP, shown in Tables 5-2 and 5-3.

Table 5-2. Encryption algorithms

Rule	Algorithm
MUST	NULL (1)
MUST-	TripleDES-CBC (RFC 2451)
SHOULD+	AES-CBC with 128-bit keys (RFC 3602)
SHOULD	AES-CTR (RFC 3686)
SHOULD NOT	DES-CBC (RFC 2405)

Table 5-3. Authentication algorithms

Rule	Algorithm
MUST	HMAC-SHA1-96 (RFC 2404)
MUST	NULL (1)
SHOULD+	AES-XCBC-MAC-96 (RFC 3566)
MAY	HMAC-MD5-96 (RFC 2403)

Combined Mode algorithms provide both confidentiality and authentication services. They are expected to provide significant throughput and efficiency advantages. However, at the time of this book's writing, there are no such mechanisms available. AES-CCM, which has been adopted as the preferred mode for security in IEEE 802.11i, is expected to be of interest in the near future. Stay tuned.

Since ESP authentication and encryption are both optional, support for NULL algorithms must be given for both. Note that only one of them can be set to NULL at a time.

The ESP can be used in both transport and tunnel modes, as shown in Figure 5-4.

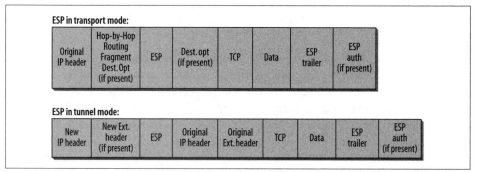

Figure 5-4. Encapsulating Security Payload Header in transport and tunnel mode

In transport mode, the IP header and the Extension headers that follow are not encrypted; otherwise the packet could not be forwarded. If the complete packet has to be encrypted, tunnel mode is the way to go. Just as with the AH in tunnel mode, the inner packet contains the IP address of sender and receiver, whereas the outer IP header contains the IP address of the tunnel endpoints.

The ESP can be used with a NULL encryption option, which is defined in RFC 2410. With NULL encryption, only the authentication option of the ESP is used, and the packet is not encrypted.

Combination of AH and ESP

The two headers can be used in combination as well. In that case, the AH header has to precede the ESP header to verify authenticity and integrity before the packet is decrypted. The authentication option has been included in the ESP header to allow for authentication of encrypted packets with only one header.

If the AH header is used in tunnel mode, the first IP header is included in the authentication. If the ESP header is used, only the part of the packet following the ESP header is authenticated. If encryption and integrity of the IP addresses are required, both headers must be combined. If both headers are used, it is obviously not necessary to use the authentication in the ESP header. On the other hand, an ESP header with NULL encryption can be used if the given authentication is sufficient.

Overview of New IPsec RFCs

Table 5-4 contains a comparison of the old and new RFCs for your reference.

Table 5-4. Overview of RFCs

Old specification	Title	New specification
RFC 2401	Security Architecture for the Internet Protocol	RFC 4301 (obsoletes 2401)
RFC 2402	IP Authentication Header	RFC 4302 (obsoletes 2402)
RFC 2404	Cryptographic Algorithm Implementation Requirements for Encapsulating Security Payload (ESP) and Authentication Header (AH)	RFC 4305 (obsoletes 2404 and 2406)
RFC 2406	IP Encapsulating Security Payload (ESP)	RFC 4303 and RFC 4305 (obsolete 2406)
RFC 2407 RFC 2408 RFC 2409	IKEv2	RFC 4306 (obsoletes 2407, 2408, 2409)
N/A	Cryptographic Algorithms for Use in the Internet Key Exchange Version 2 (IKEv2)	RFC 4307
N/A	Cryptographic Suites for IPsec	RFC 4308
N/A	Using Advanced Encryption Standard (AES) CCM Mode with IPsec Encapsulating Security Payload (ESP)	RFC 4309
RFC 2409	IKEv1	RFC 4109 (updates 2409)

Until IKEv2 is universally adopted, it is important that nodes support IKEv1 by supporting RFCs 2407, 2408, 2409, and 4109.

Interaction of IPsec with IPv6 Elements

The mandatory presence of IPsec in IPv6 is a great step for security in the Internet. But there are some areas where IPsec cannot easily be combined with other services:

- *Tunneling*, a fundamental element of both IPsec and multiple transition mechanisms, creates difficulties for existing firewalls and security gateways at the edge of the internal network. An encrypted IPsec tunnel built through a firewall providing end-to-end security for hosts on either side makes it impossible for the firewall to detect dangerous or unauthorized content. To solve this issue, the SAs have to be defined between the security gateways, not between the end nodes. Another issue is that the inner packet can contain information that presents a threat for the internal network. This could be routing information or network control messages (e.g., ICMP redirect).

- A similar problem exists when using NATs, which we all know are very common, especially in places where we would like to use IPsec (e.g., access to the company network from home or from a hotel/airport). NAT does address translation and, in many cases, port translation in the IP header. This creates a problem when authentication and/or encryption are used. RFC 3947, "Negotiation of NAT-Traversal in the IKE," provides a solution for IKEv1. IKEv2 includes improved NAT traversal support. Some vendors offer proprietary solutions. In the future, when we create IPv6 networks without NAT, this issue will go away.

- Quality of Service (QoS) allows a router to discard packets based on information in certain fields (e.g., Class and Flow label). Packet loss is a security violation with IPsec. This situation can lead to a certain service being unable to get established (e.g., IKE exchange).

- The extended mobility options with constantly changing IP addresses can lead to situations that are difficult to manage and control in IPsec environments. Dynamic addresses create difficulties if they are used for IKE identity checks.

IPv6 Security "Gotchas"

Security in an IPv6 network is not substantially different from security in an IPv4 network. Many of the existing well-known IPv4 attacks can be performed with IPv6, so our means for securing data are similar. Just like in the IPv4 world, there will always be unethical hackers who find new ways to break into our networks. The designers of security concepts and the entire computer security community will have to stay alert and keep finding mechanisms to keep pace with the hackers and find ways to protect their networks from new attacks.

 If both protocols (IPv4 and IPv6) are used in a network, each protocol needs its own security concept and provisions, which need to be coordinated. IPv6-capable firewalls have filter rules for IPv4 and separate filter rules for IPv6.

Another point to observe is that IPv6 is included in most operating systems and is usually rather simple to configure. Sometimes tunnel mechanisms are activated by default. IPv4 network administrators may believe that they do not have to worry about IPv6, but they don't realize that there may be IPv6 traffic in their network already. This fact is used by IPv6 hackers to intrude into IPv4 networks.

 Find the IPv6 traffic in your network by filtering your trace files for 0x86DD in the MAC header or for protocol 41 in the IPv4 protocol type field. You may find a surprising number of Neighbor Discovery messages—a good indicator that you have active IPv6 nodes on your network.

IPsec, while being a good security mechanism, is not the end-all, be-all for security. Most security professionals agree that there is no "silver bullet" in securing a network from internal or external attacks. Combinations of best practices and user training can minimize risks. If you are deploying IPv6 in the near future, there are some security concerns that should be addressed. Be advised that this is not a complete list, as entire volumes of information could be written on the subject.

Native IPv6

When connecting to IPv6 natively, some security issues that should be considered are discussed in the following sections.

Public Key Infrastructure (PKI)

While RFC 4301 specifies the requirement for IPSec in the IPv6 protocol, it does not cover how the keys will be exchanged. You could manually set up preshared keying, but in large enterprises, this task becomes tedious and time-consuming. In such environments, using a central certificate server is ideal. With IPv6, there were no such centralized certificate servers until recently. This has changed with servers that are based on the IKEv2 protocol, which is specified in RFC 4306. Benefits of IKEv2 are its usability on both IPv4 and IPv6 and its simpler implementation. It is not compatible with the first version of IKE, but both versions' header formats are similar enough to run them both unambiguously over the same UDP port.

Firewalls and intrusion detection/prevention systems

While end-to-end IPSec is considered one of the major advantages of IPv6, it also introduces new problems with existing firewalling and IDS/IPSes if ESP is used with encryption turned on. If the packets are encrypted from end to end, how does a border device inspect the packets without decrypting them? Storing all the encryption keys in a central location leaves both a central point of failure and a central location for a blackhat hacker to break into and steal all the encryption keys for the network. One of the ideas that has been presented to the community is a client server model for IDS/IPS (similar to current enterprise-level antivirus protection). A central server or servers keeps a database of attack signatures or network anomaly analysis. A client downloads the signatures locally and the client computer scans the packets itself, alerting the central server if it finds a signature match. Issues in current IPv4 IDS/IPS systems include lack of detection of tunneled IPv6 protocols and a general lack of attack signatures for IPv6-based attacks, although as IPv6 proliferates to more networks, these issues should eventually be solved.

Firewalls that support IPv6 are included in most of the major operating systems, but firewalls that keep the state of connections (*Stateful firewalls*) are not available in older implementations of Linux or in Windows XP/2003. Cisco, Checkpoint, and Netscreen (Juniper), among others, have Stateful inspection of IPv6 packets in newer versions of their software.

Implementation issues

Vendor IPSec implementations themselves can also cause security issues. For example, in several current IPv6 IPsec implementations, only authentication and integrity services are available using ESP with Null encryption or AH. Not all ESP implementations support the confidentiality pieces, which could provoke a false assumption of the security services available to be deployed if you don't check your vendor implementation.

Many IPv6 implementations are fairly new. This leads to two other possible security issues. The first issue is the lack of IPv6 assessment tools. It is a common practice in the information security field to audit your own network with well-known security auditing tools, and then secure the flaws found with those tools. Many of these popular tools have not been ported to audit IPv6 networks. The second issue is untested code in IPv6 implementations (which also ties into not having the tools to test the implementations). Code that has not been "put through the wringer" is probably going to have more security flaws than code that has been used in production environments.

Neighbor Discovery issues

Other security concerns to be aware of are abuses of the Neighbor Discovery Protocol (NDP), Duplicate Address Detection, and Router Advertising. A quote from RFC 2462 (IPv6 Stateless Autoconfiguration) states:

> "If a node determines that its tentative link-local address is not unique, autoconfiguration stops and manual configuration of the interface is required."

This poses a possible Denial of Service attack, as multiple IPv6 addresses can be assigned to a single interface. A rogue workstation could be assigned several thousand addresses and deny other workstations the ability to acquire a link-local address. Or even much simpler, a software responder can be built that always responds with "address in use."

Another point is that link-local addresses can be acquired without preconfiguration. An attacker can get access to a link without any further knowledge about the network. This feature gives a malicious node the opportunity to mount an attack on any other node attached to this link. Possible ways to protect from this are either link-layer authentication or the use of Cryptographically Generated addresses.

Router Advertisement spoofing is another security concern. Since multiple addresses are allowed on a single interface, multiple routes are allowed as well. A booting node sends a Router Solicitation to the all-routers multicast address (FF02::2). Each router on the link replies with a Router Advertisement containing configuration information for the client. This offers up the possibility of sending traffic through a router through which it's not supposed to be sent (allowing traffic sniffing on the rogue router). Obviously, this type of attack happens in the IPv4 world also; it differs only in the mechanisms used. Using the IPsec's AH component or SEcure Neighbor Discovery is a good way to mitigate this risk, among others.

The specification in NDP suggests using IPsec to protect from attacks, without providing more detailed information on how to do this. In many cases, especially in public and wireless networks, the key management used with IPsec is too complex and impractical.

A great reference that outlines the possible threats with NDP and provides guidelines is in RFC 3756, "IPv6 Neighbor Discovery (ND) Trust Models and Threats."

A new specification has been published in RFC 3971 to secure NDP without using IPsec. It is called *SEcure Neighbor Discovery* (SEND). This approach involves the use of new NDP options to carry public key-based signatures. A zero-configuration mechanism is used for showing address ownership on individual nodes; routers are certified by a trust anchor.

You can find a description of SEND and Cryptographically Generated Addresses (CGA) in Chapter 4.

ARP in IPv4 has been replaced with ICMP messages in IPv6. Without using IPsec AH or SEND, however, NDP has many of the security problems that ARP presented in IPv4, such as redirect attacks (malicious nodes redirecting packets away from legitimate receivers), Denial of Service (DoS) attacks, and flooding attacks (redirecting other hosts' traffic to a victim node creating a flood of bogus traffic).

Port scanning

Port scanning has become much more complex, if not impractical. The interface identifier in IPv6 has 64 bits. *draft-ietf-v6ops-nap-02.txt* states that "an attacker has to send out a simply unrealistic number of pings to map the network, and virus/worm propagation will be thwarted in the process. At full rate 40Gbps (400 times the typical 100Mbps LAN, and 13,000 times the typical DSL/Cable access link) it takes over 5,000 years to scan a single 64 bit space." Go figure. If autoconfiguration is used without the Privacy Option, some parts of the address (e.g., Vendor ID) can be guessed, but it is still a vast space. A simple and good protection is to avoid easy-to-guess addressing schemes, not using words such as BEEF, F00D, CAFE, 1234, and ABCD as part of an IPv6 address, and not using sequentially numbered or easy-to-guess addresses to key infrastructure devices (such as x::1 for routers).

Multicast issues

IPv6 supports multicast addresses with site scope, which can potentially allow an attacker to identify certain important resources on the site if misused. Particular examples are the All Routers (FF05::2) and All DHCP Servers (FF05::1:3) addresses. An attacker that is able to infiltrate a message destined for these addresses onto the site will potentially receive in return information identifying key resources on the site. This information can then be used for directed attacks ranging from simple flooding to more specific mechanisms designed to subvert the device. The risk can be minimized by ensuring that all firewalls and site boundary routers are configured to drop packets with site scope Destination addresses. Also, nodes should not join multicast groups for which there is no legitimate use on the site, and site routers should be configured to drop packets directed to these unused addresses.

Transition and Tunneling Mechanisms

IPv4 is not expected to go away anytime soon. It is very likely that there will be IPv4 nodes on networks for many years to come. IPv4 hosts cannot communicate with IPv6 hosts without some sort of transitioning or tunneling mechanism, which can add complexity to the existing network topology and the underlying code for the network stack. Transitioning and tunneling mechanisms can also be used as backdoors into normally IPv4-only networks.

Using IPv6 as a back door into IPv4 networks has been a known practice since 2002. On December 17, one of the HoneyNet Project's (*http://www.honeynet.org*) Solaris 8 servers was compromised. The difference between this attack and earlier ones was that this attacker set up an IPv6 tunnel to another country and tunneled out the data he was trying to steal. This bypassed many intrusion detection systems of the time, and it would do so today. This practice has been made easier with the advent of UDP-based tunneling mechanisms designed to allow IPv6 from behind NATs (a practice that was almost impossible before these mechanisms were available). Teredo and Tunnel Setup Protocol (TSP) are two such mechanisms.

Generally, with tunneling one has to make sure that packets that enter the network through a tunnel cannot circumvent incoming packet filters. An attacker from the Internet could, for instance, send an IPv4 packet to the tunnel endpoint (the entry point to our network) that contains an IPv6 packet with an IPv6 Source address out of the range of our internal network. The tunnel endpoint decapsulates the packet and forwards the IPv6 packet to the internal network. The receiver believes that this packet originates from a host from the internal network. One example is that some IPv6 security mechanisms rely on checking that the hop limit is 255 and that a link-local Destination address is used. Such a packet can be introduced in an IPv6 network through a tunnel. Automatic tunnels are more dangerous in that respect because they have to accept packets from any source. So a partial protection can be to configure the tunnel endpoint to accept only packets from a configured tunnel entry point or to use only manually configured tunnels. But the attacker can still spoof that address. Additional filter mechanisms have to be implemented on the tunnel endpoint. *draft-ietf-v6ops-ipsec-tunnels-02.txt*, "Using IPsec to Secure IPv6-in-IPv4 Tunnels," goes into more details and gives guidance on securing manually configured IPv6-in-IPv4 tunnels using IPsec.

In the 6to4 scenarios, there are special considerations discussed in RFC 3964, "Security Considerations for 6to4." The issues here are that: a) all 6to4 routers must accept and decapsulate IPv4 packets from every other 6to4 router and from 6to4 relays, and b) all 6to4 relay routers must accept traffic from any native IPv6 node. The routing scenarios to be analyzed are as follows:

- From 6to4 to 6to4
- From native IPv6 to 6to4
- From 6to4 to native IPv6

Please refer to the RFC for a detailed discussion of the scenarios and best practices to protect your network.

6to4 tunneling is a well-known transition mechanism for networks that do not currently have native IPv6 connectivity. It consists of using a dual-stacked border router with a routable IPv4 address (refer to Chapter 10 for a detailed discussion of 6to4). The 6to4 router can be used for a Distributed Denial of Service (DDoS) attack using a tool called *4to6DDoS*. 4to6DDoS does not require an IPv6 stack to be installed on either the attacking or the victim host. It sends IPv6 in IPv4 encapsulated packets directly from v4 to v4. The routers used for 6to4 tunneling can also be DoS attacked by simply connecting to the router several times with a private IPv4 address. These routers must accept and decapsulate IPv4 packets even if they are forged. They must also accept traffic from any native IPv6 node. 6to4 also does not guarantee symmetric routing, meaning that traffic can take one routing path going to its destination, and take a completely different path upon return. This situation may not be optimal from a security standpoint.

Mapped IPv4 addressing can also cause security issues. For example, if an attacker transmits an IPv6 packet with Source address of `::ffff:127.0.0.1` or `::ffff:10.1.1.1` in the IPv6 Source address field, it is possible to bypass Access Control Lists (ACLs) of the border router or firewall.

 A good reference with an overview of security issues is *draft-ietf-v6ops-security-overview-04.txt*.

Enterprise Security Models for IPv6

End-to-end transparency and security has been lost in many IPv4 networks due to the need to introduce NAT because of the shortage of IPv4 addresses. IPv6 can restore the transparency. However, some people have become used to seeing NAT and private addressing schemes to provide security in enterprise networks by hiding the network topology from the outside. These people may perceive the IPv6 transparency as a threat to their network and may even plan to deploy IPv6 networks with private local addressing schemes and translators only for this reason.

The goal with IPv6 is to restore end-to-end connectivity by using the abundant address space. To secure an IPv6 network, a security concept has to be created and the security mechanisms have to be implemented. NAT should no longer be used with IPv6. If hiding network topology from the outside is a requirement, other mechanisms should be used, such as private addressing (RFC 3041), unique local addresses (ULAs), or untraceable IPv6 addresses. Find a detailed description and discussion of these options in *draft-ietf-v6ops-nap-02.txt*, "IPv6 Network Architecture Protection" (NAP).

The New Model

In IPv4 networks, the favored model for security is to have perimeter firewalls and integrate NATs. Applying this same approach in an IPv6 network may be a good starting point, but is limiting in the long term. In IPv6 networks, you should aim to design an improved security model that increases the overall security of the network but also facilitates end-to-end communication. IPv6 provides IPsec capability in each node. Relying on one perimeter firewall can be dangerous. An attacker who manages to get behind the firewall will usually find an open unsecured field. The optimal security concept for IPv6 networks will most likely be "defense in depth," a combination of centralized security policy repositories and distribution mechanisms that, in conjunction with trusted hosts, will allow network managers to place more reliance on security mechanisms at the end points and allow end points to influence the behavior of perimeter firewalls. Perimeter firewalls will be responsible for securing the network from general attacks, and the end node will be responsible for securing itself from node-related attacks. The new security policy model for IPv6/IPsec networks must be an identity-based model in order to separate security policy from network IDs. This is crucial for networks that want to allow for automation, auto-configuration, and mobility without compromising security. This new distributed security model is emerging, and some of the technologies required are still under development, including protocols to allow end nodes to control and inform firewalls. Initial IPv6 deployments probably make use of similar firewall and intrusion detection techniques as used in today's IPv4 networks (with the exception of NATs, which should not be used at all in IPv6 networks). But the final goal to introduce a new type of distributed security concept should be kept in mind as you go along, and the development of these technologies should be followed closely.

There may be two types of managed security models depending on the size of the network to be secured:

End Node Distributed Firewall Model

A site security manager server authenticates end nodes on a network and then distributes firewall policies to end-node firewalls. This includes firewall configuration, access policies, IPsec keys, virus protection, etc. No site-level access control is required. Once an end node is authenticated and updated with a security policy, it is solely responsible for its own security.

Hybrid Distributed Firewall Model

A site-level security manager server may handle end-node authentication and distribution of firewall policies to both site firewalls and end-node firewalls. Once end nodes are authenticated, they can be granted varying levels of privilege by the security manager. The security manager's set of policies determines who has access to the outside, who has access to each other internally, which types of services and protocols may be run by different nodes, and who gets IPsec keys. The perimeter firewalls do some light access control while distributing the heavy work to the end-node firewalls. Various levels of coordination and control are possible in this model. In a simple version, end-node firewalls may run independently after being given the local firewall rule set by the security management service. In a more tightly managed version for high-security networks, the controller may coordinate between Intrusion Detection Systems (IDS), the site firewall, and end-node firewalls to detect attacks and shut off access to dangerous users inside or outside the corporate network.

One main source of information for the new model is a presentation by David B. Green, given at the North American IPv6 Task Force (NAv6TF) Technologist Seminar in November 2004 at the George Mason University, Washington, D.C. We thank David for the permission to present it in this book.

IPv6 Firewall Filter Rules

When you live in a dual-stack network, you will have two security concepts: one for the IPv4 world and another for the IPv6 world. And the two concepts do not have to match; they have to be designed according to the requirements of each protocol. Your firewalls may support both protocols, having two separate filter sets (one for each protocol), or you may have two boxes, one being the firewall for the IPv4 network and the other being the firewall for your IPv6 network.

Without trying to provide a full-fledged Security and Firewall Guide, here are some ideas for IPv6 security provisions and firewall filters that should be considered:

- Ingress filter at perimeter firewall for internally used addresses.
- Filter unneeded services at the perimeter firewall.
- Deploy host-based firewalls for a defense in depth.
- Critical systems should have static, nonobvious (randomly generated) IPv6 addresses. Consider using static neighbor entries for critical systems (versus letting them participate in ND).
- Hosts for Mobile IPv6 operations should be separate systems (to protect them by separate rules).
- Ensure that end nodes do not forward packets with Routing Extension headers.
- Layer 3 firewalls should never forward link-layer multicast packets.
- Firewalls should support filtering based on Source and Destination address, IPv6 extension headers, and upper-layer protocol information.
- Check your network for external packets that did not enter through your main perimeter firewall as an indication of "backdoor" connections of surreptitious tunneling.

In IPv6 networks, ICMPv6 plays a fundamental role and provides great functionality. Uncontrolled forwarding of ICMP messages also creates security risks. *draft-ietf-v6ops-icmpv6-filtering-bcp-01.txt*, Best Current Practice for Filtering ICMPv6 Messages in Firewalls, provides recommendations for the configuration of ICMPv6 firewall filtering rules (specifically, allowing the forwarding of messages that are important for the functioning of the network and dropping messages that are potential security risks).

Let's move on from security to Chapter 6, which covers another interesting topic—Quality of Service.

References

Here's a list of the most important RFCs and drafts mentioned in this chapter. Sometimes I include additional subject-related RFCs for your personal further study.

RFCs

- RFC 1828, "IP Authentication using Keyed MD5," 1995
- RFC 1829, "The ESP DES-CBC Transform," 1995
- RFC 1918, "Address Allocation for Private Internets," 1996
- RFC 2085, "HMAC-MD5 IP Authentication with Replay Prevention," 1997
- RFC 2104, "HMAC: Keyed-Hashing for Message Authentication," 1997
- RFC 2401, "Security Architecture for the Internet Protocol," 1998
- RFC 2402, "IP Authentication Header," 1998
- RFC 2403, "The Use of HMAC-MD5-96 within ESP and AH," 1998
- RFC 2404, "The Use of HMAC-SHA-1-96 within ESP and AH," 1998
- RFC 2405, "The ESP DES-CBC Cipher Algorithm With Explicit IV," 1998
- RFC 2406, "IP Encapsulating Security Payload (ESP)," 1998
- RFC 2407, "The Internet IP Security Domain of Interpretation for ISAKMP," 1998
- RFC 2408, "Internet Security Association and Key Management Protocol (ISAKMP)," 1998
- RFC 2409, "The Internet Key Exchange (IKE)," 1998
- RFC 2410, "The NULL Encryption Algorithm and Its Use With IPsec," 1998
- RFC 2411, "IP Security Document Roadmap," 1998
- RFC 2412, "The OAKLEY Key Determination Protocol," 1998
- RFC 2451, "The ESP CBC-Mode Cipher Algorithms," 1998
- RFC 2462, "IPv6 Stateless Address Autoconfiguration," 1998
- RFC 2553, "Basic Socket Interface Extensions for IPv6," 1999
- RFC 3056, "Connection of IPv6 Domains Via IPv4 Clouds," 2001
- RFC 3068, "An Anycast Prefix for 6to4 Relay Routers," 2001
- RFC 3526, "More Modular Exponential (MODP) Diffie-Hellman groups for Internet Key Exchange (IKE)," 2003
- RFC 3602, "The AES-CBC Cipher Algorithm and Its Use with IPsec," 2003
- RFC 3631, "Security Mechanisms for the Internet," 2003
- RFC 3715, "IPsec-Network Address Translation (NAT) Compatibility Requirements," 2004
- RFC 3739, "Internet X.509 Public Key Infrastructure: Qualified Certificates Profile," 2004
- RFC 3740, "The Multicast Group Security Architecture," 2004
- RFC 3748, "Extensible Authentication Protocol (EAP)," 2004

- RFC 3754, "IP Multicast in Differentiated Services (DS) Networks," 2004
- RFC 3756, "IPv6 Neighbor Discovery (ND) Trust Models and Threats," 2004
- RFC 3765, "NOPEER Community for Border Gateway Protocol (BGP) Route Scope Control," 2004
- RFC 3947, "Negotiation of NAT-Traversal in the IKE," 2005
- RFC 3948, "UDP Encapsulation of IPsec ESP Packets," 2005
- RFC 3964, "Security Considerations for 6to4," 2004
- RFC 3971, "SEcure Neighbor Discovery (SEND)," 2005
- RFC 3972, "Cryptographically Generated Addresses (CGA)," 2005
- RFC 4033, "DNS Security Introduction and Requirements," 2005
- RFC 4035, "Protocol Modifications for the DNS Security Extensions," 2005
- RFC 4106, "The Use of Galois/Counter Mode (GCM) in IPsec Encapsulating Security Payload (ESP)," 2005
- RFC 4107, "Guidelines for Cryptographic Key Management," 2005
- RFC 4109, "Algorithms for Internet Key Exchange version 1 (IKEv1)," 2005
- RFC 4285, "Authentication Protocol for Mobile IPv6," 2005
- RFC 4301, "Security Architecture for the Internet Protocol," 2005
- RFC 4302, "IP Authentication Header," 2005
- RFC 4303, "IP Encapsulating Security Payload (ESP)," 2005
- RFC 4305, "Cryptographic Algorithm Implementation Requirements for Encapsulating Security Payload (ESP) and Authentication Header (AH)," 2005
- RFC 4306, "Internet Key Exchange (IKEv2) Protocol," 2005
- RFC 4307, "Cryptographic Algorithms for Use in the Internet Key Exchange Version 2 (IKEv2)," 2005
- RFC 4308, "Cryptographic Suites for IPsec," 2005
- RFC 4309, " Using Advanced Encryption Standard (AES) CCM Mode with IPsec Encapsulating Security Payload (ESP)," 2005
- RFC 4359, "The Use of RSA/SHA-1 Signatures within Encapsulating Security Payload (ESP) and Authentication Header (AH)," 2006
- RFC 4380, "Teredo: Tunneling IPv6 over UDP through Network Address Translations (NATs)," 2006

Drafts

Drafts can be found at *http://www.ietf.org/ID.html*. To locate the latest version of a draft, refer to *https://datatracker.ietf.org/public/pidtracker.cgi*. You can enter the draft name without a version number and the most current version will come up. If a draft does not show up, it was either deleted or published as an RFC. Alternatively, you can go to the new Internet drafts database interface at *https://datatracker.ietf.org/public/idindex.cgi*. *http://tools.ietf.org/wg* is also a very useful site. More information on the process of standardization, RFCs, and drafts can be found in the Appendix.

Here's a list of drafts I refer to in this chapter, as well as interesting drafts that relate to the topics in this chapter:

- *draft-ietf-v6ops-ipsec-tunnels-02.txt*, Using IPsec to Secure IPv6-in-IPv4 Tunnels
- *draft-blanchet-v6ops-tunnelbroker-tsp-03.txt*, IPv6 Tunnel Broker with the Tunnel Setup Protocol (TSP)
- *draft-ietf-v6ops-security-overview-04.txt*, IPv6 Transition/Co-existence Security Considerations
- *draft-ietf-mip6-ikev2-ipsec-05.txt*, Mobile IPv6 Operation with IKEv2 and the revised IPsec
- *draft-ietf-mobike-protocol-08.txt*, IKEv2 Mobility and Multihoming Protocol (MOBIKE)
- *draft-ietf-mobike-design-08.txt*, Design of the MOBIKE Protocol
- *draft-ietf-v6ops-nap-02.txt*, IPv6 Network Architecture Protection
- *draft-ietf-bmwg-ipsec-term-08.txt*, Terminology for Benchmarking IPsec Devices
- *draft-ietf-bmwg-ipsec-meth-01.txt*, Methodology for Benchmarking IPsec Devices
- *draft-ietf-v6ops-icmpv6-filtering-bcp-01.txt*, Best Current Practice for Filtering ICMPv6 Messages in Firewalls

CHAPTER 6

Quality of Service

In the beginning, the Internet was designed to be a simple communications platform, mainly used to support file transfer and email. Over the past 25+ years, it has grown to be a very complex global communications infrastructure with a multitude of applications and services. IPv4 is based on a simple packet switching model, delivering packets with best effort and no guarantee for delivery. TCP adds guaranteed delivery but has no options to control parameters such as delay and jitter or to do bandwidth allocation.

Emerging multimedia services (such as Voice over IP and videoconferencing) can have significant bandwidth demands and are often very sensitive to timely delivery. The Type of Service Byte (ToS) in the IPv4 header was designed to provide prioritized treatment of certain traffic. However, it was never widely implemented, one reason being that its use would delay the forwarding of packets on routers. As there were almost no real-time services in those days, there was little pressure to find better solutions.

The development of IPv6, combined with the growing demand for real-time services—and, therefore, Quality of Service (QoS) features—was an opportunity to look for other solutions. Despite the availability of several different approaches, the topic of QoS is still a matter of research, and there are many ideas under development.

This chapter aims to discuss the features in IPv6 that support QoS.

QoS Basics

The current IP model treats all packets alike. They are all forwarded with best effort treatment according to the "first-come, first-served" principle. Which path a packet takes through the network depends on the available routers, routing tables, and general network load.

QoS protocols have the task of providing different data streams with priorities and guaranteeing qualities such as bandwidth and delay times. There are currently two main architectures: Integrated Services (IntServ) and Differentiated Services (Diff-Serv). Both architectures use traffic policies and can be combined to allow for QoS in the LAN as well as in the WAN.

Traffic policies can be used to make the transmission of data dependent on certain criteria—for example, whether there are enough resources available to forward the data according to its QoS requirements. Traffic policies can also monitor data streams and make adjustments or restrictions if necessary. Besides ensuring QoS requirements for delay-sensitive traffic, they can also be used for commercial reasons, such as controlling cost depending on different service levels.

Integrated Services

The Integrated Services Architecture (IntServ) is based on the paradigm that bandwidth and all related resources per flow are reserved on an end-to-end basis. This presupposes that routers store information about flows and analyze each packet to determine whether it belongs to a specific flow in order to forward the packet according to the criteria for that specific flow.

RSVP (Resource Reservation Protocol, RFC 2205) is part of the IntServ architecture. RFC 2210, "The Use of RSVP with IETF Integrated Services," describes the use of RSVP with IntServ. RSVP is a signaling protocol used to reserve bandwidth and other QoS resources across an IP network. IntServ combined with RSVP can be complex to implement and, because of its limited scalability, is inadequate to offer a general QoS solution for the global Internet.

To find an updated list of IntServ service and parameter names and their associated values, go to *http://www.iana.org/assignments/integ-serv*.

If you are interested in further reading about RSVP and other QoS signaling protocols, refer to the informational RFC 4094," Analysis of Existing Quality-of-Service Signaling Protocols."

Differentiated Services

While IntServ offers the capability to allocate bandwidth to different flows, the Differentiated Services (DiffServ) architecture was designed to make a less granular differentiation of classes in order to increase its scalability and usability in large networks and in the Internet.

Differentiated Services is specified in RFCs 2474 and 2475. RFC 2474, "Definition of the Differentiated Services Field (DS Field) in the IPv4 and IPv6 Headers," specifies the DS field. This is implemented in the ToS field in the IPv4 header and the Traffic Class field in the IPv6 header. The DS field is used by DiffServ routers to determine the QoS forwarding requirements of packets. Communicating nodes can categorize their communication through a so-called Per-Hop Behavior (PHB). Based on the PHB, packets receive specific treatment on DiffServ routers.

A DiffServ (DS) *domain* is a contiguous group of DS routers that work with a common service policy implemented on all routers. A DS domain is defined by DS boundary routers. The boundary routers classify incoming data streams and ensure that all packets traversing the domain are labeled appropriately and use a Per-Hop Behavior from the set available for the domain. Routers within the domain choose the forwarding rules based on the DiffServ values in packets, which they map to the corresponding PHBs. The Differentiated Services Codepoint (DSCP; refer to Figure 6-1, shown later) value can use either the default mapping (DSCP=0) or an individually configured mapping for the domain. A DS domain usually consists of one network or a set of networks, which constitute an administrative unit.

A DS *region* is a set of contiguous DS domains. DS regions can ensure DS services for domain spanning paths. The single domains can use individual PHB definitions and PHB-codepoint mappings internally. Between the domains within a region, Traffic Conditioners are responsible for providing correct translation of the different PHBs and mappings. If the policies, PHB groups, and codepoint mappings are the same in all the domains within the region, no Traffic Conditioners are needed.

Packet Classifiers choose packets from a data stream based on information in the packet headers and according to predefined rules. There are two types of classifiers: the Behavior Aggregate Classifier (BA) classifies packets based on the DS field, and the Multi Field Classifier (MF) classifies packets based on either different header fields or a combination of header fields, such as Source or Destination address, DS field, protocol number, source or destination port, or information such as incoming interface.

QoS in IPv6 Protocols

The designers of IPv6 have focused not on requiring specific mechanisms for QoS, but on offering as much flexibility as possible to support different QoS mechanisms. This section describes the elements in the IPv6 header and the Extension headers that can be used for QoS services.

IPv6 Header

There are two fields in the IPv6 header that can be used for QoS: the Traffic Class and the Flow Label field.

Traffic Class

The use of the 1-byte Traffic Class field is specified in RFC 2474. As already mentioned, this RFC introduces the term "DS field" for the Traffic Class field. The goal of this specification is that DiffServ routers have a known set of DS routines, which are determined by the value in the DS field. These DSCP values are mapped to Per-Hop Behaviors (PHB) and can be either performance- or class-based. Figure 6-1 shows the DS field.

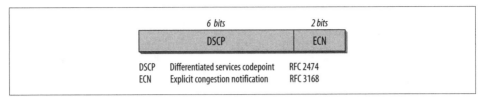

Figure 6-1. Format of the DS field

The DSCP field within the DS field (the six most significant bits of the DS field) is used for the codepoint, which specifies the PHB. With this field, 64 different codepoints can be specified. This codepoint pool has been divided into three parts to control the assignment of PHBs. Table 6-1 shows the division of the DSCP pools.

Table 6-1. The codepoint pools

Pool	Codepoint space	Assignment policy
1	xxxxx0	Standard use
2	xxxx11	Experimental/local use
3	xxxx01	Experimental/local use; potential standard use in the future

A pool of 32 recommended codepoints (pool 1) is assigned through formal standardization; a pool of 16 more codepoints (pool 2) is reserved for experimental or local use; the final pool of 16 codepoints (pool 3) is initially available for experimental or local use but should be used as an overflow pool if pool 1 is used up.

The PHBs specify how packets should be forwarded. A default PHB denominated by an all-zeros DS codepoint must be provided by any DS router. The default PHB describes the common, best-effort forwarding behavior available in existing routers. Such packets are forwarded without adhering to any priority policy; in other words, the network will deliver as many of these packets as possible as soon as possible, based on existing resources such as memory or processing capacity. Packets received with an undefined codepoint should also be forwarded as though they were marked for the default behavior.

The DS field does not specifiy PHBs; it specifies codepoints. The number of codepoints is limited to 64, whereas the number of PHBs is unlimited. There are recommended mappings of codepoints to PHBs. These mappings can be defined individually within administrative domains, which makes the number of possible PHBs unlimited. The coding rules for PHB IDs are specified in RFC 3140, "Per Hop Behavior Identification Codes." RFC 2597 defines a PHB group called Assured Forwarding (AF); RFC 3246 defines a PHB called Expedited Forwarding (EF).

Recommended codepoints and PHB IDs are assigned by IANA. The list of code-points can be found at *http://www.iana.org/assignments/dscp-registry*, and the list of PHB IDs at *http://www.iana.org/assignments/phbid-codes*.

Figure 6-2 shows the DS field in a trace file.

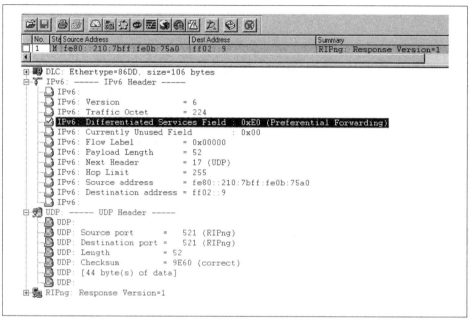

Figure 6-2. The DS field in a trace file

This is a RIPng (RIP Next Generation) Response from our Cisco router. It is sent to the RIP Routers Multicast address of FF02::9. The DS field is set to 0xE0 (decimal notation 224, binary notation 1110 0000), which is decoded by Sniffer with Preferential Forwarding.

The remaining two bits of the DS field (see Figure 6-1) are not used according to RFC 2474, and are specified in RFC 3168, "The Addition of Explicit Congestion Notification (ECN) to IP." They provide four possible codepoints (00 to 11) that are used for Congestion Notification. Usually the overload of a router could only be determined based on packet loss. With the use of these Congestion Notification Codepoints, a router can signal overload before packet loss. This method is similar to Frame Relay's use of BECNs and FECNs (Backwards and Forwards Explicit Congestion Notification).

The two bits are used as follows:

- 00: Packet does not use ECN.
- 01/10: Sender and receiver are ECN-enabled.
- 11: Router signals congestion.

Flow Label

The 20-bit Flow Label field in the IPv6 header may be used by a source to label packets for which it requests special handling by the IPv6 routers, such as nondefault QoS or real-time service. A flow label is assigned to a flow by the flow's source node. Between a sender and a receiver, there can be multiple flows active in parallel, along with the exchange of packets with no QoS requirements. New flow labels must be chosen randomly from the range 00001 to FFFFF. The purpose of the random allocation is to make any combination of bits within the Flow Label field suitable for use as a hash key by routers for looking up the state associated with the flow.

Hosts or routers that do not support the functions of the Flow Label field (most of today's applications, which will not be modified to use the Flow Label, or which do not need QoS handling) are required to set the field to all zeros when sending a packet, to pass the field on unchanged when forwarding a packet, and to ignore the field content when receiving a packet.

All packets belonging to the same flow must be sent with the same IP Source address, IP Destination address, identical source and destination ports, and a non-zero flow label. If any of these packets includes a Hop-By-Hop Options header, they all must be originated with the same Hop-By-Hop Options header contents (excluding the Next Header field of the Hop-By-Hop Options header, which is allowed to differ). If any packet includes a Routing Extension header, they all must be created with the same contents in all Extension headers up to and including the Routing Extension header (again excluding the Next Header field in the Routing Extension header). The routers or receivers are allowed to verify that these conditions are satisfied. If a violation of these consistency rules is detected, a corresponding error message is returned, indicating the exact location of the rule violation.

The handling of the flow label on routers is efficient, and when IPsec is used, it is always available because the IPv6 header is not encrypted by ESP or authenticated by AH (in transport mode). This implies that the integrity of the information in the DS field cannot be guaranteed by IPsec.

RFC 3697, "IPv6 Flow Label Specification," is a new specification of the Flow Label. A *flow* is defined as a sequence of packets from a sender to a specific unicast, anycast, or multicast address labeled as a flow by the sender. A flow is not necessarily associated with a transport connection. A host running multiple sessions with another host should be able to assign a different flow label to each session. Where the original specification defines a flow based on five criteria, the new specification definies a flow based on three criteria (Source and Destination address and flow label). The reason for this is that these three fields are always available for examination by routers, whereas the source and destination port number can be hidden by ESP.

IPv6 Extension Headers

As outlined earlier, two IPv6 Extension headers can be used to signal QoS requirements:

- The Routing Extension header can be used to request a specific route by indicating a sequence of nodes to be used (a "loose source route" in IPv4 terminology). However, use of this Extension header requires the requester to have knowledge about the preferred route (i.e., the network topology and QoS-sensitive parameters, such as possible throughput, etc.). To discourage attacks on the routing system, a packet sent in response to a received packet that included a routing header must not include a routing header that was automatically generated by "reversing" the received routing header (as is often done in IPv4 loose source routing) unless the integrity and authenticity of the received source IP address and routing header can be verified (e.g., via an Authentication Extension header in the received packet).

- The Hop-By-Hop Options header can be used to transport a maximum of one router alert signaling message per IP packet (RFC 2711) to every router on the path of QoS-sensitive traffic, indicating that each router should specifically process the IP packet. The use of the Hop-By-Hop Options header allows fast processing by the router because no analysis of higher-level protocol headers is required. Routers that are unable to recognize the router alert option type are required to ignore this option and continue processing the header. Also, routers are not allowed to change the option while the packet is in transit. Router alert types that have been defined so far are shown in Table 6-2.

Table 6-2. Currently defined router types

Value	Description
0	IP packet contains a Multicast Listener Discovery message.
1	IP packet contains an RSVP message.
2	IP packet contains an Active Networks message—the sender is attempting to load a program into the router for executing customized functions.
3–35	IP packet contains an Aggregated Reservation Nesting Level (RFC 3175, RSVP)
36–65,535	Reserved to IANA for future use.

A detailed description of these headers can be found in Chapter 2. An updated list of router alert types can be found at *http://www.iana.org/assignments/ipv6-routeralert-values*.

IPv6 Label Switch Architecture (6LSA)

One new proposal using the Flow Label field is the IPv6 Label Switch Architecture (6LSA). A new usage of the Flow Label field is proposed, the 6LSA architecture is described, and a method of binding packets to Forwarding Equivalence Classes (FECs) is discussed.

The 6LSA architecture is similar in many respects to Multiprotocol Label Switching (MPLS). Labels are assigned to IPv6 packets, which are then used to provide QoS services across a 6LSA domain. 6LSA uses the Flow Label field instead of a shim header, however, to carry the label information, thus avoiding fragmentation and certain performance issues, as well as providing an end-to-end layer 3 tag for QoS.

The 6LSA architecture is still a very new concept and will need to go through peer review in the IETF before it is finalized. While its ultimate acceptance and deployment are unknown, its development is a sign that the QoS community for IPv6 continues to work on providing better models.

Using QoS

The 6net project in Europe has conducted IPv6 QoS tests, the main focus of which was on IPv6 Differentiated Services. The document that describes these QoS tests is called "Report on IPv6 QoS Tests" and can be found at *http://www.6net.org/publications/deliverables*. The management summary states:

> "…the performed QoS tests in 6NET backbone indicated that this IPv6 QoS model can be the basis for production services. The mechanisms under test operated efficiently, as the experimental results prove, without any performance degradation on backbone routers. The above observations remained true even in heavy network congestion and the final performance results that a user or an application experienced correspond to the QoS service's specification."

While new methods of implementing QoS in IPv6 are designed and tested, there is a plethora of real-world experience that proves that a DiffServ-based QoS implementation can provide adequate, scalable QoS features for enterprises and service providers. With the increased popularity of Voice over IP, an underlying QoS-enabled infrastructure is a must, and in most cases the model chosen is DiffServ. The 6net testing further validates this architecture as ready for implementation on IPv6 to support real-time applications such as voice and video. It has to be noted that when it comes to QoS deployment, technical aspects are not the only critical factors. Cooperation between operators in terms of strategy, policy, rules, and accounting is required and can become an impediment to QoS deployment.

The next chapter describes IPv6's flexibility in supporting different physical networks.

References

Here's a list of the most important RFCs and drafts mentioned in this chapter. Sometimes I include additional subject-related RFCs for your personal further study.

RFCs

- RFC 2205, "Resource ReSerVation Protocol (RSVP)—Version 1 Functional Specification," 1997
- RFC 2210, "The Use of RSVP with IETF Integrated Services," 1997
- RFC 2430, "A Provider Architecture for Differentiated Services and Traffic Engineering (PASTE)," 1998
- RFC 2474, "Definition of the Differentiated Services Field (DS Field) in the IPv4 and IPv6 Headers," 1998
- RFC 2475, "An Architecture for Differentiated Services," 1998
- RFC 2597, "Assured Forwarding PHB Group," 1999
- RFC 2884, "Performance Evaluation of Explicit Congestion Notification (ECN) in IP Networks," 2000
- RFC 2914, "Congestion Control Principles," 2000
- RFC 2963, "A Rate Adaptive Shaper for Differentiated Services," 2000
- RFC 2983, "Differentiated Services and Tunnels," 2000
- RFC 2998, "A Framework for Integrated Services Operation over Diffserv Networks," 2000
- RFC 3006, "Integrated Services in the Presence of Compressible Flows," 2000
- RFC 3086, "Definition of Differentiated Services Per Domain Behaviors and Rules for their Specification," 2001
- RFC 3124, "The Congestion Manager," 2001
- RFC 3140, "Per Hop Behavior Identification Codes," 2001
- RFC 3168, "The Addition of Explicit Congestion Notification (ECN) to IP," 2001
- RFC 3246, "An Expedited Forwarding PHB," 2002
- RFC 3247, "Supplemental Information for the New Definition of the EF PHB (Expedited Forwarding Per-Hop Behavior)," 2002
- RFC 3260, "New Terminology and Clarifications for Diffserv," 2002
- RFC 3289, "Management Information Base for the Differentiated Services Architecture," 2002
- RFC 3290, "An Informal Management Model for Diffserv Routers," 2002
- RFC 3317, "Differentiated Services Quality of Service Policy Information Base," 2003
- RFC 3697, "IPv6 Flow Label Specification," 2004
- RFC 4094, "Analysis of Existing Quality-of-Service Signaling Protocols," 2005

CHAPTER 7

Networking Aspects

IP sits between the Data Link layer and the Transport layer. One of the goals in the development of IPv6 was to be able to support as many different physical networks as possible and to require no changes in the Transport layer. This approach is called "IP over Everything." To make IP as independent as possible from the Data Link layer, it needs an interface to this layer, which can be Ethernet, ATM, Token Ring, or any other media. The interface needs to be flexible and must be able to adapt to different requirements. For this purpose, features such as Path MTU discovery and fragmentation have been optimized. For UDP and TCP, it should not matter whether IPv4 or IPv6 is used. Obviously, changes are needed whenever IP addresses are used because of the difference in the address format. All these requirements lead to changes built into the IP layer itself. Multicast has been enhanced, and broadcast will not be used with IPv6. This chapter discusses the interface to the Data Link layer.

Layer 2 Support for IPv6

Different terms are used when the Data Link layer is discussed. The TCP/IP model has four layers, the first of which is called the Link layer. The OSI model has seven layers. It subdivides the Link layer of the TCP/IP model into two layers: the Physical layer and the Data Link layer. Thus, the term "Layer 2" refers to the second layer of the OSI model.

IPv6's independency of the physical network media is important. When a packet is sent from one network to another, we do not usually know in advance the kind of physical networks through which the packet will travel. IP cares only about the Destination address and finding a way to get there regardless of the network hardware used. IP then passes the packet to the Data Link layer. In 802 networks, the interface driver on the Data Link layer applies a Media Access Control (MAC) header to the datagram and sends it out to the physical network. The interface driver needs to be aware of the physical requirements for transmission. Each network's hardware technology defines a specific addressing mechanism. Neighbor Discovery, as described in Chapter 4, is used to map between IPv6 addresses and MAC addresses.

The rules and packet sizes for the transport of IPv6 datagrams differ depending on the topology. There is an RFC covering each topology in detail. This chapter summarizes the main points to consider; a complete list of the RFCs can be found in the Appendix B.

Ethernet (RFC 2464)

Ethernet is a widely used LAN technology developed in the early 1970s at Xerox. There are many different variants used these days: Twisted Pair Ethernet, also known as 10Base-T and operating at 10 Mbps; Fast Ethernet, also known as 100Base-T and operating at 100 Mbps; Gigabit Ethernet, also known as 1000Base-T and operating at 1 Gbps; and now even 10 Gigabit Ethernet, also known as 10GE and operating at 10 Gbps. The Institute of Electrical and Electronic Engineers (IEEE) together with a number of IT and telecom companies have defined a new standard called "Ethernet for the First Mile" (EFM, IEEE 802.3ah), which could allow usage of the Ethernet standard for first-mile connections to homes and companies.

RFC 2464 describes the format of IPv6 datagrams transmitted over Ethernet and how link-local and stateless autoconfigured addresses are formed. It obsoletes RFC 1972 and supports all Ethernet variants and VLAN technologies, such as 802.1Q and Cisco's Inter-Switch Link (ISL).

Ethernet hardware addresses use a 48-bit addressing scheme. Ethernet hardware manufacturers are assigned blocks of Ethernet addresses, known as *OUI* or *company ID*. No two Ethernet hardware interfaces have the same address, because each vendor assigns the addresses within its block in sequence. An Ethernet frame can be of variable size, but it can be no smaller than 64 bytes and no larger than 1518 bytes (header, data, and CRC). Packets over Ethernet have a default MTU of 1500 bytes. A smaller MTU can be configured through Router Advertisements containing an MTU option or through manual configuration of each device. If a Router Advertisement contains an MTU larger than 1500 bytes or larger than a manually configured MTU, the Router Advertisement must be ignored.

The Ethernet header contains the source and destination Ethernet addresses and the Ethernet type code. The Ethernet type code for IPv6 is 0x86DD. Figure 7-1 shows the Ethernet header for an IPv6 datagram.

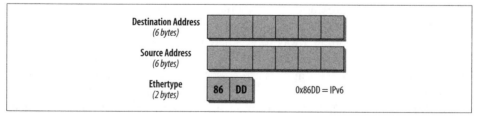

Figure 7-1. The Ethernet header for an IPv6 datagram

The Destination and Source Address fields each have six bytes, and the Ethernet Type field takes two bytes, containing the value 86DD for IPv6.

For Stateless autoconfiguration, the MAC address is used to build the IPv6 address. Chapter 3 explains how this process works. If the Destination address is a multicast address, the first two bytes of the MAC address are set to 3333 and the last four bytes are the last four bytes of the IPv6 destination multicast address. Figure 7-2 shows the format.

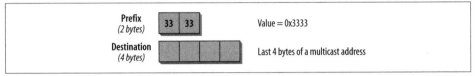

Figure 7-2. Relation of the IPv6 multicast address to Ethernet MAC address

Figure 7-3 shows how this looks in a trace file.

Figure 7-3. MAC header for an IPv6 multicast Destination address

In the summary line at the top of the figure, you can see the IPv6 Source address, which is the address of my Cisco router. The Destination address is the all-nodes multicast address. The Ethernet destination prefix shows 3333, which identifies this MAC address as a multicast address, and the remaining four bytes contain the last four bytes of the IPv6 Destination address—in this case 00-00-00-01. The Ethernet Source address contains the MAC address of the Cisco router, and the Ethertype has the value for IPv6, which is 0x86DD.

> For useful information about Ethernet, refer to Charles E. Spurgeon's site at *http://www.ethermanage.com/ethernet/ethernet.html*. He is also the author of *Ethernet: The Definitive Guide* (O'Reilly).

FDDI (RFC 2467)

Fiber Distributed Data Interconnect (FDDI) is a LAN technology operating at 100 Mbps over optical fiber using light pulses. FDDI is a Token Ring protocol, using a token to control transmission. A station that wants to transmit waits for the token circulating the ring sends the packet and passes the token to the next station in the ring. Like Token Ring, FDDI has a lot of built-in self-healing mechanisms. An FDDI frame has fields measured in 4-bit units called *symbols*.

RFC 2467 describes the format of IPv6 datagrams transmitted over FDDI. It also describes how link-local and Stateless autoconfigured addresses are formed and specifies the content of the Source/Target Link-layer Address option that is used in Router Solicitation, Router Advertisement, Neighbor Solicitation, Neighbor Advertisement, and Redirect messages when transmitted over an FDDI network. It obsoletes RFC 2019.

An FDDI hardware address can be either 4 or 12 symbols long. The maximum packet size for FDDI is 4500 bytes (9,000 symbols). 22 bytes are used for Data Link encapsulation when long-format addresses are used, and another 8 bytes are used for the LLC/SNAP header. This leaves a maximum size of 4470 bytes for the IPv6 packet. The default MTU size for IPv6 packets on FDDI networks has been set to 4352 bytes to allow for possible future extensions. This size can be reduced either by Router Advertisements containing an MTU option or by manual configuration of each device. If a Router Advertisement contains an MTU value higher than 4352 bytes or higher than a manually configured value, this option is ignored. The IPv6 datagrams are transmitted in asynchronous frames using unrestricted tokens and with a LLC/SNAP frame using 48-bit long-format addresses. Figure 7-4 shows the format of the FDDI header.

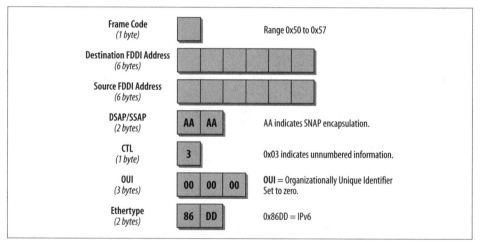

Figure 7-4. The FDDI header for an IPv6 datagram

The Frame Code field (FC) has a size of 1 byte and contains a value in the range 0x50 to 0x57. The three low-order bits indicate the frame priority. Both the Destination Service Access Point (DSAP) and the Source Service Access Point (SSAP) fields contain the value AA, which indicates SNAP encapsulation. The Control field (CTL) is set to 0x03, indicating Unnumbered Information. The Organizationally Unique Identifier (OUI) is set to 0. The Ethertype field contains the value 0x86DD for IPv6.

The rules that govern how a Stateless autoconfigured IPv6 address is built from the MAC address and the rules that govern how IPv6 multicast Destination addresses are converted to MAC addresses are the same as those used and described in the earlier discussion on Ethernet.

For tutorials and resources on FDDI, refer to *http://www.iol.unh.edu/ training/fddi*.

Token Ring (RFC 2470)

Token Ring is a well-known LAN technology developed by IBM. It is a token-ring protocol using a token for transmission control as described for FDDI. It operates at either 4 or 16 Mbps. The frame size of a Token Ring packet varies depending on the time a node can hold the token.

RFC 2470 describes the format of IPv6 datagrams transmitted over Token Ring. It also describes how link-local and Stateless autoconfigured addresses are formed, and specifies the content of the Source/Target Link-layer Address option that is used in Router Solicitation, Router Advertisement, Neighbor Solicitation, Neighbor Advertisement, and Redirect messages when transmitted over a Token Ring network.

A Token Ring hardware address uses a 48-bit format. Because the frame size is variable, it should be configured either through Router Advertisements or manually. In the absence of information, a default size of 1500 bytes should be used. As is always the case when working with Token Ring, we have to consider that Token Ring adapters read the address in noncanonical rather than canonical form, meaning that they read the bits in reverse order (last bit first). Thus, when analyzing and troubleshooting Token Ring in mixed environments, we need to make sure that implementations process the addresses correctly.

The Token Ring header is shown in Figure 7-5.

The first three fields for Starting Delimiter (SD), Access Control (AC), and Frame Control (FC) each have a size of one byte. The Source and Destination Address fields each have six bytes. The DSAP and SSAP fields are set to the value AA, which indicates SNAP encapsulation. The Control field (CTL) is set to the value 0x03, indicating Unnumbered Information. The OUI is set to 0, and the Ethertype field contains the value for IPv6: 0x86DD.

The rule governing how a Stateless autoconfigured IPv6 address is built from the MAC address is the same as the one described in the earlier discussion on Ethernet. Multicast addresses are treated differently with Token Ring, as described in RFC 2470. Packets with multicast Destination addresses are sent to Token Ring

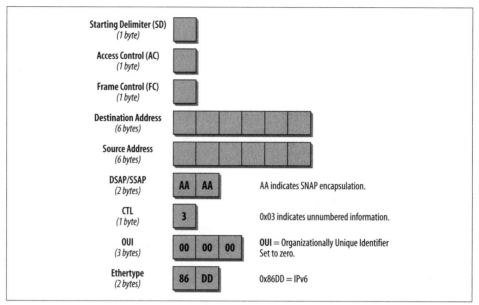

Figure 7-5. The Token Ring header for an IPv6 datagram

Functional Addresses. The RFC states 10 different functional addresses, and multiple IPv6 multicast addresses are mapped to each. Table 7-1 lists the mappings that have been defined.

Table 7-1. Mapping IPv6 multicast addresses to Token Ring Functional Addresses

MAC Functional Address (canonical)	Multicast addresses
03-00-80-00-00-00	All-nodes (FF01::1 and FF02::1) Solicited-node (FF02:0:0:0:0:1:FFxx:xxxx)
03-00-40-00-00-00	All-routers (FF0X::2)
03-00-00-80-00-00	Any other multicast address with three least significant bits = 000
03-00-00-40-00-00	Any other multicast address with three least significant bits = 001
03-00-00-20-00-00	Any other multicast address with three least significant bits = 010
03-00-00-10-00-00	Any other multicast address with three least significant bits = 011
03-00-00-08-00-00	Any other multicast address with three least significant bits = 100
03-00-00-04-00-00	Any other multicast address with three least significant bits = 101
03-00-00-02-00-00	Any other multicast address with three least significant bits = 110
03-00-00-01-00-00	Any other multicast address with three least significant bits = 111

You can find a Token Ring Tutorial at *http://www.techtutorials.info/tokenring.html*.

Point-to-Point Protocol (RFC 2472)

Point-to-Point Protocol (PPP) is a mechanism for running IP and other network protocols over a serial link. It supports synchronous and asynchronous lines. RFC 2472 describes the method for transmitting IPv6 packets over PPP and how IPv6 link-local addresses are formed on PPP links.

PPP's control protocol for IPv6, IPV6CP, is responsible for establishing and configuring IPv6 communication over PPP. One IPv6 packet can be encapsulated in a PPP Data Link layer frame, and the protocol field is set to 0x0057 for IPv6. If the PPP link is to support IPv6, the MTU size must be configured to IPv6's minimum MTU size of IPv6, which is 1280 bytes. A higher value (1500 bytes) is recommended.

IPV6CP has a distinct set of options for the negotiation of IPv6 parameters. The Options field has the same format as that which is defined for the standard Link Control Protocol (LCP). Currently the only defined options for IPV6CP are Interface-Identifier and IPv6-Compression Protocol. A PPP interface does not have a MAC address. The Interface-Identifier option provides a way to negotiate a 64-bit interface identifier, which must be unique within the PPP link. The IPv6-Compression option is used to negotiate a specific packet compression protocol, which applies only to IPv6 packets transmitted over the PPP link. The option is not enabled by default.

IPv6 address negotiation is different from IPv4. It is done through ICMPv6 Neighbor Discovery and not through PPP, as it is with IPv4. For ISPs, PPP in combination with IPv6 offers many advantages. For instance, it is no longer a problem to assign static addresses to customers, because the IPv6 address space is large enough. With IPv4, due to the shortage of addresses, ISPs often have to use dynamic addresses. The IPv6 functionality for address autoconfiguration supports easy administration and customer configuration with minimal cost. Prefix assignment to the customer site can be done through router discovery or through IPv6 Prefix Options for Dynamic Host Configuration Protocol (DHCP) Version 6 (RFC 3633). To get IPv6 to work over ADSL, ISPs need to choose an encapsulation that meets their needs, such as PPP over ATM (PPPoA) or PPP over Ethernet (PPPoE). IPv6 also has an impact on the Authentication, Authorization, Accounting (AAA) process. With IPV6CP, the address assignment occurs after the authentication. ISPs should note that Radius must support IPv6 attributes.

ATM (RFC 2492)

Asynchronous Transfer Mode (ATM) is a connection-oriented, high-speed network technology that is used in both LANs and WANs. It works over optical fiber and operates at up to gigabit speed by using special hardware and software mechanisms. An ATM network uses fixed-size frames called *cells*. Each cell is exactly 53 bytes long, and because it always has the same size, processing is very fast. An ATM cell has a header length of 5 bytes and 48 bytes of data. The ATM Adaptation layer (AAL5, RFC 2684) is the mechanism responsible for dividing a big packet, such as an IP packet, into small cells. This process can be compared to the way fragmentation works. The sender divides the packet into a set of 53 byte cells, and the receiver verifies that the packet has been received intact without errors and puts it back together again. If one cell is lost in transit, the whole set has to be resent. Because ATM does not support hardware broadcast and multicast, another mechanism that emulates it has been defined. All hosts in an ATM network register with the ATMARP server. If a host on the subnet sends a broadcast or multicast, the packet is sent to the ATMARP server, which distributes the packet to all registered hosts on the subnet/link. ATMARP is a variant of ARP and is defined in RFC 2225.

RFC 2492 describes the transmission of IPv6 packets over an ATM network in a companion document to RFC 2491, "IPv6 over Non-Broadcast Multiple Access (NBMA) Networks."

When the ATM network is used as a Permanent Virtual Circuit (PVC), each PVC connects two nodes, and the use of Neighbor Discovery is limited. IPv6 ATM interfaces have only one neighbor on each link. Multicast and broadcast are transmitted as a unicast on the ATM level. PVCs do not have link-layer addresses, so the link-layer address option is not used in Neighbor Discovery messages. IPv6 unicast and multicast packets sent over ATM are encapsulated using the LLC/SNAP encapsulation. Just as with FDDI and Token Ring, the DSAP and SSAP fields contain the value AA, and the CT field contains the value 0x03. The OUI field is set to 0 and the Ethertype field contains the value for IPv6, 0x86DD (see Figures 7-4 and 7-5). The default MTU size for an ATM PVC link is 9180 bytes.

If the ATM network is used as a Switched Virtual Circuit (SVC), unicast packets are transmitted using LLC/SNAP encapsulation, as described for PVC. For the transmission of multicast packets over SVC, the OUI field is set to 0x00005E, and the Ethertype field to 0x0001.

 A good site for information about ATM can be found at
http://cell-relay.indiana.edu.

There were a lot of discussions going on about whether IP was necessary on ATM networks: why not write applications to run natively on ATM? Finally, "IP over Everything" was developed. With the growing popularity of Fast Ethernet and Gigabit Ethernet, application designers have decided not to port their applications for transport over ATM directly. By writing their applications for IP, they needed only to write one interface and use the layer 2 functionality to run on all physical networks.

Frame Relay (RFC 2590)

Frame Relay is a connection-oriented, high-speed network technology used in WANs. It was developed in the Bell Labs in the late 1980s as part of the ISDN specification. The standard was refined in the early 1990s. By using a short, two-byte header, Frame Relay is very efficient in forwarding packets.

RFC 2590 specifies how IPv6 packets are transmitted over Frame Relay links, how IPv6 link-local addresses are formed, and how IPv6 addresses are mapped to Frame Relay addresses. It applies to Frame Relay devices that act as end stations (Data Terminal Equipment [DTEs]) on public or private Frame Relay networks. The Frame Relay Virtual Circuits can be PVCs or SVCs, and they can be point-to-point or point-to-multipoint. The default IPv6 MTU size for a Frame Relay interface is 1592 bytes.

Figure 7-6 shows the header of an IPv6 packet transmitted over Frame Relay.

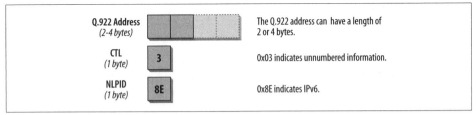

Figure 7-6. The Frame Relay header for an IPv6 datagram

The field for the Q.922 Address can be 2 or 4 bytes, depending on the address. The Control field (CTL) is set to 0x03, indicating Unnumbered Information. The Next Level Protocol ID (NLPID) contains the value 0x8E, indicating IPv6. The mapping of IPv6 addresses follows the specification for Neighbor Discovery as described in Chapter 3. A discussion of the details regarding addressing mechanisms and formats of Frame Relay addresses is in RFC 2590.

Detecting Network Attachment (DNA)

This section is not about your genetic code; it is about the issues surrounding how a host detects link changes.

The DNA working group works on defining better mechanisms for detecting IPv6 network attachment and link changes. When an IPv6 node detects or suspects that its underlying link layer connectivity has changed, it needs to check whether its IP addressing and routing configurations are still valid or must be changed. If the IP connectivity has changed, the node needs IP reconfiguration, and in the case of mobility, the initiation of mobility mechanisms such as sending binding updates (refer to Chapter 11 for information on mobility). Rapid attachment detection is important for a device that changes subnet while maintaining ongoing sessions. The current IPv6

Stateless and Stateful autoconfiguration procedures may take a fairly long time due to delays associated with Router Discovery and Duplicate Address Detection. The new mechanisms should avoid or reduce such delays wherever possible.

 The DNA working group can be found at *http://www.ietf.org/html. charters/dna-charter.html.*

RFC 4135, "Goals of Detecting Network Attachment in IPv6," describes the scope and goal of DNA. There are several drafts related to DNA in the "Drafts" section.

References

Here's a list of the most important RFCs and drafts mentioned in this chapter. Sometimes I list additional subject-related RFCs for your personal further study.

RFCs

- RFC 2149, "Multicast Server Architectures for MARS-based ATM multicasting," 1997
- RFC 2464, "Transmission of IPv6 Packets over Ethernet Networks," 1998
- RFC 2467, "Transmission of IPv6 Packets over FDDI Networks," 1998
- RFC 2470, "Transmission of IPv6 Packets over Token Ring Networks," 1998
- RFC 2472, "IP Version 6 over PPP," 1998
- RFC 2491, "IPv6 over Non-Broadcast Multiple Access (NBMA) networks," 1999
- RFC 2492, "IPv6 over ATM Networks," 1999
- RFC 2590, "Transmission of IPv6 Packets over Frame Relay Networks Specification," 1999
- RFC 3162, "Radius and IPv6," 2001
- RFC 3633, "IPv6 Prefix Options for Dynamic Host Configuration Protocol (DHCP) version 6," 2003
- RFC 3717, "IP over Optical Networks: A Framework," 2004
- RFC 3769, "Requirements for IPv6 Prefix Delegation," 2004
- RFC 4135, "Goals of Detecting Network Attachment in IPv6," 2005
- RFC 4282, "The Network Access Identifier," 2005
- RFC 4338, "Transmission of IPv6, IPv4, and Address Resolution Protocol (ARP) Packets over Fibre Channel," 2006

Drafts

Drafts can be found at *http://www.ietf.org/ID.html*. To locate the latest version of a draft, refer to *https://datatracker.ietf.org/public/pidtracker.cgi*. You can enter the draft name without a version number, and the most current version will come up. If a draft does not show up, it was either deleted or published as an RFC. Alternatively, you can go to the new Internet drafts database interface at *https://datatracker.ietf.org/public/idindex.cgi*. *http://tools.ietf.org/wg* is also a very useful site. More information on the process of standardization, RFCs, and drafts can be found in Appendix A.

Here's a list of drafts that I refer to in this chapter, Along with interesting drafts that are related to the topics in this chapter.

- *draft-shin-ipv6-ieee802.16-02.txt*, Scenarios and Considerations of IPv6 in IEEE 802.16 Networks
- *draft-ietf-dna-link-information-03.txt*, Link-layer Event Notifications for Detecting Network Attachments
- *draft-ietf-dna-cpl-02.txt*, DNA with unmodified routers: Prefix list based approach
- *draft-ietf-dna-hosts-02.txt*, Detecting Network Attachment in IPv6—Best Current Practices for hosts
- *draft-ietf-dna-routers-02.txt*, Detecting Network Attachment in IPv6—Best Current Practices for Routers
- *draft-ietf-dna-frd-00.txt*, Fast Router Discovery with L2 support

CHAPTER 8

Routing Protocols

Forwarding an IPv6 datagram beyond a directly attached subnet requires a router. Routers look at the datagram's destination IPv6 address and search for a matching prefix in their local routing tables. The first section of this chapter explains the routing table. It is very important for the router to have all relevant destinations in its routing table. But how do they get there? Entering them manually on all routers would not be very economical. A much more efficient automatic approach can be achieved by deploying routing protocols. *Routing protocols* define exchange procedures to synchronize the routing table between routers dynamically. Routing information needs to be distributed either within an *autonomous system* (AS) or between autonomous systems. An AS is defined as a set of networks governed by a single authority. Routing protocols that distribute information within an AS are called *Interior Gateway Protocols* (IGP). OSPF for IPv6, RIPng, IPv6 support on integrated IS-IS, and EIGRP for IPv6 belong to this category. Protocols that distribute information between ASes are called *Exterior Gateway Protocols* (EGP). BGP-4 and its extensions for IPv6 represent such a protocol.

This chapter explains the routing protocols RIPng, OSPF for IPv6, and BGP-4 support for IPv6 in detail. They represent the most important routing protocols in use today. The last section, "Additional Routing Protocols for IPv6," gives a brief description of IS-IS for IPv6 and EIGRP for IPv6, and also upcoming multicast routing for IPv6.

Most of the routing protocols discussed here can be used only for the exchange of IPv6 routing information. If IPv4 and IPv6 are deployed on the same network, separate routing protocols must be implemented: one for IPv4 and one for IPv6—for example, OSPFv2 for IPv4 routing and OSPFv3 for IPv6 routing. The only exceptions are the routing protocols BGP-4 and IS-IS. They can exchange routing information for both IP protocols within the same instance.

 The term *router* in this document stands for any device capable of IPv6 packet forwarding and/or processing the appropriate routing protocol (e.g., endsystems).

The Routing Table

Each router maintains a routing table (also known as forwarding table). Each entry represents an IPv6 destination, from now on called an IPv6 route. Each IPv6 route in the table is stored in the form of an IPv6 address prefix and its length. For each IPv6 route, additional information is stored in the routing table. The next hop information, for instance, tells the router where to forward a packet destined for this particular IPv6 route. Another type of information would be the metric of the IPv6 route, allowing the router to select the best path (smallest metric) to each IPv6 route in case of multiple entries.

> There is no distinction between network, subnet, and host routes in the routing table, because an IPv6 address prefix is unambiguous. Throughout this document, IPv6 routes will also be referred to as "routes."

Routing Table Lookup and Content

For each incoming IPv6 packet, the router inspects the Destination address and looks it up in the routing table. For each IPv6 route in the routing table, the router applies the prefix length to the Destination address to calculate a Destination address prefix. If this calculated prefix corresponds with the prefix of the IPv6 route, a match was found. To optimize the lookup, the searching algorithm looks through the entries based on prefix length, starting with longest prefix. If a match was found, the rest of the routing table can be ignored, as the longest matched prefix is always the preferred IPv6 route. Of course, this is a simplified representation of the lookup process. The actual algorithms behind it are complex and highly optimized.

Once the router has found a matching entry, the datagram is forwarded according to the next-hop information associated with this entry. In addition, the value of the hop limit within the datagram's IPv6 header is decremented by one. If no match is found in the routing table or the hop limit value has reached zero, the datagram is dropped. Figure 8-1 shows an example of such a routing table.

For each route, the router keeps the following entries in the routing table:

IPv6 prefix and prefix length
> The prefix length defines the number of relevant bits of the IPv6 prefix. Normally the nonrelevant bits are set to zero in the routing table. The prefix length is also used to determine whether the Destination address of an incoming datagram matches this route.

Next Hop address
> The IPv6 address (normally link-local) of the first router along the path to the IPv6 route. If the route is directly connected to the router through a local interface, there is no need for a Next Hop address.

```
                                                            Next Hop
                 Prefix                      Protocol   Intf.
-------------------------------------------  ----------  -------
FEC0::0008:0000/112                          DIRECT      3
   RIPv6 Metric: 3, Prefix on a directly attached link
   Last updated 3865 seconds ago

FEC0::0080:0000:0000:0000:0000/64            DIRECT      2
   RIPv6 Metric: 1, Prefix on a directly attached link
   Last updated 4703 seconds ago

FEC0::0004:0000:0000:0000:0000/64            DIRECT      1
   RIPv6 Metric: 1, Prefix on a directly attached link
   Last updated 4745 seconds ago

FEC0::0000/112                               RIPv6       3
   RIPv6 Metric: 5, Nexthop: FE80::0002
   Last updated 17 seconds ago

FEC0::0004:0000/112                          RIPv6       2
   RIPv6 Metric: 2, Nexthop: FE80::0003:A209:A348
   Last updated 2 seconds ago

FEC0::0001:0000:0000:0000:0000/64            RIPv6       2
   RIPv6 Metric: 2, Nexthop: FE80::0003:A209:A348
   Last updated 2 seconds ago

FEC0::0002:0000:0000:0000:0000/64            RIPv6       2
   RIPv6 Metric: 2, Nexthop: FE80::0003:A2E0:BEF2
   Last updated 9 seconds ago

FEC0::0003:0000:0000:0000:0000/64            RIPv6       3
   RIPv6 Metric: 4, Nexthop: FE80::0002
   Last updated 17 seconds ago

FEC0::0005:0000:0000:0000:0000/64            RIPv6       1
   RIPv6 Metric: 2, Nexthop: FE80::0280:2DFF:FE41:C90B
   Last updated 10 seconds ago
```

Figure 8-1. An IPv6 routing table

Next Hop interface

The local interface of the router that is used to reach the Next Hop address.

Metric

A number indicating the total distance to the destination. This metric depends on the routing protocol that has put this entry into the routing table. Metric calculations done by the different routing protocols cannot be compared to each other. If the same route is known by different routing protocols, the router must prefer one routing protocol over the other. This is done by assigning a priority value to each routing protocol (e.g., Cisco Systems calls this priority the "administrative distance"). Directly connected routes always have the best priority and are assigned the metric of the Next Hop interface (normally set to zero).

Timer
> The amount of time since the information about the route was last updated.

Route Source, also known as protocol
> The entity that provided information for this entry. For example, this may be a static entry, a directly connected route, or a route from a routing protocol, such as RIPng, OSPF for IPv6, BGP, etc.

Default Route

A *default route* represents a route to all Destination addresses that are not explicitly listed in the routing table. It can be used when a router does not need to know all destinations specifically—for example, a router connecting a remote branch office to the main site. It does not need to know all routes of the entire autonomous systems. It only needs to know the local routes of the remote office; all other routes can be reached only via the connection to the main site, hence a default route.

A default route must be entered into the routing table just like any other route. The Next Hop address of the default route is also called the *default router or default gateway*. The entire data traffic for unknown routes is sent to the default router. It is assumed that the default router knows all the routes or has a default router itself. It is at the discretion of the network designer to determine whether and how such a chain of default routers should be implemented. The top router of such a chain is typically a boundary router to another network area or autonomous system. It is here that the default route is entered statically and then distributed over the appropriate network area via a routing protocol. The advantage of distributing the default route is to reduce the number of routing updates to be distributed throughout the network area. Default routes should not be propagated further than intended—that is, they should not leave the network area or the autonomous system. A metric is assigned to the default route at its origin to establish precedence among multiple default routers. Default routes and distribution must be planned and implemented with care to avoid routing inconsistencies.

Any prefix with a length of zero is considered to be a default route, but normally an IPv6 prefix of 0:0:0:0:0:0:0:0 (or simply ::) with a prefix length of zero is used. A Destination address of an incoming datagram will always match the default route, as the number of relevant bits for comparison is zero. The default route, however, is always the last route in the routing table, and hence a match is found only if no other routes in the routing table produce a match.

> The most common use of a default route is on the endsystems attached to the network, such as PCs, servers, printers, etc. Each system must have a *default gateway* to send traffic to destinations outside the local subnet.

RIPng

History is repeating itself. Just as with IPv4, the first dynamic routing protocol to reach productivity is RIP, in this instance called *RIPng*. RIPng is a routing protocol based on a distance-vector algorithm known as the Bellman-Ford algorithm. I outline the theory and math behind this algorithm briefly in this section. Most of the concepts for RIPng have been taken from RIPv1 and RIPv2, which have been implemented for IPv4 for quite some time.

 RIPv1 is defined in RFC 1058, RIPv2 in RFC 2453. RIPng is defined in RFC 2080 (January 1997).

Distance-Vector Algorithm for RIPng

RIPng uses a simple mechanism to determine the metric (cost) of a route. It basically counts the number of routers (hops) to the destination. Each router counts as one hop. Routes with a distance greater than or equal to 16 are considered to be unreachable. The router periodically distributes information about its routes to its directly connected neighbors using RIPng response messages. Upon receiving RIPng response messages from its neighbor, the router adds the distance between the neighbor and itself (usually one, as in one hop) to the metric of each route received. The router then processes the newly received route entry using the Bellman-Ford algorithm.

Figure 8-2 provides a closer look at the Bellman-Ford algorithm, and its implementation for RIPng is explained below.

The RIPng process within each router maintains specific RIPng parameters for each route. To illustrate the distance vector algorithm, two of these parameters are briefly explained here. They are the route change flag, indicating a change of information of the corresponding route, and the time-out timer, indicating the lifetime of the route. The periodic updates prevent the route from expiring. Let's assume Router A and Router B are running RIPng. Router A receives a routing update from Router B and has already added the distance of 1 to each route r_i advertised by B. The next hop address for route r_i is Router B. For each route r_i, the router steps through the algorithm depicted in Figure 8-2. According to Figure 8-2, the routing table will be updated if the following criteria are true; otherwise, route r_i is discarded:

Route r_i is new and reachable. The route is added as a new entry to the routing table. The time-out timer is set to zero, and the Route Change flag is raised.

Route r_i is already in the routing table, and the next hop address corresponds to the one in the routing table. The route has just been refreshed. The time-out timer is reset to zero. If the metric has changed, it is updated and the Route Change flag is raised.

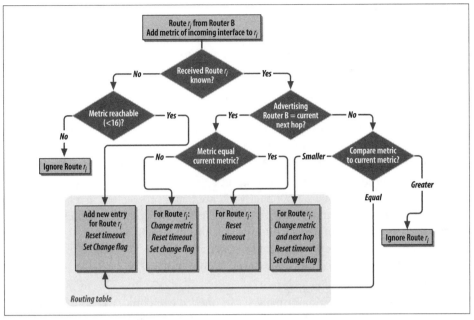

Figure 8-2. The Bellman-Ford algorithm

***Route r_i is already in the routing table, but the next hop address is different and the
metric is smaller than the one in the routing table.*** A different path to the route has
been found. The metric and next hop address are updated. The time-out timer is
set to zero, and the Route Change flag is raised.

***Route r_i is already in the routing table, but the next hop address is different and the
metric is equal to the one in the routing table.*** If the routing process allows for multiple equal-cost paths to the same destination in the routing table, the route is
treated as a new entry (see earlier item). If the routing process does not provide
for multiple equal-cost paths, route r_i is discarded. Multiple equal-cost paths
allow for load sharing of IPv6 traffic among multiple paths. The algorithm for
distributing traffic among these paths is at the discretion of the routing process
itself, normally based on the source and destination IPv6 addresses to ensure
that datagrams between two particular systems always take the same path.

The next hop address of r_i is taken either from the information within the routing
update message or from the source IPv6 address of the RIPng packet. In this case it
was Router B. See the "Next Hop Information" section for more information.

When the routers are first initialized, they know only their directly connected routes.
This information is passed to all neighbors, processed, and then distributed to their
neighbors. Eventually, all IPv6 routes are known by all routers. The routers keep
sending response messages periodically to prevent valid routes from expiring. The
time it takes for all routers to learn about the new routes is called *convergence time*.

Limitations of the Protocol

RIPng, like the earlier versions of RIP, is primarily designed for use as an IGP in networks of moderate size. The limitations specified for RIP versions 1 and 2 apply to RIPng as well. They are described in the following list:

The RIPng diameter is limited.
> The longest path to any IPv6 route is limited to a metric of 15 when propagated with RIPng. Normally this corresponds with a path over a maximum of 15 hops. The protocol allows for larger costs to be assigned to any link, limiting the number of hops even further. Routes with a metric of 16 or greater are unreachable.

Routing loops can cause high convergence time.
> When IPv6 routes that are no longer valid are being propagated in a looped environment, RIPng continues to increase the metric by one. The routes would be passed around indefinitely ("counting to infinity"). The mechanism of limiting the metric to 16 prevents this from happening. The routes will circle until they reach the maximum metric and are eventually eliminated.

The metric does not reflect line speed.
> RIPng uses a fixed metric normally set to one for each link crossed. A route cannot be chosen based on bandwidth or real-time parameters such as measured delay, load, or reliability.

Changes in Topology and Preventing Instability

A change in topology happens when a route is newly added or has gone down. Newly added routes are advertised within the next response message sent by the router having the direct connection to that route. Its neighbors process the route and pass it on to their neighbors. Eventually, all routers know about the newly added route.

What happens if a route goes down or a router crashes? These routes will eventually time out, as they are no longer being advertised. The questions are just how long this process will take and whether this time is acceptable for the network. To keep the convergence time to a minimum, several measures can be introduced.

Route poisoning and the hold-down timer

If an interface goes down on a router, the router does not remove the route(s) associated with that interface immediately. Instead, the router keeps the route in the routing table and raises the metric to 16 (unreachable). A *garbage-collection timer*, also known as a hold-down timer, determines how long the router keeps this unreachable route in the routing table. The route is now advertised to the neighbors with a metric of 16. The neighbors are running a hold timer as well, so they keep the route in the routing table to inform their respective neighbors about the invalidity of the route. This process is called *route poisoning*.

Split horizon, with or without poison reverse

Let's assume route r_1 is directly connected to router A, as shown in Figure 8-3.

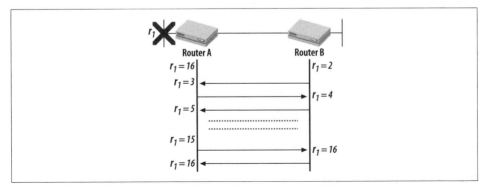

Figure 8-3. Convergence of route r_1 without split horizon

Router A advertises r_1 to its neighbor, Router B, with a cost of 1. Router B adds 1 to the cost and lists r_1 in its routing table using Router A as the next hop. Now r_1 goes down. Router A poisons r_1 and waits for the update timer to expire before advertising r_1 to B with a cost of 16. In the meantime, however, Router B advertises r_1 back to A with a cost of 2. Router A changes the entry for r_1 using B as the next hop with a metric of 3. Now Router A advertises r_1 with a cost of 3 (not 16) to Router B. Router B adds 1 to the cost and lists r_1 in its routing table with a cost of 4. The routers send r_1 back and forth, each time raising the cost by 1 until counting to infinity strikes and both reach a cost of 16, declaring r_1 invalid. This will take quite some time, however. The core problem lies in the fact that Router B advertises routes learned from A back to A.

Split horizon prevents this scenario from happening. With split horizon, a router never advertises a route back over its next hop interface. An additional option is *split horizon with poison reverse*. With this option, a router always advertises a route back over its next hop interface with a metric of 16. In the very unlikely situation that both Routers A and B have the same route pointing to each other, the routers don't have to wait for a timeout to eliminate this route, because poison reverse invalidates each of them immediately. Poison reverse can, however, have the disadvantage of increasing the size of routing messages, especially if many destinations have to be advertised back as poisoned.

There are very few situations in which split horizon (with or without poison reverse) cannot be used at all. If there is a point-to-multipoint (also called hub-and-spoke) topology using a single common IPv6 network, split horizon prevents the spoke routers from learning routes advertised by other spoke routers. Split horizon must be turned off at the central router (the hub router).

Triggered updates

Any changes in the routing table have to wait to be advertised until the update timer has expired. Triggered updates speed up the process by allowing the changed route entry to be advertised almost immediately. A very small hold timer is introduced before sending the update. Because only the changes are advertised, regular periodic updates need to stay in place.

All these measures speed up convergence, but the world is not perfect. Erroneous information may always come back over larger loops, especially within a large network with a topology containing many loops. The process of counting to infinity with a maximum metric will, however, always prevail to eliminate the erroneous information.

RIPng Message Format

RIPng is a UDP-based protocol using UDP port number 521; let's call it the RIPng port. The RIPng routing process always listens to messages arriving on this port. With the exception of specific requests, all RIPng messages set the source and destination port to the RIPng port. Specific requests are discussed later in this chapter.

The RIPng message format is shown in Figure 8-4.

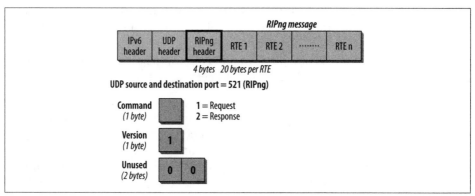

Figure 8-4. RIPng message format

The fields of the RIPng message are explained in the following list:

Command (1 byte)

1 = Request: A request message is asking the responding system to send all or part of its routing table.

2 = Response: A response message containing all or part of the sender's routing table. It may be sent as a response to a previous request or as an unsolicited response used in periodic or triggered routing updates.

Version (1 byte)

The version field is set to a value of 1.

Route Table Entry (RTE) (20 bytes each)

The RIPng header is followed by one or more Route Table Entries using the format depicted in Figure 8-5.

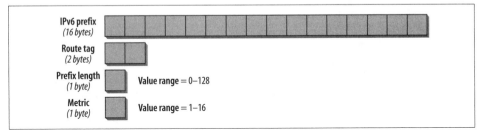

Figure 8-5. Format of a Route Table Entry

Each RTE describes the route to be advertised by using the IPv6 Prefix (16 bytes) and its Prefix Length (1 byte). The metric field (1 byte) contains the metric used by the sender for this route. A valid metric has a value between 1 and 15. A metric of 16 describes the route as unreachable by the sending router.

Each RTE contains a Route Tag field as well. It may be used to carry additional information about a route learned from another routing protocol—e.g., BGP. A router importing external routes into RIPng may set this tag. RIPng will preserve and redistribute this tag within its routing domain. Information within this tag can be used to redistribute the route out of the RIP domain. RIPng itself makes no use of this tag.

The number of RTEs within a single RIPng message depends on the physical MTU (Maximum Transfer Unit) of the medium between two neighboring routers. The formula is as follows:

number of RTEs = Integer value ((MTU – length of IPv6 headers – length of UDP header – length of RIPng header) / size of RTE)

Next Hop Information

If you are familiar with RIPv2, you probably miss the field for the next hop address. Not to worry: RIPng provides this feature too. With RIPv2, each entry has a designated field specifying the Next Hop address. This would not be very economical for RIPng because it would nearly double the size of each RTE. As shown in Figure 8-6, a specially constructed RTE, the Next Hop RTE, is introduced. It contains the next hop's IPv6 address. All subsequent RTEs use this IPv6 address for the next hop identification until the end of the message has been reached or another next hop RTE is encountered.

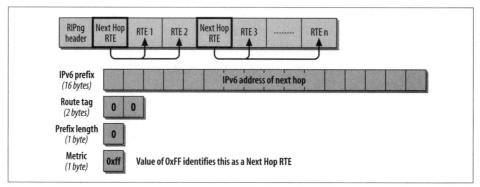

Figure 8-6. The Next Hop RTE

The Next Hop RTE is identified by a value of 0xFF in the metric field of the RTE. The IPv6 address within the RTE is now identified as the Next Hop IPv6 address to be used by the subsequent RTE. The route tag and the prefix length are set to 0 on sending and ignored on reception.

Specifying a value of 0:0:0:0:0:0:0:0 (or simply ::) in the prefix field of the Next Hop RTE indicates that the Next Hop IPv6 address should be set to the source IPv6 address of the RIPng message. The purpose of naming a specific next hop is to eliminate unnecessary routing hops. For example, Routers A, B, and C are directly connected on a common subnet. Router C does not run RIPng. Assume that Router A somehow knows a route r_i using Router C as its next hop. Router A could advertise r_i to B with the Next Hop address of Router C. Router B can now forward traffic for r_i directly to Router C, therefore avoiding the unnecessary hop through Router A.

The next hop IPv6 address must always be a link-local address (starting with a prefix of FE80). If there is no Next Hop RTE, or if the received next hop address is not link-local, it should be considered 0:0:0:0:0:0:0:0 (or simply ::).

Timers

RIPng implements different timers to control updates of the routing information. The name and purpose of these timers are specified in the following list:

Update timer
> By default, every 30 seconds the RIPng process wakes up on each interface to send an unsolicited response message to the neighboring routers. This response contains the entire routing table known to the RIP process, except for routes that follow the split horizon rule. One or more response messages may be needed. This timer is kept for each router interface.

Timeout timer
> Each time a route entry is updated, the timeout time for this route entry is reset to zero. If the route entry reaches 180 seconds (default value) without another

update, it is considered to have expired. The metric is set to 16, and the garbage collection process begins. In addition, the Route Change flag is raised to indicate a change. The output process uses this flag to trigger an update. This timer is kept for each routing table entry.

Garbage-collection timer (sometimes referred to as hold-down timer)
This timer is set for 120 seconds for each route entry that has timed out (see timeout timer) or has been received with a metric of 16. Only upon expiration of this timer will the route entry finally be removed from the routing table. If a new update to this route arrives before the garbage collection timer expires, the route is replaced and the garbage collection timer is cleared. This timer is kept for each routing table entry.

Packet Processing

Let's look at how the router processes incoming and outgoing RIPng messages.

Request message

A *request message* asks a router to respond with all or part of its routing table by specifying the requested RTE. The incoming request is processed as follows.

If there is exactly one RTE with a prefix of zero, a prefix length of zero, and a metric of 16, the request is for the entire routing table, and the router responds by sending the entire routing table. Figure 8-7 shows a trace of such a request message.

Otherwise, the request message is processed one RTE at a time. If the RTE's corresponding prefix is found in the routing table, the RTE's metric is placed into the metric field of the RTE; otherwise, a metric of 16 is placed into the metric field, indicating that the route is unknown. Once all RTEs have been processed, the command field in the RIPng header is changed to "response," and the newly formed response message is sent back to the requestor.

There are two types of request messages, General and Specific, which are handled differently by the receiving router.

A General Request is sent by a router that has just come up and wants to fill its routing table quickly. The router sends out a General Request message asking all directly connected neighbors to send their entire routing tables. The neighbors each reply with a response message that contains their entire routing tables using the split horizon rule.

A Specific Request message is sent by a monitoring station asking for all or part of the routing table. The queried router replies to the requestor by sending the requested information from its routing table. Split horizon is not used, because it is assumed that the requestor is using the requested information for diagnostic purposes only.

```
Sniffer - Local, Ethernet (Line speed at 10 Mbps) - [rip6book.cap: Decode, 1/3 Ethernet Frames]
 File  Monitor  Capture  Display  Tools  Database  Window  Help

   ▶ ||  ■ ▣ ▥ ◬  Default          ▼

  ▣▤ ▦▨ ▧▨▩▨▧ ▨▤ ▨◩◪ ▨ ▧ ▨

 No.  Status  Source Address       Dest Address        Summary
 1    M       fe80::280:2dff:ff02::9                    RIPng: Request Version=1
 2            fe80::200:a2ff:fe80::280:2dff:            RIPng: Response Version=1
 3            fe80::280:2dff:ff02::9                    RIPng: Response Version=1

 DLC:  ----- DLC Header -----
   DLC:
   DLC:  Frame 1 arrived at  19:36:12.4960; frame size is 86 (0056 hex) bytes.
   DLC:  Destination = Multicast 333300000009
   DLC:  Source      = Station Xylogi41C90B
   DLC:  Ethertype   = 86DD
   DLC:
 IPv6:  ----- IPv6 Header -----
   IPv6:
   IPv6:  Version          = 6
   IPv6:  Priority         = 7 (Internet Control Traffic)
   IPv6:  Flow Label       = 0x000000
   IPv6:  Payload Length   = 32
   IPv6:  Next Header      = 17 (UDP)
   IPv6:  Hop Limit        = 255
   IPv6:  Source address   = fe80::280:2dff:fe41:c90b
   IPv6:  Destination address = ff02::9
   IPv6:
 UDP:  ----- UDP Header -----
   UDP:
   UDP:  Source port      = 521 (RIPng)
   UDP:  Destination port = 521 (RIPng)
   UDP:  Length           = 32
   UDP:  Checksum         = 0532
   UDP:  [24 byte(s) of data]
   UDP:
 RIPng:  ----- RIPng -----
   RIPng:
   RIPng:  Command          = 1 (Request)
   RIPng:  Version          = 1
   RIPng:  Reserved         = 0x0000
   RIPng:  IPv6 Prefix      = ::
   RIPng:  Route tag        = 0
   RIPng:  Prefix length    = 0
   RIPng:  Metric           = 16 (infinity: destination unreachable)
```

Figure 8-7. RIPng request message asking for the entire routing table

Table 8-1 summarizes the characteristics of the two types of requests.

Table 8-1. RIPng request messages

Request type	IPv6 Source address	IPv6 Destination address	Source UDP port	Destination UDP port	Use split horizon in response?
General	Link-local address of the requestor's sending interface	ff02::9 (multicast)	RIPng port (521)	RIPng port (521)	Yes
Specific	Global or local unicast address of the requestor	Global or local unicast address of the queried router	Any except the RIPng port	RIPng port (521)	No

RFC 2080 still uses the term "site-local address" instead of "local address." Site-local addresses have been deprecated in the meantime. For more information, refer to the sections in Chapter 3 about IPv6 addressing.

Response message

A response message carries routing information to be processed by the receiving router using the Bellman-Ford Algorithm (see the earlier section "Distance-Vector Algorithm for RIPng"). A response message is accepted by a router only if the IPv6 Source address is a link-local address of a directly connected neighbor and the UDP source and destination ports are set to the RIPng port. In addition, the hop limit value must be equal to 255. This indicates that the response message has not traveled over any intermediate node.

Once the response message is accepted, each RTE must be checked for its validity. The test includes the prefix itself (not a multicast or link-local address), the prefix length (between 0 and 128), and the metric (between 1 and 16). If the RTE is accepted, the metric of the incoming interface is added to the metric of the RTE. The RTE is now passed to the Bellman-Ford process, as described in the earlier section "Distance-Vector Algorithm for RIPng." Figure 8-8 shows a trace of a response message.

These rules for receiving and validating a response message do not apply for a response to a specific query. The hop limit value may be less than 255, and the source IPv6 address is not a link-local address. The diagnostic station uses the received RTE(s) not for routing, but to provide input into its diagnostic software. It is entirely up to the implementer of such software to determine the validity of a response message.

There are two types of response messages: Unsolicited and Solicited. An Unsolicited Response message is sent by a periodic or triggered update process. The periodic update process examines the entire routing table on expiration of the Update Timer on any given interface. The triggered update process wakes up as soon as the Route Change flag is raised and examines only routes with the Route Change flag set. Both processes then proceed with the following: if the examined route entry has a link-local address or should not be used because of split horizon processing, skip it. Otherwise, put the prefix, prefix length, and metric into the RTE, and put the RTE into the response message. If the maximum MTU has been reached, send the packet and build a new packet.

A Solicited Response message is sent as a response to a request message.

Table 8-2 summarizes the characteristics of the two types of responses.

```
Sniffer - Local, Ethernet (Line speed at 10 Mbps) - rip6book.cap: Decode, 3/3 Ethernet Frames
File   Monitor   Capture   Display   Tools   Database   Window   Help

    ▶ ‖ ▪ ▒ ▒ ▒  Default     ▾

    ▒ ▒ ▒ ▒   ▒ ▒ ▒ ▒ ▒ ▒ ▒ ▒ ▒ ▒ ▒ ▒ ▒ ▒

No.  Status  Source Address    Dest Address      Summary
□ 1   M       fe80::280:2dff:  ff02::9            RIPng: Request Version=1
□ 2           fe80::200:a2ff:  fe80::280:2dff:   RIPng: Response Version=1
□ 3           fe80::280:2dff:  ff02::9            RIPng: Response Version=1

⊞-▥ DLC: Ethertype=86DD, size=246 bytes
⊟-♈ IPv6: ----- IPv6 Header -----
    └🗋 IPv6:
    ├🗋 IPv6: Version            = 6
    ├🗋 IPv6: Priority           = 7 (Internet Control Traffic)
    ├🗋 IPv6: Flow Label         = 0x000000
    ├🗋 IPv6: Payload Length     = 192
    ├🗋 IPv6: Next Header        = 17 (UDP)
    ├🗋 IPv6: Hop Limit          = 255
    ├🗋 IPv6: Source address     = fe80::280:2dff:fe41:c90b
    ├🗋 IPv6: Destination address = ff02::9
    └🗋 IPv6:
⊟-▥ UDP: ----- UDP Header -----
    └🗋 UDP:
    ├🗋 UDP: Source port       = 521 (RIPng)
    ├🗋 UDP: Destination port  = 521 (RIPng)
    ├🗋 UDP: Length            = 192
    ├🗋 UDP: Checksum          = 3D29
    ├🗋 UDP: [184 byte(s) of data]
    └🗋 UDP:
⊟-▥ RIPng: ----- RIPng -----
    └🗋 RIPng:
    ├🗋 RIPng: Command          = 2 (Response)
    ├🗋 RIPng: Version          = 1
    ├🗋 RIPng: Reserved         = 0x0000
    ├🗋 RIPng: IPv6 Prefix      = fec0::4:0:0:0:0
    ├🗋 RIPng: Route tag        = 0
    ├🗋 RIPng: Prefix length    = 64
    ├🗋 RIPng: Metric           = 1
    ├🗋 RIPng: IPv6 Prefix      = fec0::5:0:0:0:0
    ├🗋 RIPng: Route tag        = 0
    ├🗋 RIPng: Prefix length    = 64
    ├🗋 RIPng: Metric           = 1
    ├🗋 RIPng: IPv6 Prefix      = fec0::80:0:0:0:0
    ├🗋 RIPng: Route tag        = 0
    ├🗋 RIPng: Prefix length    = 64
    ├🗋 RIPng: Metric           = 16 (infinity: destination unreachable)
    ├🗋 RIPng: IPv6 Prefix      = fec0::1:0:0:0:0
    ├🗋 RIPng: Route tag        = 0
    └🗋 RIPng: Prefix length    = 64
```

Figure 8-8. RIPng response message

Table 8-2. RIPng response messages

Request type	IPv6 Source address	IPv6 Destination address	Source UDP port	Destination UDP port
Unsolicited (periodic update or triggered update)	Link-local address of the sending interface	ff02::9 (multicast)	RIPng port (521)	RIPng port (521)
Solicited (answer a request)	Link-local address (general request), global or local address (specific request)	Source IPv6 address of the request message	RIPng port (521)	Source UDP port of the request message

Sending the Unsolicited Response message to the multicast address ensures that the response message reaches all neighbors on any particular directly connected network. There are cases in which this may not work—e.g., on a non-broadcast-capable network. A static list of all neighbors on such a network must be configured to send the messages directly to each neighbor.

Control Functions and Security

RIPng does not provide specifications for administrative control. However, experience with existing RIP implementations suggests that such controls may be important. Administrative controls are filters that allow or disallow certain routes to be advertised or received. In addition, a list of valid neighbors could be specified, and a router would accept or announce routes only to neighbors on this list. These filters can be used to change the update behavior so it complies with routing policies set within an autonomous system. Again, RIPng does not need such controls to function, but it is strongly recommended that the implementer provide such controls. Cisco Systems, for example, implements RIPng distribution lists, and Nortel implements RIPng Announce and Accept Policies.

RIPng provides no encryption option. To ensure integrity and authentication of routing exchanges, it must rely on the IP Authentication Header and the IP Encapsulating Security Payload. In practice, this method is hardly ever used.

OSPF for IPv6 (OSPFv3)

OSPF for IPv6 modifies the existing OSPF for IPv4 to support IPv6. The fundamentals of OSPF for IPv4 remain unchanged. Some changes have been necessary to accommodate the increased address size of IPv6 and the changes in protocol semantics between IPv4 and IPv6. OSPF for IPv6 is defined in RFC 2740, which emphasizes the differences between OSPF for IPv4 and OSPF for IPv6. It contains a large number of references to the documentation of OSPF for IPv4, which makes it hard to read. This chapter tries to concatenate the two worlds to make the reading a little bit more comfortable. It starts with an overview of OSPF, including the area structure and external routes. After the overview, it opens up the protocol to get down to the implementation details: it starts with the OSPF message format, proceeds to the neighbor relationship, and finishes with the actual link state database and the calculation of the routing table.

Overview of OSPF for IPv6

OSPF for IPv4 (OSPFv2) is standardized in RFC 2328. In addition to this document, several extensions to OSPF have been defined. RFC 1584 describes IPv4 multicast extensions to OSPF. RFC 3101 (which used to be RFC 1587) adds not-so-stubby areas (NSSAs) to OSPF. RFC 2740 modifies OSPF to support the exchange of routing information for IPv6. OSPF for IPv6 has a new version number: version 3.

OSPF is classified as an IGP, which are used within autonomous systems. It was designed to overcome some of the limitations introduced by RIP, such as the small diameter, long convergence time, and a metric that does not reflect the characteristics of the network. In addition, OSPF handles a much larger routing table to accommodate large number of routes.

Differences between OSPF for IPv4 and OSPF for IPv6

Most of the concepts of OSPF for IPv4 have been retained; following is a brief overview of the changes:

Protocol processing per-link, not per-subnet
> IPv6 connects interfaces to links. Multiple IP subnets can be assigned to a single link, and two nodes can talk directly over a single link even if they do not share a common IP subnet. OSPF for IPv6 runs per-link instead of per-subnet. The terms "network" and "subnet" used in OSPF for IPv4 should be replaced with the term "link," i.e., an OSPF interface now connects to a link instead of an IP subnet.

Removal of addressing semantics
> IPv6 addresses are no longer present in OSPF packet headers. They are only allowed as payload information.
>
> Router-LSA and Network-LSA (yes, they still exist) do not contain IPv6 addresses. OSPF Router ID, Area ID, and Link State ID remain at 32 bits, so they cannot take the value of an IPv6 address. Designated Routers (DRs) and Backup Designated Routers (BDRs) are now always identified by their Router ID and not their IP address.

Flooding scope
> Each LSA type contains an explicit code to specify its flooding scope. This code is embedded in the LS type field. Three flooding scopes have been introduced: link-local, area, and AS.

Explicit support for multiple instances per link
> Multiple OSPF protocol instances can now run over a single link. This allows for separate ASes, each running OSPF, to use a common link. Another use of this feature is to have a single link belong to multiple areas.

Use of link-local addresses
> OSPF assumes that each interface has been assigned a link-local unicast address. All OSPF packets use the link-local address as the Source address. The routers learn the link-local addresses of all their neighbors and use these addresses as the next hop address. Packets sent on virtual links, however, must use either the global or local IP address as the source for OSPF packets.

RFC 2740 still uses the term "site-local address" instead of "local address." Site-local addresses have been deprecated in the meantime. For more information, refer to the sections in Chapter 3 about IPv6 addressing.

Authentication

Because OSPF for IPv6 runs over IPv6, it relies on the IP Authentication Header and the IP Encapsulating Security Payload to insure integrity and authentication of routing exchanges. The authentication of OSPF for IPv4 has been removed. One integrity check remains, which comes in the form of the checksum that is calculated over the entire OSPF packet.

OSPF packet format changes

See the section "Message Format of OSPF for IPv6."

LSA format changes

Type 3 (Summary Link) has been renamed Inter-Area-Prefix-LSA.

Type 4 (AS Summary Link) has been renamed Inter-Area-Router-LSA.

Two new LSAs carry IPv6 prefix information in their payload. Link-LSA (Type 8) carries the IPv6 address information of the local links, and Intra-Area-Prefix-LSA (Type 9) carries the IPv6 prefixes of the router and network links.

For other changes, such as Link State ID and the Options field, see the section "The Link State Database."

Handling unknown LSA types

Instead of simply discarding them, OSPF for IPv6 introduces a more flexible way of handling unknown LSA types. A new LSA handling bit has been added to the LS Type field to allow flooding of unknown LSA types.

Stub area support

The concept of stub areas has been retained in OSPF for IPv6. An additional rule specifies the flooding of unknown LSAs within the stub area.

Link state–based protocol

Each router maintains a database describing the link states within the autonomous system. This database is being built by exchanging Link State Advertisements (LSAs) between neighboring routers. Depending on its contents, an LSA is flooded to all routers in the autonomous system (AS flooding scope), all routers within the same area (area flooding scope), or simply to its neighbors. The flooding always occurs along a path of neighboring routers, so a stable neighbor relationship is extremely important for OSPF to work properly. The neighbor relationship is called *adjacency*. The exact process of forming an adjacency is described later in the section "Forming Adjacencies."

Each router originates router LSAs advertising the local state of its interfaces to all routers within the same area. Additional LSAs are originated to identify links with multiple routers (multi-access networks), IPv6 routes from other areas, or IPv6 routes external to the OSPF autonomous system. All LSA types and the flooding mechanism are described in the sections "The Link State Database" and "LSA Flooding," respectively. Each router puts the received LSA into its LSA database, called the Link-State Database (LSDB).

Using the LSDB as the input, each router runs the same algorithm to build a tree of least-cost paths (shortest-path-first tree [SPF tree]) to each route. The LSDB is like having a map of the network used to plot the shortest paths to each destination. The cost is described by a single dimensionless metric, which is configurable on each interface of the router. The metric assigned to the interface is usually inversely proportional to its line speed, i.e., higher bandwidth means lower cost. A common formula was to divide 10^8 by the line speed in bits per second. This formula is outdated, as interface speed today is in the range of 10^9 (e.g., Gigabit Ethernet) or even 10^{10}. Most vendors today apply a nonlinear formula. You can always choose and implement your own cost metrics according to corporate standards.

OSPF can put multiple equal-cost paths to the same route into the routing table. The algorithm for distributing traffic among these paths is at the discretion of the routing process itself, normally based on the source and destination IPv6 addresses. I discuss the process of building the SPF and its routing table in detail later in this chapter, in the section "The Link State Database."

OSPF areas and external routes

The LSDB can become quite large, and processing such a large database can be CPU- and memory-intensive because changes to the database affect every router in the AS. OSPF allows the AS to be partitioned into areas to reduce processing overhead. In addition, OSPF can import routes derived from external sources (e.g., RIP, BGP, and static routes) into OSPF.

OSPF Areas and External Routes

Within an autonomous system, routers can be grouped together to form areas. Each area is assigned a unique *Area ID*, a 32-bit integer typically noted as a dotted decimal number. It has no addressing significance other than uniquely identifying the area. An LSA with area flooding scope will never be flooded outside the area. Together, they form the area data structure, also known as the area LSDB. The Router-LSA and Network-LSA belong to this category. Routers and networks from one area are hidden in other areas. It is similar to splitting the map of the network into multiple maps, each of which represents the topology of one area. Each router within one area calculates the SPF tree to all routes within the same area. These routes are called intra-area routes. Routers with all interfaces belonging to a single area are called internal routers. To find paths to routes outside the area, "exit points" are provided in the form of area border routers (ABR). To provide connectivity between all areas, each area must always be directly attached to a single common area called the backbone area. This is achieved by the ABR having at least one interface in the backbone area and one interface in the local area. The ABR advertises all routes of the local area to the backbone area. In return, it advertises all the routes of the backbone area to the local area. This ensures that all routes are distributed within the AS. The backbone area collects and redistributes all routes from and to all areas.

Routing within the AS takes place at two levels. If the Source and Destination IP address of a packet belong to the same area, the packet is forwarded solely on information obtained from the area LSDB. This is called intra-area routing. If the Destination address is outside the area, the packet will have to be forwarded along the path to the ABR of the local area. The ABR knows all destinations and forwards the packet either across the backbone to the ABR of the destination area or to the backbone area. This is called inter-area routing.

The advantage of having areas is the reduction of processing overhead. Because the topology of each area is smaller than the entire AS, the calculation of the SPF tree takes less time. In addition, changes in the topology stay local, and only the routers in the local area need to recalculate the SPF tree. Routers in other areas are less affected because their area topology is not changed. Internal routers profit the most from splitting the AS into areas because their LSDB is much smaller.

The backbone area

The backbone area is a special area with an assigned Area ID of 0. The backbone area contains all ABRs of the autonomous system. If the AS is not split into areas, the backbone area is usually the one configured area. If the AS is split into areas, the backbone area is the collection of all routes from all nonbackbone areas. The backbone area must be contiguous: each router within the same area has at least one direct link to another router in the same area, and that link belongs to the area. However, with the introduction of virtual links, a backbone area doesn't have to be physically contiguous. A transit area can be used to create a tunnel (a virtual link) belonging to the backbone area. This will be further discussed later in the section "OSPF Areas and External Routes."

Nonbackbone areas

Nonbackbone areas are assigned unique Area IDs other than 0. They must be physically contiguous. Each nonbackbone area must have an ABR connected to the backbone using either a physical link or a virtual link. An ABR advertises all routes of the nonbackbone into the backbone area. In reverse, an ABR advertises all the routes known to the backbone area into the nonbackbone area. Normally, the ABR uses one LSA (called the Inter-Area-Prefix-LSA) for each route advertised. The ABR can be configured to summarize routes using a shorter IPv6 prefix representing some or all of the routes to be advertised. This reduces the number of advertisements, as well as memory and processing requirements. If you want to compress the number of routes in this way, it is very important to carefully plan the assignment of IPv6 prefixes within the area.

A nonbackbone area can have multiple ABRs. Figure 8-9 explains ABRs advertising Inter-Area-Prefix-LSAs.

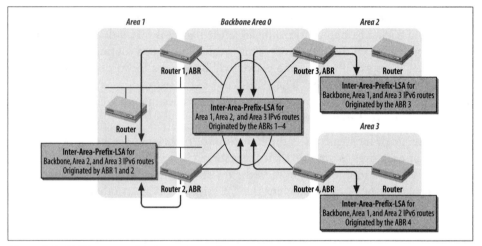

Figure 8-9. OSPF areas and their routing updates

Virtual links

A *virtual link* is a logical link that tunnels backbone traffic through a nonbackbone area. It can be configured between two ABRs by using a common nonbackbone area called a transit area. A virtual link belongs to the backbone and can cross only a single transit area. The transit area must not be a stub area (more on stub area in the subsection below). A remote area without a physical interface to the backbone area can be connected to the backbone by using virtual links. Virtual links can also be used to create redundant connections to the backbone. OSPF considers a virtual link a point-to-point link. The shortest path between the ABRs through the transit area determines the actual endpoint addresses of the tunnel. These addresses must be global or local unicast IPv6 addresses. Figure 8-10 shows an example of virtual links.

External routes

A router can learn about IPv6 routes from different sources, such as RIP, static entries, BGP, IS-IS, etc. Every route from a non-OSPF source is considered to be an OSPF external route and can be imported into OSPF. To import external routes into OSPF, a router must have at least one interface configured with OSPF and know about at least one non-OSPF network. This router is called an *autonomous system*

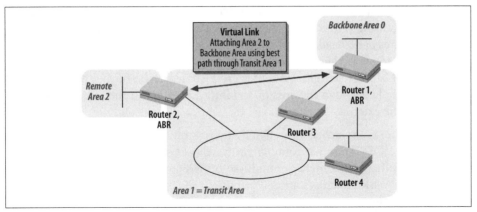

Figure 8-10. Virtual link connecting a remote area

border router (ASBR). External routes are imported using a single AS-External-LSA for each external route. Depending on the implementation, an ASBR can summarize a range of external routes to a single external LSA. Figure 8-11 explains how external routes are imported into OSPF.

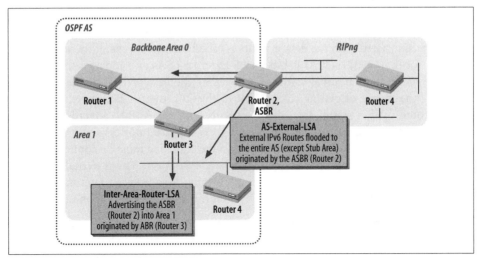

Figure 8-11. External routes imported into OSPF

AS-External-LSAs must be flooded throughout the autonomous system. Any router within the AS forwards packets to external networks to the ASBR or to an optional forwarding address specified by the ASBR. Therefore, there must be an entry to the ASBR in the Area-LSDB, or the forwarding address must be in the local routing table. If the ASBR is not within the local area, the ABR is responsible for advertising the existence of the ASBR to the local area. This is done using an Inter-Area-Router-LSA. Figure 8-11 shows the usage of the Inter-Area-Router-LSA.

Metrics of external routes are not compatible with OSPF metrics. ASBRs advertise external routes using one of two types of metrics: external-1 and external-2 routes. External-1 routes are considered to be close to the ASBR. Routers within the AS add the OSPF cost to reach the ASBR or the advertised forwarding address to the metric of the external-1 route. External-2 routes are assumed to be further away from the ASBR. A metric larger than the cost of any intra-AS path will therefore be added to the metric of the external-2 route.

If the same route is advertised as an OSPF internal route as well as an external route, the path to the OSPF internal route is always chosen over the path to the external route. This can happen if there are multiple ASBRs connected to the same external network. One ASBR advertises an OSPF route to the external routing protocol, and the other ASBR imports the same route back to OSPF.

Stub areas

In short, a *stub area* is a zone free of AS-External-LSAs. These LSAs would normally be flooded throughout the entire AS, which could result in quite a large LSDB consisting of many external advertisements. To reduce the size of the LSDB, an ABR can block AS-External-LSAs into the local area. As the ABR deprives the area of knowledge about external routes, it must make up for it by advertising a replacement route in the form of the default route. It uses the Inter-Area-Prefix-LSA to advertise the default route. The metric associated with the default route is called the *stub metric*. If there are multiple ABRs for that area, each ABR blocks AS-External-LSAs and replaces them with a default route. Routers internal to the area calculate the best path of the default route by adding the metric of getting to the ABR to the stub metric. Because there are no external routes within a stub area, there is no need for the ABR to advertise the presence of the ASBR into a stub area. The ABR therefore does not originate Inter-Area-Router-LSAs into a stub area. All routers within the stub area must be configured to be in a stub area by turning off the external-capability option. This external-capability option is crucial to forming adjacencies (see "Forming Adjacencies," later in this chapter), as all routers within an area have to agree on the same external-capability option.

There are some restrictions for stub areas. They cannot be configured as transit areas for virtual links. In addition, no ASBR can be placed in a stub area because the routers in a stub area cannot import external information. The backbone area can never be a stub area. To prevent unknown LSA types from being flooded into a stub area, certain measures must be taken. An unknown LSA can be flooded only if the LSA has link-local or area flooding scope and the handling bit (called the U bit) for flooding unknown LSAs is set to 0. Refer to "LSA Flooding," later in this chapter, for details.

As the ABR advertises a default route into the stub area, it could optionally stop originating routes to other areas as well. This can be useful if it is not crucial for the internal routers of a stub area to know the details of all routes to other areas. As long as they have the default route, they are happy. Such an area is sometimes called a *totally stubby area*. Figure 8-12 gives an example of stub areas.

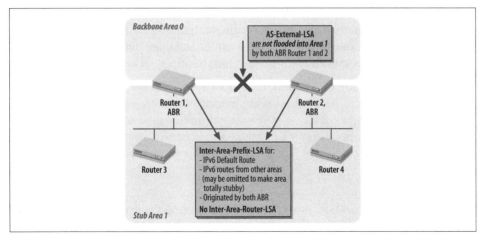

Figure 8-12. Stub area

Not-so-stubby areas

There are cases when stub areas need to connect to routers that have non-OSPF routes. The implementer does not want to revert the area to a normal area to allow these external routes to be imported. Because no AS-External-LSAs are allowed in a stub area, the OSPF designers came up with a new type of LSA called Type-7-LSA. Type-7-LSAs are exactly like AS-External-LSAs, but they can exist in a stub area. Stub areas in which Type-7-LSAs exist are humorously referred to as *Not-So-Stubby Areas*, or NSSAs. Type-7-LSAs are flooded only within the NSSA. An NSSA ASBR issues one Type-7-LSA per external route. ABRs of the NSSA can translate Type-7-LSAs into AS-External-LSAs to advertise them to the rest of the AS. In addition, these ABRs still behave like ABRs in a stub area, and they advertise a default route by using a Type-7-LSA in this case. All routers within the NSSA must be configured to be in an NSSA by turning on the NSSA capability option. This option must be set on all routers to form adjacencies (see "Forming Adjacencies"). In addition, the external-capability option still must be turned off on all routers within the NSSA. The NSSA has the same restrictions as the stub area. In addition, it cannot be a totally stubby area.

Message Format of OSPF for IPv6

Let's now have a closer look at the protocol implementation starting with the actual OSPF packet encapsulation. The routers use OSPF packets to exchange LSA information and to establish and maintain neighbor relations (adjacencies).

Encapsulation in IP datagrams

OSPF packets are directly encapsulated in IPv6, specified by protocol number 89 in the Next Header field of the IPv6 header. This means that OSPF does not run over TCP or UDP.

OSPF doesn't use fragmentation, therefore relying entirely on IP fragmentation when sending packets larger than the MTU. Fragmentation should be avoided whenever possible. Potentially large OSPF packets such as Database Description packets or Link State Update packets can easily be split into multiple packets by OSPF itself.

OSPF messages normally use the link-local IPv6 address of the outgoing interface as their Source addresses. The exceptions are messages sent on a virtual link. They use the local or global unicast address of the virtual link as their source. Depending on the situation, OSPF messages can be sent as a unicast to a specific neighbor or as a multicast to multiple neighbors. The following two multicast addresses are set aside for this purpose:

AllSPFRouters (FF02::5)
> All routers running OSPF must listen to this multicast address. Hello packets are always sent to this address, with the exception of non-broadcast-capable networks. This address is also used for some packets during LSA flooding.

AllDRouters (FF02::6)
> Both the DR and the BDR (see the section "Forming Adjacencies") on a multi-access medium must listen to this multicast address. This address is used for some packets during LSA flooding.

OSPF packets sent to the multicast address have link-local scope, and their IPv6 hop limit is set to 1. They will never be sent over multiple hops.

OSPF header

There are five different packet types used by OSPF. All OSPF packets begin with a standard 16-byte header, shown in Figure 8-13.

 OSPF uses the word "type" in many instances. Carefully distinguish between OSPF packet type, LSA types, and Link type. This book uses the name of a particular type rather than the type number.

The fields of the OSPF header are explained in detail in the following list:

Version (1 byte)
> OSPF for IPv6 uses version number 3.

Type (1 byte)
> Defines the type of OSPF messages. Table 8-3 lists all possible types.

Table 8-3. OSPF for IPv6 packet types

Packet type	Name	Description
1	Hello	Initializes and maintains adjacencies. Also used to elect DR and BDR. See the section "Forming Adjacencies."
2	Database Description	Exchanges database description during the formation of adjacencies. See the section "Forming Adjacencies."

Table 8-3. OSPF for IPv6 packet types (continued)

Packet type	Name	Description
3	Link State Request	Requests missing or changed LSAs. See the section "Forming Adjacencies."
4	Link State Update	Transmits LSAs either responding to requests when forming adjacencies or during LSA flooding. See the sections "Forming Adjacencies" and "LSA Flooding."
5	Link State Acknowledgment	Acknowledges the reception of an LSA. Every LSA must be acknowledged. See the sections "Forming Adjacencies" and "LSA Flooding."

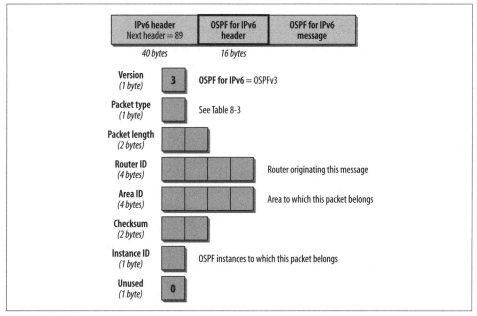

Figure 8-13. The OSPF for IPv6 packet header

Packet length (2 bytes)

This is the length of the OSPF protocol packet in bytes, including the OSPF header.

Router ID (4 bytes)

The Router ID of the router originating this packet. Each router must have a unique Router ID, a 32-bit number normally represented in dotted decimal notation. The Router ID must be unique within the entire AS.

Area ID (4 bytes)

The Area ID identifies the area to which this OSPF packet belongs. The area is normally based on the area of the outgoing interface of the router. The Area ID is a 32-bit integer. Area 0 represents the backbone area.

Checksum (2 bytes)

OSPF uses the standard checksum calculation for IPv6 applications. The checksum is computed using the 16-bit one's complement of the one's complement sum over the entire packet. If the packet's length is not an integral number of 16-bit words, the packet is padded with zeros before checksumming. Before computing the checksum, the checksum field in the OSPF packet header is set to 0.

Instance ID (1 byte)

Identifies the OSPF instance to which this packet belongs. The Instance ID is an 8-bit number assigned to each interface of the router. The default value is 0. The Instance ID enables multiple OSPF protocol instances to run on a single link. If the receiving router does not recognize the Instance ID, it discards the packet. For example, routers A, B, C, and D are connected to a common link n. A and B belong to an AS different from the one to which C and D belong. To exchange OSPF packets, A and B will use a different Instance ID from C and D. This prevents routers from accepting incorrect OSPF packets. In OSPF for IPv4, this was done using the Authentication field, which no longer exists in OSPF for IPv6.

Processing OSPF packets

When a router sends an OSPF protocol packet, it fills in the header fields as described earlier. The Area ID and Instance ID are taken from the data structure of the outgoing interface. If authentication is required, it is the responsibility of IPv6 to add the necessary headers.

When a router receives an OSPF protocol packet, IPv6 validates it first by checking the IPv6 headers (IPv6 addresses, Next Header field, and authentication). The packet is then given to the OSPF process. OSPF checks the version number (which must be 3), the checksum, the Area ID, and the Instance ID. The Area ID must match the Area ID configured on the incoming interface. If there is no match, but the Area ID is 0, the incoming interface must be the endpoint of a virtual link. The Instance ID must match the interface's Instance ID. If the packet's destination IPv6 address is the AllDRouters multicast address, the router must be either a DR or a BDR on this link. (DR and BDR will be explained in the next section.) If the packet passes all of these tests, it is passed to the appropriate OSPF process for further processing. Otherwise, it must be dropped.

Forming Adjacencies

In order to exchange LSAs, the routers must create reliable channels, called adjacencies, to its neighbors. These channels allow the routers to synchronize the LSDB upon initialization and to flood the LSA in case of a change.

The neighbors need to be discovered first. This is done using the Hello protocol. Each interface on an OSPF router is assigned one of four link types: point-to-point, transit, stub, or virtual. On point-to-point or virtual links, only one neighbor can be discovered. Transit links correspond to multi-access networks (e.g., Ethernet); multiple routers can be connected to this network, and therefore more than one neighbor could be discovered. Forming adjacencies with all routers on transit links is not necessary. Each transit link elects a DR to form adjacencies with all routers on the transit link. This guarantees that all routers on this link have a synchronized LSDB. To ensure uninterrupted operation, a BDR is elected as well; it forms adjacencies with all routers on the transit link, too. Figure 8-14 shows adjacencies on point-to-point links and transit links. If no neighbor is discovered on any given link, the link is declared to be a stub link, and obviously no adjacencies are being formed on such a link.

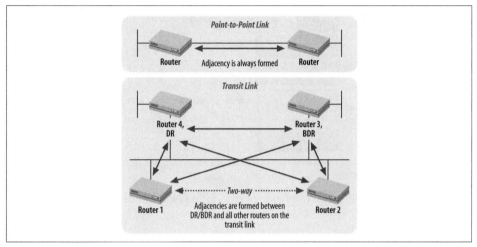

Figure 8-14. Adjacencies on point-to-point and transit links

The Hello packet

The Hello Protocol is responsible for initializing and maintaining adjacencies as well as electing a DR/BDR. It ensures that communication between two routers is bidirectional. Hello packets are sent out through each interface at regular intervals. On point-to-point or broadcast-capable transit networks, OSPF Hello packets are sent to the multicast address AllSPFRouters. The neighbors are discovered dynamically. Multi-access networks not capable of transmitting broadcast or multicast packets (e.g., X.25 and some Frame Relay implementations) are called *non-broadcast-multi-access networks* (NBMA). NBMA networks can be configured as either point-to-multipoint links or transit links. Point-to-multipoint links are actually point-to-point links as separate logical links are created to each neighbor. As in point-to-point links, no DR or BDR is needed. NBMA networks configured as transit links have static IPv6 address entries for each neighbor. A DR and BDR is elected. OSPF messages are sent as unicast to these statically configured neighbors.

Figure 8-15 shows the Hello packet format. It is an OSPF packet type 1, as explained earlier in Table 8-3.

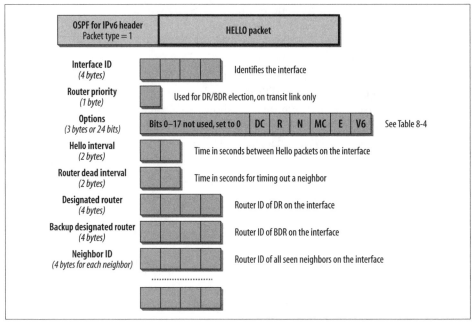

Figure 8-15. The Hello packet

The following list explains all the fields of the Hello packet in detail:

Interface ID (4 bytes)
Identifies the interface of the Hello packet. Each interface of an OSPF router is assigned an Interface ID. The Interface ID must be unique within the same router. Some implementations use the MIB-II Interface Index as specified in RFC 2863.

Within the field explanations, the terms "interface" and "router" always refer to the originating router and its interface over which the packet was sent.

Router priority (1 byte)
Identifies the router priority number assigned to the interface. It is used for the election of the DR or BDR. This field is meaningful only on transit links. The router with the highest priority becomes the DR or BDR, but only if a DR or BDR has not already been elected. If this field is set to 0, the router of the interface can never be a DR or BDR.

Options (3 bytes)
Describes the optional capabilities of the router. This field is set in OSPF Hello packets, Database Description packets, and the following LSAs: Router-LSA, Network-LSA, Inter-Area-Router-LSA, and Link-LSA. Table 8-4 explains the bits used in the Options field. Only 6 bits are currently used.

Table 8-4. The Options field

Bit	Name	Description
0–17	Not used	Reserved for future use.
18	DC	Handling of Demand Circuits, as described in RFC 1793.
19	R	Indicates that the originator of the Hello packet is an active router. If this bit is set to 0, the originator will not forward packets: for example, a multihomed host that wants to build an OSPF routing table without actually routing packets.
20	N	All routers within an NSSA must set this bit. In addition, the E bit must be set to 0 (see RFC 3101).
21	MC	Multicast capability, as defined in RFC 1584.
22	E	External-routes capability of the router. All members of an area must agree on the external capability. In a stub area, all routers must set this bit to 0 to achieve adjacency. The E bit is meaningful only in Hello packets (similar to the N bit).
23	V6	Indicates that the router supports OSPF for IPv6. If set to 0, this router/link should be excluded from IPv6 routing calculation.

Hello interval (2 bytes)

Specifies the number of seconds between Hello packets sent by the router on the link. The default is 10 seconds.

Router Dead Interval (2 bytes)

Specifies the number of seconds before the router declares a silent router on the link to be down. (A silent router is no longer sending Hello packets.) The default is 40 seconds. On a transit link, the Router Dead Interval also determines the waiting timer during the election of the DR or BDR. Upon initialization of a transit link, the interface enters a waiting state to determine whether a DR or BDR has already been elected.

Designated Router ID (4 bytes)

Specifies the Router ID of the DR from the router's perspective on the link. This field is useful only on transit links. It is set to 0.0.0.0 when no DR has yet been elected, or on point-to-point links.

Backup Designated Router ID (4 bytes)

Specifies the Router ID of the BDR from the router's perspective on the link. This field is useful only on transit links. It is set to 0.0.0.0 when no BDR has yet been elected, or on point-to-point links.

Neighbor ID (4 bytes)

Specifies the Router ID of each router from which the router has received valid Hello packets on the link during the last Router Dead Interval.

Interface status and election of DR/BDR

As soon as IPv6 on an OSPF interface is operational (link up) the processing of Hello packets begins. A point-to-point link changes its state to point-to-point and is immediately active.

A transit link first enters the waiting state to discover the DR/BDR. Each transit link needs a DR and a BDR, which form adjacencies with all routers on that particular transit link. For each transit link the router does the following: during the waiting period, the router listens to Hello packets to determine whether a DR/BDR already exits. It also sends Hello packets with the DR/BDR field set to 0 to indicate that it is in discovery mode. If a router already claims to be the DR, no election of a DR takes place. If no router declares itself as the DR (all Hello packets contain a zero in their DR field), the router with the highest router priority declares itself the DR. If the priorities are equal, the router with the highest Router ID wins the election. The BDR is elected in exactly the same way. Routers that were not elected as DR/BDR are called DR-Other. The interface status changes to either DR, BDR, or DR-Other and becomes active. Routers with a priority of zero never become DR/BDR. Their interface status changes immediately to DR-Other without entering the waiting state.

If the DR goes silent (not sending Hellos for Router Dead Interval), the BDR becomes the DR, and a new BDR is elected. Because the BDR has already formed all adjacencies, there is no disruption of the synchronized LSDB on that transit link. If the original DR comes back online, it recognizes that there is already a DR and a BDR, and it enters the DR-Other state. If the BDR goes silent, a new BDR is elected.

Processing of Hello packets

Before a Hello packet is accepted, a number of criteria must be met. Figure 8-16 shows the decision process to accept a Hello packet.

The OSPF input process has already accepted the packet as described in the section "Message Format of OSPF for IPv6." Now the Hello Interval and Router Dead Interval are checked. They must match the values set on the receiving interface. Next, the E and N bits in the Options field are examined. The settings of these bits must match the value set on the receiving interface.

At this point, if all the criteria matched, the packet is accepted and the neighbor is identified by its Router ID. The router keeps a neighbor state table for each interface. If there is already a full adjacency with this neighbor, the Hello timer is simply reset. Otherwise, the state of this neighbor changes to initialize (Init). The router examines the list of neighbors proclaimed in the received Hello packet. If the router identifies its own Router ID in that list, bidirectional communication has been established, and the neighbor's state changes to two-way. The router decides whether to form an adjacency with this neighbor. If the interface is a point-to-point state, an adjacency is formed with this neighbor. On a transit link, if the router itself or this neighbor is the DR/BDR, an adjacency is formed. If the router decides not to form an adjacency, this neighbor stays in a two-way state.

Figure 8-17 explains the different phases of forming an adjacency and the corresponding neighbor states.

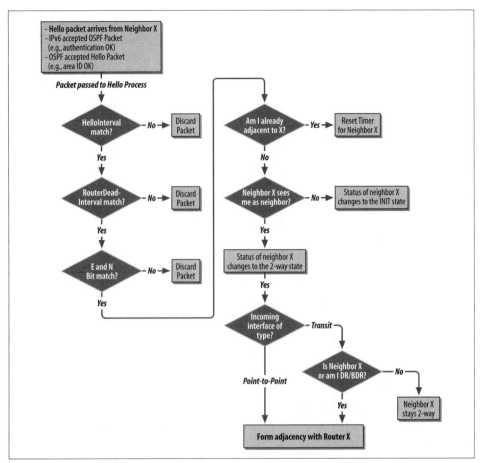

Figure 8-16. Processing a Hello packet

The two routers forming an adjacency start communicating the contents of their LSDB. This phase is called the database description exchange. Once the routers know the contents of each other's databases, they request the missing or outdated information. This is the loading phase. After completing the loading phase, the routers are fully adjacent. Continuous sending of Hello packets prevents the adjacency from timing out.

Database description exchange

The routers change their neighbor state to exchange-start and send an initial Database Description packet without data. They establish a master-slave relationship to achieve an orderly exchange. Each router declares itself as the master in the initial Database Description packet. The only relevant information within the initial Database Description packet is the database description (DD) sequence number issued by each side. The router with the higher Router ID stays master during the entire DD exchange phase.

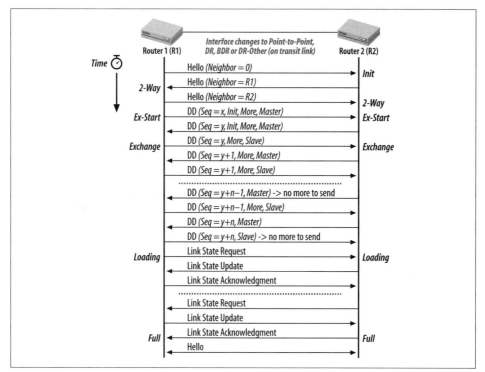

Figure 8-17. Forming an adjacency

The neighbors now enter the Exchange state. Starting with the slave, a series of packets describing the contents of their LSDB are exchanged. The master always increments the sequence number and the slave always uses the master's sequence number in its packet. Each router indicates that it has more data to send by setting the more bit (see Figure 8-17). If one router has sent its entire database description but the other hasn't yet, the first router is obliged to send empty packets to keep the sequence numbers matched. To describe the LSDB, the router only sends the database headers (LSA headers) as described in Figure 8-18. The LSA header is discussed later in "The Link State Database." All Database Description packets are sent to the neighbor as unicast. The unicast addresses are discovered by looking at the source IPv6 address of the Hello packet sent by the neighbor. As soon as both routers have nothing more to send, the routers enter the loading phase.

The following list explains all the fields of the Database Description packet in detail.

Options (3 bytes)
> The optional capabilities supported by the router according to Table 8-4. They should be the same options advertised in the Hello packet. Changes in the Options field during DD exchange will stop the exchange, and the routers revert back to exchange-start.

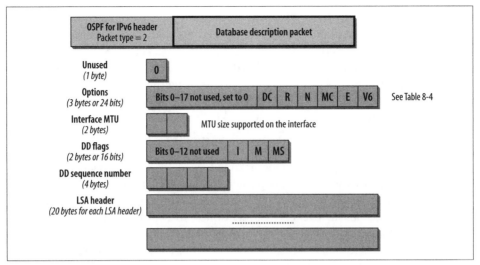

Figure 8-18. Database Description packet

Interface MTU (2 bytes)
   The largest frame size that can be sent through the interface without fragmentation. If the router receives a DD packet stating an MTU larger than it can handle
   on the receiving interface, the packet is rejected. On virtual links, this should be
   set to 0.

Init bit (I bit)
   When set to 1, this bit indicates the first Database Description packet sent by the
   router. This packet contains no data and starts the exchange process. The M/S
   bit is set as well.

More bit (M bit)
   When set to 1, this bit indicates that there are more Database Description packets to follow. When set to 0, it indicates that all database descriptions have been
   delivered.

Master/slave bit (M/S bit)
   When set to 1, this bit indicates the router to be the master; otherwise, it's the
   slave.

DD sequence number (4 bytes)
   This number makes the exchange reliable. The master increments the sequence
   number by one for each Database Description packet sent. The slave always
   quotes the last sequence number received by the master. A mismatch in
   sequence number causes the DD exchange to fail and the routers to revert back
   to exchange-start.

List of LSA headers (20 bytes for each header)
   This list describes the entry in the LSDB. See "The Link State Database."

The loading phase

The routers are now requesting the missing or outdated LSAs learned during the exchange of database descriptions. Link State Request packets (OSPF packet type 3) identify the requesting LSA by its LSA header. Multiple requests can be sent using a single packet. A router replies to the request by sending the corresponding LSA from its database. The LSA is sent using Link State Update packets (OSPF packet type 4). Multiple LSAs can be sent in a single packet. Each Link State Update must be acknowledged by using a Link State Acknowledgment packet (OSPF packet type 5). The Link State Acknowledgment packet contains the LSA header of the LSA to be acknowledged. Multiple LSAs can be acknowledged in a single packet. The Link State Request and Acknowledgment packets simply contain a list of requested or acknowledged LSA headers, so I won't discuss them in more detail. Like Database Description packets, all the packets just mentioned are sent to the unicast address of the neighbor. The neighbors now enter the full state. Hello packets keep the adjacency alive. Adjacencies must stay alive, as they are used for flooding LSAs. Refer to "LSA Flooding," later in this chapter.

The Link State Database

The *link state database* (LSDB) is the most important component of OSPF. Figure 8-19 illustrates the components of the LSDB.

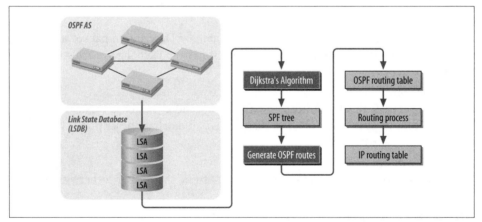

Figure 8-19. Components of the LSDB

The LSDB is a data structure consisting of LSAs exchanged in the AS. The link state information is structured to allow the building of a tree whose branches and leaves represent the shortest paths to all routes within the AS. Each router builds such a tree from its point of view. Most commonly, the routers use the algorithm developed by Dijkstra to build this tree of shortest paths (SPF tree). First, the router builds the intra-area tree to all destinations within its own area. Inter-area and external routes are then attached to the branch representing an ABR or ASBR. At the end, each route within the tree is added to one of four sections of the OSPF routing table: the intra-area routes, inter-area routes, external-1 routes, and finally, external-2 routes. The next hop is always the link-local address of first router in the shortest path to the route. The following sections describe each of these components, starting with the contents of the LSDB. Then I'll discuss how Dijkstra calculates the SPF tree and puts the routes into the routing table.

Contents of the LSDB

RFC 2328 describes the SPF as a system of directed graphs using vertices to build a tree. This basically describes the network topology as a set of pointers building a tree. There are three basic pointers within the tree:

Router-to-router
> Describes a router's point-to-point interface identifying the Router ID of the neighboring router on a point-to-point link. In LSDB terminology, it points from a Router-LSA to another Router-LSA.

Router to transit link
> Describes a router's interface to a transit link by identifying the Interface ID of the DR for this transit link. In LSDB terminology, it points from a Router-LSA to a Network-LSA.

Transit link to routers
> Describes a transit link and points to all its attached routers. In LSDB terminology, it points from a Network-LSA to one or many Router-LSAs.

There are also informational elements. They provide complementary information associated to particular branches. It is like adding leaves to branches. Unlike the three previous pointers, which build the actual tree, the informational element just adds information to the tree. LSAs representing an informational element are Inter-Area-Prefix-LSA, Inter-Area-Router-LSA, AS-External-LSA, Type-7-LSA, Link-LSA, and Intra-Area-Prefix-LSA.

Figure 8-20 shows the basic pointers and the informational element in a sample tree structure.

LSAs

Each LSA within the LSDB incorporates one or more of the previously mentioned pointers or informational elements. It consists of an LSA header and an LSA body. The LSA header identifies each LSA uniquely.

LSA header

Each LSA starts with a common 20-byte header. Figure 8-21 shows the details of this header. The Link State (LS) type, LS ID, and Advertising Router together uniquely identify the LSA.

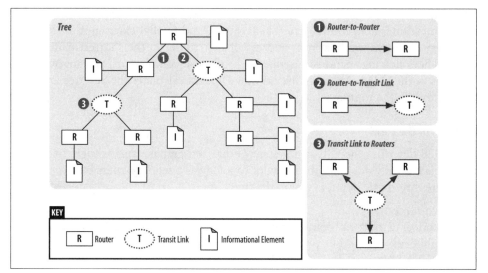

Figure 8-20. LSDB structural pointers

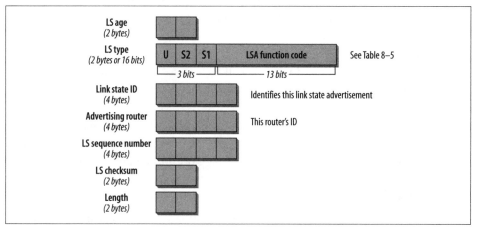

Figure 8-21. LSA header

The LSA header fields are fully detailed in the following list:

LS Age (2 bytes)

LS Age is the time in seconds since the LSA was originated. If it has reached *MaxAge* (3,600 seconds), the LSA is no longer considered for the SPF tree calculation. The originating router of this LSA must renew the LSA and increment the sequence number before MaxAge is reached, to prevent the LSA from aging out. It is recommended to renew an LSA after MaxAge/2.

LS type (2 bytes)

This is the type of this advertised LSA. The first three bits of the LSA type field indicate special properties of the LSA.

U bit (handling of unknown LS type)

Identifies the handling of unknown LSA types by the routers. If the bit is set, the LSA must be stored and flooded as if the type were understood. Otherwise, if the bit is 0, the LSA has to be treated as if it had link-local flooding scope.

S2 and S1 bit (flooding scope)

Define the flooding scope of the LSA. The four values are:

00 = Link-local, flooded only on the link on which it originated
01 = Area, flooded to all routers in the originating area
10 = AS, flooded to all routers in the AS
11 = Reserved

The last 13 bits represent the actual LSA Function Code. See Table 8-5 for details on link state types. The LS type is represented in hexadecimal notation to reflect the flooding scope.

Table 8-5. Link state (LS) types

LS type	Name	Flooding scope	Advertised by	Link State ID
0x2001	Router-LSA	Area	Each router	Router ID
0x2002	Network-LSA	Area	DR	DR's Interface ID of the transit link
0x2003	Inter-Area-Prefix-LSA	Area	ABR	A locally unique ID set by ABR
0x2004	Inter-Area-Router-LSA	Area	ABR	A locally unique ID set by ABR
0x4005	AS-External-LSA	AS	ASBR	A locally unique ID set by ASBR
0x2006	Group-Membership-LSA	Area	See RFC 1584	See RFC 1584
0x2007	Type-7-LSA	Area	See RFC 3101	See RFC 3101
0x0008	Link-LSA	Link	Each router for each link	Locally unique Interface ID
0x2009	Intra-Area-Prefix-LSA	Area	Each router	A locally unique ID set by router

Link State ID (4 bytes)

The Link State ID is part of the link state identification. With Router-LSA and Network-LSA, the Link State ID serves as a value for a pointer in the tree to identify this router or network. For all other LSAs, the originating router uses a locally unique ID.

Advertising Router (4 bytes)

The Advertising Router is the Router ID of the router originating this LSA.

LS Sequence Number (4 bytes)

The LS Sequence Number identifies the instance of this LSA. It is used to determine which LSA is newer in case of multiple occurrences of the same LSA. The higher the sequence number, the newer the LSA is. The starting sequence number is always 0x80000000. The highest sequence number possible is 0x7FFFFFFF. If this number has been reached, the LSA is aged out (LS Age equals MaxAge) and flooded before a new instance of the LSA (now using 0x80000000) is issued.

Checksum (2 bytes)
This is the Fletcher checksum of the complete contents of the LSA, including the LSA header but excluding the LS Age field.

Length (2 bytes)
This is the length of the entire LSA in bytes.

The following paragraphs explain all types of LSA in detail, with the exception of Group-Membership-LSAs and Type-7-LSAs. Group-Membership-LSAs are defined in RFC 1584, which has not yet been updated for IPv6. Type-7-LSAs are explained in RFC 3101, which introduces the concept of NSSA. Type-7-LSAs are very similar to As-External-LSAs.

Router-LSA (type 0x2001)

Router links describe the router's point-to-point, virtual, or transit links. Basically, it includes all links having at least one neighbor. Unlike OSPF for IPv4, stub links are no longer advertised within a router link. An ABR must originate separate router links for each attached area, containing only links belonging to that particular area. Virtual links always belong to area 0 and are advertised only by ABR. Figure 8-22 outlines a Router-LSA.

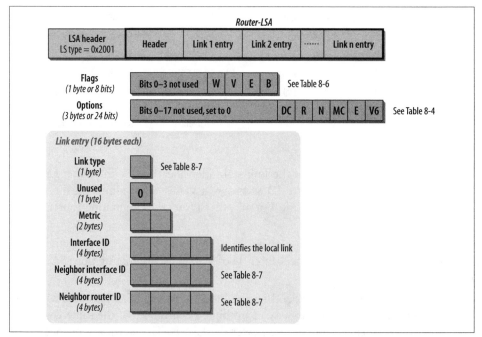

Figure 8-22. Router-LSA

The fields of the Router-LSA are fully detailed in the following list:

Flags (1 byte)

The Flags field indicates the special function of the router originating the LSA. Table 8-6 shows the possible values and their corresponding functions.

Table 8-6. Flags in Router-LSA

Bit	Name
W bit	The router is a wildcard multicast receiver. See RFC 1584 for more information.
V bit	The router is the endpoint of a virtual link using the area to which this packet belongs as a transit area.
E bit	The router is an ASBR.
B bit	The router is an ABR.

Options (3 bytes)

This field describes the optional capabilities supported by the router, as outlined in Table 8-4.

Link Entry (16 bytes per link)

Each link entry describes an interface of the router. A link entry has five relevant sub-fields. The link types are shown in Table 8-7 describing the possible link types of an interface. The Neighbor Interface ID and Router ID are learned through the Hello protocol. In addition, there is the actual Interface ID and the metric assigned to the interface. The Link Entries are used as pointers to build the intra-area tree. Interface types 1 and 4 point to the Router-LSA specified in the Neighbor Router ID (LS-ID and Advertised Router). Interface type 2 points to Network-LSA, as specified in the Neighbor Interface ID (LS-ID) and Neighbor Router ID (Advertised Router).

Table 8-7. Link type supported in a Router-LSA

Link type	Name	Neighbor Interface ID	Neighbor Router ID
1	Point-to-point	Interface ID of the neighbor on the other end of the point-to-point link	Router-ID of the neighbor on the other end of the point-to-point link
2	Transit	Interface ID of the DR on this link	Router ID of the DR on this link
3	Reserved	N/A	N/A
4	Virtual	Interface ID of the neighbor on the other end of the virtual link	Router ID of the neighbor on the other end of the virtual link

Network-LSA (type 0x2002)

The designated router of each transit link in the area originates a Network-LSA. The Link State ID is set to the Interface ID of the DR's interface to the transit link. Figure 8-23 outlines the Network-LSA. It simply contains the Options field (see Table 8-4 earlier in this chapter), followed by a list of Router IDs identifying all routers attached to this particular transit link. This represents a pointer to all routers attached to this transit link.

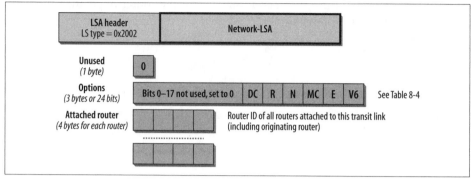

Figure 8-23. Network-LSA

The Options field in the Network LSA is set to the logical OR of the options received from each Link-LSA of all the routers attached to this transit link. This provides the common optional capabilities supported by all routers on this link.

Inter-Area-Prefix-LSA (type 0x2003)

Inter-Area-Prefix-LSAs are originated by the ABR to advertise IPv6 prefixes from other areas into the area of this LSA. A separate Inter-Area-Prefix-LSA is originated for each route. An ABR could summarize a contiguous range of IPv6 prefixes into a single advertisement. For a stub area, the ABR advertises the default route using this LSA. Inter-Area-Prefix-LSA is the equivalent to Summary-LSA in OSPFv2 and is outlined in Figure 8-24.

In the tree-building process, this LSA represents an informational element associated with the ABR for attaching inter-area routes to the SPF tree. The Inter-Area-Prefix-LSA fields are detailed in the following list:

Metric (20 bits)
> Defines the cost from the ABR to the IPv6 address prefix advertised with this Inter-Area-Prefix-LSA. If this route represents a summary, the metric should be taken from the highest metric of the member prefixes.

IPv6 Prefix Representation (0 to 20 bytes in multiples of 4)
> Defines the actual IPv6 prefix advertised. It consists of four fields: the Prefix Length, the Prefix Options, an unused field (set to 0), and the actual IPv6 Address Prefix. The Prefix Length defines the length of the address prefix. The default route is represented by a prefix length of 0. Table 8-8 explains the prefix options. The address prefix represents the IPv6 address. If necessary, it is padded with zero bits to the next full 32-bit word.

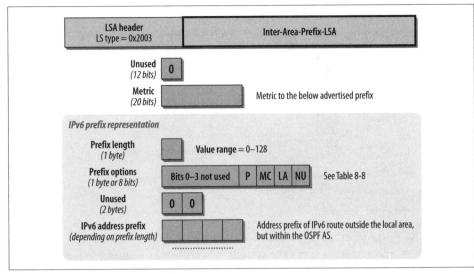

Figure 8-24. Inter-Area-Prefix-LSA

Table 8-8. Prefix options starting with the leftmost bit

Bit	Name	Description
0–3	Reserved	N/A
4	P bit	Propagate bit: if set, the NSSA ABR readvertises the prefix into the backbone. Used only in Type-7-LSA.
5	MC bit	Multicast bit: if set, the prefix should be included in IPv6 multicast routing calculations.
6	LA bit	Local address bit: if set, the prefix is actually a local IPv6 address of the originating router.
7	NU bit	No unicast bit: if set, the prefix should be excluded from IPv6 unicast calculation.

Inter-Area-Router-LSA (type 0x2004)

Inter-Area-Router-LSAs are originated by ABRs to advertise ASBRs from other areas into the area of this LSA. A separate Inter-Area-Router-LSA is originated for each ASBR. This is necessary to inform all routers in this area of the existence of an outside ASBR. Inter-Area-Router-LSA is the equivalent to AS-Summary-LSA in OSPFv2. As shown in Figure 8-25, the Inter-Area-Router-LSA contains the Options field (refer back to Table 8-4), the Metric field, and the Router ID of the ASBR. The Metric field represents the cost from the ABR to the ASBR.

In the tree-building process, this LSA represents an informational element associated with the ABR for attaching an ASBR to the SPF tree.

AS-External-LSA (type 0x4005)

AS-External-LSAs are advertised by ASBRs to import external IPv6 prefixes into the AS. Each AS-External-LSA represents one IPv6 prefix external to OSPF—i.e., learned

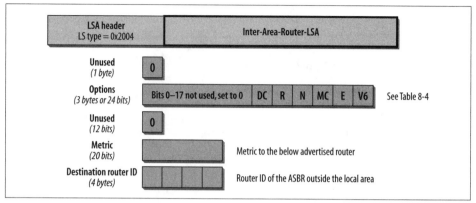

Figure 8-25. Inter-Area-Router-LSA

from RIP, BGP, static, etc. They are flooded throughout the entire AS and are therefore known to every router except the routers in a stub area. Figure 8-26 explains the AS-External-LSA.

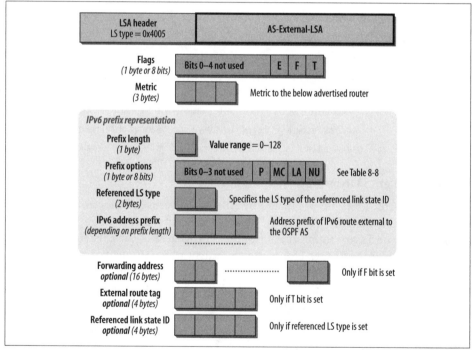

Figure 8-26. AS-External-LSA

In the tree-building process, this LSA represents an informational element associated with the ASBR for attaching external routes to the SPF tree. The AS-External-LSA fields are described in the following list:

E bit

If set, the specified metric is a Type 2 external metric as explained in "Overview of OSPF for IPv6." The metric is considered larger than any path to any route within the AS. If set to 0, the metric is a Type 1 external metric. It is expressed using the same units as the metric used in Router-LSA, Inter-Area-Prefix-LSA, and Intra-Area-Prefix-LSA.

F bit

If set, a forwarding address has been included in the LSA.

T bit

If set, an external router tag has been included in the LSA.

Metric (3 bytes)

Defines the cost from the ASBR to the external IPv6 prefix. The interpretation of the metric value depends on the E bit.

IPv6 Prefix Representation (0 to 20 bytes in multiples of 4)

Defines the actual IPv6 prefix advertised. It consists of four fields: the Prefix Length, the Prefix Options, the Referenced LS Type, and the actual IPv6 Address Prefix. The Prefix Length defines the length of the address prefix. The default route is represented by a 0 length prefix. Table 8-8 explains the prefix options. The Address Prefix represents the IPv6 address. If necessary, it is padded with zero bits to the next full 32-bit word.

Referenced LS Type (part of the IPv6 Prefix Representation)

If set to a value other than zero, an additional LSA is associated with this external route. This LSA is specified in the Referenced Link State ID field.

Forwarding address (4 bytes)

If the F bit is set, any router in the AS forwards data traffic (to the external IPv6 prefix specified with this LSA) to this forwarding address. If the F bit is not set, data traffic is forwarded to the ASBR originating this LSA. This field must never be set to the IPv6 unspecified address (0:0:0:0:0:0:0:0). If any router within the AS cannot reach the forwarding address or the ASBR, the IPv6 prefix of the external route is not added to the routing table.

External Route Tag (4 bytes)

If the T bit is set, this field contains additional information about the external route. This information, however, will never be used within the OSPF AS.

Referenced Link State ID (4 bytes)

If and only if the Referenced LS Type is set to a value other than zero, the Referenced LS Type, Referenced Link State ID (this field), and the advertising router of this LSA represent an existing LSA in the LSDB, providing additional information for this external IPv6 prefix. This information, however, is not used by the OSPF protocol itself. The precise nature of such information is not part of the OSPF specification.

Link-LSA (type 0x0008)

Link-LSAs are originated by each router, one for each link of the router. They are never flooded beyond this link. The Link State ID is set to the Interface ID of this link. The Link-LSA serves three purposes. It provides:

- The router's link-local address to all other routers attached to this link
- A list of IPv6 prefixes associated with this link
- A list of options to be used by the designated router for this link

Figure 8-27 outlines the Link-LSA

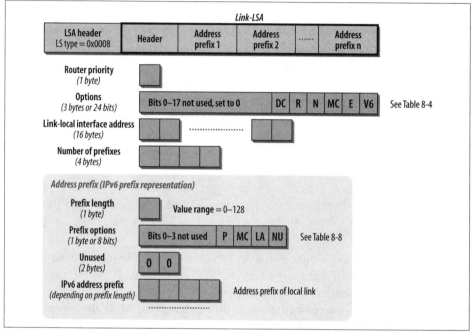

Figure 8-27. Link-LSA

In the tree-building process, this LSA represents an informational element associated with each link from or to a Router-LSA. It attaches the link-local address of the link to the SPF tree. The Link-LSA fields are described in the following list:

Router Priority (1 byte)
> The priority number given to the router on the interface.

Options (3 bytes)
> The router would like to use the options specified here (see Table 8-4). This is an indication (to the DR on this transit link) of which options it should use.

Link-local address (16 bytes)
> The link-local address of the interface.

Number of prefixes (4 bytes)

The number of prefixes to be advertised with this LSA.

IPv6 Prefix Representation (4 to 20 bytes in multiples of 4)

All IPv6 prefixes will be listed here according to the number of prefixes. It consists of four fields: the Prefix Length, the Prefix Options, an unused field (set to 0), and the actual IPv6 Address Prefix. The Prefix Length defines the length of the address prefix. Table 8-8 explains the prefix options. The Address Prefix represents the IPv6 address. If necessary, it is padded with zero bits to the next full 32-bit word.

Intra-Area-Prefix-LSA (type 0x2009)

A router uses the Intra-Area-Prefix-LSA to advertise one or more IPv6 prefixes associated with either the router or a Network-LSA. As OSPF for IPv6 has removed all addressing semantics from the Router-LSAs and Network-LSAs, the Intra-Area-Prefix-LSA provides this information. Each address prefix advertised is associated with a Router-LSA or a Network-LSA. Figure 8-28 shows the contents of an Intra-Area-Prefix-LSA. Particular attention should be paid to the Referenced LS Type, Link State ID, and Advertising Router fields, as explained next.

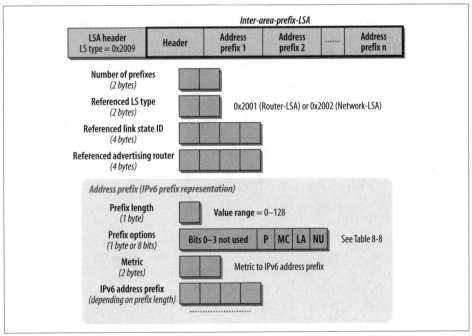

Figure 8-28. Intra-Area-Prefix-LSA

In the tree-building process, this LSA represents an informational element associated with a router, attaching IPv6 prefixes of its interfaces to the SPF tree. It can also be associated with a transit link, attaching its IPv6 prefixes to the SPF tree. The Intra-Area-Prefix-LSA fields are detailed in the following list:

Number of prefixes (2 bytes)
> The number of prefixes to be advertised with this LSA.

Referenced LS Type, Link State ID, Advertising Router (10 bytes)
> If the Referenced LS Type is set to 0x2001, the address prefixes are associated with this router. The Referenced Link State ID is set to 0, and the Referenced Advertising Router is set to the Router ID of the router originating this LSA. If the Referenced LS Type is set to 0x2002, the address prefixes are associated with the Network-LSA. The Referenced Link State ID is set to the Interface ID of the link's DR, and the Referenced Advertising Router is the Router ID of the DR.

IPv6 Prefix Representation (4 to 20 bytes in multiples of 4)
> All IPv6 Prefixes are listed here according to the length of prefixes. It consists of four fields: the Prefix Length, the Prefix Options, the Metric, and the actual IPv6 Address Prefix. The Prefix Length defines the length of the address prefix. Table 8-8 earlier in this chapter explained the prefix options. The Address Prefix represents the IPv6 address. If necessary, it is padded with zero bits to the next full 32-bit word. The Metric field defines the cost of this prefix.

Calculation of the OSPF Routing Table (Dijkstra Algorithm)

Using the LSDB as a base, each router builds an SPF tree and adds the routes to the routing table. Each router keeps multiple LSDBs. The Link LSDB contains all LSAs with link-local flooding scope, the Area LSDB contains all LSAs with area flooding scope, and finally, the AS LSDB contains all LSAs with AS flooding scope. The ABR has one Area LSDB for each locally attached area. The tree-building is based on Dijkstra's shortest path first (SPF) algorithm. It involves the three-step process described in the following subsections. The sample network depicted in Figure 8-29 illustrates the process. Steps 1 and 2 must be performed on the Area LSDB. The ABR has to perform them for each local area as it builds one SPF tree for each area.

Step 1: Intra-area routes

In Step 1, the router builds the core tree using the Router-LSA and Network-LSA for this area. Remember that these two LSAs contain actual pointers. Each router places its own Router-LSA at the root of the tree. Each link entry in the Router-LSA represents a pointer to another Router-LSA (link type 1 or 4) or to a Network-LSA (link type 2). The Neighbor ID and, on link type 2, the Interface ID identify the LSA at the end of the pointer. Each adjacent LSA (called a *candidate*) is placed temporarily in the tree as a branch, and their metric is noted on the branch. The least-cost branch is made permanent because it represents the shortest path. Its LSA is examined next. Based on the type of LSA, the following happens:

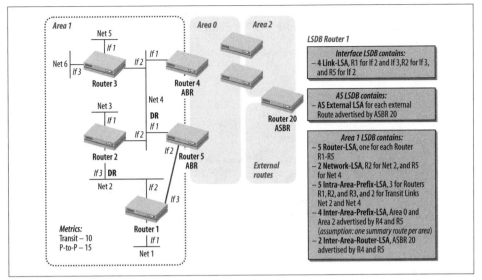

Figure 8-29. Sample network and its LSDB

Router-LSA

Each link entry of this router LSA provides a new set of LSAs as candidates. The candidates are added to the tree temporarily unless the candidate is already permanently in the tree and can therefore be ignored. The metrics are added to the branches.

Network-LSA

Each attached router provides a new set of LSAs as candidates. The candidates are added to the tree temporarily unless the candidate is already permanently in the tree and can therefore be ignored. The metrics are not added to the tree, because the metric to this transit link has already been determined and noted in the tree.

All paths to all candidates are being examined. The LSA with the smallest path cost (accumulated metric from the root) is made a permanent branch. If this particular LSA exists as a temporary branch anywhere else in the tree, the temporary branch(es) can be eliminated. In case of two or more branches having the same least costs, each branch is made permanent. The LSA of the newly made permanent branch is examined and these steps are repeated.

This process continues until there are no more Network-LSAs or Router-LSAs to be added. The SPF core tree is now built. The tree, however, contains no addressing information. This address information is provided by the Intra-Area-Prefix-LSA. The router simply adds the Intra-Area-Prefix-LSA to the Router-LSA or Network-LSA according to the referenced LSA. The last step is to find the next hop information. Next hop addresses are the link-local addresses of directly connected routers. This information is provided by the Link-LSA originated by the directly connected routers.

The router has now found all routes within the area and adds them to the OSPF routing table as Intra-area routes. Figure 8-30 explains the building of the SPF tree of area 1 for Router R1.

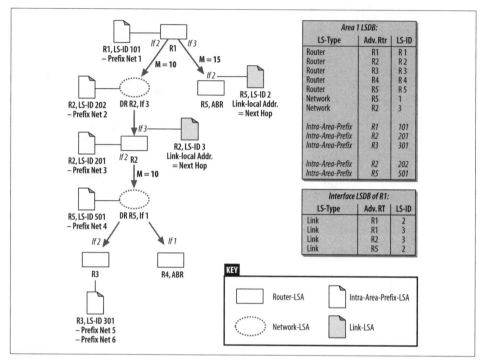

Figure 8-30. Intra-area tree for router R1 in area 1

Step 2: Inter-area routes

The router identifies all Inter-Area-Link-LSAs of the local area as they represent routes from areas other than the local area. In addition, all ABRs of the local area are identified based on the intra-area tree constructed in step one. The Inter-Area-Link LSAs are now associated with the corresponding ABRs and added to the tree with the advertised metric. This attaches IPv6 prefixes of routes to the tree. The total cost to these routes consists of the cost to the ABR added to the cost advertised in the Inter-Area-Link-LSA. If the same prefix appears more than once, the one with the best total path cost is considered. If the costs are equal, all equal-cost prefixes must be accepted into the inter-area routing table. The next hop is determined as the directly connected router on the shortest intra-area path to the ABR. Figure 8-31 illustrates this process for Router R1.

If the router itself is an ABR, only Inter-Area-Link-LSAs originated by other ABRs are considered. All Inter-Area-Link-LSAs that represent routes for directly attached areas

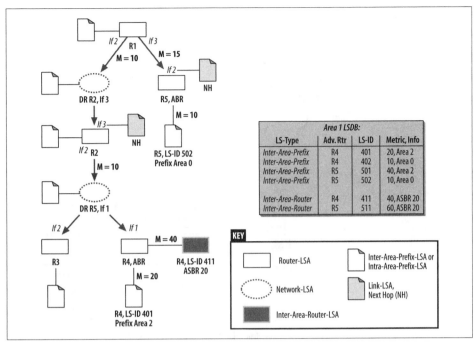

Figure 8-31. Inter-area routes for Router R1

are ignored because there is always an intra-area path to that destination, and intra-area paths are always preferred.

Step 3: External routes

The router first identifies all Inter-Area-Router-LSAs and associates them with the ABRs as described in step 2. This ensures that all ASBRs outside the local area have been identified. The ASBRs of the local area are identified based on the intra-area tree constructed in step one. Next, the router associates all AS-External-LSAs with their corresponding ASBR and adds them to the SPF tree. This attaches the IPv6 prefixes of the external routes to the tree. Depending on the external metric type, the router enters these routes into the external-1 or external-2 routing table. If the same prefix appears more than once, external-1 routes are preferred over external-2 routes. If the same prefix still appears more than once, the one with the best total cost is considered. If the costs are equal, all equal-cost prefixes must be accepted. The next hop is determined as the directly connected router on the shortest intra-area path to the ASBR or to the forwarding address, if the F bit has been set within the LSA. Figure 8-32 illustrates this process for Router R1.

The calculation of the OSPF routing table is now finished, and its content is handed to the internal routing process of the router.

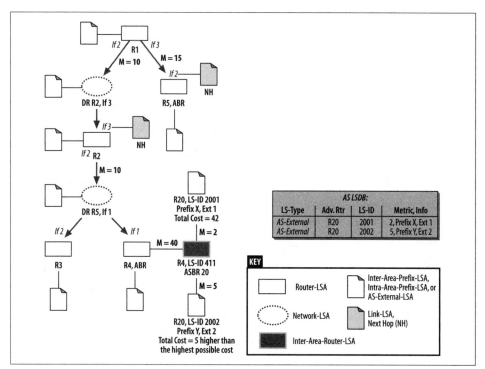

Figure 8-32. External routes for Router R1

LSA Flooding

Any change in the network causes certain link state information to change. Examples of such changes include the following:

- The state of a router's OSPF interface changes.
- A neighbor transitions to full state.
- A neighbor loses full adjacency.
- The DR on a transit link changes.
- A new IPv6 prefix is added or deleted on any given interface configured for OSPF.
- An interface configured for OSPF is added or deleted on a router.
- An area's summary information changes.
- An external route is added or withdrawn at the ASBR.
- The renewal timer (MaxAge/2) of an LSA requires an updated LSA.

The router detecting the change rewrites the LSA accordingly, increases the sequence number, and gives the LSA to the flooding process. According to Table 8-5, the LSA is then flooded to a neighbor only (link scope), to all neighbors in the same area (area scope), or to all neighbors (AS scope).

Flooding means that the LSA is passed from the advertising router to its adjacent neighbors. Depending on the flooding scope of the LSA, the neighbors then pass it on to their neighbors, and so on. Each router receiving an LSA first evaluates whether the LSA is new or has a higher sequence number than the one already installed in the LSDB. If either of these two conditions is true, the LSA is added or replaced in the LSDB. Now the router considers the interfaces to be used for further flooding. It will not flood the LSA out the incoming interface with one exception: if the router is a DR for the incoming interface of the LSA and the LSA was not sent by the BDR, it must be flooded back out the same interface. The DR is responsible for sending LSAs to all its neighbors. Another reason not to flood the LSA is, if the LSA is older than or the same age as the one already installed. This prevents LSAs from looping in the network. LSAs are normally sent to the AllSPFRouters multicast address with the following exceptions:

- On transit networks, routers in the DR-Other state send LSAs to the address All-DRouters. The update reaches the DR/BDR, which in turn sends it back to all other routers on this transit link using the AllSPFRouter multicast address.

- If a router requests a link state update sending a Link State Request packet, the LSA uses the unicast address of the requesting router.

- On NBMA, all LSAs are sent unicast to the statically configured neighbors.

- LSA retransmissions (unacknowledged LSAs) are sent to the unicast address of the neighbor.

Figure 8-33 shows the process of a DR receiving new or changed LSAs and flooding them to all routers.

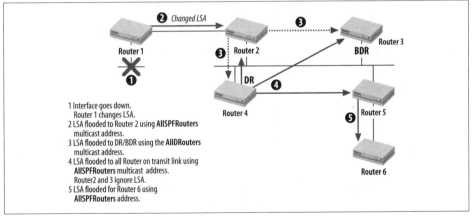

Figure 8-33. LSA flooding

Each router receiving a new or changed LSA has to acknowledge this LSA. Sending a Link State Acknowledgment packet usually accomplishes this. It could also be acknowledged by sending back the LSA if the received LSA is older or the same age as the one already installed in the LSDB. In that case, the sequence number is set to the one already installed. Unacknowledged LSAs have to be retransmitted. Each router keeps track of which neighbor has acknowledged which LSA. Retransmissions are always sent to the unicast address of the neighboring router.

A sequence number is assigned to the LSA by the advertising router to keep track of the most recent instance of this particular LSA. The sequence number is incremented by the advertising router each time the LSA is changed. When a new or changed Router-LSA or Network-LSA is received and accepted, the router installs it in the LSDB. It then recalculates the SPF tree. If a new or changed LSA of another type is received, it is not necessary to recalculate the SPF tree, because these LSAs represent only informational elements. They replace or remove the existing information. The new information is used to reevaluate the best path for the intra-area, inter-area, or external routers.

Aging an LSA

In addition to the sequence number, each LSA maintains an Age field. The age is expressed in seconds. Each router increments the Age field of its LSA by one every second. If an LSA is transmitted to the neighbor router, a transmit delay must be added to the Age field. An LSA can never age beyond a Maximum Age (*MaxAge*), which is an architectural constant set to 3,600 seconds. Usually a router is flooding an update (increment sequence number) of its own LSA when it has reached MaxAge/2. LSAs that have reached MaxAge are not considered for the SPF tree and are eventually deleted from the LSDB. The advertising router can prematurely age an LSA to flush it from the OSPF area or AS. It simply sets the Age field to MaxAge. This would be done if, for example, an external route were withdrawn. Another reason to prematurely age an LSA might occur if the LSA has reached the biggest sequence number possible. Before wrapping the sequence number (starting again), the LSA has to be flushed. This is very unlikely to happen. If there were to be a change of the LSA every second, it would take over 136 years to reach the biggest sequence number.

Self-originating LSAs

A router may receive an LSA that it has issued itself. This could happen if there are redundant links within the area, forming a loop. Self-originated LSAs are normally discarded unless the self-originated LSA is newer. Obviously, this should not happen because only the advertising router can increment the sequence number of the LSA. If, however, the router has been rebooted, previously issued LSA are still held in the other router's LSDB. If a newer, self-originated LSA is received, the router prematurely ages that LSA, thereby flushing it from the area or AS.

Handling of unknown LSAs

OSPF for IPv6 has added the capability to handle unknown LSAs. Each LSA header contains the U bit in its LSA Type field. If the U bit is set, the unknown LSA is flooded according to the encoded flooding scope. A U bit set to 0 indicates link-local flooding scope. The exception to the previous rule is flooding into a stub area. To prevent unnecessary flooding of LSAs into a stub area, the following rule applies: if the LSA is unknown and either its flooding scope is set to AS or its U bit is set, the LSA is discarded and not flooded into a stub area.

BGP-4 Support for IPv6

There is no actual BGP for IPv6. The IPv6 support derives from the capability of BGP-4 to exchange information about network layer protocols other than IPv4. These multiprotocol extensions of BGP-4 are defined in RFC 2858, which obsoletes RFC 2283. RFC 2283 is mentioned here because it is the base document for RFC 2545, which defines the IPv6 extensions for BGP-4. It is important to understand BGP-4 fully before looking at its multiprotocol extensions. The following sections start with a short overview of BGP-4 and its operations as defined in RFC 4271 (formerly RFC 1771). BGP message types are then discussed. The last part covers the implementation of IPv6 information carried within BGP-4.

BGP-4 Overview

Each AS runs its interior routing protocol (RIP, OSPF, etc.) to distribute all routing information within the AS. The BGP is an exterior routing protocol whose primary function is to exchange information about the reachability of networks between ASes. Each AS receives a unique AS number assigned by the numbering authority. Figure 8-34 shows the different types of ASes that can be interconnected using BGP-4.

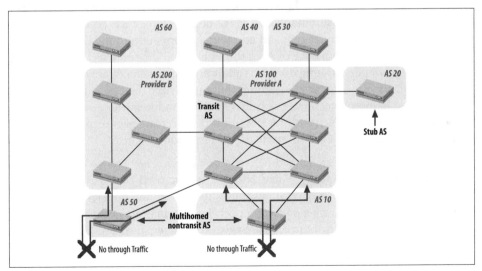

Figure 8-34. BGP traffic and AS types

The AS types are further explained in the following list:

Transit AS

> A *transit* AS has multiple connections to other ASes. Routing updates from any AS arriving at the transit AS may be passed through the AS and distributed out to other neighboring ASes. A transit AS can forward traffic to any other AS based on the routing information received. The AS of larger ISPs are usually of this type.

Stub AS

> A *stub* AS has a single connection to another AS. All traffic to or from the stub AS passes through this link. Smaller ISPs and campus or corporate networks use this kind of AS. Most stub ASes don't have a unique AS number assigned, as they don't really have any use for BGP. Their network addresses are treated as part of the parent AS.

Multihomed nontransit AS

> A *multihomed nontransit* AS has multiple connections to one or more other ASes. It does not pass routing updates through. Traffic not belonging to this AS is therefore never forwarded. A multihomed nontransit AS allows multiple entry/exit points to be used for load sharing of inbound and outbound traffic.

Two routers exchanging routing information with BGP are called BGP peers, BGP speakers, or BGP neighbors. They first establish a TCP connection to ensure reliable transport. The peers then open the actual BGP connection to exchange BGP messages. The most important BGP message is the UPDATE message, which contains the routes to be exchanged. A *BGP route* is defined as a unit of information consisting of the Network Layer Reachability Information (NLRI) and a set of path attributes. The NLRI is basically an IPv4 prefix and its prefix length. Any concept of IPv4 class information has been eliminated. The NLRI may represent a single network or, more commonly, an aggregate (summary) of a range of addresses. Each NLRI is accompanied by a set of path attributes that add additional information to the BGP route, i.e., the next hop address, a sequence of ASes through which the route has passed during its update, or its origin. Routing decisions and traffic management are often based on these path attributes. One attribute must be emphasized here, as it plays a very important role in loop detection: it is called AS_PATH, and it carries a sequence of AS numbers through which the route has passed. If the receiving peer recognizes its own AS number within the AS_PATH, it rejects the corresponding route.

BGP routing updates are exchanged between two peers. They are governed by policies. Outbound policies specify which NLRIs are advertised to a particular peer. A router can advertise only the BGP routes it uses itself. Inbound policies specify which BGP routes are accepted from a particular peer. Policies may also be used to modify a BGP route (including its attributes), to change its characteristics.

Establishing a BGP connection

In order to exchange routing updates, two peers first have to establish a BGP connection. Figure 8-35 illustrates the steps needed to establish a BGP connection, including the different BGP messages exchanged and the peer state. The entire state machine is explained in detail in RFC 4271. Each message and its fields are explained in the upcoming section "BGP Message Header."

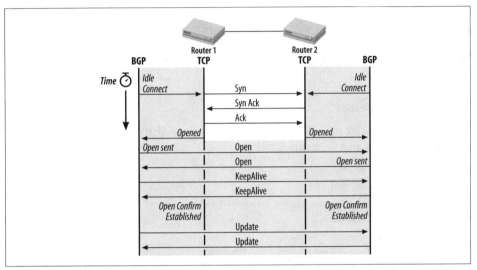

Figure 8-35. Establishing a BGP connection

To initiate and establish a BGP connection, the peers use the BGP OPEN message. If both routers simultaneously try to establish a BGP connection to each other, two parallel connections might well be formed. To avoid this connection collision, one router has to back down. The connection initiated by the router with the higher BGP Identifier prevails. The BGP Identifier is uniquely assigned to each BGP router and is exchanged during the OPEN message. Once the open is confirmed, the routers exchange the entire routing table based on their policies. Only changes in the routing table are exchanged from now on. Routing exchanges are done using BGP UPDATE messages. BGP KEEPALIVE messages prevent the connection from timing out. The TCP session guarantees reliable delivery of each BGP message.

BGP distinguishes between the following peer connections:

IBGP connection
> The peers are in the same AS and are called *internal peers*. BGP routes learned from internal peers must not be sent back to other internal peers; they can be sent only to external peers. Each internal peer must have a connection to all other internal peers so internal peers are fully meshed. The introduction of AS confederation for BGP (RFC 3065) or BGP route reflection (RFC 2796) relaxes

this rule. The AS_PATH and NEXT_HOP attributes must not be modified when passing updates to internal peers.

EBGP connection

The peers are in different ASes and are called external peers. BGP routes learned from external peers can be updated to all other peers. When sending an update to an external peer, the AS_PATH and NEXT_HOP attributes are modified. The sending router adds the local AS number to the AS_PATH and sets the NEXT_HOP field to its local IPv4 address.

BGP NOTIFICATION messages inform the peers of any errors during the open or update process. The connection can be shut down in a controlled fashion using a cease NOTIFICATION message.

Route storage and policies

BGP routes are stored in a Routing Information Base (RIB). Figure 8-36 shows the three different RIBs and their interactions.

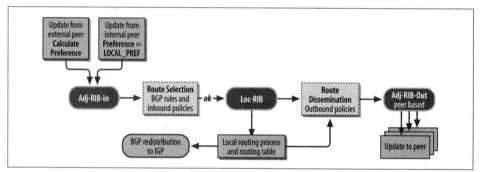

Figure 8-36. BGP RIBs and their interactions

Incoming messages could contain new feasible routes, replacement routes of earlier updates, or routes that have been withdrawn by the advertising peer. All these routes are placed into the Adj-RIB-In. For each new or changed route, a degree of preference is calculated based on the inbound policy. This preference is placed into the attribute LOCAL_PREF. If the route arrives from an internal peer, the LOCAL_PREF is already carried in the update and should not be recalculated. Each route in the Adj-RIB-In is now processed by the route selection process and entered into the Loc-RIB. The selection process first looks at the NEXT_HOP and AS_PATH attributes of the route. The IP address specified by the NEXT_HOP must be reachable through an entry in the local routing table. The AS_PATH must not contain the local AS number. If the two attributes comply, the route is accepted or ignored based on the inbound policy; otherwise, the route is ignored. In case of multiple routes to the same destination, the route with the highest preference is accepted. In case of the same preference, a complex tie-breaking rule ensures that only one of the routes to the same destination is accepted. See RFC 4271 for more details on this tie-breaking rule.

Routes in the Loc-RIB are now placed into the local routing table. The true next hop address is taken from the local route entry to the IPv4 address specified in the NEXT_HOP attribute.

All routes in the Loc-RIB and all routes in the local routing table are eligible to be advertised to external peers of this router. Only routes in the Loc-RIB learned from external peers are eligible to be advertised to all internal peers of this router unless route reflection is enabled (see RFC 2796). The outbound policy disseminates the routes to a peer-specific Adj-RIB-Out. The outbound policy may perform route aggregation or path attribute modification. Changes in the Adj-RIB-Out cause the update process to send an update to the peer.

BGP Message Header

BGP messages are carried on top of TCP connections, which can be established over either IPv4 or IPv6. The source and destination IP addresses of the datagram depend on the peer configuration. They are always unicast. BGP connections use the well-known TCP port 179. Remember that only one TCP connection is established between two peering routes. Figure 8-37 shows the BGP message header format. The header has a fixed size of 19 bytes.

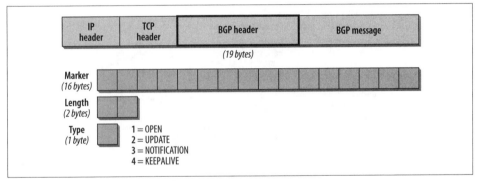

Figure 8-37. BGP message header format

The fields of the BGP header are explained in detail in the following list:

Marker (16 bytes)
> Contains authentication data if authentication was negotiated between the peers. All bits are set to one if no authentication is used or in the OPEN message.

Length (2 bytes)
> The total length of the BGP message, including headers. The value must be between 19 and 4096. The maximum message size of any BGP message is 4096 bytes.

Type (1 byte)
> Indicates the BGP message types as listed in Table 8-9.

Table 8-9. BGP message types

Type	Name	Description
1	OPEN	Initializes BGP connection and negotiates session parameters
2	UPDATE	Exchanges feasible and withdrawn BGP routes
3	NOTIFICATION	Reports errors or terminates BGP connections
4	KEEPALIVE	Keeps the BGP connection from expiring

OPEN Message

As soon as the TCP connection between two BGP peers has been established, the routers send OPEN messages to initialize the BGP connection. This message verifies the validity of the peer and negotiates parameters used for the session using the fields illustrated in Figure 8-38. To verify the validity of a peer, each side of the connection must configure the IP address and the AS number of the peer.

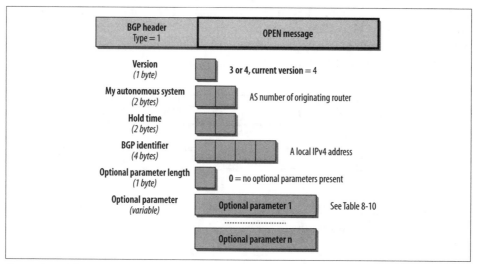

Figure 8-38. The BGP OPEN message

The following list details of the fields of the OPEN message:

Version (1 byte)
> Indicates the BGP version used by the sending peer. The current version is 4. Both peers have to agree on the same version. The version can be negotiated. Each peer usually indicates the highest version it supports. If the receiving peer does not support this version, it notifies the peer and terminates the session.

My Autonomous System (2 bytes)
> Indicates the AS number of the sending router. The receiving router must verify this number to be the peer's AS number. If it is incorrect, the peer is notified and

the session is terminated. If the AS number is the same as the receiving router's AS number, the peer is internal (IBGP); otherwise, the peer is external (EBGP).

Hold time (2 bytes)

Proposes a maximum time in seconds that may elapse before any BGP message must arrive on this interface. The hold timer is negotiated to the smaller value advertised by either peer. To keep a BGP connection from expiring, the peers send KEEPALIVE messages once every *HoldTime*/3 seconds. A hold time of 0 indicates that no KEEPALIVE messages need to be sent. The value of the hold time is 0 or greater than 2.

BGP Identifier (4 bytes)

Each router must be identified by a unique, globally assigned BGP identifier. At startup, the BGP Identifier is set to an IPv4 address of a local interface. The message is rejected if the BGP Identifier equals the BGP Identifier of the receiver or if the BGP Identifier is illegal. During route selection, the BGP Identifier may be used to break a tie.

Optional Parameter Length (1 byte)

Indicates the length of optional parameters to be negotiated. A length of 0 indicates that there are no optional parameters.

Optional Parameters

Each Optional Parameter consists of a <Type, Length, Value> (TLV) triplet. Both routers must know and agree on the optional parameter; otherwise, the peer is notified of the rejection of the parameter. This could lead to the termination of the session. At the moment, two parameters are specified, as explained in Table 8-10. The optional parameter BGP Capability is very important for IPv6 support.

Table 8-10. Optional parameters

Type	Name	Description
1	Authentication	The parameter consists of two fields: Authentication Code and Authentication Data. The Authentication Code defines the authentication mechanism used and how the marker and authentication data fields are to be computed.
2	BGP Capability	The parameter consists of one or more <Code, Length, Value> triplets identifying different BGP Capabilities. It is defined in RFC 3392. The capability parameter may appear more than once in the OPEN message.
		The Capability Code set to 1 indicates the Multiprotocol Extension Capability as defined in RFC 2858.

The authentication for BGP connection is currently mostly based on the MD5-signature-option and implemented directly in TCP. This authentication does not use the authentication data subfield.

The multiprotocol capability is used in conjuntion with IPv6. It has a 4-byte value field. The first 2 bytes identify the Address Family Identifier (AFI), byte 3 is reserved, and byte 4 defines the Subsequent Address Family Identifier (SAFI). AFI defines the network layer protocol used in the multiprotocol extension. SAFI defines additional information about the protocol, such as whether the protocol uses unicast forwarding (SAFI=1), multicast forwarding (SAFI=2), or both (SAFI=3). To support IPv6, the Multiprotocol Extension Capability is set to <Code=1, Length=4, Value=hexadecimal 0x0002 0001>.

UPDATE Message

An UPDATE message carries BGP route(s) advertised by the originating peer. It is divided into three sections, as outlined in Figure 8-39. The first section specifies the IPv4 NLRI that the sending peer is withdrawing. The second section defines all path attributes associated with the feasible IPv4 NLRI followed in section three. Multiple NLRI with the exact same set of path attributes can be placed in a single UPDATE message.

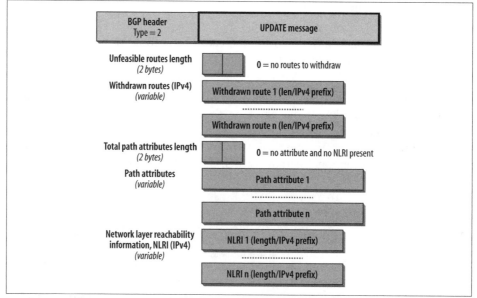

Figure 8-39. The BGP UPDATE message

The fields of the UPDATE message are detailed in the following list:

Unfeasible Routes length (2 bytes)
> Defines the length of the Withdrawn Routes field. When set to 0, it indicates that the originating peer has no route to withdraw with this message.

Withdrawn Routes
> A list of IPv4 NLRIs that are no longer valid. Each NLRI is encoded as <length, prefix> and represents an IPv4 prefix. The 1-byte Length field defines the length of the corresponding Prefix field. The Prefix field is padded to the full octet.

Because the NLRIs are IPv4 prefixes, this field can never be used to withdraw IPv6 routes. See "BGP Multiprotocol Extension for IPv6" for further details.

Total Path Attribute length (2 bytes)
Defines the length of the Path Attributes field.

Path attributes
Contains a list of path attributes that belong to the feasible NLRI advertised. Attributes are further explained in the next section.

Network Layer Reachability Information
A list of IPv4 NLRI that are advertised with this update. Each NLRI is encoded as <length, prefix> and represents an IPv4 prefix. The 1-byte Length field defines the length of the corresponding Prefix field. The Prefix field is padded to the full octet. The total length of this field is calculated as follows:

UPDATE message length – 23 – Unfeasible Routes Length – Total Path Attribute Length

Because the NLRIs are IPv4 prefixes, this field can never be used to advertise IPv6 routes. See "BGP Multiprotocol Extension for IPv6" for further details.

BGP Attributes

Path attributes provide additional information about the advertised NLRI. Each path attribute has a 2-byte attribute header, as depicted in Figure 8-40.

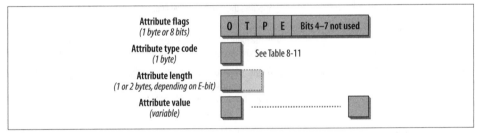

Figure 8-40. The BGP path attributes

The following list explains the Path Attribute in detail:

O bit (Optional bit)
Defines whether the attribute is optional (set to 1) or well-known (set to 0). A well-known attribute must be recognized and supported by each BGP router. Optional attributes may not be recognized by some routers.

T bit (Transitive bit)
Defines whether the attribute is transitive (set to 1) or nontransitive (set to 0). Transitive attributes must always be passed on when the NLRI is advertised to another peer. Well-known attributes must always be transitive.

P bit (Partial bit)

Applies only to optional transitive attributes. If any router along the update path does not recognize the optional transitive attribute, it must set the P bit to 1. This setting indicates that at least one router in the path to the route does not recognize this attribute. This bit must always be set to 0 for optional nontransitive or well-known attributes.

E bit (Extended length bit)

Defines whether the attribute length field is 1 byte (set to 0) or 2 bytes (set to 1). Extended length may be used if the attribute's data is longer than 255 bytes.

Attribute code (1 byte)

Defines the type of attribute. Table 8-11 lists and explains some of the most common attributes. Detailed explanations should be taken directly from RFC 4271 or any RFC extending BGP (e.g., BGP Route Reflection defines attribute types 9 and 10).

Table 8-11. BGP attributes

Type	Name/flags	Description
1	ORIGIN (well-known)	Defines the original source of this route. 0=IGP, 1=EGP, 2=Incomplete
2	AS_PATH (well-known)	A sequence of AS numbers that this route has crossed during its update. The rightmost AS number defines the originating AS. Each AS crossed is prepended. Prevents loops and can be used for policies.
3	NEXT_HOP (well-known)	Specifies the next hop's IPv4 address. Cannot be used for IPv6.
4	MED (optional nontransitive)	The MULTI_EXIT_DISC (MED) indicates a desired preference (4-byte) of the route to the peer—the lower the better. Designed for multiple EBGP connections between two ASes to load-share inbound traffic.
5	LOCAL_PREF (well-known)	Defines a local preference (4 byte) of the route. The higher the better. It is usually calculated on routes arriving from external peers and preserved to internal peers. Designed for multiple EBGP connections to any AS to manage outbound traffic.
6	ATOMIC_AGGREGATE (well-known)	Specifies that one of the routers has selected the less-specific route over a more-specific route.
7	AGGREGATOR (optional transitive)	The BGP Identifier of the router that aggregated routes into this route.
8	COMMUNITY (optional transitive)	Carries a 4-byte informational tag. Can be used by the route selection process. Defined in RFC 1997.
14	MP_REACH_NLRI (optional nontransitive)	Advertises multiprotocol NLRI. Used for IPv6 prefixes. See "BGP Multiprotocol Extension for IPv6."
15	MP_UNREACH_NLRI (optional nontransitive)	Withdraws multiprotocol NLRI. Used for IPv6 prefixes. See "BGP Multiprotocol Extension for IPv6."

NOTIFICATION and KEEPALIVE Messages

NOTIFICATION messages are used to report errors. A 1-byte Error Code field specifies the main category of the error. A Subcode field providing the actual error follows the

Error Code field. For troubleshooting reasons, additional data about the error is placed in the Data field. See RFC 4271 for all error codes. Additional documents extending BGP add error subcodes. Error messages for the BGP Extension for IPv6 are specified in RFC 2858.

KEEPALIVE messages contain no data whatsoever, just the BGP message header with the message type 4. They are used to prevent a BGP connection from timing out.

BGP Multiprotocol Extension for IPv6

BGP-4 carries only three pieces of information that are truly IPv4-specific:

- NLRI (feasible and withdrawn) in the UPDATE message contains an IPv4 prefix.
- NEXT_HOP path attribute in the UPDATE message contains an IPv4 address.
- BGP Identifier is in the OPEN message and in the AGGREGATOR attribute.

To make BGP-4 available for other network layer protocols, the multiprotocol NLRI and its next hop information must be added. RFC 2858 extends BGP to support multiple network layer protocols. IPv6 is one of the protocols supported, as emphasized in a separate document (RFC 2545). To accommodate the new requirement for multiprotocol support, BGP-4 adds two new attributes to advertise and withdraw multiprotocol NLRI. The BGP Identifier stays unchanged. BGP-4 routers with IPv6 extensions therefore still need a local IPv4 address. To establish a BGP connection exchanging IPv6 prefixes, the peering routers need to advertise the optional parameter BGP capability to indicate IPv6 support. BGP connections and route selection remain unchanged. Each implementer needs to extend the RIB to accommodate IPv6 routes. Policies need to take IPv6 NLRI and next hop information into consideration for route selection.

An UPDATE message advertising only IPv6 NLRI sets the unfeasible route length field to 0 and carries no IPv4 NLRI. All advertised or withdrawn IPv6 routes are carried within the MP_REACH_NLRI and MP_UNREACH_NLRI. The UPDATE must carry the path attributes ORIGIN and AS_PATH; in IBGP connections it must also carry LOCAL_PREF. The NEXT_HOP attribute should not be carried. If the UPDATE message contains the NEXT_HOP attribute, the receiving peer must ignore it. All other attributes can be carried and are recognized.

An UPDATE message can advertise both IPv6 NLRI and IPv4 NLRI having the same path attributes. In this case, all fields can be used. For IPv6 NLRI, however, the NEXT_HOP attribute should be ignored. IPv4 and IPv6 NLRI are separated in the corresponding RIB.

MP_REACH_NLRI path attribute

This optional nontransitive attribute allows the exchange of feasible IPv6 NLRI to a peer, along with its next hop IPv6 address. The NLRI and the next hop are delivered in one attribute, as depicted in Figure 8-41.

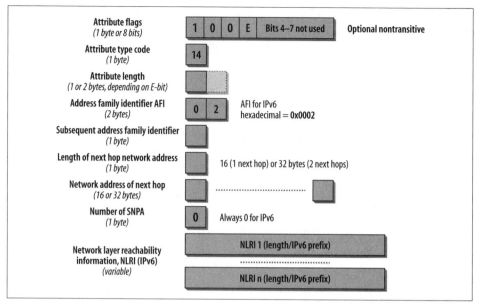

Figure 8-41. The MP_REACH_NLRI path attribute for IPv6

The fields comprising the MP_REACH_NLRI path attribute are detailed in the following list:

Address Family Identifier (AFI) (2 bytes)
> Defines the network layer protocol. IPv6 uses the value 0x0002 (hexadecimal) as specified at *http://www.iana.org/numbers.html* (see RFC 3232).

Subsequent Address Family Identifier (SAFI) (1 byte)
> Defines whether the protocol uses unicast forwarding (SAFI=1), multicast forwarding (SAFI=2), or both (SAFI=3).

Length of the next hop network address (1 byte)
> Defines the number of bytes used for the Next Hop Address field. IPv6 sets this field to either 16 or 32, depending on the number of the next hop address provided.

Network address of next hop
> Contains the next hop IPv6 address of this IPv6 route. This field is updated when advertising this route to an external peer. The router chooses its own IPv6 global/local address of the link to the external peer. This field is generally not updated when advertising this route to an internal peer. If the next hop IPv6 address and the peer IPv6 address share a common link—e.g., a link between two external peers—the link-local address of the common link should be added as a second next hop address. In return, when advertising this route to an internal peer, the link-local address received from an external peer needs to be removed.

RFC 2545 still uses the term site-local address instead of local address. Site-local addresses have been deprecated in the meantime. For more information, refer to the sections in Chapter 3 about IPv6 addressing.

Number of SNPA (1 byte)
Defines the number of Subnetwork Points of Attachment (SNPA) to follow right after this field. SNPA carry additional information associated with the router associated with the next hop address. IPv6 does not use this field and sets it to 0. Therefore, no SNPA data field will follow.

Network Layer Reachability Information (NLRI)
A list of IPv6 NLRI that are advertised with this attribute. Each NLRI is encoded as <length, prefix>. The 1-byte Length field defines the length of the corresponding Prefix field. The Prefix field is padded to the full octet. The length of this field is the remaining length after deducting the length of all previous fields from the attribute length.

MP_UNREACH_NLRI path attribute

This optional nontransitive attribute allows the sending peer to withdraw multiple IPv6 routes that are no longer valid. As illustrated in Figure 8-42, it basically contains a list of IPv6 prefixes that the peer should remove from its RIB.

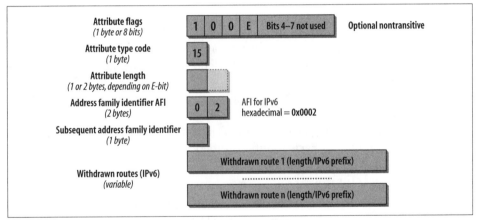

Figure 8-42. The MP_UNREACH_NLRI path attribute for IPv6

The fields comprising the MP_UNREACH_NLRI path attribute are detailed in the following list:

Address Family Identifier (AFI) (2 bytes)
Defines the network layer protocol. IPv6 uses the value 0x0002 (hexadecimal).

Subsequent Address Family Identifier (SAFI) (1 byte)
Defines whether the protocol uses unicast forwarding (SAFI=1), multicast forwarding (SAFI=2), or both (SAFI=3).

Withdrawn routes

A list of IPv6 NLRI that are withdrawn from service. Each NLRI is encoded as <length, prefix>. The 1-byte Length field defines the length of the corresponding Prefix field. The Prefix field is padded to the full octet. The length of this field is the remaining length after deducting the length of all previous fields from the attribute length.

Additional Routing Protocols for IPv6

The final section of this chapter is focused on two additional routing protocols, IS-IS and EIGRP. Both protocols have quite a broad implementation base with IPv4, and migrations to IPv6 are expected. This chapter provides only an overview for these protocols.

At the end of this chapter, multicast routing is discussed briefly to complete the routing picture.

Routing IPv6 with IS-IS

IPv6 support with IS-IS is defined in *draft-ietf-isis-ipv6-05.txt*. This document is based on the specifications for integrated IS-IS as defined in RFC 1195. Without in-depth knowledge of integrated IS-IS, the IPv6 extension cannot be understood.

Integrated IS-IS

Unlike the previous routing protocol discussions, this section gives only a very brief overview of integrated IS-IS. IS-IS originally defines the exchange of routing information between Intermediate Systems (ISes, otherwise known as routers) for the OSI network layer protocols CLNP (connectionless network protocol) and CONP (connection-oriented network protocol). Other protocols use other routing protocols. Having separate routing protocols for each network layer is sometimes referred to as "ships in the night." Each routing protocol uses (or maybe wastes) its own resources, such as CPU and memory. A misbehaving routing protocol can destabilize another routing protocol.

An integrated routing protocol uses resources efficiently and is more stable, as it introduces a single process for routing control. That is the idea behind integrated IS-IS (i/IS-IS), in which the routing protocol has been adapted to carry concurrently routing information for the OSI network protocols and for IPv4. This is achieved by introducing variable-length data fields in the form <Type, Length, Value> (TLVs). Each network layer protocol can use the TLVs according to its addressing syntax. Each supported network layer protocol is specified by its Network Layer Protocol Identifier (NLPID), assigned by ISO.

Integrated IS-IS is an interior routing protocol based on link state updates. OSPF and IS-IS have many similarities: if you know one, the other is easy to grasp. We have already explained OSPF in detail, so we can briefly compare OSPF features with i/IS-IS. OSPF runs within an AS, and i/IS-IS runs within a routing domain. An i/IS-IS routing domain can be further split into multiple areas with a common central area. Routers within the central area are called Level 2 intermediate systems, or L2 routers. Routers in all other areas are called Level 1 intermediate systems or L1 routers. In most cases, L2 routers are L1 routers as well, such as ABR in OSPF. Each area is identified by the first 13 bytes of the ISO NSAP address assigned to the router. Routers keep adjacencies with each other, initiated and maintained by IS-IS Hello packets. Routers can become adjacent only if they are on the same level. Once they have become adjacent, they advertise level 1 or level 2 Link State PDU (L1-LSP or L2-LSP). L1 routers originate L1-LSP advertising their local addresses. L2 routers originate L2-LSP advertising their local address, routes learned from directly attached areas, and external routes. Only L2 routers can advertise routes external to the routing domain, called ASBR in OSPF. To synchronize and acknowledge the most recent LSP, the routers use Sequence Number PDU (SNP), again for level 1 and level 2. An L1 router knows L1 routes in its area by calculating an SPF tree to all destinations. L1 routers have no knowledge about any route outside their own area. Anything outside the area is reached via the closest L2 router. L2 routers, however, know all the internal and external routes to the routing domain. In addition, transit links are handled in i/IS-IS by implementing pseudonodes. The designated router of a transit link originates LSP on behalf of the pseudonode.

Routing IPv6 with IS-IS

Integrated IS-IS provides for the inclusion of variable-length fields (TLVs) in all IS-IS packets (Hello, LSP, and SNP). Relevant addressing information is stored in TLV fields. Hello packets and LSP packets carry a field specifying the network layer protocols. Each supported network layer protocol is specified by its NLPID, assigned by ISO. The value of the IPv6 NLPID is 142 (0x8E).

The Internet draft proposes two new TLVs for IPv6. They are described in the following list. Remember that this is only a draft document; some of this information may change, or additional information may be added. However, interoperating implementations already exist.

The IPv6 Reachability TLV (Type 236)
> Defines the IPv6 prefix advertised within L1-LSP and L2-LSP. Within a L2-LSP, it can also be used to advertise an IPv6 prefix external to the routing domain by setting the external bit in the Control field. The following fields make up this TLV: Prefix Length, IPv6 Prefix, Metric (4 bytes), and the Control field.

IPv6 Interface Address TLV (Type 232)
> Defines the IPv6 addresses of one or more interfaces of the router. It is advertised in Hello packets, L1-LSP, and L2-LSP. For Hello packets, it must contain the link-local IPv6 address assigned to the interface that is sending the Hello packet. In LSP, it must contain the global/unique-local addresses assigned to the router.

EIGRP for IPv6

Enhanced Interior Gateway Protocol (EIGRP) is an interior routing protocol (IGP) developed by Cisco Systems, Inc. It runs in an autonomous system called EIGRP domain. The main objective of EIGRP was to eliminate limitations of a distance vector routing protocol (see the discussion of RIP, earlier in this chapter) without developing another link state based protocol. Link state protocols with their complexity and database demand higher CPU performance and more memory of the routers. EIGRP was therefore developed as a hybrid protocol combining the best of both worlds. It uses a so-called Diffuse Update Algorithm (DUAL) to calculate the routes. It allows for fast convergence and ensures loop-free operations at every instant throughout route computation. Only routers affected by a change are involved.

EIGRP has the following components: protocol dependent modules, EIGRP message protocol and its packet types, neighbor relations, and the actual algorithm (DUAL). A specialty of EIGRP is its calculation of the path costs. A mixed metric is being used. It takes the following characteristics into consideration: bandwidth, delay, load, and reliability. These parameters can be configured on each EIGRP interface. A complex formula that includes a weight factor for each parameter produces a metric for each interface. The metrics are added to get the overall path costs.

Protocol-dependent modules

EIGRP has always supported different network layer protocols. For each network layer protocol, EIGRP runs a separate instance in a "ships in the night" fashion. There are modules for IPv4, IPX, Appletalk, and now also for IPv6. The basic functions for all protocols are the same. The semantics of the the different protocols are implemented using protocol-dependent TLVs (type, length, value) fields. The TLVs will be explained further later in the chapter.

EIGRP packet types

EIGRP packets are directly encapsulated in IPv6 specified by protocol number 88 in the Next Header field of the IPv6 header. EIGRP introduces a mechanism for reliable packet delivery. It guarantees that EIGRP packets arrive in the right sequence. The EIGRP header contains a sequence and acknowledgement field to accommodate this reliable transport mechanism. EIGRP packets can be sent as either a unicast packet to a particular router or as a multicast packet to multiple routers. The multicast IPv6 address in the latter case is set to FF02::A. Acknowledgments are always sent as unicast. For efficiency reasons, reliable transport is provided only when necessary. Certain messages do not use reliable transport. In this case, the sequence number is not used and no acknowledgments are sent.

EIGRP distinguishes between the following packet types:

Hello packets
> Hello packets are used for neighbor discovery or rediscovery. They are usually not using the reliable transport.

Acknowledgment (ACK) packets
> Acknowledgment packets are used to confirm the receipt of an EIGRP packet. They are basically Hello packets with no data. They are part of the reliable transport process.

Update packets
> Update packets transmit the actual routing information. Routing information is transmitted only if it represents a change (unlike RIP). They only contain the necessary information and are only sent to routers affected by the change. They always make use of the reliable transport mechanism.

Query and replay packets
> These packets are part of the DUAL process and play an important part in the diffuse calculations. They always make use of the reliable transport.

With reliable transport, unacknowledged packets are sent again—in this case, always as a unicast packet. After 16 unsuccessful retries, the neighbor is declared dead. The waiting time for an acknowledgment depends on the transmission type (multicast or unicast). With multicast, the timer is called *multicast flow timer*; with unicast, it is called *retransmission time-out*. Both depend on the overall smooth round trip time (SRTT). The SRTT is the average time in milliseconds for a packet to travel to the neighbor and back.

EIGRP neighbors

Unlike RIP, which sends periodic updates, EIGRP sends only changes. It is of utmost importance to discover all neighbors and to rediscover them in case of temporary failures. Hello packets ensure discovery and rediscovery. They are sent at periodic intervals out of all interfaces configured for EIGRP. The Hello interval depends on the bandwidth of the network. Normally it is set to 5 seconds for LAN-like bandwidth and 60 sec for WAN-like bandwidth. The EIGRP router expects periodic Hello packets from its neighbors as well and keeps a neighbor table. This table keeps certain information about each neighbor, including up time and hold time. The *hold time* defines a maximum waiting time for a valid packet from this neighbor. If this time expires, the neighbor is declared unreachable and the DUAL process is informed about the loss of this neighbor. The default value of the hold time is three times the Hello time. If a packet from the neighbor arrives, the hold time is reset.

A neighbor can send a goodbye message to indicate its shutdown. In this case, the routers don't have to wait for the hold time to expire.

The Diffuse Update Algorithm (DUAL)

DUAL handles all route computations in EIGRP. Its main objective is to maintain a table of loop-free paths to every route. If a loop-free path is not found in the table, a route recomputation must occur, during which DUAL queries its neighbors, who, in turn, may query their neighbors. This characteristic gives the algorithm its name, as in "diffuse update." E. W. Dijkstra and C. S. Scholten first proposed the algorithm. The most important contribution to DUAL, however, came from J. J. Garcia-Luna-Aceves. DUAL is based on a few fundamental principles. The reliable transport mechanism of EIGRP enables the fulfillment of these principles. These principles are as follows:

- A router must discover the existence of loss of a neighbor within a certain time frame.
- All messages are delivered correctly and in the proper sequence.
- All messages (e.g., change of metric, loss of link, etc.) are processed in the proper sequence of their occurrence and within a certain time frame.

DUAL keeps a topology table. The topology table keeps not only the least cost instance of a route (as does RIP, for example), but also all feasible instances of a route. However, only the least cost routes are copied to the routing table.

For DUAL to work properly, the neighbor connections must be established. These connections are being used for the exchange of routing information. During the initial setup of the neighbor connection, all known EIGRP routes are passed to each other using one or more update packets. The routing information received by the neighbors contains, among other information, the reported distance RD (metric) for each route, indicating the path cost from the neighbor to the destination. The receiving router calculates the total distance for each route by adding the metric of the receiving interface to the RD. The least cost instance (called feasible distance, or FD) of each route is entered into the EIGRP topology table and is named the successor. In case a particular route has more than one instance (i.e., has been received from several neighbors), the routes with an RD smaller than the FD are added to the topology table as well. They are called feasible successors (FS). This situation is called feasibility condition (FC). The feasibility condition is a test for a loop-free route. If the FC is met, the neighbor advertising the RD must have a path to the destination not through this router. If the neighbor would route through this router, the RD would have to be higher than the FD.

Each route in the topology table contains the following information:

- The route itself (IPv6 prefix and prefix length).
- The feasible distance (FD).
- The number of successors. More than one successor indicates two or more equal cost instances of the route.

- The successor(s) neighbor IPv6 address (Next Hop), the reported metric (RD), and the local interface to reach this neighbor.
- A list of feasible successors (if any). For each successor the following information is listed: the neighbor IPv6 address, the RD (must be smaller than FD), and the local interface to reach this neighbor.
- The EIGRP status of this route.

If there is a change (e.g., an update from a neighbor, a change in the metric of a directly connected interface, or a transition in the state of a directly connected interface, such as a shut down), the router must reevaluate the topology table. DUAL first tries to find a feasible successor locally. After recalculating the metrics, it checks for feasible successors. If a feasible successor is found, the successor is determined. If the FD has changed, it will be replaced and an update is sent to all neighbors. During this phase, the route has stayed in passive state, indicating that the route is good. If a feasible successor cannot be found in the local topology table, the route will transition to the active state. During the active state, the route is "on hold" and no changes are allowed. The router sends queries to its neighbors to find feasible successors. If the neighbor doesn't have a feasible successor, it forwards the query to its neighbors. The query thus propagates (diffuses) until a reply is received. DUAL has only finished its calculations when all queries have been answered. If no feasible successor has been found, the route is set to unreachable. Otherwise, the successor is determined and the route is put back to passive. To avoid being stuck in active state, a waiting timer is introduced. If a neighbor does not reply within this time, the reply is assumed to be "no successor found" (the route is unreachable).

A complex finite state machine for DUAL governs the query and reply exchanges, and it is not explained further in this chapter.

EIGRP packet format

All EIGRP packets have a standard 20-byte EIGRP header consisting of the following fields:

Version (1 byte)
> The version of the EIGRP process.

Operations code (1 byte)
> Defines the actual packet type, such as Update (Opcode=1), Query (Opcode=3), Reply (Opcode=4), or Hello (Opcode=5).

Checksum (2 bytes)
> Standard IP checksum calculated over the entire EIGRP packet.

Flags (4 bytes)
> Indicates additional functionality of the packet. For example, the Init flag (0x00000001) indicates the initial routing update to a neighbor. During the initial

update, the entire routing table is transmitted. The conditional-receive-bit flag (0x00000002) is used for the reliable transport.

Sequence number (4 bytes)
The current sequence number of the packet. This is used during a reliable transport exchange.

Acknowledgment number (4 bytes)
Contains the sequence number of a received packet. The sender acknowledges the receipt of this packet back to the sender by setting this field in the Acknowledgment packet. This is used during a reliable transport exchange.

Autonomous system number (4 bytes)
Identifies the EIGRP domain and with it the EIGRP process ID on the local router. It must be set to the same value throughout the entire EIGRP domain.

The EIGRP Header is followed by one or more TLV fields. Each TLV contains a type field (2 bytes), a length field (2 bytes), and finally the actual value or data field. The value field has a length specified in the length field. There are two categories of TLV:

General EIGRP TLV
Used for EIGRP parameters which are independent of the network layer protocol. An example of TLVs belonging to this category is the EIGRP parameter TLV used to exchange metric weights and hold times. TLVs used for the reliable transport mechanism are part of this category as well.

Network-layer-specific TLV
There are TLVs for IPv4, Appletalk, IPX, and now also for IPv6. Each network layer has at least two TLVs. One of them contains the internal EIGRP routes. The other contains external routes that have been imported into EIGRP from other routing protocols. Additional TLVs exist for each network layer protocol.

EIGRP support for IPv6

At the time of this writing, Cisco Systems has not yet officially released EIGRP for IPv6. It is currently available only on test releases. There will be an additional EIGRP protocol module for IPv6, along with the IPv6-specific TLVs.

Multicast Routing for IPv6

Until now, we have looked only at unicast routing. This section briefly outlines the general basics of multicast routing and how IPv6 makes use of it.

Multicast routing forwards IPv6 datagrams addressed to a multicast IPv6 address, from now on called *multicast packets*. Multicast packets are used for data streams originated from a source (called a sender) to a group of receivers. Each group is addressed using a specific multicast IPv6 address. Some of these addresses can be officially registered. With multicast, routing data packets do not have to be sent individually to each receiver. A single multicast packet can reach all receivers and therefore reduces the number of packets significantly, especially with a large number of receivers. Each multicast data stream is uniquely identified by its Source address (IPv6 unicast address) and its group or multicast IPv6 address. Multicast routing ensures packet delivery from the sender to all receivers. It must be enabled on all routers between the sender and the receivers. The router receives the multicast packet on the receiving interface and forwards it out over all other interfaces with registered receivers. The tricky part is to avoid duplication of multicast packets and the process of receivers joining a multicast group. Next I explain how it works.

For each multicast data stream, only a single receiving interface is allowed on any given router. If a data stream were accepted over multiple interfaces, packet duplication would occur. The receiving interface is selected as the interface having the least cost path back to the sender. This ensures that the data has reached this router over the shortest path. In order to determine the least cost path, the router examines the local unicast routing table and looks up the route to the sender. The next hop interface of this route will be the receiving interface, also called the reverse path forwarding (RPF) interface. If multiple least cost paths exist, an arbitration mechanism ensures that only one RPF interface is selected. Each incoming multicast datagram is now checked for whether it has arrived over its RPF interface. This is called the RPF check. Datagrams failing the RPF check are rejected. The first part of the puzzle is now solved. But how does the router know where the receivers are? It could simply not care and forward the multicast packets out every interface except the RPF interface, but this would not be very efficient. To avoid this flooding of packets, receiver registration is introduced. Receivers wanting to receive a multicast data stream register themselves with the local router using the Multicast Listener Discovery (MLD) protocol. These routers keep a list of registered receivers for each multicast group, or in case of a more granular registration, for each data stream (sender/group). They also add the outgoing interface to reach the receivers to this list. This information must now be passed to other multicast routers using a multicast routing protocol. The most important multicast routing protocol in use today is called PIM (protocol independent multicast), which is specified in RFC 2362. PIM basically distributes information about multicast groups and their receivers. Many multicast features requiring special IPv6 consideration are still in draft.

As just mentioned, MLD defines mechanisms for end-systems to join and leave multicast groups or multicast data streams (sender/group).

Now we have all the information within a multicast routing table. Each entry represents a multicast data stream defined by its sender address and the multicast group address. Each maintains the RPF interface and all outgoing interfaces (where there are receivers).

This was a brief introduction into multicast functionality. To fully understand multicast routing, the protocols MLD and PIM should be studied in-depth.

References

Here's a list of the most important RFCs and drafts mentioned in this chapter. Sometimes I include additional subject-related RFCs for your personal further study.

- RFC 1058, "Routing Information Protocol," 1988
- RFC 1195, "Use of OSI IS-IS for Routing in TCP/IP and Dual Environments," 1990
- RFC 1584, "Multicast Extensions to OSPF," 1994
- RFC 1793, "Extending OSPF to Support Demand Circuits," 1995
- RFC 1997, "BGP Communities Attribute," 1996
- RFC 2080, "RIPng for IPv6," 1997
- RFC 2328, "OSPF Version 2," 1998
- RFC 2362, "Protocol Independent Multicast-Sparse Mode (PIM-SM): Protocol Specification," 1998
- RFC 2365, "Administratively Scoped IP Multicast," 1998
- RFC 2453, "RIP Version 2," 1998
- RFC 2545, "Use of BGP-4 Multiprotocol Extensions for IPv6 Inter-Domain Routing," 1999
- RFC 2710, "Multicast Listener Discovery (MLD) for IPv6," 1999
- RFC 2740, "OSPF for IPv6," 1999
- RFC 2796, "BGP Route Reflection," 2000
- RFC 2858, "Multiprotocol Extensions for BGP-4," 2000
- RFC 2863, " The Interfaces Group MIB," 2000
- RFC 2908, "The Internet Multicast Address Allocation Architecture," 2000
- RFC 3065, "Autonomous System Confederations for BGP," 2001
- RFC 3101, "The OSPF Not-So-Stubby Area (NSSA) Option," 2003
- RFC 3232, " Assigned Numbers: RFC 1700 is Replaced by an On-line Database," 2002
- RFC 3306, "Unicast-Prefix-based IPv6 Multicast," 2002
- RFC 3307, "Allocation Guidelines for IPv6 Multicast Addresses," 2002
- RFC 3392, "Capabilities Advertisement with BGP-4," 2002
- RFC 3569, "An Overview of Source-Specific Multicast (SSM)," 2003
- RFC 3590, "Source Address Selection for the Multicast Listener Discovery (MLD) Protocol," 2003
- RFC 3765, "NOPEER Community for Border Gateway Protocol (BGP) Route Scope Control," 2004

- RFC 3810, "Multicast Listener Discovery Version 2 (MLDv2) for IPv6," 2004
- RFC 4271, "A Border Gateway Protocol 4 (BGP-4)," 2006

Drafts

Drafts can be found at *http://www.ietf.org/ID.html*. To locate the latest version of a draft, refer to *https://datatracker.ietf.org/public/pidtracker.cgi*. You can enter the draft name without a version number and the most current version will come up. If a draft does not show up, it was either deleted or published as an RFC. Alternatively, you can go to the new Internet drafts database interface at *https://datatracker.ietf.org/public/idindex.cgi*. *http://tools.ietf.org/wg* is also a very useful site. More information on the process of standardization, RFCs, and drafts can be found in Appendix A.

Here's a list of drafts that I refer to in this chapter, along with interesting drafts that are related to the topics in this chapter:

- *draft-ietf-pim-sm-v2-new-12.txt*, Protocol Independent Multicast—Sparse Mode (PIM-SM): Protocol Specification (Revised)
- *draft-ietf-pim-bidir-08.txt*, Bi-directional Protocol Independent Multicast
- *draft-ietf-pim-sm-bsr-07.txt*, Bootstrap Router (BSR) Mechanism for PIM
- *draft-ietf-isis-ipv6-06.txt*, Routing IPv6 with IS-IS
- *draft-ietf-isis-wg-multi-topology-11.txt*, M-ISIS: Multi Topology (MT) Routing in IS-IS

CHAPTER 9

Upper-Layer Protocols

The impact of IPv6 on upper-layer protocols is minimal because the datagram service has not changed substantially. This chapter discusses UDP and TCP over IPv6 and describes changes for upper-layer protocols, such as DNS, DHCP, SLP, FTP, Telnet, and HTTP when used over IPv6. The most important changes are always needed where an IP address is used. Any process or application that uses an IP address needs to be updated to be able to handle the extended 128-bit address format. Applications that use a hardcoded 32-bit IPv4 address should be updated to use a DNS name instead, so that DNS can return either an IPv4 or an IPv6 address to make the IP protocol fully transparent.

UDP/TCP

Checksumming is done on different layers. Remember, the IPv6 header does not have a checksum. But a checksum is important on the transport layer to determine packet delivery problems. Other upper-layer protocols may use a checksum, too. All checksum calculations that include the IP address in the calculation must be modified for IPv6 to accommodate the new 128-bit address.

Transport protocols such as UDP and TCP attach checksums to their packets. A checksum is generated using a pseudoheader. The TCP and UDP pseudoheader for IPv6 contains fields for Source and Destination address, payload length, and Next Header value (RFC 2460). If the IPv6 packet contains a routing header, the Destination address used in the pseudoheader is the address of the final destination. If the Source or Destination address was changed in transit, the value of the pseudoheader at the destination will not match the value of the initial packet, which causes checksum calculation failure and an error report.

Because the IPv6 address is so much longer than the IPv4 address, the IPv6 specification includes a new version of the pseudoheader. The IPv6 pseudoheader specification takes into account that an unknown number of extension headers can be present before the UDP or TCP layer, which is essential when calculating the payload length for the pseudoheader. With IPv4, a checksum in the UDP header was optional. With IPv6, the computation of a checksum is mandatory for UDP. IPv6 nodes that receive a UDP packet with a value of 0 in the checksum field should discard the packet and log the error.

The source node calculates and stores the checksum, and the destination node verifies it. Figure 9-1 shows the format of the pseudoheader that is built and used to calculate TCP and UDP checksums.

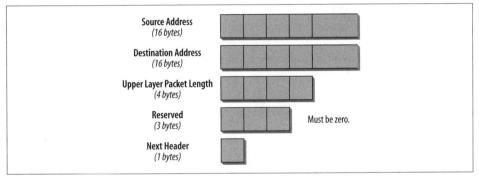

Figure 9-1. Format of the pseudoheader

The following list describes each of the fields:

Source Address (16 bytes)
> The Source address of the IPv6 packet.

Destination Address (16 bytes)
> The Destination address of the IPv6 packet. If there is a routing header in the packet, the address of the final destination is used for the checksum calculation. On the first node, this address is the last address in the list of the routing header. At the final destination, this is the Destination address in the IPv6 header.

Upper Layer Packet Length (4 bytes)
> This field contains the length of the Upper-Layer Protocol header plus data.

Next Header (1 byte)
> The Next Header field identifies the type of the header using the values listed in Table 2-1.

The same algorithm used with IPv4 is used to calculate the checksum with IPv6. The 16-bit checksum is computed over the entire pseudoheader. By including the source and Destination addresses in the checksum calculation, any alteration of the addresses en route would be detected.

DHCP

DHCP is widely used to configure hosts with their IPv4 addresses and additional information. If you have an IPv6 network, you do not need DHCP to configure your hosts with address information. The Stateless autoconfiguration mechanism will configure your hosts for their IPv6 addresses without the need to set up a DHCP server. All you need to do is configure your IPv6-enabled routers with the prefix information for the links to which they are attached. But you might still choose to have DHCP servers in some cases. Host configuration that includes the assignment of IPv6 addresses using DHCP is called *Stateful autoconfiguration* or *Stateful DHCPv6*. Maybe you have a specific IPv6 addressing scheme; or you need dynamic assignment of DNS servers; or you choose not to have the MAC address as a part of the IPv6 address; or you wish to implement dynamic updates to DNS (RFC 2136). In these cases, you can use DHCP for address configuration. You can also combine Stateless and Stateful autoconfiguration by using Stateless autoconfiguration for the IPv6 address configuration and DHCP servers to provide additional configuration information including but not limited to DNS server IP addresses or DNS domains.

RFC 3736 offers an additional configuration option. It defines a Stateless DHCP service for IPv6. A Stateless DHCP server can configure hosts that already have an IP address with additional information such as DNS or SIP servers. It cannot do address assignment, though. Stateless DHCP is explained later in this chapter, after the section on stateful DHCPv6.

DHCPv6 and DHCPv4 are independent. If you want to configure hosts with DHCP in a dual-stack network, currently you will need two separate DHCP services running, one for each protocol. In this case, you will also have to watch out for configuration conflicts. In the DHCPv4 world, the client is configured to know whether to use DHCP. In the DHCPv6 world, the Router Advertisement has options to inform the client whether to use DHCP. There may be differing configuration information arriving at the client from different sources, or a node may have multiple interfaces, e.g., one being IPv4-only and one being dual-stacked. DHCPv6 uses a unique identifier (DUID), which does not exist for DHCPv4. In the realm of DHCPv4, MAC address and client ID resemble the DUID in DHCPv6 but are not synonymous. There is work going on to make the DUID available for DHCPv4 also.

The DHCP working group is further assessing requirements and evaluating solutions, which will allow dual-stack hosts to be configured for both protocols by one or more DHCP server. *Draft-ietf-dhc-dual-stack-04.txt* goes into more detail and describes issues identified with dual IP version DHCP interactions. The most important aspect is how to handle potential problems in clients processing configuration information received from both DHCPv4 and DHCPv6 servers.

On the humorous side, according to Steve Deering from Cisco, one of the key persons in the design of IPv6, no other specification had as many revisions as the DHCPv6 draft. So rest assured that there is a lot of hard work in this specification.

DHCPv6 is specified in RFC 3315. All references in this chapter relate to DHCPv6.

For the development of DHCPv6, the following guidelines were originally defined:

- It must be possible to combine DHCP and Stateless autoconfiguration.
- The configuration of DHCP and the interaction with other mechanisms (e.g., Stateless autoconfiguration) are the responsibility of the administrator.
- The clients do not need to be configured manually.
- DHCP must be able to configure multiple addresses per interface.
- A DHCP server is not needed in every subnet. Relay agents must be able to forward DHCP packets.
- A client must be able to deal with multiple DHCP replies coming back from different DHCP servers.
- It must be possible to have subnets where only some of the clients are configured by DHCP.
- DHCP does not depend on the presence of a router. Routers are needed only if Stateless autoconfiguration is used.
- DHCP must be able to do dynamic DNS updates to register allocated addresses in DNS. The administrator can decide to update DNS manually.
- DHCP must support and simplify the renumbering of a network.

DHCP Terms

Let us define some common terms used for DHCPv6:

DHCP Client
 A DHCP client sends requests to a DHCP server to get configuration information.

DHCP Server
 A DHCP server is preconfigured to reply to client requests. It knows the configuration for each client. When it receives a client request, it sends the information back to the client. A DHCP server may or may not be on the same link as the client.

DHCP Relay Agent
 If there is no DHCP server on the client link, a relay agent must be configured on the client link. The relay agent receives the client request and forwards it to one or more DHCP server(s) on another subnet. When the relay agent receives the

answer from the DHCP server, it forwards it to the client. A relay agent is called an *IP helper* in the Cisco world. I use the term *relay agent* in this chapter.

DHCP Unique Identifier (DUID)

Each DHCP client and server has a DUID. DHCP servers use DUIDs to identify clients for the selection of configuration parameters and in the association of IAs with clients. DHCP clients use DUIDs to identify a server in messages where a server needs to be identified.

Identity Association (IA)

A collection of addresses assigned to a client. Each IA has an associated Identity Association Identifier (IAID), which is assigned by the client. A client can have multiple IAs—for example, one for each interface.

Identity Association Identifier (IAID)

An identifier for an IA chosen by the client. Each IA has an IAID, which is chosen to be unique among all IAIDs for IAs belonging to that client.

Transaction ID

A value used to match requests and replies.

DHCP uses the following multicast addresses:

All_DHCP_Relay_Agents_and_Servers (FF02::1:2)

All DHCP agents (servers and relays) are members of this multicast group. DHCP clients use this link-scoped multicast address to reach DHCP agents on their link. So clients do not need to know the agent's link-local address.

All_DHCP_Servers address (FF05::1:3)

All DHCP servers within a site are members of this multicast group. This site-scoped address is used by DHCP relays to reach all DHCP servers within a site. They either do not know the server's unicast address, or they want to reach all DHCP servers within the site.

The following UDP ports are used with DHCPv6:

UDP port 546—Client port

Clients listen on port 546 for DHCP messages. DHCP servers and relays use it as the destination port to reach DHCP clients.

UDP port 547—Server/Agent port

DHCP servers and relays listen on port 547 for DHCP messages. DHCP clients use this port as the destination port to reach DHCP servers and relay agents. DHCP relays use this port as the destination port to reach DHCP servers.

The messages types shown in Table 9-1 have been specified in RFC 3315.

Table 9-1. DHCPv6 message types

Message type	Description
SOLICIT (1)	Used by clients to locate DHCP servers.
ADVERTISE (2)	Used by servers as a response to Solicit.

Table 9-1. DHCPv6 message types (continued)

Message type	Description
REQUEST (3)	Used by clients to get information from servers.
CONFIRM (4)	Used by clients to verify that their address and configuration parameters are still valid for their link.
RENEW (5)	Used by clients to extend the lifetime of their IP address and renew their configuration parameters with their original DHCP server when their lease is about to expire.
REBIND (6)	Used by clients to extend the lifetime of their address(es) and renew their configuration parameters with any DHCP server when their lease is about to expire and they have not received a reply to their Renew message.
REPLY (7)	Used by DHCP servers to respond to Solicit messages with a Rapid Commit Option, as well as to Request, Renew, and Rebind messages. A Reply to an Information Request message contains only configuration parameters, but no IP address. A Reply to a Confirm message contains a confirmation that the client's IP address(es) are still valid for the link (or a decline). A server sends a Reply as an acknowledgment for a Release or Decline message.
RELEASE (8)	Used by clients to release their IP address. The message is sent to the server, from which the address was received.
DECLINE (9)	Used by clients to indicate to the server that one or more addresses assigned to them are already in use on the link. This is determined by the client through Duplicate Address Detection (DAD).
RECONFIGURE (10)	Used by DHCP servers to inform clients that the server has new or updated configuration information. The clients then must initiate a Renew or Information Request message in order to obtain the updated information.
INFORMATION REQUEST (11)	Sent by clients to request additional configuration parameters (without IP address information).
RELAY-FORW (12)	Used by DHCP relays to forward client messages to servers. The relay encapsulates the client message in an option in the Relay Forward message. The message can be sent directly to a DHCP server or via other relay agents. If a DHCP message is relayed multiple times, it is encapsulated multiple times.
RELAY-REPL (13)	Used by DHCP servers to send messages to clients through a relay. The client message is encapsulated as an option in the Relay Reply message. The relay decapsulates the message and forwards it to the client. The Relay Reply message takes the same path back through which the Relay Forward message traveled and may therefore also be encapsulated multiple times if there is more than one relay agent on the path.

The DHCP server-initiated configuration exchange is a great new feature. It can be used, for example, when links in the DHCP domain have to be renumbered or when new services or applications have been added and need to be configured on the clients. When services or applications need to be configured on the client, the DHCP server sends out a Reconfigure message (type 10). A client receiving this message must initiate a Renew or Information Request message exchange to get the updated information. Haven't we been waiting for this?

This could also be done with DHCPv4, but it has rarely been implemented. The IPv4 way of doing this is defined in RFC 3203. A DHCPv4 server sends a DHCPforcerenew message, which triggers the client to the Renew state in which it tries to renew its lease.

DHCPv6 Header Format

The general DHCPv6 header format is much simpler than the one used with DHCPv4. I describe it next.

Client-Server messages

All DHCP messages exchanged between server and client have a fixed header with a variable part for options.

Figure 9-2 shows the header format.

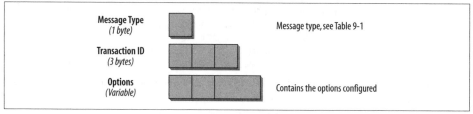

Figure 9-2. Format of the DHCP header

The Message Type field defines the type of message. You saw the list of message types in Table 9-1. For each request, the client generates a new transaction ID and writes it into the Transaction ID field. It is used in all messages relating to this specific request. When troubleshooting DHCP, it is important to check the transaction ID and make sure to associate the corresponding requests and replies.

Options are used to provide configuration information and parameters. The options fields have an identical base format, which is shown in Figure 9-3.

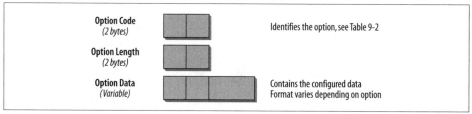

Figure 9-3. DHCP option fields

The Option Code field defines the type of the option. Find an overview of the available option types in Table 9-2. The Option Length field indicates the length of the option in bytes. The Option Data field finally contains the information configured for the option. Its format and length varies depending on the option type.

The options defined in RFC 3315 are a base set of options. In the future, additional options will be defined and specified in separate RFCs. Table 9-2 shows an overview.

Table 9-2. DHCP options

Option	Value	Description
Client Identifier	1	Used for the client DUID. A DUID is a unique identifier (described later in this chapter).
Server Identifier	2	Used for the server DUID.
Identity Association for Nontemporary Addresses (IA_NA)	3	Used to indicate the IA_NA, the parameters, and the nontemporary addresses associated with it.
Identity Association for Temporary Adresses (IA_TA)	4	Used to indicate the IA_TA, the parameters, and the temporary addresses associated to it. All addresses contained in this option are used as temporary addresses by the client (according to RFC 3041 on Privacy Extensions for Stateless Address Autoconfiguration).
IA Address	5	Used to indicate the addresses associated with an IA_NA or IA_TA.
Option Request	6	Used in a message between client and server to identify a list of options. Can be contained in a Request, Renew, Rebind, Confirm, or Information Request message. The server can use this option in a Reconfigure message to indicate which options have been changed or added.
Preference	7	Sent by the server to influence the choice of a client for a DHCP server.
Elapsed Time	8	Contains the time when the client started the DHCP transaction. Indicated in hundredths of a second. In the first message sent by a client it is set to 0. Can be used by a secondary DHCP server to detect whether a primary server responds in time.
Relay Message	9	Contains the original message in a Relay Forward or Relay Reply message (remember that the original message is encapsulated in a Relay Forward or Reply message).
Authentication	11	Contains information to authenticate the identity and the content of DHCP messages.
Server Unicast	12	The server sends this option to the client to indicate that unicast can be used for communication. The option contains the IP address of the DHCP server, which is to be used by the client.

Some specifications with additional options have already been published:

RFC 3319, "Dynamic Host Configuration Protocol (DHCPv6) Options for Session Initiation Protocol (SIP) Servers"

The Session Initiation Protocol (SIP) is defined in RFC 3261. It is a control protocol for the establishment, modification, and termination of multimedia sessions or calls. The components are a SIP server and a SIP client. RFC 3319 defines two DHCPv6 options for the configuration of a SIP client for a local SIP server. The client will use this server for all outgoing SIP requests. The first option (option code 21) contains a list of domain names, and the second option (option code 22) is a list of 128-bit IP addresses. The servers have to be listed in the order of their preference. The client has to choose the first server in the list; if it does not answer, the client chooses the second server in the list. The client can request both options. It then has to use the domain list first and use the IP address list only if that is unsuccessful.

RFC 3633, "IPv6 Prefix Options"

This RFC defines options that can be used to send prefix information from a delegating router or a DHCPv6 server to a requesting router that has DHCPv6 client functionality. It is useful in environments where the delegating router has no information about the topology of a network connected to the requesting router. A delegating router or a DHCPv6 server in an ISP network uses this option to configure a router in a customer network for its prefix. The delegating router can, for example, assign a /48 prefix to the border router in the customer network. The border router can subdivide the /48 prefix to /64 subnets and advertise these prefixes with Router Advertisements. DHCP prefix delegation (DHCP-PD) is independent from DHCP address assignment, but the two can be combined.

RFC 3646, "DNS Configuration Options"
RFC 3646 defines two DHCPv6 options for the client configuration of DNS name servers (option code 23) and domain search lists (option code 24).

RFC 3898, "Network Information Service (NIS) Configuration Options"
This RFC defines four options for Network Information Service (NIS) related configuration information: NIS Servers (option type 27), NIS+ Servers (option type 28), NIS Client Domain Name (option type 29), and NIS+ Client Domain name (option type 30). They can be used only for the configuration of NIS services that can be reached over IPv6. The two options for NIS and NIS+ servers provide a list of IPv6 addresses for the respective servers. The lists are ordered according to their preference.

RFC 4014, "DHCPv6 Relay agent RADIUS Attributes Option"
This option enables the network access system (NAS), which also serves as a DHCPv6 relay agent, to pass along attributes for the user of a device (received during RADIUS authentication) to a DHCP server. The NAS, using RADIUS as an authentication authority, will receive attributes from a RADIUS server that may be used by the DHCP server in the selection of configuration parameters to be delivered to the device requesting access.

RFC 4075, "Simple Network Time Protocol (SNTP) Configuration Option for DHCPv6"
The Simple Network Time Protocol servers option provides a list of one or more IPv6 addresses of SNTP servers available to the client for synchronization. The clients use these SNTP servers to synchronize their system time to that of the standard time servers.

This is the status at the time of writing, but active development is underway. If you want to get up to speed with the latest status at the time of your reading, refer to the DHCP working group at *http://www.ietf.org/html.charters/dhc-charter.html*. There you will also find all the drafts that are underway.

Relay Agent—Server Message Format

Relay Agents forward client and server messages if the two are not on the same link. A DHCP message can be forwarded by more than one Relay Agent to one or more server(s). The reply by the server has to follow the same path back through which the original request came in, and it has to be forwarded by the same Relay Agents. Figure 9-4 shows the header fields in the Relay Agent and server messages.

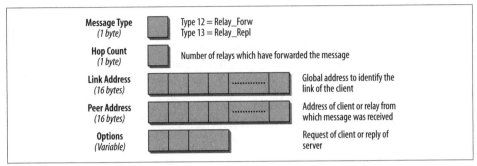

Figure 9-4. Header fields in Relay Agent and server messages

Relay Forward and Relay Reply messages have the same format and are identified by the value in the Message Type field. Type 12 is a Relay Forward message, type 13 a Relay Reply message.

The Hop Count field in a Relay Forward message shows how many Relays have already forwarded this message. Each forwarding Relay increases the value by one. The Relay can be preconfigured with a Hop Count Limit to limit the number of Relays that forward the message. When a Relay receives a message in which the Hop Count has reached the value configured in the Hop Count Limit, it discards the message. The default value for the Hop Count Limit is 32. In a Relay Reply message, the Hop Count field value is taken from the Hop Count field in the corresponding Relay Forward message.

The Link Address field contains a global IPv6 address. Based on this field in a Relay Forward message, the server can identify the link where the requesting client sits. The RFC also mentions the site-local address as a possible value for this field because the DHCPv6 RFC was published before the site-local address was deprecated. In a Relay Reply message, the value in this field is taken from the corresponding Relay Forward message.

The Peer Address field contains the address of the client or the Relay from which the message was received. This field is copied from the Relay Forward message into the corresponding field in the Relay Reply message.

The variable size Options field contains a Relay Message Option (option type 9). In a Relay Forward message, it contains the client request; in a Relay Reply message, it contains the server reply. This field can contain additional information that can be preconfigured on Relay Agents and that they insert when forwarding the message.

DHCP Unique Identifier

Each DHCP client and server has a DHCP Unique Identifier (DUID) that is used to identify each other. A server uses the client DUID to choose the corresponding client configuration to be sent. The DUID has to be unique across all servers and clients and should not be changed after initial assignment. RFC 3315 specifies three different types of DUIDs. Additional types may be specified in the future. A DUID contains a 2-byte type code followed by a variable number of bytes containing the identifier. The three types specified currently are as follows:

- Link-layer address plus time (DUID-LLT)
- Vendor-specific unique ID based on enterprise number (DUID-EN)
- Link-layer address (DUID-LL)

Identity Association

An *Identity Association* (IA) is an object used by the server and the client to identify and manage a group of addresses. Each IA is identified by a corresponding IAID and contains individual configuration information. A client has at least one IA per interface, which is to be configured by a DHCP server. The client uses the IA to get the right configuration for the interface from the server. Each IA has to be associated to only one interface. It is the client that chooses the IAID, and it must be unique. The configuration information of an IA contains one or more IPv6 addresses plus the T1/T2 timers (Renewal and Rebinding timers, explained in "Renew/Rebind," later in this chapter).

A DHCP server chooses the configuration information for the IA according to the address allocation policies defined by the administrator. It chooses the configuration based on the following criteria:

- The link to which the client is connected
- The DUID of the client
- Other information provided by the options from the client
- Other information taken from the options, which have been added by Relay Agents

DHCP Communication

There are different processes in the DHCP communication. There is the client-server interaction and the forwarding of messages over Relay Agents. The following sections describe these processes in more detail. Many processes are similar to DHCPv4, differing only in IPv6-related adaptation. Other processes are new—for instance, the way messages are forwarded over Relay Agents.

Client and server communication

A client uses multicast Solicit messages to find a DHCP server. If a client wishes to contact a specific DHCP server, it uses the server DUID in a Server Identifier Option (option type 2). All DHCP servers will receive this message, but only the server specified by the DUID will reply. In some cases, a client can use a unicast address to reach a specific server. This is possible only if the server is configured to send a Server Unicast Option (option type 12) indicating that unicast communication is possible and stating the IP address to be used. In this case, it has to be considered that these unicast messages will not be forwarded over Relay Agents, so any configuration done on the Relay Agent will not be inserted into the unicast DHCP messages.

The client receives one or more Advertise messages in answer to its Solicit message. If it receives more than one, it applies the following criteria to choose a DHCP server:

- The message with the highest Server Preference value is preferred.
- If there are several messages with an equal Server Preference value, it chooses the one with the preferred configuration.
- The client may also choose a message with a lower Server Preference value if it contains more appropriate configuration parameters.

The list of servers and their corresponding Preference values are stored at the client. Should it not receive replies from its preferred DHCP server, it will choose the next one in the list. If a client does not receive an answer from a DHCP server within a certain amount of time, it either initiates a new Discovery process by sending out another Solicit message or ends the configuration and creates an error message.

In reply to the Advertise message, the client sends a Request message to one of the DHCP servers including its IA Option, its client DUID, and an Option Request option, which contains the desired DHCP options. The server replies with a Reply message containing the requested options. If the server received the Request forwarded by a Relay Agent in a Relay Forward message, it will reply with a Relay Reply message forwarded over the same Relay Agents like the incoming Request message. The server flags the addresses given out in the Reply message as allocated. If the client receives multiple Replies, it chooses the most appropriate one and uses these addresses. The addresses allocated by other servers through their Advertise messages remain allocated but are not used. They will be reused by the DHCP server when their lifetimes have expired.

The client has to perform Duplicate Address Detection (DAD) for each address allocated by the DHCP server. For an explanation of DAD, refer to "Neighbor Discovery (ND)" in Chapter 4. A typical DHCP communication performed by a client that does Stateful address autoconfiguration looks as follows:

1. Client sends Solicit message.
2. Server(s) reply with Advertise message.

3. Client sends Request message to one server.

4. Server replies with Reply message.

This communication can be shortened to only two messages with the Rapid Commit option. In this case, the client sends a Solicit message with the Rapid Commit option included. The server replies with a Reply message that also contains the Rapid Commit option. If the client sent out a Solicit message with a Rapid Commit option, it will ignore any Replies that do not contain a Rapid Commit option. If the client does not receive any Reply including a Rapid Commit option, it may accept an incoming Advertise message and continue the regular configuration process. If a server receives a Solicit message with a Rapid commit option and is not configured to use it, it replies with a regular Advertise message. While it is true that Rapid Commit offers a more efficient approach to address assignment by using only two messages, it has to be chosen carefully. Depending on the configuration and the number of DHCP servers, it could result in wasted address space or a situation where multiple DHCPv6 servers believe that they each assigned addresses to requesting clients. Once a DHCP server has allocated an address in a Reply message with a Rapid Commit option, it has to commit the IP address to the client.

A client uses Request, Renew, Rebind, Release, and Decline messages as necessary for the lifetime of its server-assigned addresses. If the client switches link or subnet (for instance, in a wireless network or after waking up from sleep mode), it has to initiate a Confirm/Reply exchange. It does this by sending its IAs and the corresponding addresses and options. If the client does not receive an answer to its Confirm message, it should continue to use the previously allocated addresses.

To release one or more of its addresses, a client sends a Release message, which contains the IA and the corresponding addresses and options. The server answers with a Reply. If the client does not receive a Reply, it sends another Release message. This is not possible in all cases—for instance, if the client is shutting down. If a DHCP server did not receive a Release message, it will reuse the addresses when their lifetimes have expired.

If a client notices that an allocated address is already in use (for instance, through DAD), it sends a Decline message to the server. This message contains a Transaction ID, the client identifier, the server identifier, and the address(es).

If a DHCP server receives a unicast message from a client to which it has not sent the Unicast option, it replies with a Reply message containing the Status Code "use multicast" (option 13, code 5).

Renew/Rebind

If a client wants to refresh the lifetime of its valid and preferred addresses, it sends a Renew (type 5) message containing the IA Address option and the addresses corresponding to this IA. The server identifies the corresponding lifetimes and sends a

Reply message to the client. Doing this it may also add new addresses or remove old addresses by setting their lifetime to 0.

If a server receives a Renew message for an IA for which it has no entry, it replies with a Reply message setting the Status code to "no binding" (option 13, code 3). If the client wants to renew an address that is not valid for its link, the server sends a Reply message setting the lifetimes for the addresses to 0.

The server controls the intervals in which a client has to renew its addresses through the Timers T1 and T2 preconfigured and associated to each IA. When the client reaches the time indicated by T1, it has to start the Renew process. When a client reaches the time indicated by T2, this indicates that its Renew messages have not been answered. In this case, it sends a Rebind message to all DHCP servers. The Rebind message contains an IA option with the currently allocated addresses and an Option Request option with all desired DHCP options.

When a server receives a Rebind message and finds the corresponding IA, it answers with a Reply message. If the addresses are not valid for the link anymore, it sets the lifetimes to 0. If the client does not receive an answer to a Rebind message, it cannot make further use of the address(es). In this case, it has two options:

- Restart the address configuration by sending out a Solicit message to find a DHCP server.
- If the client has other valid IAs, it can ignore the expired IA and use other addresses.

Information Request

If the client already has IP addresses but wants to get other DHCP information, it sends an Information Request message. This message contains an Option Request option to indicate the desired DHCP options. If, for instance, the client is configured by Stateless address autoconfiguration and the router is configured to set the O-flag (other Stateful configuration) in the Router Advertisement, this causes the client to send an Information Request message to get additional information such as DNS, NTP, or SIP server configuration. The Information Request message is also sent by the client in answer to a Reconfigure message from the server.

Reconfigure process

The server sends a Reconfigure message to trigger the client to send a Renew or an Information Request message. This is useful when the server has been updated with new or modified information, to make sure the new information is propagated as quickly as possible. In the Reconfigure message, the Transaction ID is set to 0 and contains a Server Identifier option including the server DUID and a Client Identifier option containing the client DUID. Additionally, an Option Request option can be sent along to indicate to the client which options have changed or been added. The Option Request option contains an IA Address option (type 5) if the client needs to reconfigure its IP address. With the Reconfigure message option (type 19), the server indicates whether the client has to send a Renew or an Information Request message.

Because of the danger of DoS attacks, the use of security mechanisms is mandatory in Reconfigure messages, which means that the server has to use DHCP authentication. The server sends a Reconfigure message to a unicast IPv6 address of each client. If it doesn't know the unicast address of the client, it sends the message as a Relay Reply message to a Relay agent. While a client is in a Reconfigure process, it does not accept further Reconfigure messages. A new process can be started only once the initial process has been completed.

Relay Agent communication

The way a Relay Agent forwards DHCP messages with DHCPv6 is quite different from the way it is done with DHCPv4. The following section describes the Relay Agent communication in detail. A Relay Agent is often called an IP helper in the Cisco world.

A Relay Agent uses the All_DHCP_Severs multicast address (FF05::1:3) to forward messages to DHCP servers. It can be configured to use a unicast address. The Relay Agent takes the message coming from the client and builds a Relay Forward message. Figure 9-4 shows the header of this message. In the Link Address field, it sets its global IPv6 address with the prefix for the link on which the client resides. From this address, the DHCP server determines for which prefix it has to allocate addresses. The Hop Count is set to 1. The Source address from the original address (i.e., the client IP address) is copied into the Peer Address field of the Relay Forward message. The original DHCP message is copied into the Relay Message Option field. The Relay Agent can now add other information that has been preconfigured by the administrator.

When a Relay Agent receives a Relay Forward message from another Relay Agent and the value of the Hop Count field reaches the preconfigured value for the Hop Count Limit, it ignores the message. With the Hop Count Limit, the number of Relay Agents that forward a DHCP message can be limited. If the Hop Count is smaller than the Hop Count Limit, the message is forwarded. It encapsulates the packet into another Relay Forward header, increases the Hop Count by one, and copies the Source address of the previous Relay Agent into the Peer Address field. The Link Address field is set to 0. The message received is copied into the Relay Message Option.

As already mentioned, the Relay Reply message has to be forwarded over the same Relay Agents as the Relay Forward message. With the process just described, each Relay Agent encapsulates the received message into a new Relay Forward header, which makes it possible for the DHCP server to track the way back. In the last Relay Message Option, the server finds the original request from the client. It replies to it and copies the answer into the Relay Message Option of a Relay Reply message. It encapsulates this reply into as many Relay Reply headers as the Relay Forward message has received. So the Relay Reply travels the same way back through the same Relay Agents. Each Relay Agent on the path decapsulates the exterior header and forwards the message to the next Relay Agent. The last Relay Agent on the path receives a Relay Reply message, which contains the server reply in the Relay Message Option field. It removes the Relay Reply header and forwards the server reply to the client.

Table 9-3 shows the entries in the header fields for a packet that has been forwarded over two Relays, Relay A and Relay B.

Table 9-3. The headers in Relay Forward and Relay Reply messages

Header field	Packet 2	Packet 3	Packet 4	Packet 5
	Relay A to Relay B	Relay B to Server	Server to Relay B	Relay B to Relay A
Message Type	Relay Forward (Type 12)	Relay Forward (Type 12)	Relay Reply (Type 13)	Relay Reply (Type 13)
Hop Count	1	2	2	1
Link Address	Relay A	0	0	Relay A
Peer Address	Client C	Relay A	Relay A	Client C
Relay Message Option	Client Request	Packet 2	Packet 5	DHCP Reply

The communication looks as follows:

1. Client C sends a DHCP Request (Packet 1, not shown in Table 9-3).

2. Relay Agent A forwards the client request in a Relay Forward message (type 12) to Relay Agent B (packet 2). It copies its address into the Link Address field. The client request is copied into the Relay Message Option.

3. Relay Agent B forwards the message to the DHCP server (packet 3). It sets the Link Address field to 0 and copies the address of Relay Agent A into the Peer Address field. Packet 2 received from Relay Agent A is copied into the Relay Message Option.

4. The DHCP server sends a Relay Reply (type 13) to Relay Agent B (packet 4). The Hop Count, Link Address, and Peer Address fields are copied from the Relay Forward message. The Relay Message Option contains the packet, which has to be sent from Relay Agent B to Relay Agent A (packet 5).

5. Relay Agent B decapsulates packet 5 and forwards it to Relay Agent A.

6. Relay Agent A takes the server reply from the Relay Message Option and forwards it to Client C.

Security Considerations

Attacks based on DHCP functionality are possible in the IPv4 world as well as in the IPv6 world. The points of attack to be watched are the same:

• External, unknown DHCP servers allocating false addresses to DHCP clients

• Faulty or malicious DHCP servers in the intranet that assign false addresses or other false configuration information to DHCP clients

- Unknown, external clients that attach to the corporate network and receive internal addresses
- Intentional exhaustion of IP addresses by malicious clients, resulting in valid clients being unable to obtain a valid IP address and/or configuration options
- Malicious client(s) transmitting such high volumes of requests that a DHCP server is unable to respond to valid requests

To protect your network from external DHCP servers from outside the corporate network, a firewall closing the ports for DHCP is a good protection. It is important to protect your network from internal DHCP servers. It doesn't even need to be a malicious attack. Very often the problems come from improperly configured test servers. A client can be attacked by a malicious DHCP server configuring it with false information. For instance, a bad DNS or NTP server can be configured, or it can be configured in a way that it cannot communicate in the local network anymore. To protect from such attacks, Authentication should be used.

With DHCPv4, the ways to protect from such attacks are limited. Firewalls only protect from outside attacks. The possibility to use Authentication for DHCP communication exists only in the form of vendor solutions in addition to DHCPv4.

The specification for DHCPv6 includes an Authentication mechanism, which is based on Authentication for DHCPv4 (RFC 3118). New hosts must be authorized and authenticated before they receive configuration information from a DHCP server, the sender of a message must be authenticated, and the content of the message must be protected.

The following section gives an overview of the Authentication mechanisms specified in RFC 3315. If you are not familiar with security concepts and terms, please refer to Chapter 5 first.

Security for messages between Relay Agents and DHCP servers

For a secure exchange of messages between Relay Agents and DHCP servers, IPsec (in transport mode with ESP) is used. Between each Relay Agent and its communication peers, an independent two-way trust relationship has to be established. If the content of the message is not considered confidential, encryption is not required (null encryption). As the Relay Agents and the DHCP servers are within the corporate network, private keys can be used.

In addition to this, DHCP servers and Relay Agents are configured with the addresses of trusted communication peers. It is therefore not possible for an unknown DHCP server or Relay Agent to intrude into the communication.

DHCP Authentication

The authentication of DHCP messages can be accomplished through the use of the Authentication option (option 11). The authentication information carried in the

Authentication option can be used to reliably identify the source of a DHCP message and to confirm that the contents of the DHCP message have not been changed. Multiple authentication protocols can be used with the Authentication option. Two such protocols are specified in RFC 3315: the Delayed Authentication Protocol and the Reconfigure Key Authentication Protocol (section 21 in RFC 3315). Additional protocols may be specified in the future with separate RFCs.

Dynamic Updates to DNS

With the widespread use of DHCP and autoconfiguration for dynamic IP address configuration, the need for a dynamic update of DNS for addition and deletion of records arose. RFC 2136 introduced the mechanism called Dynamic DNS (DDNS). It is supported by BIND Versions 8 and 9 and many popular DNS implementations. The update functionality is usually used by applications such as DHCP, but it can be implemented on hosts as well. With IPv6, dynamic addresses are often assigned using Stateless autoconfiguration, which means there may not be a DHCP server in the network. A DNS update mechanism is necessary on each host to update its DNS records. There are important security aspects to consider when DDNS updates are made. It is important that you can control which nodes are authorized to make changes to your DNS records. Update policies must be implemented and Transaction Signatures (TSIG; see RFC 2845) or Domain Name System Security Extensions (DNSSEC; see RFCs 3007, 4033, 4034, and 4035) mechanisms should be used. RFC 4339, "IPv6 Host Configuration of DNS Server Information Approaches," discusses some of these general DNS aspects for IPv6 hosts.

Stateless DHCP

In environments where Stateless autoconfiguration is used for IP address information, there was no way to configure additional information on the client, such as DNS information or other options. Several solutions were discussed, one being to add such options to the Router Advertisement. Finally, RFC 3736 specified a new service called Stateless DHCP Service for IPv6. A Stateless DHCP server has an implementation of only a subset of the DHCPv6 specification. Its use requires that hosts are already configured for an IPv6 address. A Stateless DHCP server replies to Information Request messages (message type 11) that contain an Option Request option (option type 6) with a Reply message (message type 7). The Stateless DHCP server can also act as a relay agent. This allows configuration of a part of the clients on a link using Stateless address autoconfiguration while getting additional information from the Stateless DHCP server. Meanwhile, other clients use Stateful address autoconfiguration, and their DHCP messages are forwarded by the Stateless DHCP server acting as a relay agent.

DNS

DNS is used in the IPv4 world to do name-to-address mappings and vice versa. This is not changing in the IPv6 world. The need for DNS is actually much greater because of the length of IPv6 addresses. Mixed IPv4/IPv6 environments need multiple host entries in DNS. A host communicating with both versions of TCP/IP needs at least two entries in DNS—one with its IPv4 address and the other with its IPv6 address. A new DNS record type has been defined for IPv6 hosts. RFC 3596 defines the AAAA type record (called "quad-A"). RFC 2874 defines the A6 type record, which was designed to make renumbering of networks and prefix changes easier to administer. A6 has been moved to experimental status and is not used. The other DNS record types (NS and PTR records) remain unchanged, adjusting only to the IPv6 address format.

AAAA Records (RFC 3596)

RFC 3596 describes DNS extensions for IPv6 implementations based on AAAA records. This record type can store a 128-bit IPv6 address, and the DNS value for this type of record is 28 (decimal notation). A host that has more than one IPv6 address has an AAAA record for each address. The corresponding reverse lookup domain is IP6.ARPA. The reverse lookup records are PTR records of type 12.

An AAAA type record can look like this:

```
moon.universe.com   IN   AAAA   4321:0:1:2:3:4:567:89ab
```

For reverse lookups, each subdomain level under IP6.ARPA represents 4 bits of the 128-bit address. The least significant bit appears at the far left of the domain name. Omitting leading zeros is not allowed in this case, so the PTR record for the previous example looks like this:

```
b.a.9.8.7.6.5.0.4.0.0.0.3.0.0.0.2.0.0.0.1.0.0.0.0.0.0.0.1.2.3.4.IP6.ARPA.IN
PTR   moon.universe.com
```

Note that there are several ways to represent reverse IPv6 addresses in DNS. It depends on the implementation, so refer to your vendor's documentation to find out which format is expected.

 Originally, the reverse domain was called IP6.INT. It has been deprecated (RFC 4159) and replaced by IP6.ARPA. IP6.INT is still operational, as there are some applications using it, but it will be phased out in the future. New applications are supposed to use the IP6.ARPA domain.

DNS Servers

BIND implements IPv6 DNS in versions of BIND 8.4 and higher and in BIND Version 9. For BIND 8.2.3, a patch that adds some IPv6 support is available.

DNS implementations based on these versions of BIND support IPv6. A good reference site for BIND is the Internet Systems Consortium homepage at *http://www.isc.org/products/BIND*. The same site has a list of vendor implementations based on BIND. There are also links to versions of BIND that run on different versions of the Microsoft operating system.

The most important file for configuring a name server on Unix is */etc/named.conf*. The file itself contains detailed information on how to configure it. To make name resolution work over IPv6, you need to add one important entry: listen on ipv6 { any }. This entry tells the name server to listen for IPv6 queries. Then update */var/named* with the entries for all IPv6 hosts.

The entries in our zone record file are shown in Figure 9-5.

```
$TTL 3h
$ORIGIN universe.com.
@      IN     SOA     ford.universe.com. mail.universe.com. (
       20011017    ; Serial
       3h          ; Refresh
       1h          ; Retry
       1w          ; Expire
       1h )        ; Minimum

universe.com.  IN NS  ford.universe.com.

ford   IN A   192.168.0.99
       IN AAAA fe80:0:0:0:2a0:24ff:fec5:3256
       IN A6 0 fe80:0:0:0:2a0:24ff:fec5:3256

arthur      IN A   192.168.0.66
       IN AAAA fe80:0:0:0:a00:20ff:fe20:adc2
       IN A6 0 fe80:0:0:0:a00:20ff:fe20:adc2

marvin      IN A   192.168.0.20
       IN AAAA fe80:0:0:0:202:b3ff:fe1e:8329
       IN A6 0 fe80:0:0:0:202:b3ff:fe1e:8329
```

Figure 9-5. The zone record file

Obviously, you would not usually put link-local addresses into your DNS. I did it in my lab just to show how DNS replies to my queries.

 For a detailed explanation of BIND and DNS configuration, refer to the latest edition of *DNS and BIND*, by Paul Albitz and Cricket Liu (O'Reilly). It is a masterpiece, and I have nothing to add.

DNS Resolvers

Resolvers are the client part in DNS communication. The resolver sends out DNS requests for IP addresses to DNS servers. It can be part of an operating system or an application. DNS servers also have a resolver implemented to send out DNS requests to other DNS servers.

Resolvers in an IPv4/IPv6 network must be able to handle all record types: the A record type for IPv4 and the AAAA record type for IPv6. In the future, resolvers also need a mechanism for choosing the protocol on a dual-stack host. When the DNS server replies with a set of different addresses, resolvers need to implement a feature for a default choice of address, and this should be configurable. If the DNS reply contains an IPv4 and an IPv6 address, the resolver can either forward both addresses to the requesting application and let the application make the choice or make a choice on behalf of the application. If the resolver forwards the IPv4 address, the application will communicate over IPv4; if it forwards the IPv6 address, the application will communicate over IPv6. Applications written for dual-stack hosts should be able to determine whether they communicate with IPv6 or IPv4 peers.

When people talk about IPv6 support in DNS, they are usually referring to two different aspects that are sometimes not pointed out clearly. One aspect is whether your DNS server supports IPv6 address records (AAAA). A DNS server supporting AAAA records does not necessarily have to be queried over IPv6. It can reply to such requests using IPv4. The other aspect is whether the resolver and the DNS server can use IPv6 as a transport for DNS queries and replies. For instance, if you have Windows XP with the IPv6 stack running, it does lookups for IPv6 records but uses IPv4 as the transport for the query. The support for resolving DNS names over IPv6 in the case of Windows XP is planned for the next major release. The DNS service in the Windows 2003 server family supports IPv6 transport.

DNS Lookup

For the DNS lookup of IPv6 records, your client needs a resolver that supports the new record type. In my case, I used SuSE Linux host Ford with BIND 9 utilities and my Windows XP host Marvin with the IPv6 stack.

I used *nslookup* to play with my new DNS server. You can also use *dig* and *host* for DNS lookups; they are installed with BIND 9. *nslookup* has many configuration options. It can be run in interactive mode, and you can specify the types of records you want to query. You can set the query mode to either A type records for IPv4 or AAAA type records for IPv6, or set it to "any," in which case *nslookup* will request all records. The *nslookup* version I used did not support the A6 type. The DNS server still sends the information back, which is why you see the "unrecognized record" type in the answer.

 Here is a hint for using *nslookup*: if you want to do a reverse lookup, you cannot use the abbreviated version for an IPv6 address. You have to type the address as, for example, fe80:0:0:0:a00:20ff:fe20:adc2. You can skip leading zeros, but you cannot replace a sequence of zeros with two colons. Newer implementations may change this. Use *nslookup* in debug mode to get additional information.

Figure 9-6 shows the output of nslookup on Marvin.

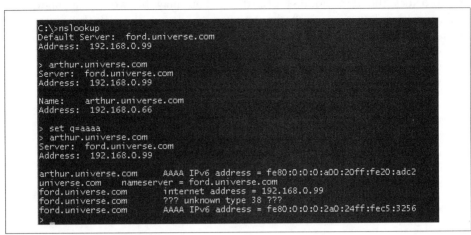

Figure 9-6. Output of nslookup

We first used *nslookup* in interactive mode with the default options. *nslookup* defaults to query type A. Looking up *arthur.universe.com* with the default returned the IPv4 address of arthur (192.168.0.66). Next, we changed the query type to AAAA. The reply returned the IPv6 address of arthur plus additional information about our name server, Ford: its IPv4 address, AAAA type IPv6 address, and A6 type entry. Because this version of *nslookup* did not support A6 type records, the answer was shown as "unknown type 38."

Being curious by nature, I traced the whole communication with Sniffer. Figure 9-7 shows how the same query looks in the trace file.

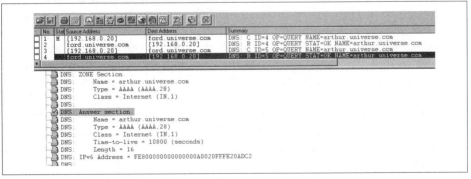

Figure 9-7. DNS lookup in the trace file

The first pair of request-replies is the standard query for the A type record returning the IPv4 address 192.168.0.66. Frame number 3 is the query for which we set the query type to AAAA. Figure 9-7 shows the part of the DNS reply that refers to Arthur's IPv6 address. In the zone section, you can see what we requested. We did *nslookup* for *arthur.universe.com* with the query type set to AAAA. The answer section provides the IPv6 address of Arthur. You may be wondering about the "unknown type" message and the question marks in the *nslookup* output in Figure 9-6. Let's see what's actually in the reply coming from the server. Figure 9-8 shows the authority and additional record section in the same frame.

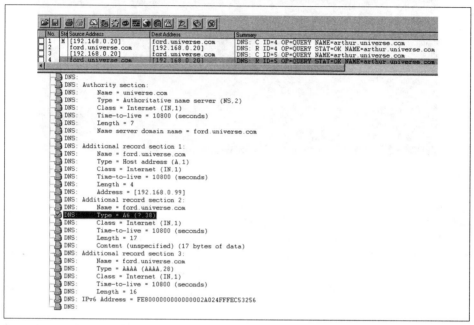

Figure 9-8. Authority and additional record section

The authority section states that the name server for the domain *universe.com* is *ford.universe.com*. The content in the authority section can be seen in the *nslookup* screenshot (Figure 9-6), on the line just after the IPv6 address for the AAAA record of Arthur (near the bottom of the screenshot). Next, in the trace file, we see the additional record section 1. It contains the IPv4 address (A record) for the name server *ford.universe.com*. This refers to the third line in the nslookup output in Figure 9-6. The fourth line in the *nslookup* output is the one beginning with the three question marks and the "unknown type 38" comment. This can also be seen in the trace file. Look at the additional record section 2. Sniffer doesn't decode type 38, but we know that type 38 is the A6 record type. I checked the hexadecimal part of the reply packet in the trace, and following the A6 type value, the IPv6 address for *ford.universe.com* can be seen. The additional record section 3 contains the AAAA record (type 28 decimal, 1C in hex) for *ford.universe.com*, containing the IPv6 address for Ford. This corresponds to the last line in the *nslookup* output.

Issues with DNS Lookups

In practice, there are some issues with DNS lookups where DNS servers do not react as expected when queried for AAAA records. This can lead to unexpected behavior on the client: for instance, a web browser that cannot connect to a web server although connectivity is available because it queries DNS for an AAAA record and, if there is no entry, fails to fall back to IPv4 even though the web server would have an A record with an IPv4 address. There are different causes and cases and, accordingly, different troubleshooting scenarios. If you want to explore this issue further, refer to RFC 4074, "Common Misbehavior Against DNS Queries for IPv6 Addresses."

SLP

The Service Location Protocol (SLP) discovers and selects services in IP networks. SLP Version 2 is specified in RFC 2608. RFC 3111 describes how SLPv2 can be used in IPv6 networks. SLP uses UDP and TCP, so only minor changes are necessary to use SLP on IPv6 networks. SLPv1, which was defined in RFC 2165, does not support IPv6. If you want to use SLP over IPv6, you have to use SLPv2.

SLP is based on three components. A *User Agent* (UA) sends out service requests to find services. *Service Agents* (SA) reply to service requests from UAs. An SA can register its services with a *Directory Agent* (DA). UAs can then send their service requests to the DA, which will answer on behalf of the SAs with a list of the registered services. Most SLP communication is based on multicast messages. SLP also knows scopes that can be used to group services into administrative units.

 For a detailed discussion of SLP concepts, refer to my book *Guide to Service Location Protocol* (*http://www.podbooks.com*). Readers in Europe can order the book at *http://www.sunny.ch*.

The changes made for SLPv2 can be summarized as follows:

- The use for broadcasting of SLP requests was eliminated.
- The format of SLP URLs (service entries) must be able to hold IPv6 addresses.
- SLP must be able to use IPv6 multicast addresses and multicast scopes.
- The propagation of Service Advertisements must be restricted.

When SLP is used over IPv4, it can be configured to use broadcasts for service requests, but this is not recommended. IPv6 no longer supports broadcasts, so if SLP is used over IPv6, it has to use multicast addresses to discover service or directory agents.

Table 9-4 shows the multicast addresses that have been defined for SLP over IPv6.

Table 9-4. Multicast addresses for SLP over IPv6

Multicast address	Description
FF0X:0:0:0:0:0:0:116	Service Agent (SA), used for Service Type and Attribute Request Messages.
FF0X:0:0:0:0:0:0:123	Directory Agent (DA), used by User Agents (UAs) and SAs to discover DAs. Also used by DA for sending unsolicited DA Advertisement messages.
FF0X:0:0:0:0:0:1:1000 to FF0X:0:0:0:0:0:1:13FF	Service Location, used by SAs to join the groups that correspond to the Service Types of the services they advertise. The Service Type string is used to determine the corresponding value in the 1000 to 13FF range, which has been assigned by IANA for this purpose. For an explanation of the algorithm used to calculate the group ID, refer to RFC 3111.

The X in FF0X is the placeholder for the multicast scope to be used for this group ID. For instance, 2 would be link-local scope and 5 would be site-local scope. For a list of the multicast scopes, refer to Table 3-6.

SLP also uses scopes. All SLP agents (i.e., User Agents, Service Agents, and Directory Agents) support scopes, and Service Registration and Service Requests work only if the SLP scope is configured on all agents. Using SLP over IPv6 adds multicast scopes to this scenario. For instance, an SLPv2 agent cannot join a multicast group with a greater multicast scope than itself. If the SA has only a link-local address, it will join multicast scope FF01 and FF02. If the SA is configured with a site-local or global address, it will join multicast groups in the range FF01 to FF05. An SLPv2 agent issues requests using a Source address with a scope no less than the scope of the multicast group it addresses. This prevents, for example, a site-local multicast message being sent from a link-local Source address. An SA and a DA must join all multicast scopes to which an SLP agent may send a message. The maximum scope for SLPv2 messages is site-local (FF05). The service URL in an SLP message can contain a hostname instead of an IP address, in which case the agent has to resolve the name to a set of addresses using DNS.

FTP

FTP has been designed to work over IPv4 supporting 32-bit addresses. With RFC 2428, "FTP Extensions for IPv6 and NATs," a specification was made that allows FTP to work over IPv4 and IPv6. During the time in which both protocols coexist (and this will be a long time), it is important that FTP servers have a mechanism to negotiate the network protocol that should be used for a session.

The RFC specifies two new FTP commands to replace the PORT and PASV commands from the earlier FTP specification (RFC 959). The PORT command is used in active mode to specify a port different from the default ports used for the data connection. It contains IPv4 address information and therefore cannot be used with IPv6 without modification. The PASV command is used to put the server into passive mode, which means the server listens on a specific data port rather than initiating the transfer.

This command includes the host and port address of the FTP server and therefore does not work over IPv6 without modification.

The PORT command is replaced by the EPRT command, which allows the specification of an extended address for the data connection. The extended address specifies the network protocol (IPv4 or IPv6, for instance), as well as the IP address and the port to be used. The EPSV command replaces the PASV command. The EPSV command has an optional argument that allows it to specify the network protocol, if necessary. The server's reply contains only the port number on which it listens, but the format of the answer is similar to the one used for the EPRT command and has a placeholder for network protocol and address information that might be used in the future. The new commands not only accommodate IPv6; they also provide greater flexibility in using FTP through firewalls and NATs (RFC 2428).

The FTP extensions specified in RFC 2428 work with both IPv4 and IPv6. If your FTP implementation supports the new extensions, you are ready to use FTP over IPv6.

Figure 9-9 shows an FTP login over IPv6.

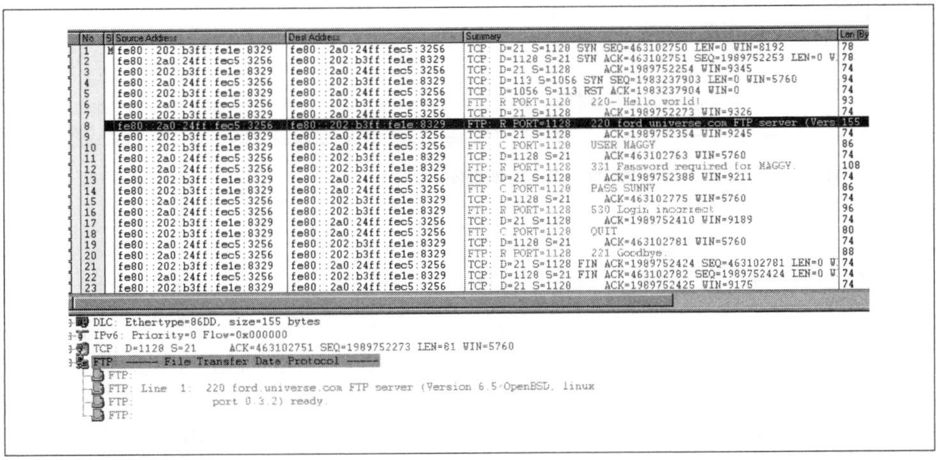

Figure 9-9. FTP session over IPv6

We installed an FTP server on our Linux host, Ford. Then we logged into FTP from our Windows XP host, Marvin. In the detail window, you can see the layers. On the MAC layer, the Ethertype is set to 86DD for IPv6. The IPv6 layer specifies a value of 6 for TCP in the Next Header field (not seen in the figure). On the TCP layer, you can see the port number for FTP, 21. Now you know Maggy's password, right? But who is Maggy?

There are other applications such as Secure Copy (SCP) that provide encrypted file transfers, thus protecting your passwords. These are also ready for IPv6 and have been working in the IPv4 world.

Telnet

Telnet is a virtual terminal protocol used to log into a computer across the Internet or an intranet. RFC 854 contains the Telnet protocol specification, and RFC 855 contains the Telnet options specification. Telnet connects to a remote host by establishing a TCP connection over port 23 and passing keystrokes from the user's keyboard to the remote machine, as if they had been entered on a keyboard attached to the remote host. The Telnet protocol uses TCP for transport. No modifications have to be made to Telnet, because Telnet does not embed addresses in its protocol.

I had a Telnet server running on Windows, accessing it from the Linux host Ford, and also did the opposite—running an IPv6-enabled Telnet server on the Linux host and accessing it with the Microsoft Telnet client. Both ways are no problem. The Telnet protocol works over TCP over IPv6 with the standard Telnet port number 23. Figure 9-10 shows the Telnet session.

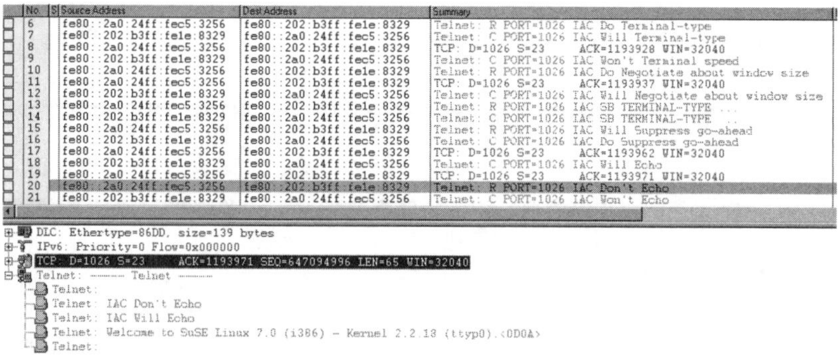

Figure 9-10. A Telnet session over IPv6

The figure shows the negotiation of the Telnet session. In the detail window, you can see the layers: the MAC layer with Ethertype 86DD, the IPv6 layer using TCP value 6 in the Next Header field, the TCP layer using port 23 for Telnet, and the Telnet header. Telnet also sends passwords and all session data in clear text that an intermediary may discover. Software such as SSH provides an encrypted terminal for security. SSH is IPv6-ready today and available on many platforms.

Web Servers

If you want to surf the Internet over IPv6, you need web servers and a browser that support IPv6.

There are different HTTP servers that already support IPv6. Probably the most common one is Apache, which has supported IPv6 since version 2. Version 1.3 can be patched to support IPv6. Whichever HTTP server you use, you must be able to configure it to listen on the HTTP port (usually 80) over IPv6. If you are using proxy servers, you need to make sure that they are enabled for IPv6, too.

If you are looking for references on how to set up Apache 2 on Linux, refer to the web site of the Linux Documentation Project (LDP) at *http://www.tldp.org*. There is one chapter that explains configuration of different daemons, including BIND (*named*) and Apache 2 (*httpd2*).

Browser Support

To browse IPv6 sites, you need a browser that sends out DNS requests for AAAA records and DNS to return an IPv6 address for the name of the web server you are trying to access. In some cases, you can also enter a literal IPv6 address (described in RFC 2732) in your browser. It has the format *http://[2001:DB8:4179::836B:4179]*. Some browsers can use this format. Internet Explorer, included in Windows XP, no longer supports literal IPv6 addresses; however, other browsers on Windows XP can use literal addresses. As an aside, consider how the vast majority of nontechnical Internet users would react or even adapt to having to use the URL cited above to surf the Internet. The colon hexadecimal format of IPv6 addresses will certainly be cumbersome for most users and is very error-prone. This is yet another illustration of the value DNS brings to IPv6 deployments.

If your browser is configured for a proxy server that is not enabled for IPv6, it cannot browse local or remote IPv6 web sites. In this case, you will have to disable the use of the proxy for your IPv6 trips.

If you want to experiment, you can find a list of IPv6-accessible web sites at *http://www.ipv6.org/v6-www.html*. Many of these sites are dual-stack; some can be reached only over IPv6. For Linux users, the best link will probably be *http://www.bieringer.de/linux/IPv6/status*. If you want to test your IPv6 connectivity, try our IPv6-only web site at *http://ipv6.sunny.ch* and say hi when you get there!

Proxy Support and Scenarios

One important goal in a heterogeneous network is to make all services available over as many channels as possible. The question of whether a corporate network will use IPv4 or IPv6 in the near future is the wrong question. Reality for the coming years will be that people/customers use both protocols. In the Internet, there will be web sites available only over IPv4, others available only over IPv6, and hopefully most of them available over both protocols. Internet surfers will use one or the other, or in some cases both protocols. If you want to offer services or a web site to the whole community, you will not get around making it available over both protocols.

In the case of a web site, the easiest way to go may be dual-stack. There may be cases where the addition of IPv6 to your web server cannot be accomplished within a short time for different reasons. In this case, proxies can help you fulfill the protocol requirement.

Proxies can be used in different ways:

- Your hosts in the corporate network are IPv4-only, but you want them to be able to view IPv6-only web sites also. Configure your proxy dual-stack to the outside world, and let your internal users view IPv6 content over IPv4. Obviously this works the other way, too—let IPv6-only clients view IPv4 content over IPv6 through the dual-stack proxy.

- Your web site is IPv4-only for the moment, and you currently cannot add IPv6 support. But you want IPv6 Internet users to be able to view it. Set up a proxy in front of the web server that is dual-stacked. Internet users can use IPv6 to view content on your IPv4-only web server.

If you cannot set up a proxy to provide your IPv4 web site over IPv6 for any reason, use *http://www.6gate.com*. This is the simplest (and free) way to immediately add IPv6 access to your web site. The only thing it requires is a DNS entry. But don't forget, these are temporary solutions. The goal is to configure your web site to be dual-stack as soon as possible.

The next chapter describes integration and transition mechanisms and scenarios that allow for a smooth, step-by-step introduction of IPv6 into your network.

References

Here's a list of the most important RFCs and drafts mentioned in this chapter. Sometimes I list additional subject-related RFCs for your personal further study.

RFCs

- RFC 854, "TELNET PROTOCOL SPECIFICATION," 1983
- RFC 855, "TELNET OPTION SPECIFICATIONS," 1983
- RFC 959, "FILE TRANSFER PROTOCOL (FTP)," 1985
- RFC 1321, "The MD5 Message Digest Algorithm," 1992
- RFC 2104, "HMAC: Keyed-Hashing for Message Authentication," 1997
- RFC 2136, "Dynamic Updates in the Domain Name System," 1997
- RFC 2324, "Hyper Text Coffee Pot Control Protocol (HTCPCP/1.0)," 1998
- RFC 2428, "FTP Extensions for IPv6 and NATs," 1998
- RFC 2608, "Service Location Protocol, Version 2," 1999
- RFC 2845, "Secret Key Transaction Authentication for DNS (TSIG)," 2000

- RFC 3007, "Secure Domain Name System (DNS) Dynamic Update," 2000
- RFC 3008, "Domain Name System Security (DNSSEC) Signing Authority," 2000
- RFC 3111, "Service Location Protocol Modifications for IPv6," 2001
- RFC 3118, "Authentication for DHCP Messages," 2001
- RFC 3315, "Dynamic Host Configuration Protocol for IPv6 (DHCPv6)," 2003
- RFC 3319, "Dynamic Host Configuration Protocol (DHCPv6) Options for Session Initiation Protocol (SIP) Servers," 2003
- RFC 3596, "DNS Extensions to Support IP Version 6," 2003
- RFC 3633, "IPv6 Prefix Options for Dynamic Host Configuration Protocol (DHCP) version 6," 2003
- RFC 3646, "DNS Configuration options for Dynamic Host Configuration Protocol for IPv6 (DHCPv6)," 2003
- RFC 3736, "Stateless Dynamic Host Configuration Protocol (DHCP) Service for IPv6," 2004
- RFC 3898, "Network Information Service (NIS) Configuration Options for Dynamic Host Configuration Protocol for IPv6 (DHCPv6)," 2004
- RFC 3901, "DNS IPv6 Transport Operational Guidelines," 2004
- RFC 4033, "DNS Security Introduction and Requirements," 2005
- RFC 4034, "Resource Records for the DNS Security Extensions," 2005
- RFC 4035, "Protocol Modifications for the DNS Security Extensions," 2005
- RFC 4074, "Common Misbehavior Against DNS Queries for IPv6 Addresses," 2005
- RFC 4075, "Simple Network Time Protocol (SNTP) Configuration Option for DHCPv6," 2005
- RFC 4076, "Renumbering Requirements for Stateless Dynamic Host Configuration Protocol for IPv6 (DHCPv6)," 2005
- RFC 4159, "Deprecation of "ip6.int," 2005
- RFC 4242, "Information Refresh Time Option for Dynamic Host Configuration Protocol for IPv6 (DHCPv6)," 2005
- RFC 4243, "Vendor-Specific Information Suboption for the Dynamic Host Configuration Protocol (DHCP) Relay Agent Option," 2005
- RFC 4280, "Dynamic Host Configuration Protocol (DHCP) Options for Broadcast and Multicast Control Servers," 2005
- RFC 4339, "IPv6 Host Configuration of DNS Server Information Approaches," 2006
- RFC 4472, "Operational Considerations and Issues with IPv6 DNS," 2006

Drafts

Drafts can be found at *http://www.ietf.org/ID.html*. To locate the latest version of a draft, refer to *https://datatracker.ietf.org/public/pidtracker.cgi*. You can enter the draft name without a version number and the most current version will come up. If a draft does not show up, it was either deleted or published as an RFC. Alternatively, you can go to the new Internet drafts database interface at *https://datatracker.ietf.org/public/idindex.cgi*. *http://tools.ietf.org/wg* is also a very useful site. More information on the process of standardization, RFCs, and drafts can be found in Appendix A.

Here's a list of interesting drafts related to the topics or drafts to which I referred in this chapter:

- *draft-ietf-dhc-dual-stack-04.txt*, DHCP: IPv4 and IPv6 Dual-Stack Issues
- *draft-ietf-dhc-dual-stack-merge-01.txt*, Dual-stack clients and merging of data from DHCPv4 and DHCPv6
- *draft-ietf-dhc-ddns-resolution-12.txt*, Resolution of FQDN Conflicts among DHCP Clients
- *draft-ietf-dhc-v6-relay-radius-02.txt*, DHCPv6 Relay agent RADIUS Attribute Option
- *draft-ietf-dhc-dhcpv6-subid-01.txt*, DHCPv6 Relay Agent Subscriber-ID Option
- *draft-ietf-dhc-dhcpv6-remoteid-01.txt*, DHCPv6 Relay Agent Remote ID Option
- *draft-ietf-dhc-dhcpv6-ctep-opt-02.txt*, Configured Tunnel End Point Option for DHCPv6
- *draft-ietf-dhc-dhcpv6-fqdn-05.txt*, The DHCPv6 Client FQDN Option
- *draft-ietf-dhc-dhcpv6-opt-dnsdomain-02.txt*, Domain Suffix Option for DHCPv6
- *draft-ietf-dhc-dhcpv6-agentopt-delegate-00.txt*, DHCP Relay Agent Assignment Notification Option

CHAPTER 10

Interoperability

IPv6 and IPv4 will coexist for many years, and there are a wide range of techniques that make coexistence possible and provide an easy transition. These techniques are separated into three main categories:

Dual-stack techniques
> Allow IPv4 and IPv6 to coexist in the same devices and networks

Tunneling techniques
> Allow the transport of IPv6 traffic over the existing IPv4 infrastructure

Translation techniques
> Allow IPv6-only nodes to communicate with IPv4-only nodes

These techniques can and likely will be used in combination with one another. The migration to IPv6 can be done step-by-step, starting with a single host or subnet. You can migrate your corporate network or parts of it while your ISP still runs only IPv4, or your ISP can upgrade to IPv6 while your corporate network still runs IPv4. This chapter describes the techniques available today for each of these categories. RFC 4213, "Basic Transition Mechanisms for IPv6 Hosts and Routers," describes the dual-stack technique and configured tunneling. As IPv6 grows into our networks, there will be new tools and mechanisms to ease the transition further.

Dual-Stack Techniques

A *dual-stack node* has complete support for both protocol versions. This type of node is often referred to as an *IPv6/IPv4 node*. In communication with an IPv6 node, such a node behaves like an IPv6-only node; in communication with an IPv4 node, it behaves like an IPv4-only node. Implementations may have a configuration switch to enable or disable one of the stacks, so this node type can have three modes of operation. When the IPv4 stack is enabled and the IPv6 stack is disabled, the node behaves like an IPv4-only node. When the IPv6 stack is enabled and the IPv4 stack disabled, it behaves like an IPv6-only node. When both the IPv4 and IPv6 stacks are enabled, the node can use both protocols. An IPv6/IPv4 node has at least one address for each protocol version. It uses IPv4 mechanisms to be configured for an IPv4 address (static configuration or DHCP) and uses IPv6 mechanisms to be configured for an IPv6 address (static configuration or autoconfiguration).

DNS is used with both protocol versions to resolve names and IP addresses. An IPv6/IPv4 node needs a DNS resolver that is capable of resolving both types of DNS address records. The DNS A record resolves IPv4 addresses, and the DNS AAAA (referred to as quad-A) record resolves IPv6 addresses.

 For a detailed discussion of IPv6 DNS record types, refer to Chapter 9.

In some cases, DNS has been configured to advertise only an IPv4 or an IPv6 address. If the host that is to be resolved is a dual-stack host, DNS might return both types of addresses. Hopefully, in this case, both the DNS resolver on the client and an application using DNS will have configuration options that let us specify orders or filters of how to use the addresses (i.e., preferred protocol settings). Generally, applications that are written to run on dual-stack nodes need a mechanism to determine whether they are communicating with an IPv6 peer or an IPv4 peer. Note that the DNS resolver may run over an IPv4 or IPv6 network, but the worldwide DNS tree will only become fully reachable over IPv6 over time.

A *dual-stack network* is an infrastructure in which both IPv4 and IPv6 forwarding is enabled on routers. The disadvantage of this technique is that you must perform a full network software upgrade to run the two separate protocol stacks. All tables (e.g., routing tables) are kept simultaneously with routing protocols being configured for both protocols. For network management, on some operating systems you may still have separate commands depending on the protocol (e.g., *ping* for IPv4 and *ping6* for IPv6), and it takes more memory and CPU power.

Tunneling Techniques

Tunneling mechanisms can be used to deploy an IPv6 forwarding infrastructure while the overall IPv4 infrastructure is still the basis and either should not or cannot be modified or upgraded.

Tunneling is also called *encapsulation*. With encapsulation, one protocol (in our case, IPv6) is encapsulated in the header of another protocol (in our case, IPv4) and forwarded over the infrastructure of the second protocol (IPv4). The process of encapsulation has three components:

- Encapsulation at the tunnel entry point
- Decapsulation at the tunnel exit point
- Tunnel management

So tunneling can be used to carry IPv6 traffic by encapsulating it in IPv4 packets and tunneling it over the IPv4 routing infrastructure. For instance, if your provider still has an IPv4-only infrastructure, tunneling allows you to have a corporate IPv6 network and tunnel through your ISP's IPv4 network to reach other IPv6 hosts or networks. Or you can deploy IPv6 islands in your corporate network while the backbone is still IPv4. IPv6 packets traveling from one IPv6 island to another can traverse the backbone encapsulated in IPv4 packets. The tunneling techniques and the encapsulation of IPv6 packets in IPv4 packets are defined in several RFCs, such as RFC 2473, "Generic Packet Tunneling in IPv6 Specification," RFC 4213, "Basic Transition Mechanisms for IPv6 Hosts and Routers," and RFC 3056, "Connection of IPv6 Domains via IPv4 Clouds (6to4)," which differentiate two general types of tunneling:

Manually configured tunneling of IPv6 over IPv4
> IPv6 packets are encapsulated in IPv4 packets to be carried over IPv4 routing infrastructures. These are point-to-point tunnels that need to be configured manually.

Automatic tunneling of IPv6 over IPv4
> IPv6 nodes can use different types of addresses, such as 6to4 or ISATAP addresses, to dynamically tunnel IPv6 packets over an IPv4 routing infrastructure. These special IPv6 unicast addresses carry an IPv4 address in some parts of the IPv6 address fields.

How Tunneling Works

The concepts discussed in this section apply to tunneling in general. The next two paragraphs discuss the difference between configured tunnels and automatic tunneling. Figure 10-1 shows two IPv6 networks connected through an IPv4-only network.

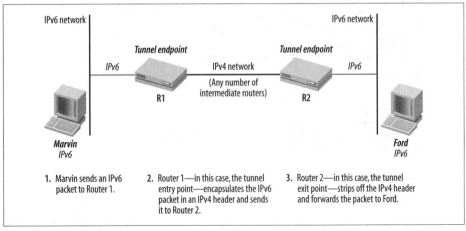

Figure 10-1. Encapsulation and tunneling

Host Marvin is on an IPv6 network and wants to send an IPv6 packet to host Ford on another IPv6 network. The network between router R1 and router R2 is an IPv4-only network. Router R1 is the *tunnel entry point*. Marvin sends the IPv6 packet to router R1 (step 1 in Figure 10-1). When router R1 receives the packet addressed to Ford, it encapsulates the packet in an IPv4 header and forwards it to router R2 (step 2 in Figure 10-1), which is the *tunnel exit point*. Router R2 decapsulates the packet and forwards it to its final destination (step 3 in Figure 10-1). Between R1 and R2, any number of IPv4 routers is possible.

A tunnel has two endpoints: the tunnel entry point and the tunnel exit point. In the scenario in Figure 10-1, the tunnel end points are two routers, but the tunnel can be configured in different ways. It can be set up router-to-router, host-to-router, host-to-host, or router-to-host. Depending on which scenario is used, the tunnel entry and exit point can be either a host or a router.

The steps for the encapsulation of the IPv6 packet are the following:

1. The entry point of the tunnel decrements the IPv6 hop limit by one, encapsulates the packet in an IPv4 header, and transmits the encapsulated packet through the tunnel. If necessary, the IPv4 packet is fragmented.

2. The exit point of the tunnel receives the encapsulated packet. It checks whether the source of the packet (tunnel entry point) is an acceptable source (according to its configuration). If the packet was fragmented, the exit point reassembles it. Then, the exit point removes the IPv4 header and processes the IPv6 packet to its original destination.

Figure 10-2 shows the encapsulation of an IPv6 packet in an IPv4 packet.

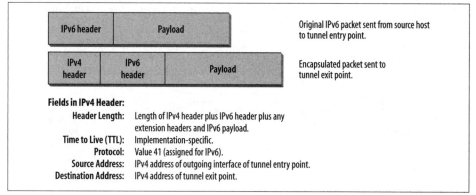

Figure 10-2. Encapsulation

The following fields in the IPv4 header are interesting to note: the Total Length field in the IPv4 header contains the length of the IPv4 header plus the length of the IPv6 packet, which is treated as the payload. If the encapsulated packet has to be fragmented, there will be corresponding values in the Flags and Fragment Offset fields.

The value of the Time to Live (TTL) field depends on the implementation used. The Protocol Number is set to 41, the value assigned for IPv6. Thus, if you want to analyze your tunneled IPv6 traffic, you can set a filter in your analyzer to display the packets containing the value 41 in the Protocol Number field. The IPv4 Source address is usually the address of the outgoing interface of the tunnel entry point. It should also be configurable for cases where automatic address selection may produce different results over time (multiple addresses/interfaces). The IPv4 Destination address is the IPv4 address of the tunnel exit point. The IPv6-over-IPv4 tunnel is considered a single hop. The Hop Limit field in the IPv6 header is therefore decremented by one. This hides the existence of a tunnel to the end user, and is not detectable by common tools such as *traceroute*. Figure 10-3 shows an encapsulated IPv6 packet in the trace file.

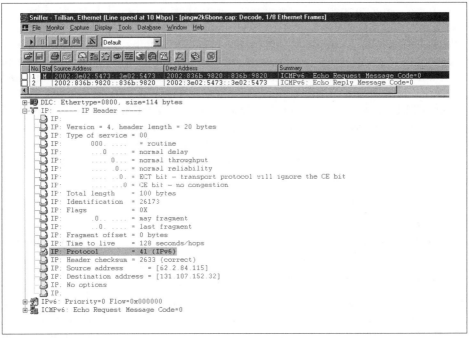

Figure 10-3. Encapsulation in the trace file

This is a ping generated on Marvin, our Windows host. We were pinging a host on the 6Bone. The TTL is set to 128. The Protocol field shows value 41 for IPv6, which identifies this packet as an encapsulated packet. The Source address 62.2.84.115 is the IPv4 address of Marvin, which was configured for this address by a DHCP server. It is the tunnel entry point. The Destination address is the IPv4 address of a 6to4 relay router (explained later in this chapter) in the 6Bone, the tunnel exit point. This router can forward the packet to an IPv6 network, the 6Bone in this case. Compare these IPv4 addresses with the IPv6 Source and Destination addresses (which can be seen in the highlighted summary line above the detail screen). Use your Windows calculator to find out that the IPv6 Source and Destination addresses have the 6to4 prefix of 2002 plus the IPv4 address in hexadecimal notation in the low-order 32 bits. This is an example of a host-to-host automatic tunnel because we were actually pinging the 6to4 router.

If an IPv4 router from within the tunnel generates an ICMPv4 error message, the router sends the message to the tunnel entry point because that host is the source of that packet. If the packet contains enough information about the original, encapsulated IPv6 packet, the tunnel entry point may send an ICMPv6 message back to the original source of the packet.

When the tunnel exit point receives an IPv4 datagram with a protocol value of 41, it knows that this packet has been encapsulated. Before forwarding a decapsulated IPv6 packet, the tunnel endpoint must verify that the tunnel Source address is acceptable. Thus, unacceptable ingress into the network can be avoided. If the tunnel is a bidirectional configured tunnel, this check is done by comparing the Source address of the encapsulated packet with the configured address of the other side of the tunnel. For unidirectional configured tunnels, the tunnel must be configured with a list of source IPv4 address prefixes that are acceptable. By default, this list is empty, which means that the tunnel endpoint has to be explicitly configured to allow forwarding of decapsulated packets. In the case of fragmentation, it reassembles the packets and removes the IPv4 header. Before delivering the IPv6 packet to the final destination, it checks to see if the IPv6 Source address is valid. The following Source addresses are considered invalid:

- All multicast addresses (FF00::/8)
- The loopback address (::1)
- All IPv4-compatible IPv6 addresses (::/96), excluding the unspecified address for Duplicate Address Detection (::/128)
- All IPv4-mapped IPv6 addresses (::ffff:0:0/96)

Both tunnel endpoints need to have a link-local IPv6 address. The IPv4 address of that same interface may be the interface identifier for the IPv6 address. For example, a host with an IPv4 address of 192.168.0.2 may have a link-local address of FE80::192.168.0.2/64.

The specification contains rules that apply tunnel Source address verification and ingress filtering (RFCs 2827 and 3704) in general to packets before they are decapsulated. If further security mechanisms are desirable, a tunneling scheme with authentication can be used—for example, IPsec (preferable) or Generic Routing Encapsulation (GRE) with a preconfigured secret key (RFC 2890). Since the configured tunnels are set up manually, setting up the keying material is not a problem.

Automatic Tunneling

Automatic tunneling allows IPv6/IPv4 nodes to communicate over an IPv4 infrastructure without the need for tunnel destination preconfiguration. In a previous specification (RFC 2893, obsoleted by RFC 4213), the tunnel endpoint address was determined by an IPv4-compatible Destination address. RFC 4213 removes the description of automatic tunneling and IPv4-compatible addresses and refers to 6to4 (discussed later in this chapter), which does not use IPv4-compatible IPv6 addresses. 6to4 has its own IPv6 address format, which includes the IPv4 address of the tunnel endpoint in the prefix and therefore allows for automatic tunneling.

Configured Tunneling (RFC 4213)

Configured tunneling is IPv6-over-IPv4 tunneling where the IPv4 tunnel endpoint addresses are determined by configuration information on the tunnel endpoints. All tunnels are assumed to be bidirectional. The tunnel provides a virtual point-to-point link to the IPv6 layer using the configured IPv4 addresses as the lower layer endpoint addresses. The administrative work to manage configured tunnels is higher than with automatic tunnels, but for security reasons, it may be desirable, as it provides more possibilities to control the forwarding path of IPv6 packets.

RFC 4213 discusses the configuration and issues to be taken care of, such as determination of valid tunnel endpoint addresses (ingress filtering), how to deal with ICMPv4 or ICMPv6 messages, tunnel MTU sizes, fragmentation, the header fields, Neighbor Discovery (ND) over tunnels, and security considerations.

IPv6/IPv4 hosts connected to network segments with no IPv6 routers can be configured with a static route to an IPv6 router in the Internet at the other side of an IPv4 tunnel; this enables communication with a remote IPv6 world. In this case, the IPv6 address of an IPv6/IPv4 router at the other end of the tunnel is added into the routing table as a default route. Now all IPv6 Destination addresses match the route and can be tunneled through the IPv4 infrastructure. This default route has a mask of zero and is used only if there are no other routes with a more specific matching mask.

Encapsulation in IPv6 (RFC 2473)

RFC 2473 specifies the model and the generic mechanisms for encapsulation with IPv6. Most of the rules discussed in this chapter about tunneling in IPv4 apply to tunneling in IPv6. The main difference is that in tunneling in IPv6, the packets are encapsulated in an IPv6 header and sent through an IPv6 network. The packet being encapsulated can be an IPv4 packet, an IPv6 packet, or any other protocol. The tunnel entry point prepends the IPv6 header and, if needed, one or a set of Extension headers in front of the original packet header. Whatever the tunnel entry point prepends are called the *Tunnel IPv6 headers*. Figure 10-4 shows the Tunnel IPv6 headers in the packet view.

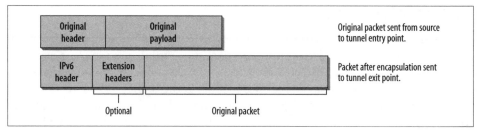

			Original packet sent from source to tunnel entry point.
Original header	Original payload		

| IPv6 header | Extension headers | | Packet after encapsulation sent to tunnel exit point. |

Optional   Original packet

Figure 10-4. Tunnel IPv6 headers from the packet view

In the IPv6 header applied by the tunnel entry point, the Source address is the address of the tunnel entry point node, and the Destination address is the address of the tunnel exit point node. The source node of the original packet can be the same node as the tunnel entry point. The original packet, including its header, becomes the payload of the encapsulated packet. The header of the original packet is treated according to standard forwarding rules. If the header is an IPv4 header, the TTL field is decremented by one. If it is an IPv6 header, the Hop Limit field is decremented by one. The network between the tunnel entry point and the tunnel exit point is thus virtually just one hop, no matter how many actual hops there are in between.

The Tunnel IPv6 header is processed according to the IPv6 protocol rules. Extension headers, if added, are processed as though the packet were a standard IPv6 packet. For example, a Hop-by-Hop Options header would be processed by every node listed in the Hop-by-Hop Options field. A Destination Options header would be processed by the destination host—i.e., the tunnel exit point. All these options are configured on the tunnel entry point. An example of the use of a Destination Options header is the configuration of a Tunnel Encapsulation Limit Option (RFC 2473). This option may be used when tunnels are nested. One hop of a tunnel can be the entry point of another tunnel. In this case, we have *nested tunnels*. The first tunnel is called the *outer tunnel*, and the second tunnel is called the *inner tunnel*. The inner tunnel entry point treats the whole packet received from the outer tunnel as the original packet and applies the same rules as shown in Figure 10-6. The only natural limit to the number of nested tunnels is the maximum IPv6 packet size. Every encapsulation adds the size of the tunnel IPv6 headers. This would allow for something around 1,600 nested tunnels, which is not realistic. Also, consider the case in which the packet has to be fragmented. If it has to be fragmented again because the additional tunnel IPv6 headers have increased the packet size, the number of fragments is doubled. So a mechanism was needed to limit the number of nested tunnels. It is specified in RFC 2473 and is called the Tunnel Encapsulation Limit Option. This option is carried in a Destination Option header and has the format shown in Figure 10-5.

The Option Type field has 1 byte and the decimal value 4, specifying the Tunnel Encapsulation Limit Option. The Option Data Length field has the decimal value 1, specifying the length of the following Option field. In this case, the Option field has a size of 1 byte and contains the actual value for the Tunnel Encapsulation Limit Option. The value in this field specifies how many further levels of encapsulation are

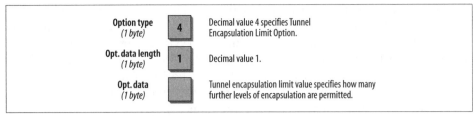

Figure 10-5. Format of the Tunnel Encapsulation Limit Option

permitted. If the value is zero, the packet is discarded and an ICMP Parameter Problem message is sent back to the source (the tunnel entry point of the previous tunnel). If the value is nonzero, the packet is encapsulated and forwarded. In this case, a new Tunnel Encapsulation Limit Option has to be applied with a value of one less than the limit received in the packet being encapsulated. If the packet received does not have a tunnel encapsulation limit, but this tunnel entry point has one configured, the tunnel entry point must apply a destination options header and include the configured value.

Loopback encapsulation should be avoided. Loopback encapsulation happens when a node encapsulates a packet originating from itself and destined to itself. IPv6 implementations should prevent this by checking and rejecting configurations of tunnels where both the entry and exit points belong to the same host. Another undesirable situation is a *routing-loop nested encapsulation*. This situation happens if a packet from an inner tunnel reenters an outer tunnel from which it has not yet exited. This can be controlled only by a combination of the original packet's hop limit and the configuration of tunnel encapsulation limits.

Let's have a closer look at a Tunnel IPv6 Header (Figure 10-6).

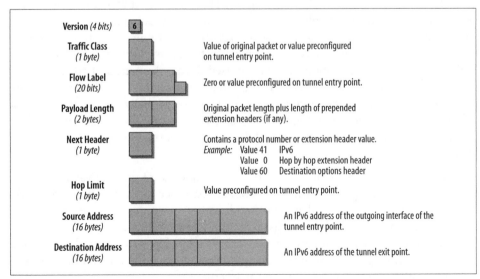

Figure 10-6. The Tunnel IPv6 header

The fields of a standard IPv6 header were discussed in Chapter 2. Interesting values here are the following: the values for Traffic Class, Flow Label, and Hop Limit can be preconfigured on the tunnel entry point. The Payload Length has the value for the packet length of the original packet plus the size of any Extension headers prepended by the tunnel entry point. The Source and Destination Addresses of the Tunnel IPv6 header contain the IPv6 addresses of the tunnel entry and exit points, respectively. Note that a host configured as a tunnel entry point must support fragmentation of packets that it encapsulates. Encapsulated packets may exceed the Path MTU of the tunnel. Because the tunnel entry point is considered the source of the encapsulated packet, it must fragment it if needed. The tunnel exit point node will reassemble the packet. If the original packet is an IPv4 packet with the Don't Fragment bit set, the tunnel entry point discards the packet and sends an ICMP Destination Unreachable message with the code "fragmentation needed and DF set" back to the source of the packet.

Transition Mechanisms

The next sections describe other transition mechanisms available today. They are to be seen as a toolbox. Analyze your environment and your requirements to find the optimal tools or combination of tools that meet your goals. Some of these mechanisms are already standardized, such as 6to4 and Teredo; others, such as DSTM, are still in draft.

6to4 (RFC 3056)

RFC 3056, "Connection of IPv6 Domains via IPv4 Clouds," specifies a mechanism for IPv6 sites to communicate with each other over the IPv4 network without explicit tunnel setup. This mechanism is called *6to4*. The wide area IPv4 network is treated as a unicast point-to-point link layer, and the native IPv6 domains communicate via 6to4 routers, also referred to as 6to4 gateways. Note that only the gateway needs to be 6to4 aware. No changes have to be made to the hosts within the 6to4 network. This is intended as a transition mechanism used during the period of coexistence of IPv4 and IPv6. It will not be used as a permanent solution. The IPv6 packets are encapsulated in IPv4 at the 6to4 gateway. At least one globally unique IPv4 unicast address is required for this configuration. The IANA has assigned a special prefix for the 6to4 scheme: 2002::/16. Figure 10-7 shows the format of the 6to4 prefix in detail.

The 32 bits after the prefix 2002::/16 are the IPv4 address of the gateway in hex representation. This leaves you with 80 bits of address space for your internal network. 16 bits are used for the local network addressing, so you can create 65,536 networks! The remaining 64 bits are used for the interface identifier of the nodes on your network; that is, 2^{64} nodes per network. It looks like getting familiar with the extended address space has some advantages. Now all the hosts on your network can communicate with other 6to4 hosts on the Internet.

3 bits	13 bits	32 bits	16 bits	64 bits
FP 001	TLA 0x0002	IPv4 Addr.	SLA ID	Interface ID

Prefix length: 48 bits
Notation: 2002:V4ADDR::/48

Figure 10-7. Format of the 6to4 prefix

 In Figure 10-7, there are terms such as FP (Format Prefix), TLA (Top Level Aggregator), and SLA (Site Level Aggregator). They come from an older IPv6 address architecture specification (RFC 2374). At the time when 6to4 was specified, RFC 2374 was still valid.

When a node in a 6to4 network wants to communicate with a node in another 6to4 network, no tunnel configuration is necessary. The tunnel entry point takes the IPv4 address of the tunnel exit point from the IPv6 address of the destination. To communicate with an IPv6 node in a remote IPv6 network, you need a *6to4 relay router*. The relay router is a router configured for 6to4 and IPv6. It connects your 6to4 network to the native IPv6 network. It announces the 6to4 prefix of 2002::/16 into the native IPv6 network.

Figure 10-8 shows the 6to4 components and how they play together.

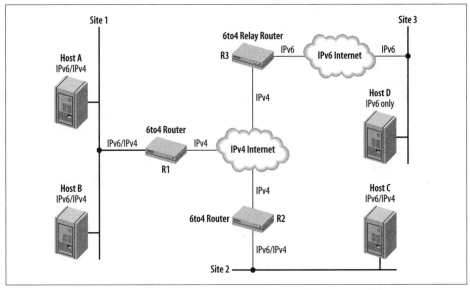

Figure 10-8. 6to4 components

The figure shows the different possible communication paths. Within site 1, hosts A and B can communicate using IPv6. To communicate with host C in site 2 (another

6to4 site), the packets are sent to router R1 in site 1. Router R1 encapsulates them in IPv4 and forwards them to Router R2 in site 2. Router R1 learns the IPv4 address of Router R2 from the IPv6 Destination address. Router R2 decapsulates the packet and forwards the original IPv6 packet to host C. To communicate with an IPv6-only host in the Internet, host A or B sends its IPv6 packets to Router R1. Router R1 encapsulates them in IPv4 and forwards them to the Relay Router R3. Router R3 decapsulates the packet and forwards the original IPv6 packet over the IPv6 routing infrastructure to host D.

Router R1 internally advertises the 6to4 prefix in its Router Advertisements (if configured to do so). The IPv6 hosts in site 1 can use the RA for Stateless autoconfiguration of their IPv6 address. The prefix announced has the format `2002:IPv4-address-R1:subnet::/64`.

To connect a 6to4 network with the IPv6 Internet, a convenient 6to4 relay can be evaluated and manually configured. The manual configuration has the advantage of providing control over the relays used but creates more administrative work. In case the preconfigured relay is not available, another relay needs to be configured.

 There are a number of public 6to4 relay routers in the Internet that you can use. For a list, go to *http://www.kfu.com/~nsayer/6to4/*.

RFC 3068 defines a 6to4 relay router anycast address to simplify the configuration of 6to4 gateways that need a default route to find a 6to4 relay router on the Internet. IANA assigned an IPv4 6to4 Relay anycast prefix of `192.88.99.0/24`. The assigned anycast address corresponds to the first node in the prefix, e.g., `192.88.99.1`. The 6to4 routers have to be configured with a default route pointing to this anycast address. Using this address means that 6to4 packets are routed to the nearest available 6to4 relay router automatically. If one 6to4 relay goes down, you do not need to reconfigure your 6to4 gateway; packets will automatically be rerouted to the next available relay. With the ongoing deployment of IPv6 in commercial networks, the number of public 6to4 relay routers will increase. If a host wishes to communicate with a node on a native IPv6 subnet (i.e., Destination address `3ffe:b00:c18:1::10`), the IPv4 header Destination address will be the reserved anycast address `192.88.99.1` and will be delivered to the nearest 6to4 relay router. In the reverse, a native IPv6 host that wants to send packets to a host in a 6to4 cloud will route its packets to the nearest 6to4 relay router advertising the prefix `2002::/16`.

ISATAP

The Intra-Site Automatic Tunnel Addressing Protocol (ISATAP) is designed to provide IPv6 connectivity for dual-stack nodes over an IPv4-based network. It treats the IPv4 network as one large link-layer network and allows those dual-stack nodes to automatically tunnel between themselves. You can use this automatic tunneling mechanism regardless of whether you have global or private IPv4 addresses. ISATAP addresses embed an IPv4 address in the EUI-64 interface identifier. Note that all nodes in an ISATAP network need to support ISATAP. ISATAP is experimental and specified in RFC 4214.

Figure 10-9 shows the format of the ISATAP address.

64 bits	32 bits	32 bits
Prefix	00 00 5E FE / 02 00 5E FE	IPv4 address

00: private IPv4 address
02: public IPv4 address
00 00 5E: IANA's OUI
FE: Identifies IPv6 address with embedded IPv4 address

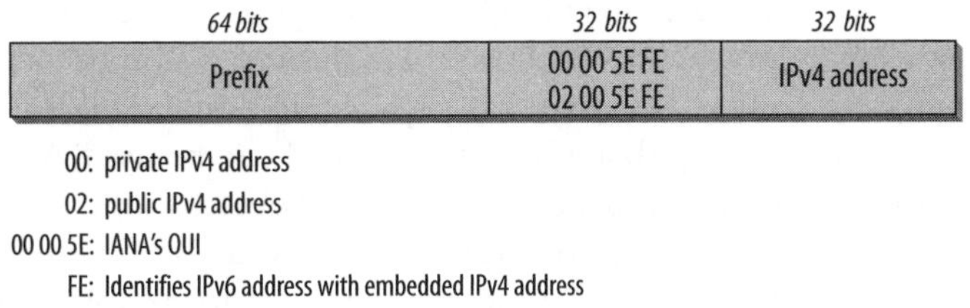

Figure 10-9. The format of the ISATAP address

The ISATAP address has a standard 64-bit prefix that can be link-local, site-local, a 6to4 prefix, or can belong to the global unicast range. The Interface identifier is built using the IANA OUI 00-00-5E, which follows the prefix. The following byte is a type field, and the value FE indicates that this address contains an embedded IPv4 address. The last four bytes contain the IPv4 address, which can be written in dotted decimal notation. The format of the address can thus be summarized as 64bitPrefix: 5EFE:IPv4address. For instance, if you have an assigned prefix of 2001:DB8:510::/64 and an IPv4 address of 62.2.84.115, your ISATAP address is 2001:DB8:510::200: 5EFE:3e02:5473. Alternatively, you can write 2001:DB8:510::200:5EFE:62.2.84.115. The corresponding link-local address would be FE80::200:5EFE:62.2.84.115.

ISATAP interfaces form ISATAP interface identifiers from their IPv4 addresses and use them to create link-local ISATAP addresses. The neighbor discovery mechanisms specified in RFC 2461 are used (router and prefix discovery).

Using ISATAP, IPv6 hosts within an IPv4 intranet can communicate with each other. If they want to communicate with IPv6 hosts on the Internet, such as 6Bone hosts, a border router must be configured; it can be an ISATAP router or a 6to4 gateway. The IPv4 addresses of the hosts within the site do not need to be public. They are embedded in the address with the standard prefix and are therefore unique and routable. Large numbers of ISATAP hosts can be assigned to one ISATAP prefix. If you deploy IPv6 on a segment in your corporate network, you configure one of the native IPv6 nodes with an ISATAP interface, and it acts as a router between the native IPv6 segment and ISATAP hosts in the IPv4 segments.

Teredo

6to4 makes IPv6 available over an IPv4 infrastructure using public IPv4 addresses. ISATAP enables deployment of IPv6 hosts within a site regardless of whether it uses public or private IPv4 addresses. Teredo is designed to make IPv6 available to hosts through one or more layers of NAT by tunneling packets over UDP. It is specified in RFC 4380.

Many Internet users, especially many home users, can access the Internet only through NATs (Network Address Translation). NATs create issues when tunneling IPv6 over an IPv4 infrastructure mainly for two reasons: first, NAT users have a private IPv4 address, and second, many NATs are configured to perform ingress filtering and do not allow many types of payload to go through. With tunneling, the IPv6 packet is the payload of IPv4. Mechanisms such as 6to4 often fail in these environments because they require a public IPv4 address. 6to4 can be used in NAT environments if the 6to4 router runs on the same box as NAT. In all other cases, other mechanisms have to be chosen. In our future IPv6 world, we will no longer need NATs, but for the coming transition time, we will have to deal with them. Therefore, IPv6 developers are working on mechanisms to allow users sitting behind NATs to access the IPv6 world by tunneling IPv6 packets in UDP. One of these mechanisms is Teredo.

The following terms are used with Teredo:

Teredo Service
    The transmission of IPv6 packets over UDP.

Teredo Client
    A node that has access to the IPv4 Internet and needs access to the IPv6 Internet.

Teredo Server
    A node that has access to the IPv4 Internet through a public IPv4 address and is used to provide IPv6 connectivity to Teredo clients.

Teredo Relay
    An IPv6 router that can receive traffic destined to Teredo clients and forward it using the Teredo service.

Teredo IPv6 Service Prefix
    An IPv6 addressing prefix used to construct the IPv6 address of Teredo clients. The global Teredo prefix assigned by IANA is 2001:0000::/32.

Teredo UDP Port
    The UDP port number at which Teredo Servers are waiting for packets. The value of this port is 3544.

Teredo Bubble
    A minimal IPv6 packet made of an IPv6 header and a null payload (payload type is set to 59, No Next Header). Teredo clients and relays use bubbles to create a mapping in a NAT.

Teredo Service Port
    The port from which the Teredo client sends Teredo packets. This port is attached to one of the client's IPv4 addresses.

Teredo Server Address
The IPv4 address of the Teredo Server.

Teredo-mapped Address and Teredo-mapped Port
A global IPv4 address and a UDP port that results from the translation of the IPv4 address and UDP port of a client's Teredo service port by one or more NATs. The client learns these values through the Teredo protocol.

Teredo IPv6 Client Prefix
A global IPv6 prefix composed of the Teredo IPv6 service prefix and the Teredo server address.

Teredo Node Identifier
A 64-bit identifier that contains the UDP port and IPv4 address at which a client can be reached through the Teredo service. A flag indicates the type of NAT through which the client accesses the IPv4 Internet.

Teredo IPv6 Address
A Teredo IPv6 address obtained by combining a Teredo IPv6 client prefix and a Teredo node identifier.

Teredo Refresh Interval
The interval during which a Teredo IPv6 address is expected to remain valid in the absence of "refresh" traffic. The interval depends on configuration parameters of the local NAT(s) in the path to the Teredo server. By default, clients assume an interval value of 30 seconds.

Teredo Secondary Port
A UDP port used to send or receive packets in order to determine the appropriate value of the refresh interval, but not used to carry any Teredo traffic.

Teredo IPv6 Discovery Address
An IPv4 multicast address used to discover other Teredo clients on the IPv4 subnet. The multicast address is 224.0.0.253.

The Teredo service transports IPv6 packets a payload of UDP, which has been chosen over TCP for performance reasons.

Research has shown that most implemented NATs are either of type Cone NAT or Restricted Cone NAT. Teredo supports Cone NATs, Restricted Cone NATS, and Port-restricted Cone NATs. Symmetric NATs are not supported by Teredo.

RFC 2663, "IP Network Address Translator (NAT) Terminology and Considerations," provides a good overview of the terminology and the different types of NAT. *Draft-ietf-v6ops-nap-02.txt* goes into more details about NAT issues, IPv6 networks, and Network Architecture Protection (NAP).

The Teredo design aims to provide robust access to IPv6 networks. This design creates some overhead. Teredo is only to be used if no other, more direct access is possible.

For instance, if it is possible to implement a 6to4 gateway on a NAT, this is the preferable solution.

A Teredo address has the format shown in Figure 10-10.

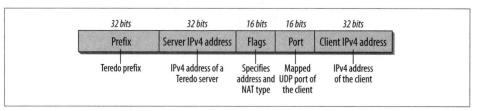

Figure 10-10. Format of the Teredo Address

The Teredo Service Prefix has 32 bits and is 2001:0000::/32. The Server IPv4 field has a length of 32 bits and contains the IPv4 address of the Teredo server. The Flags field has 16 bits and defines the address and the NAT type used. The 16-bit Port field contains the mapped UDP port of the Teredo Service on the client; the Client IPv4 field contains the mapped IPv4 address of the client. The bits in the Port and Client address field are all obfuscated. Each bit in the address and port number is reversed.

A Teredo client must be preconfigured with the IPv4 address of its Teredo Server. On booting, it sends a Router solicitation to the All-Routers multicast address from its link-local IPv6 address. The Router solicitation is sent to the IPv4 address of the Teredo server over UDP. The Router advertisement coming back from the Teredo Server contains the Teredo IPv6 Service prefix. The client builds its Teredo IPv6 address by combining the prefix with the reversed values for address and port.

When the Teredo Server forwards packets from Teredo clients, it encapsulates the IPv6 packet in a UDP packet. It builds the IPv4 address and the UDP port for the destination from the destination IPv6 address. It uses its own IPv4 address as Source address and the Teredo UDP port (3544) as source port. The Teredo Server's job is to forward packets from Teredo clients over UDP to the right Destination address and to forward packets for Teredo clients coming from outside to the right client internally.

The Teredo Relay is an IPv6 router announcing the Teredo Service prefix to the outside world using regular IPv6 routing mechanisms.

Silkroad

Silkroad is a new mechanism under development that also allows nodes sitting behind a NAT to access the IPv6 Internet. It uses a Silkroad Navigator and a Silkroad Access router. The main difference from Teredo is that Silkroad supports all types of NAT, including Symmetric NATs, and does not need a special prefix.

The Silkroad draft is in an early stage and we do not know of any implementations so far, so I don't go into more details in describing the specification. The future will show whether and how it is implemented and used.

Proto 41 Forwarding

Some NAT implementations allow the configuration of IPv6 tunnels from inside of the private LAN to routers or tunnel servers in the Internet. This is a simple and helpful way to provide IPv6 nodes and IPv6 networks behind a NAT with access to the IPv6 Internet. This should only be used if no other mechanisms such as 6to4 or native IPv6 are possible.

A tunnel client (host or router) with a private IPv4 address and a connection to the Internet through an IPv4-only NAT box can use a Tunnel Broker or an IPv6 router to create an IPv6 tunnel. Many NAT boxes can be configured to forward packets based on the protocol value of 41 (for IPv6) in the IPv4 header. This provides an opportunity to rapidly deploy a huge number of IPv6 nodes and networks.

Most of the existing solutions for the transition to IPv6 rely in tunnels assuming that the client endpoint is an IPv6-capable router. However, nowadays the installed base of IPv4-only NAT boxes/routers is still quite large, while most of the client operating systems already support IPv6.

Tunnel Broker

Tunnel Brokers can be seen as virtual IPv6 providers providing IPv6 Internet connectivity to users that already have an IPv4 connection to the Internet. The Tunnel Broker is specified in RFC 3053.

Figure 10-11 illustrates how the Tunnel Broker works.

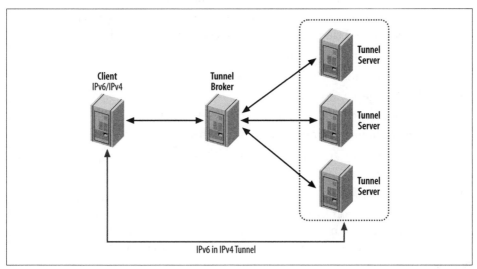

Figure 10-11. How the Tunnel Broker works

A user desiring an IPv6 connection registers with the Tunnel Broker. The Tunnel Broker manages the establishment, maintenance, and deletion of the tunnel on behalf of the user. The Tunnel Broker can share the data load across several Tunnel Servers. The Tunnel Broker sends the configuration information to a Tunnel Server when it wants to establish, change, or delete a tunnel. The Tunnel Broker also registers the addresses in DNS if it is configured to do so. A Tunnel Broker must be reachable with an IPv4 address. It can also have an IPv6 address, but it is not required. The communication between Tunnel Broker and Tunnel Server can run over either IPv4 or IPv6.

A Tunnel Server is a dual-stack router connected to the global Internet. When it receives configuration information from the Tunnel Broker, it establishes, changes, or deletes the server part of the tunnel.

The client is a dual-stack host or router connected to the Internet over IPv4. When it wants to register for an IPv6 connection with the Tunnel Broker, it should authenticate with standard procedures (e.g., with RADIUS). This way, unauthorized use of the tunnel service can be avoided. So the Tunnel Broker provides access control to the tunnel service. Once the client is authorized, it provides its IPv4 address, a name for the registration of its IPv6 address in DNS, and an indication of whether it is a host or a router. If the client is a router, it should send additional information about the number of IPv6 addresses that it wants to be served. The Tunnel Broker needs this information in order to assign an appropriate prefix to the client.

The Tunnel Broker fulfills the following tasks:

- Choosing a Tunnel Server as a tunnel exit point. If it has more than one option, it chooses based on preconfigured load-sharing criteria.
- Choosing a prefix for the client. The prefix can be of any length. The most common values are /48 (site prefix), /64 (subnet prefix) or /128 (single host).
- Defining a Lifetime for the tunnel.
- Registering the global IPv6 addresses it has assigned in DNS.
- Configuring the Tunnel Server.
- Sending the configuration information back to the client. This information includes the tunnel parameters and DNS names.

This concludes the tunnel configuration. The clients now have access to all IPv6 networks to which the Tunnel Server has access.

There are a number of ISPs that offer Tunnel Broker services. Often, users can register through the browser by filling out a form and receiving the configuration information displayed or sent by email. The client can now manually configure its tunnel entry point or use script files from the provider, that automate the configuration process.

The Tunnel Broker model is designed for smaller and isolated IPv6 networks and especially for single, isolated IPv6 hosts. It works only with public IPv4 addresses. If private addresses are used, another mechanism such as Teredo or Protocol 41 Forwarding must be used.

 Find a worldwide list of Tunnel Brokers at The IPv6 Portal: *http://www.ipv6tf.org*. Go to "Using IPv6" and choose "Connectivity."

Dual-Stack IPv6 Dominant Transition Mechanism (DSTM)

The Dual-Stack IPv6 Dominant Transition Mechanism (DSTM) allows the transport of IPv4 packets over an IPv6-dominant network by encapsulating the IPv4 packets in IPv6 packets. The specification defines a method to assign dual-stack nodes a temporary IPv4 address. DSTM is designed to allow IPv6 nodes the communication with IPv4 nodes and applications without using translation (NAT-PT). Find the current description in *draft-bound-dstm-exp-04.txt*.

The main goal of this specification is in providing the possibility for early adopters to move to an IPv6-only network as soon as possible but still be able to support communication with the IPv4 world.

The following terms are used with DSTM:

DSTM Domain
> The network domain within an intranet where IPv6/IPv4 nodes use DSTM to communicate with IPv4 nodes. An IPv4 Address Allocation Server can be implemented to manage an IPv4 address pool. Within a DSTM domain, there is usually no IPv4 routing access.

DSTM Client
> An IPv4/IPv6-capable client with DSTM client software.

DSTM Server
> An IPv4/IPv6-capable node with DSTM Server software implemented. It maintains the IPv4 address pool and configures the DSTM clients with the tunnel endpoint (TEP) parameters. Alternatively, the DSTM clients can be configured manually.

DSTM Border Router
> An IPv4/IPv6-capable node with DSTM Border Router software. It connects the IPv6 network with the IPv4 network and manages the address mapping (IPv6 to IPv4 addresses).

Dynamic Tunnel Interface
> An interface on a DSTM Client that will permit the sending of IPv4 packets within IPv6 to a DSTM Border Router and receive IPv4 packets within IPv6 from an IPv4 node or application.

A DSTM Client acts as a tunnel endpoint (TEP) by encapsulating IPv4 packets in IPv6 packets and sending them to a DSTM Border Router, the other tunnel endpoint, which decapsulates the IPv6 packet and forwards the IPv4 packet to the IPv4 destination. The

DSTM Border Router caches the IPv6 path for the IPv4 address back to the DSTM client to encapsulate incoming IPv4 packets and forward them to the DSTM client.

The DSTM Address server manages the allocation of IPv4 addresses and configures the clients for the tunnel endpoint. The DSTM Server and Border Router software can be installed on the same hardware. This mechanism allows for the communication of IPv4 nodes with IPv4 applications without changing anything on the IPv4 side.

The allocation of IPv4 addresses to DSTM clients can be done with the Tunnel Setup Protocol (TSP) described in the framework of the Tunnel Broker (*draft-blanchet-v6ops-tunnelbroker-tsp-03.txt*). With the DSTM Tunnel Endpoint option (*draft-ietf-dhc-dhcpv6-opt-dstm-01.txt*), the DSTM client can receive its tunnel endpoint configuration from DHCPv6. This is important, as DSTM is designed to support an IPv6-dominant infrastructure and to eliminate as many IPv4 dependencies as possible and as early as possible. Being able to use DHCPv6 for allocating IPv4 addresses to DSTM clients further reduces the dependency of IPv4 and therefore supports a quicker migration to an IPv6-dominant infrastructure while still supporting IPv4 applications and services. The advantage is that supporting an IPv6-dominant infrastructure is simpler and less costly than supporting a dual-stack infrastructure.

 Even though DSTM is still in draft, there are several DSTM implementations available for Windows XP, Linux, FreeBSD, and Sharp Zaurus.

IPv4/IPv6 coexistence by using VLANs

VLANs, which are quite common in enterprise networks, can be used to deploy IPv6 in a situation where IPv6-capable router and switch equipment is not available yet. The VLAN standard allows separate LANs to be deployed over a single bridged LAN. It uses virtual LAN tagging or membership information, which is inserted into the Ethernet frames. So to introduce IPv6 in such an environment, a parallel IPv6 routing infrastructure can be deployed, and the IPv6 links can be overlayed onto the IPv4 infrastructure by using VLAN technology. This setup doesn't require any changes to the IPv4 environment. Find a detailed description of this scenario and possible configurations in *draft-ietf-v6ops-vlan-usage-01.txt*.

IPv6 in MPLS networks

Different universities in Europe have conducted studies about IPv6 in MPLS (Multiprotocol Label Switching) networks. Backbones that already have MPLS implemented can choose one of the following IPv6 scenarios:

Native IPv6 over MPLS
> In this case, IPv6 is used in parallel to IPv4. This implies that all routers in the MPLS network are dual-stack and use IPv6 routing protocols in combination with LDP (Label Distribution Protocol).

Layer 2 Tunneling over MPLS

The Layer 2 packets (e.g., Ethernet or ATM) are switched over the MPLS backbone. This is possible on most common platforms including Cisco IOS and Juniper JunOS.

IPv6 over IPv4/MPLS Core

This method is based on the distribution of IPv6 prefixes (along with the corresponding labels) between the Edge Label Switching routers using BGP4 over IPv4. The next hop is identified by an IPv4 address. Cisco calls their implementation of this mechanism 6PE (IPv6 Provider Edge Router).

The main sources of this information are documents from the 6net Project (*http:// www.6net.org*). The 6net was a collaboration of approximately 15 European research and educational networks. IPv6 has been implemented and thoroughly tested by these partners. The detailed reports of their tests and findings are documented on the 6net web site. It is well worth going there; you will find a wealth of useful guides, reports, and cookbooks that help you to plan for and implement IPv6. Go to *http:// www.6net.org/publications/deliverables*. The 6net project concluded in June 2005, but the dissemination and support activities continue in the 6DISS project (*http:// www.6diss.org*).

Cisco's 6PE

The concept for 6PE is based on the hierarchical routing structure of MPLS shown in Figure 10-12. I do not aim to discuss general MPLS technology here; the goal is to show how MPLS can support an easy introduction of IPv6.

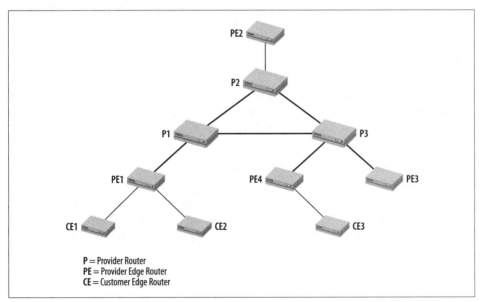

Figure 10-12. MPLS routing hierarchy

In the center of the MPLS network are the Provider routers (P). They switch the MPLS packets, which means that they do not process the layer 3 header. At the edge of the core network are the Provider Edge routers (PE). They receive regular IP packets from the Customer Edge routers (CE), apply an MPLS label, and forward them to the Provider routers. MPLS packets are sent only between Provider Edge routers and Provider routers in Figure 10-12. Routing works as follows:

- The PE and CE routers use the common routing protocols (RIP, OSPF, BGP, or static routing). The PE router learns the prefixes that it can reach through the CE routers through these routing protocols.

- PE routers distribute these prefixes among each other using IBGP sessions. Each PE router announces the prefixes learned from its CE routers over BGP to the other PE routers and inserts itself as next hop for these prefixes.

- Each PE router therefore is capable of determining the routes to the other PE routers by using an Interior Gateway Protocol such as IS-IS or OSPF.

IPv6 packets can then be routed over an MPLS infrastructure without configuring the Provider routers for IPv6. The Provider Edge routers need to be dual-stack. The Customer Edge routers can be dual-stack or IPv6-only.

Find a detailed description of 6PE on the Cisco web site at *http://www.cisco.com/ ipv6*. There are a lot of interesting publications there, including a data sheet on 6PE, case studies, and a series of white papers.

The fact that MPLS can be used to transport IPv6 packets over IPv4 does not mean that you should implement MPLS for this purpose. If you do not have an MPLS infrastructure in place, other tunneling mechanisms may be better suited to reach your goal. But if you already have MPLS, it is a great starting point.

Generic Routing Encapsulation (GRE)

Another Tunneling mechanism that can be used is Generic Routing Encapsulation (GRE). GRE is specified in RFC 2784 and is designed to encapsulate any protocol in another protocol. The protocol being encapsulated—in our case IPv6—is called the Passenger Protocol. The protocol that is used to encapsulate—in our case IPv4—is called the Carrier Protocol.

The configuration of a GRE tunnel is manual. On both tunnel endpoints (the GRE routers), the IPv4 address of the tunnel peer is preconfigured. So for each route where IPv6 has to be tunneled, a tunnel must be configured separately. In a more complex network, this can lead to a high initial configuration effort. A GRE tunnel cannot traverse NATs. It is useful when multiple protocols have to be tunneled through the same tunnel.

SSH (Secure SHell) Tunnels

You won't find SSH Tunnels as an official IPv6 transition mechanism, but they can be very practical and offer useful solutions in different situations. This section describes what they are and how you can use them in an IPv6 environment.

The aim of two projects, the commercial OpenSSH (*http://www.openssh.com*) and the closed source SSH (*http://www.ssh.com*), was to eliminate the use of unencrypted protocols such as Telnet, rlogin, and rsh. This section is by no means a complete overview of SSH, but it shows how SSH tunnels can be used as a simple transition mechanism for IPv4 to IPv6 and vice versa.

> For a more precise look at SSH, we recommend *SSH—The Secure Shell, The Definitive Guide*, Second Edition, written by Daniel J. Barrett et al (O'Reilly).

Both projects allow for a practice called "port forwarding," which essentially allows TCP ports to be forwarded between machines. It is also loosely referred to as "The Poor Man's VPN." In the scenario shown in Figure 10-13, we have an IPv4-only client connecting to a dual-stacked host running either version of SSH (both versions of SSH are IPv6 compliant).

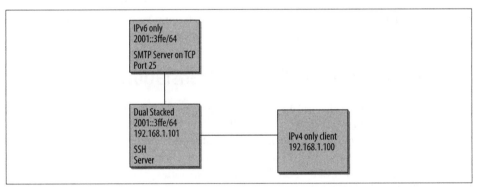

Figure 10-13. IPv4 client connects to IPv6-only server through a dual-stacked SSH host

The IPv4 client wishes to send mail via the IPv6-only server. With SSH's flexibility, this can be accomplished one of two ways, described next. The examples that follow show how to do this using the command-line SSH client available from both vendors, but this can also be easily accomplished with GUI tools (please check your vendor's documentation for your GUI tool).

Port forwarding TCP port 25 back to the client

Typing the following command on the SSH server allows a single IPv4 client to access the IPv6 mail server: `ssh -L 25:[2001::3ffe]:25 user@192.168.1.101`. After typing in a password, this command will forward TCP port 25 from the IPv6 server back to the IPv4-only client. On the client side, a simple `telnet 127.0.0.1 25` shows that the data is actually initiated on the local host, then forwarded to the IPv6-only SMTP server via the SSH server. It may sound a bit complex, but it works very well.

Port forwarding TCP port 25 to the SSH server and allowing clients to connect to port 25 on the SSH server

This method, while a bit more complex on the initial setup, can ease administration issues; the connection only has to be initiated once, and then each client can connect to the SSH server. The following commands are typed on the SSH server: `ssh -g -L 25:[2001::3ffe]:25 user@127.0.0.1`. After typing this on the server and logging in, you should be able to type `telnet 127.0.0.1 25` and get the SMTP prompt from the IPv6-only SMTP server. The difference here is the `-g` in the SSH command, which allows Gateway mode. In Gateway mode, clients other than localhost can connect to that port. Typing the command `telnet 192.168.1.101 25` at the IPv4-only workstation allows that client to connect to the IPv4 side of the dual-stacked SSH server, which relays the data to the IPv6-only SMTP server.

The flexibility of SSH tunnels allows for many other combinations, including the client being able to forward the port and the use of pregenerated keys for ease of administration (no logging in required). Disadvantages of using SSH as a transition mechanism include being able to forward only TCP connections and a possibility of high processing overhead in forwarding many ports using the same machine.

Network Address and Protocol Translation

Address and protocol translation techniques are described in RFCs 2765 and 2766. They offer transition mechanisms in addition to dual-stack and tunneling techniques. The goal is to provide transparent routing for nodes in IPv6 networks to communicate with nodes in IPv4 networks and vice versa. The Stateless IP/ICMP Translation Algorithm (SIIT; see RFC 2765) specifies algorithms that translate between IPv4 and IPv6 packet headers. It does not specify a mechanism for the assignment of IPv4 addresses. Network Address Translation—Protocol Translation (NAT-PT; see RFC 2766) uses a pool of public IPv4 addresses for assignment to IPv6 nodes on a dynamic basis as sessions are initiated across protocol boundaries.

Stateless IP/ICMP Translation

For the case in which IPv4-only hosts want to communicate with IPv6-only hosts or vice versa, RFC 2765 defines how a protocol translator has to translate the IP and ICMP headers for both parties to understand each other. For example, you might have a new network segment and want to roll out native IPv6 hosts. With the implementation of a protocol translator, it is possible to set up the new IPv6-only network internally and have those IPv6-only clients access the standard IPv4 Internet or any other IPv4-only node. For this purpose, a new address type has been introduced: the *IPv4-translatable address*. The format of the prefix for this address is 0::ffff:0:0:0/96. The host identifier is an IPv4 address that has to be taken from a special pool and assigned to the IPv6 node that wants to communicate with IPv4 nodes.

TCP and UDP headers generally do not need to be modified by the translator. One exception is UDP headers that need a checksum for IPv6 because a pseudoheader checksum is required for IPv6. The same is true for ICMPv4 messages that need a pseudoheader checksum for ICMPv6. In addition to the checksum, ICMP error messages contain the IP header of the original packet in the payload that needs to be modified by the translator; otherwise, the receiving node cannot understand it. IPv4 options and IPv6 Routing headers, Hop-by-Hop Options headers, and Destination Option headers are not translated. Also, the translation techniques cannot be used for multicast traffic, because IPv4 multicast addresses cannot be mapped into IPv6 multicast addresses and vice versa.

Just as with dual-stack nodes, applications running on nodes that use IP/ICMP translation need a mechanism to determine which protocol version to use for communication with their peers.

Translating IPv4 to IPv6

An IPv4-to-IPv6 translator receives an IPv4 datagram. Because it has been configured to know the pool of IPv4 addresses that represent the internal IPv6 nodes, the translator knows that the packet needs translation. It removes the IPv4 header and replaces it with an IPv6 header by translating all the information from the IPv4 header into the IPv6 header.

Path MTU discovery is optional in IPv4 but mandatory in IPv6. If an IPv4 host does Path MTU discovery by setting the Don't Fragment bit in the header, Path MTU discovery works even through the translator. The sender may receive Packet Too Big messages from both IPv4 and IPv6 routers. If the Don't Fragment bit is not set in the IPv4 packet, an IPv6 translator has to ensure that the packet can safely travel through the IPv6 network. It does this by fragmenting the IPv4 packet if necessary, using the minimum MTU for IPv6, 1280 bytes. IPv6 guarantees that 1280-byte packets will be delivered without a need for further fragmentation. In this case, the translator always includes a fragment header to indicate that the sender allows fragmentation. Should this packet travel through an IPv6-to-IPv4 translator, the translator knows it can fragment the packet.

For a UDP packet with a zero checksum, the translator must calculate a valid checksum for IPv6. If a translator receives the first fragment of a fragmented UDP packet with a zero checksum, it should drop the packet and generate a system message specifying the IP address and port number. Further fragments should be silently discarded.

Translating ICMPv4 to ICMPv6 and vice versa

For all ICMPv4 messages, the translator has to compute a valid checksum because it is required with ICMPv6. In addition to this, the type values have to be translated and, for error messages, the included IP header also needs to be translated. Internet Group Management Protocol (IGMP) messages are single-hop messages and should not be forwarded over routers. Therefore, they do not require translation and are silently discarded.

The same translation rules apply to the translation of ICMPv6 messages to ICMPv4 messages, only in reverse order.

Translating IPv6 to IPv4

This process is not much different from the translation discussed previously. In this case, the translator knows that it has to translate from IPv6 to IPv4 based on the IPv4-mapped Destination address. It removes the IPv6 header and replaces it with an IPv4 header. The minimum MTU for IPv4 is 68 bytes; the minimum MTU for IPv6 is 1280 bytes. If a translator receives a packet for an IPv4 network with a smaller MTU, it creates 1280-byte packets and fragments them after translation.

NAT-PT

Network Address Translation—Protocol Translation (NAT-PT) is an implementation of SIIT. The NAT gateway uses a pool of globally unique IPv4 addresses and binds them to IPv6 addresses. No changes to the end nodes are necessary. NAT-PT has been set to experimental and is not to be seen as a preferred transition mechanism, but it is implemented and used, as you will see in the case study section.

The following abbreviations are used in RFC 2766 and throughout this section:

Network Address Translation (NAT)
> Translates IP address, IP, TCP, UDP, and ICMP header checksums.

Network Address Port Translation (NAPT)
> In addition to the fields translated by NAT transport, identifiers such as TCP and UDP port numbers and ICMP message types are translated.

Network Address Translation and Protocol Translation (NAT-PT)
> Translates an IPv6 packet into an equivalent IPv4 packet and vice versa.

Network Address Port Translation and Protocol Translation (NAPT-PT)
> Allows IPv6 hosts to communicate with IPv4 hosts using a single IPv4 address.

These concepts are explained in the following sections.

NAT has widely been used, especially to overcome the limitations of the IPv4 address space. Corporate networks use IPv4 addresses from the private range and a NAT router at the border of the corporate network translates the private addresses to a single or a limited number of public addresses. NAT, as described here, provides routing between an IPv6 network and an IPv4 network. With basic NAT, a block of IPv4 addresses is set aside and the fields for IP Source addresses, IP, TCP, UDP, and ICMP header checksums are translated. With NAPT, further transport identifiers such as TCP and UDP port numbers and ICMP message types are translated. This allows a set of IPv6 hosts to share a single IPv4 address. NAT can be unidirectional (only IPv6 hosts can initiate a session) or bidirectional (the session can be initiated from both sides). Hosts in the IPv4 network use DNS to resolve names. Therefore, a DNS Application Layer Gateway (ALG) must be capable of translating IPv6 addresses into their IPv4 NAT address bindings and vice versa.

To understand how packets are translated, we'll follow a packet being sent from an IPv6 host through a NAPT gateway to an IPv4 host and back. Figure 10-14 illustrates the translation process.

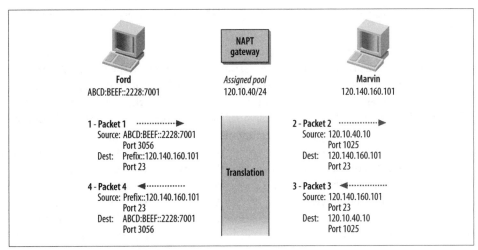

Figure 10-14. Communication flow over NAPT

In this example, Ford, the IPv6 host, has an IPv6 address of ABCD:BEEF::2228:7001. Marvin, on the other side of the NAPT router, has an IPv4 address of 120.140.160. 101. The NAPT gateway has been assigned a pool of 120.10.40/24. Ford initializes a session with Marvin by sending a packet to the Destination address prefix::120.140. 160.101, port 23. The prefix ::/96 is advertised by NAPT into the IPv6 network, and whenever a packet is sent to that prefix, it will be routed through NAPT. As Source address, Ford uses its IPv6 address with a port number of 3056 (step 1). The NAPT gateway now assigns an IPv4 address and a port number out of its pool. Let's say it uses the address 120.10.40.10. The new IPv4 packet going out from NAPT to Marvin has a Source address of 120.10.40.10, port 1025, and a Destination address of 120.140.160.101, port 23 (step 2). When Marvin replies, it sends the packet with a Source address of 120.140.160.101, port 23, to Destination address 120.10.40.10, port 1025 (step 3). NAPT translates the packet according to the parameters it has stored in its cache for the duration of the session and sends it from Source address prefix::120.140.160.101, port 23, to Destination address ABCD:BEEF::2228:7001, port 3056 (step 4).

Limitations

The NAT-PT translation mechanisms described in RFC 2766 should be used only if no other transition mechanism is possible, and dual-stack operation should be avoided for certain reasons. This mechanism has a number of disadvantages. For instance, it does not take full advantage of the advanced capabilities that IPv6 offers, and it is difficult to maintain the number of Application Level Gateways (ALG) required in NAT to keep all applications working correctly through the gateway. NAT-PT has therefore been moved to experimental status. For an explanation of the issues that led to this decision, refer to *draft-ietf-v6ops-natpt-to-exprmntl-03.txt*. There are other transition techniques, such as DSTM, to support IPv4 applications in IPv6 networks.

The same topology restrictions apply that also apply to IPv4 NATs. The inbound and outbound datagrams pertaining to one session have to traverse the same NAT router. There are applications that use IP addresses in the payload of IP datagrams. NAT is not aware of the application layer and does not look into the payload to detect IP addresses. In this case, NAT would have to be combined with an ALG to support such applications in this type of environment. RFC 2766 describes how a DNS ALG or FTP ALG would have to translate to support these applications over NAT. For instance, if a DNS request goes out from the IPv4 network to a DNS server through a NAT-PT device in the IPv6 network (or vice versa), a mechanism must be provided that translates IPv4 resource records types (A type) to IPv6 resource record types (AAAA). FTP control sessions carry IP address information in the payload, and the format of the command allows only for 32-bit addresses. RFC 2428 defines two new extensions to FTP commands to replace the PORT and PASV commands. The new commands are designed not only to allow long addresses, but also to carry additional information about the protocol to be used. These new extensions can also be used for FTP over IPv4. An FTP ALG would have to be able to translate these commands for FTP to work over NAT.

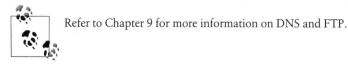 Refer to Chapter 9 for more information on DNS and FTP.

End-to-end security cannot be provided when using any form of NAT. Two end nodes that need IPsec-level security must use either IPv4 or IPv6 natively. This is a well-known limitation of NAT in general and will be one of the driving reasons to move away from NAT and start to use IPv6 natively. Because the DNS ALG translates DNS requests, the mechanisms of DNSSEC will not work either.

Other Translation Techniques

There are additional translation mechanisms, which I describe in this section.

Bump-in-the-Stack

Bump-in-the-Stack (BIS) is specified in RFC 2767. It basically corresponds to the NAT-PT mechanism described in the previous section with the difference that the translator sits within the operating system of the host. BIS is a translation interface between IPv4 applications and the underlying IPv6 network, and its goal is to support IPv4 applications within an IPv6 dominant network. The BIS interface is between the IPv4 application and the network interface driver, and translates IPv4 to IPv6 for outgoing data and IPv6 to IPv4 for incoming data. The difference from using a dual-stack node is that when using BIS, such a node does not need an IPv4 address; IPv6 packets go over the network. The BIS driver has a pool of IPv4 addresses for internal communication with the IPv4 applications, but these addresses never leave the node. From outside, the node looks like an IPv6-only node.

This mechanism is not designed to be a long-term solution, but to allow a migration to an IPv6 dominant network while still supporting IPv4 applications.

Bump-in-the-API

Bump-in-the-API (BIA) is specified in RFC 3338. It is the same mechanism as in BIS, only in this case, the translation happens internally between the IPv4 APIs and the IPv6 APIs. When an IPv4 application wants to communicate with an IPv6 node, the API translator intercepts the socket API functions and calls the corresponding IPv6 socket APIs. It also uses a pool of internal IPv4 addresses.

Again, this mechanism is not designed to be a long-term solution. The goal is the same as with BIS and DSTM: to prevent the necessity to support IPv4 applications from delaying a migration to an IPv6-dominant network.

Transport Relay Translator

The Transport Relay Translator (TRT; see RFC 3142) is a translation mechanism to be used in an IPv6-only network on the transport layer. It sits in the IPv6 network and allows the communication between IPv6 nodes and IPv4 nodes. Every communication of an IPv6 client with an IPv4 application needs to go through the Relay Translator. In case of a TCP connection, the relay terminates the connection to the client and makes a new TCP connection on the other side to the IPv4 application. Internally, the translator translates between the two sessions. In case of a UDP connection, the translator simply translates and forwards the packet.

All translation techniques should be used only if there is no other choice. The overview in this chapter aims to give an idea of the variety of mechanisms to enable coexistence and smooth transition. The most important goal the developers had in mind was to provide mechanisms to give customers the possibility to move to an IPv6 network as soon as possible. The sooner you have an IPv6-dominant network, the better, because maintaining one protocol is always less costly than maintaining two.

Comparison

Now that you have an overview of the available techniques, I'll summarize them by listing advantages and disadvantages. This summary should help you to determine which way to go and which combinations to choose.

Dual Stack

This technique is easy to use and flexible. Hosts can communicate with IPv4 hosts using IPv4 or communicate with IPv6 hosts using IPv6. When everything has been upgraded to IPv6, the IPv4 stack can simply be disabled or removed. Whenever you can, deploying dual-stack hosts and routers offers the greatest flexibility in dealing with islands of IPv4-only applications, equipment, and networks. Dual stack is also the basis for other transition mechanisms. Tunnels need dual-stacked endpoints, and translators need dual-stacked gateways. Disadvantages of this technique include the following: you have two separate protocol stacks running, so you need additional CPU power and memory on the host. All the tables are kept twice: one per protocol stack. A DNS resolver running on a dual-stack host must be capable of resolving both IPv4 and IPv6 address types. Generally, all applications running on the dual-stack host must be capable of determining whether this host is communicating with an IPv4 or IPv6 peer. In a dual-stack network, you need to have a routing protocol that can deal with both protocols (such as IS-IS) or a routing protocol for the IPv4 network (such as OSPFv2) and another routing protocol for the IPv6 network (such as OSPFv3). If you are using dual-stack techniques, make sure that you have firewalls in place that protect not only your IPv4 network, but also your IPv6 network, and remember that you need separate security concepts and firewall rules for each protocol.

Tunneling

Tunneling allows you to migrate to IPv6 just the way you like. There is no specific upgrade order that needs to be followed. You can even upgrade single hosts or single subnets within your corporate network and connect separated IPv6 clouds through tunnels. You don't need your ISP to support IPv6 in order to access remote IPv6 networks because you can tunnel through their IPv4 infrastructure. And you don't need to upgrade your backbone first. As long as your backbone is IPv4, you can use tunnels to transport IPv6 packets over the backbone. If you have an MPLS infrastructure, you have the best foundation for using this to tunnel IPv6 packets as long as you do not want to upgrade the backbone routers to support IPv6 natively.

The disadvantages are known from other tunneling techniques used in the past. Additional load is put on the router. The tunnel entry and exit points need time and CPU power for encapsulating and decapsulating packets. They also represent single points of failure. Troubleshooting gets more complex because you might run into hop count or MTU size issues, as well as fragmentation problems. Management of encapsulated traffic (e.g., per-protocol accounting) is also more difficult due to encapsulation. Tunnels also offer points for security attacks. Find more information on security issues in Chapter 5.

NAT-PT

Translation should be used only if no other technique is possible and should be viewed as a temporary solution until one of the other techniques can be implemented. The disadvantages are that it does not support the advanced features of IPv6, such as end-to-end security. It poses limitations on the design topology because replies have to come through the same NAT router from which they were sent. The NAT router is a single point of failure, and flexible routing mechanisms cannot be used. All applications that have IP addresses in the payload of the packets will stumble. The advantage of this method is that it allows IPv6 hosts to communicate directly with IPv4 hosts and vice versa. For the reasons mentioned previously, NAT as described in RFC 2765 and RFC 2766 is going to be moved to experimental.

When to Choose IPv6?

A golden rule says to "never touch a running system." This rule also applies to your IPv4 networks. As long as they do what you need them to do, let them run. But when an IPv4 network hits the limits for some reason, choose IPv6. IPv6 is mature enough to be used in corporate and commercial networks, as many case studies and deployments worldwide show. High investments in new IPv4 setups, fixes, or complex configurations for IPv4 (especially NATs) should be avoided if possible because they are investments in a technology that will slowly be phased out. When you reach the point where this becomes necessary, evaluate IPv6. Whatever you invest in IPv6 is an investment in future technology. As you can see in the findings of people who present their case studies, getting familiar with the new protocol early, taking some time to play with it before you really need it, and planning for it early saves a lot of cost and headaches.

As already mentioned in Chapter 1, here's the list of indicators that it may be time for you to consider or integrate IPv6:

- Your IPv4 network or NAT implementation needs to be fixed or extended.
- You are running out of address space.
- You want to prepare your network for applications that are based on advanced features of IPv6.

- You need end-to-end security for a large number of users and you do not have the address space, or you struggle with a NAT implementation.

- Your hardware or applications reach the end of their lifecycle and must be replaced. Make sure you buy products that support IPv6, even if you don't enable it right away.

Integration Scenarios

As this chapter shows, there are numerous mechanisms that support a step-by-step introduction of IPv6. There is no one mechanism that can cover all requirements or be optimal for all scenarios. In most cases, a combination of different mechanisms will be chosen. What the best combination and sequence are depends on the infrastructure of the current environment and the goals and requirements for the transition/integration. In the IETF, the work on the basic protocol is completed. They now focus on developing practical scenarios for different types of environments, and the results are published. We offer a summary here, not with the intent to deliver a cookbook for your environment, but rather to provide food for thought that you can apply to your requirements.

 If you want to follow what is going on in the IPv6 operational working group, refer to *http://www.ietf.org/html.charters/v6ops-charter.html*. You can also find a concise list of all relevant RFCs and drafts at *http://tools.ietf.org/wg/v6ops*.

Organizations

To connect a single host or a small network with the IPv6 Internet is not a big challenge and can be done with one of the tunnel mechanisms described earlier. It is easy to implement with most operating systems.

If you have a public IPv4 address and want access to the IPv6 Internet, 6to4 or a Tunnel Broker can be used. If you have NAT in place and make use of private IPv4 addresses, you may choose to use Teredo or Proto 41 Forwarding if the NAT box supports it. Organizations that have the privilege of their providers offering native IPv6 connections can have a dual-stack Internet connection. Dual-stack is in many cases the easiest way to go if your devices and operating systems support IPv6 (and they do if they are on an up-to-date level). If you have routers or layer 3 switches that do not support IPv6, or if you do not want to enable IPv6 on your routers for some reason, you can use ISATAP for internal IPv6 communication on your IPv4 network. You can then also add an ISATAP or 6to4 router to access the IPv6 Internet if desired.

Many organizations have a number of IPv4 Virtual LANs (VLANs). In such situations, an IPv6 router can advertise one single IPv6 prefix into all VLANs that support dual-stack communication. This is only advisable for a transition period, though. All the IPv6 nodes in the VLANs can autoconfigure for an IPv6 address using the prefix advertised by the IPv6 router.

The tunnel mechanisms do not only support the transport of IPv6 over the IPv4 Internet, but also internally over an IPv4 backbone. A backbone upgrade is not something you choose to do every year; you probably want to wait for the end of the backbone router lifecycle before touching it. This does not prevent rolling out IPv6 at the edge of the network. As long as the backbone is based on IPv4, IPv6 packets are tunneled to IPv6 islands on the other side.

RFC 4057, "IPv6 Enterprise Network Scenarios," is an RFC that assists you in identifying your enterprise transition strategy. It describes different scenarios for IPv6 deployment within enterprise networks and provides guidance and checklists of how to approach this task. This RFC includes enterprises that decide to deploy IPv6 in conjunction with IPv4, or to deploy IPv6 because of a specific set of applications that it wants to use over an IPv6 network, or to build a new network or restructure an existing network and decides to deploy IPv6 as the predominant protocol within the enterprise in coexistence with IPv4. The document then reviews a set of network infrastructure components common to most enterprises that must be analyzed.

ISPs

IPv6 is designed to enable Internet Service Providers (ISP) to meet the challenges with the exponential growth of the Internet and to provide new services to their customers. The number of devices will explode in the coming years, a challenge that can be met only with the address space of IPv6. Cable, DSL, wireless, and other always-on technologies can also benefit from the address space. Other benefits of IPv6 include the capability to enhance end-to-end security and mobile communications, and to ease system management burdens. Some examples include peer-to-peer communication without NAT traversal problems, being able to securely access devices and applications at work from home or vice versa, enhanced IP Mobility, and many more.

Therefore, ISPs have to evaluate the capabilities of IPv6 to meet these needs. Some countries have taken a lead role in this area and moved from testing and evaluation to real deployments of IPv6 in the broadband arena. Japan is a prime example, along with other countries that are looking at moving towards large-scale production deployments of IPv6.

ISPs will have to offer both IPv4 and IPv6 services in the coming years. To provide access to IPv6 networks to customers in a first phase, tunnel mechanisms can be used. This is a simpler and more economical method to start offering IPv6 services. Depending on customer needs and requirements, a native IPv6 deployment option might be more scalable and provide better service performance. You may be able to use the next due backbone upgrade and introduce dual-stack. All other services such as web hosting, email, and FTP are best if offered for both protocols (IPv4 and IPv6).

The migration steps should be well-planned, and a useful combination of mechanisms chosen and implemented. The main goal for an ISP will be to offer all of the services over both protocols: this is the only way to cover the whole market. Especially for ISPs, the introduction of IPv6 offers the possibility to create business opportunities and new service offerings.

RFC 4029, "Scenarios and Analysis for Introducing IPv6 into ISP Networks," analyzes the challenges and opportunities for ISPs and discusses different integration and transition scenarios, divided into exploring backbone transition actions, customer connection transition actions, and network and service operation actions. *Draft-ietf-v6ops-bb-deployment-scenarios-04.txt* presents the options available in deploying IPv6 services in the access part of a broadband Service Provider network, namely Cable/HFC, Broadband Ethernet, xDSL, WLAN, and PLC/BPL. It briefly discusses the other elements of a provider network as well. It provides different viable IPv6 deployment and integration techniques and models for each of the previously mentioned broadband technologies. *Draft-shin-v6ops-802-16-deployment-scenarios-00.txt* extends the discussion in the previous draft and goes into deployment scenarios for wireless broadband access networks. RFC 3574 discusses transition scenarios for 3GPP networks. RFC 4215 goes into more details for 3GPP networks and is an additional document to RFC 3574.

 Find a list of IPv6 Internet Exchange Points at *http://www.v6nap.net*. An updated list of IPv6 experiments around the world, classified by country, can be found at the UK IPv6 Resource Center at *http://www.cs-ipv6.lancs.ac.uk/ipv6/6Bone/Whois/bycountry.html*.

Case Studies

Here are some case studies that may be of interest to you. The first is an example of an ISP that has quite a few years of operational experience with IPv6 and was willing to share this information with us. Next, we have the description of two universities that have deployed IPv6, and I describe them both because they each have a completely different approach. The last case study is about my ISP in Zurich and how it offers its services over IPv6. Talking to all these people shows that a step-by-step introduction is much easier and less costly than one would anticipate. These people were kind enough to provide the information about their deployments and share their findings and experiences with us. The examples show that IPv6 is ready to be used and may give you some ideas on how to proceed with the plans and strategy for your network. I tried to find different types of deployments, and I hope that the variety of these examples inspires you to find a good and creative deployment path for your network and to enjoy getting there.

NTT Communications—An ISP Case Study

This case study focuses on NTT Communications's Internet access services. (Some of the companies that are part of the NTT Communications Group were or are known by the name Verio Inc. or other names; in this section, they are all included and referred to by the name NTT Communications.) The company also offers IPv6 web hosting and other services. NTT Communications has a long history with IPv6 that began in 1996 when NTT Labs started one of the world's largest IPv6 research networks in Japan, and just one year later, NTT Communications affiliates started operating major nodes of the 6bone. The ISP made a decision early in the IPv6 growth curve to be a leader in this industry, and in the late 1990s made a decision to productize IPv6 services as soon as practical. A policy was implemented that equipment procurement decisions needed to account for IPv6 support as far back as 1997, and by 1999, NTT Communications was pushing hard for advanced IPv6 support from major router vendors. In the meantime, the company was supporting IPv6 peering and participating in every major global IPv6 exchange. In 1999 and 2000, NTT Communications was allocated sTLAs from the APNIC and ARIN respectively. The ISP's comment regarding this early commitment to IPv6:

> "This long-sighted planning led to a much easier and less expensive transition to IPv6."

NTT Communications decided to roll out IPv6 services to its customers in three phases: a precommercial phase, a commercial phase, and follow-up releases to fill functionality gaps. This phased approach allowed for NTT Communications's IP routing infrastructure to be gradually upgraded while taking on a limited, manageable number of customers. In the meantime, internal tools were enhanced, and testing in the 6bone and in internal private labs continued. The entire process was treated as a product development process—treating IPv6 not just as a technology, but as a technology that needed to be packaged in a manner that could meet the needs of customers who desire to be on the leading edge of IPv6 deployment. No elaborate business case was developed, and NTT Communications realized that IPv6 alone would not open revenue floodgates. But a business decision to commit to providing IPv6 Internet access products was based on the premise that IPv6 could be used as a differentiator to land new customers in an ever-competitive ISP market, and to gain access to new market verticals.

The first phase of IPv6 deployment, launched in June of 2003 and called "IPv6 Precommercial Services" was relatively modest for a large ISP. Three Cisco 7206 routers running dual-stack IPv4/v6 were deployed in Los Angeles, San Jose, and the Washington, D.C. area. The majority of the NTT Communications backbone remained IPv4-based, with tunnels over the backbone between these three locations and the various IPv6 peering points. Only a handful of customers were brought on during this phase. Customers in any of these three geographic areas could receive native or dual-stack service, while customers in other locations in the United States could get IPv6 access via tunneling (RFC 2893, manually configured tunnels) to one of the three 7206 routers. The precommercial phase allowed engineers to continue testing Cisco's IOS and Juniper Networks's JunOS, and allowed time for the entire global NTT Communications backbone to be upgraded. It also allowed for provisioning and support procedures to be tested and for Network Operation Center (NOC) personnel and other support staff to be trained.

In addition to making the routing network IPv6 capable, there were a number of other pieces to consider before launching a commercial product. Customer expectations are set high when they pay for a commercial service. And from the ISP's standpoint, to make money on a product, it must be able to scale and must be supportable. Therefore, a number of other tools and systems also needed to be in place. Router configuration tools needed to be upgraded to support IPv6 as well as NTT Communications's route registry and internal address allocation database. DNS resolvers and servers needed to be upgraded to not only serve IPv6 record types, but also serve these records via either IPv4 or IPv6 transport. The customer portal needed to be upgraded to display IPv6 usage data, albeit over an IPv4 transport. NOC operational and troubleshooting tools were upgraded to accommodate a dual-stack network. Finally, the SNMP infrastructure and SLA monitoring systems were upgraded to support IPv6. The transmission of data for these systems at times still used IPv4, but they had to at least be capable of monitoring IPv6 network elements. The ISP's comment regarding these expenditures:

> "The difficulty and cost of this effort was greatly reduced by years of planning and the decisions made during software and hardware purchases."

By the end of 2003, the main support systems were in place and the entire global NTT Communications backbone (Asia, Australia, Europe, and North America) had been upgraded to run dual stack. The AS2914 core was upgraded first, followed shortly thereafter by the aggregation routing infrastructure. In December 2003, NTT Communications launched commercial IPv6 Internet access in the United States, albeit with some functionality limitations when compared to its IPv4 product suite. Outside of the United States, commercial IPv6 service had already been launched in most other NTT Communications regions. Three types of IPv6 access were supported:

- Native IPv6 (available at every NTT Communications POP)
- Manually configured IPv6 over IPv4 tunnels (RFC 2893)
- Dual-stack IPv4/IPv6 Internet access

The most popular service type was dual stack. Customers were routed both IPv4 and IPv6 address space (usually a /48) and could send either type of packet over their connection—T1, DS3, Ethernet, or whatever type of loop circuit the customer purchased. Since the NTT Communication aggregation and core routing infrastructure is completely dual stack, the aggregation router will accept all packets and will route them accordingly based on either the IPv4 or IPv6 routing tables. This method is very simple and flexible. The native IPv6 access option (only routed IPv6 address space, not IPv4) has been primarily used by organizations that wanted to keep a separate and isolated IPv6 environment—usually for testing or lab purposes. The tunneling option is still available but seldom used since the native and dual stack services offer superior performance. Figure 10-15 shows NTT's peering points.

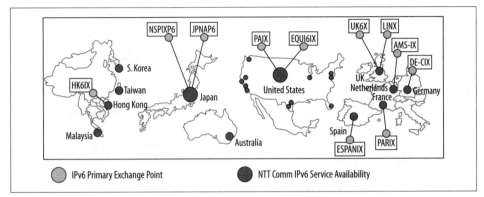

Figure 10-15. NTT Communications's IPv6 network map highlighting IPv6 peering points

At the time of the commercial launch, a few gaps still remained between NTT Communications's IPv4 and IPv6 services. This was partly due to internal development time constraints and partly due to vendor feature support. Follow-up releases have allowed NTT Communications to fill these feature gaps. These releases have added IPv6 support for enhanced IP services such as shadow circuit support, managed router services (where NTT Communications manages the customer's IPv6 or dual-stack CPE), and off-net tunneling. The latter allows customers of a third-party ISP to connect to the NTT Communications Global IP Network via a tunnel (either an RFC 2893 manually configured tunnel or GRE). This has been a popular feature since it allows customers of ISPs that do not support IPv6 to access the IPv6 Internet, and it is relatively inexpensive.

NTT Communications was the first global ISP to support commercial IPv6 Internet access services. Due to proper planning and foresight, the process was relatively painless and inexpensive. No capital budget was ever specifically allocated for the project of rolling out dual-stack IPv6 to its IP network. Changes to support IPv6 were carried out through normal upgrade cycles over the course of a couple of years. Some capital was eventually spent for Cisco 6509 sup720 card upgrades and router memory, but this was a relatively small amount. Like any product development process, there were expenses for employee training, code development to enhance internal tools to support IPv6, and testing. This phased approach allowed NTT Communications to launch IPv6 services while still solidifying internal process and tools as it bought time to continue testing on features that needed to be developed and allowed vendors to add features. Follow-up releases that could support a greater number of customers on a more flexible set of IPv6 access options were then launched.

NTT Communications's IPv6 services have been very successful. In 2005 they report more than 500 IPv6 customers globally. The IPv6 product offerings have strengthened the company's position in some market segments, such as educational institutions, and have opened the door to new verticals such as high tech manufacturing companies and the wireless industry. Cody Christman, Director of Product Engineering at NTT Communications confirms:

"The benefits have greatly outweighed the expense of deploying IPv6 services."

There is an informational RFC (RFC 4241), "A Model of IPv6/IPv4 Dual Stack Internet Access Service," that contains a digest of the user network interface specification of NTT Communications's dual-stack ADSL access service, which provides IPv6/IPv4 dual-stack services to home users. The RFC focuses on an architecture for IPv6/IPv4 dual-stack access service and an automatic configuration function for IPv6-specific parameters, such as the prefix assigned to the user and the addresses of IPv6 DNS servers. It specifies a way to deliver these parameters to Customer Premises Equipment (CPE) automatically.

University of Porto

The Faculty of Engineering at the University of Porto (Portugal) has deployed IPv6. The following sections provide a description of the deployment. The project was split into four main areas, which are described next.

Access/perimeter technology

In the beginning, when there was no IPv6 connectivity available, IPv6 tunneling was used. Very early, the university received connectivity and a /56 prefix, which was divided into /64 prefixes distributed evenly throughout the campus, providing the necessary granularity.

To give IPv6-only users connectivity to the IPv4 world, they chose to implement Network Address Translation—Port Translation (NAT-PT). The main reason for their choice was that it does not "snoop" the data payload, making it application-unaware and perfect for a heterogeneous environment such as theirs. NAT-PT does not require any modifications or extra software to be installed on any of the end user hosts of either the IPv4 or IPv6 networks. It provides the required interoperability functions within the core network, making the interoperability between hosts easier to manage and faster to deploy. The only work required is to install NAT-PT at the network boundary. Maintenance is also eased, as any alteration to NAT-PT only needs to be downstreamed to the boundary routers, not to every host that requires connectivity across an IPv6/IPv4 boundary. The two issues with NAT-PT are scalability compared with other methods and the performance hit that it has on the network equipment that implements this mechanism.

Because NAT-PT is not application-aware and because it works as a level 3 translation mechanism, there is a need to implement an Application Level Gateway (ALG) for specific protocols. These application-specific agents allow an IPv6 node to communicate with an IPv4 node and vice versa. The ALG works seamlessly and in conjunction with NAT-PT to support many mainstream applications, such as DNS-ALG, FTP-ALG, HTTP-ALG, etc.

Core and vertical distribution

The internal network consists of 80 level 2 vertical distribution switches of type Nortel Networks Baystack 450/470 and 18 core router switches of type Nortel Networks Passport 8600. They had issues with distributing the IPv6 network prefixes and the IPv6 routing initially when they tried using beta versions on the core router switches. This created too much of a performance hit on the switch-fabric processors and had a very limited level of features. So they decided to use an ISP router type, a Cisco 7609 OSR, to do the level 3 IPv6 Routing based on the level 2 VLANs. The Cisco router announces the IPv6 prefixes according to the VLAN from where the end user is located. For this mechanism, they use Router ADVertisement Daemon (RADVD), and the IPv6 addresses are created using Stateless Autoconfiguration based on the end user's MAC address.

The level 2 vertical distribution switches were implemented dual stack with a simple mechanism using protocol-based VLANs. The fact that protocol-based VLANs have a higher priority than any port-based VLANs fit perfectly, so the IPv6-based VLAN has priority over the IPv4 port-based VLAN. This was the perfect recipe for transparency with the end users. Whenever an end user activates the IPv6 protocol, he automatically gets access to his respective VLAN. To configure the clients for their default gateway and DNS servers, operating system-specific scripts are used that automatically configure these parameters according to the Prefix/VLAN.

Network services

Any network infrastructure wouldn't be complete without the services to complement the connectivity. The first and foremost service that had to be set up was a DNS Server to provide name resolution for IPv6 and IPv4 queries. After thorough testing, this service was implemented on existing internal and external DNS servers that have a separate network card for IPv6 queries only. These services were implemented using BIND 9 for Linux, providing the end user with the capability to register their workstations on both IPv4 and IPv6 DNS servers. The next step was to introduce more mainstream services, such as HTTP (*http://ipv6.fe.up.pt*), FTP (*ftp://ftp.fe.up.pt*), and NTP. The university's main web site, FEUP (*http://www.fe.up.pt/*), was a bit trickier to implement because Oracle does not yet support Apache v2.0, which is needed for IPv6 support. A dual-stack proxy was then introduced to provide the IPv6-to-IPv4 connectivity for the IPv4 web server. In addition, an IPv6 support page was created to introduce end users to the IPv6 technology and explain how to config-ure and use IPv6 inside the campus (*http://ipv6.fe.up.pt*).

The official FTP server also has a separate network card for native IPv6 communica-tion. This machine mirrors various Linux and software distributions and, in most cases, communicates with IPv6 sites. This has been very helpful in convincing the users to use IPv6, since the university has physically distinct links to the Internet (100MBit/s for IPv4 and 100MBit/s for IPv6) and the IPv6 usage is low and therefore very fast.

The diagram in Figure 10-16 represents the IPv6 servers and core equipment that connects the university to the IPv6 world.

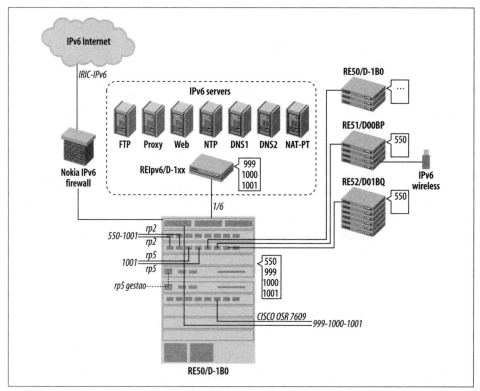

Figure 10-16. IPv6 servers and IPv6 Internet connection

Security

For security, a Nokia IP 650 Firewall running IPSO v3.8 and a Checkpoint Next Gen-eration Application Intelligence R55 are used. The firewall is a pure IPv6 firewall with only IPv6 policies and logs. Checkpoint is a well-integrated security solution for defeating and preventing both network- and application-level attacks in IPv6. This implementation was overseen directly with the help of Checkpoint. The big advantage in the adoption of Checkpoint for their border gateway security is the comprehensive interface that already exists in IPv4 security gateways.

Cost of introduction

The university states the initial cost to be pretty low. In terms of switching, all equipment was configured only for layer 2 switching. The Cisco router was expensive, but usually the backbone upgrade can be done with the next due upgrade, thereby not creating any extra cost. For testing purposes in the lab setup, a Cisco 2600 or a Free BSD server was sufficient. There were some investments in servers and secondary network interface cards for existing servers. But all in all, this wasn't an expensive project. As for human resources, there were two people (one on a part-time basis and one on a full-time basis) working on this project for about one year, between R&D (Research and Development) and deployment of the entire IPv6 network.

Conclusions

The university's conclusion is that the overall result was very good with a high satisfaction rate. They see the project as a very interesting experience with some peculiar and proactive measures to overcome various problems that had to be solved by the network administrators. This is currently and will continue to be an ongoing project, as maintenance and extension of a network always is. They believe that it will still take some time for manufacturers to ultimately implement IPv6 with the same quality and characteristics that are used today in IPv4, and that until companies such as Microsoft deploy IPv6 on their desktop operating systems fully, IPv6 won't take off like it should. They think that Windows Server 2003 is in fact a big step forward in terms of IPv6 features. They found that both MAC OS X and Linux support IPv6 out of the box, and network layers are implemented as they are defined in RFCs. In terms of applications, most of them have limited functionalities compared to native IPv4 mainstream applications.

I had an interesting conversation with Paulo Vieira from the university, and his final statement was:

> "For years, we have being saying that IPv4 would die in the near future because of obvious limitations like limited IP address space, problems with NAT, and security flaws in the IPv4 architecture. The fact is that IPv4 has overcome all these problems with developers and manufacturers working to resolve them for economic reasons. When companies/organizations feel a need to implement IPv6, then for the same reasons, IPv6 will fast become a highly used standard and protocol, even with the added complexity that is introduced in terms of deployment."

University of Strasbourg

Osiris is the name of the Metropolitan Area Network (MAN) for the education and research community in Strasbourg (France). Osiris connects 17 institutions (universities, research institutes, engineering schools, etc.) that represent about 110 buildings, all connected at 1 Gb/s via private fiber optics to the Osiris backbone. The total number of users is 50,000. Osiris is managed by a network operation center called Centre Réseau Communication (CRC), part of University Louis Pasteur (ULP), which is one of the 17 institutions.

The decision to migrate Osiris to IPv6 was made in 2002. The renewal of the backbone equipment in 2003 offered the opportunity to invest in IPv6-capable routers. Quality of IPv6 support was then one of the main criteria for the choice of Juniper M20 routers. IPv6 connectivity in parallel to IPv4 connectivity was offered from the beginning. The routing protocol was changed from OSPFv2 to IS-IS because IS-IS can be used for both IPv4 and IPv6 routing. Since all routing is done in the dual-stack backbone, IPv6 support in the core routers allows IPv6 traffic to be brought in all subnetworks without effort for either the CRC or the local network engineers.

However, IPv6 connectivity was configured in subnetworks only after the local network engineers had been properly educated about the new protocol. A one-day course about "IPv6 Principles and Client Configuration" was designed, and at the time of writing, 53 engineers have taken this course.

During the deployment of new routers, the following network services have also been configured or migrated to support IPv6:

- DNS (all DNS servers migrated to BIND 9 to fully support IPv6)
- Local host database and web application based on PostgreSQL which supports the IPv6 address format natively
- SMTP relay
- Mailbox server for about 3000 users, supporting POP3/POP3S/IMAP/IMAPS and webmail
- Web servers (Apache)
- Anonymous FTP (various mirrors)

All servers are running FreeBSD.

The new Wifi access network (approximately 100 access points at the time of writing, expected to grow to 250 access points by the end of 2005), which requires an authentication with either the 802.1X protocol or a captive portal, now fully supports IPv6.

On the client side, IPv6 Stateless autoconfiguration is used as much as possible. Manually configured addresses are assigned only on "public" servers whose addresses should not be changed. If you are interested in how the university designed their IPv6 addressing scheme, you can find the documentation at *http://www-crc.u-strasbg.fr/osiris/ipv6/plan-adressage.html*. You may need to know a few words of French, but the main structure can be understood without understanding the language. One particular subnetwork is the one where the CRC workstations for the engineers' day-to-day use are located. All these workstations are dual-stacked, being a mix of FreeBSD, Linux (gentoo, debian), and Windows XP.

Connectivity to the Internet is offered by Renater, the French National Research and Education Network (NREN) via two 2.5 Gb/s links. Renater supports native IPv6 connectivity. Thus, no complex tunnel settings are necessary.

Now the migration to IPv6 is complete for the core backbone and services. At the time of writing, 29 local sub-networks have been (partially or fully) migrated to IPv6, and around 500 different hosts on Osiris are regularly using IPv6.

The university made the choice for migration to IPv6 for various strategic reasons:

- To keep the CRC network engineers' knowledge up-to-date and to force them to increase their skills
- To keep up with users' needs since, as a NOC, you don't have the right to be late
- To contribute to providing the best knowledge to their students (especially to those in the computer science field)
- To contribute to the evolution of the Internet

Retrospectively, the migration was made possible by the enthusiasm of a small group of people and by the opportunity to renew the backbone routers. They have had the chance to be among the first to migrate on such a large scale, but they think that it would have occurred sooner or later anyway.

When asked about the cost of introduction, they say that there were no identifiable extra migration costs. The routers had to be upgraded or renewed anyway, so the key element to IPv6 connectivity has been brought without cost. The engineering cost could be the largest one after the routers, but they consider this cost to be a strategic investment towards a high-quality operated network, where ROI cannot be computed by formulae.

The overall summary of Pierre David, who kindly provided all this information, was:

> "There is no real technical challenge for moderately technical people; it is only a matter of ambition. The level of maturity of IPv6 is sufficient for implementation. Regarding the cost of introduction, we see this as an investment just as any upgrade of infrastructure. If I don't do it now, I will have to do it later. Introducing IPv6 is part of my challenge for my group to evolve. There wasn't any extraordinary cost associated with IPv6. We spent more money, but that was for investments in better redundancy, new equipment, and air-conditioning systems; they were not related to IPv6 in any way."

This Book Has Been Reviewed over IPv6

Sometimes things just happen. While we think about the pitfalls of introducing IPv6, IPv6 is already used in many cases, many of which we may not even be aware. One example is the editing process of this book—we can say it has been reviewed over IPv6. David Malone from Ireland has been reviewing it. When working on the first couple chapters, I sent David an email with questions regarding his comments. Here's the email header:

```
Received: from [IPv6:2001:8a8:20:1:202:b3ff:fe8d:c678]
        ([IPv6:2001:8a8:20:1:202:b3ff:fe8d:c678] helo=dachs.cyberlink.ch)
        by salmon.maths.tcd.ie with SMTP id <aa64060@salmon>;
        31 May 2005 21:34:32 +0100 (BST)
```

I must admit that in my office I use an IPv4-based email client, even though I have IPv6 connectivity to the outside world through a Tunnel Broker. This way, I learned that my ISP Cyberlink (*http://www.cyberlink.ch*) not only hosts my web site on a dual-stack web server, but also my email can go out over IPv6. So I asked whether they would share their setup and experience with us.

I was their first customer requesting IPv6 web hosting back in 2001 when I was working on the first edition of this book. At that time, they already had a 6bone tunnel to their private playgrounds, so they had already made their first steps and gathered some experience with IPv6. Their inventory of software and systems that needed to be IPv6-ready showed that this was true for the Cisco router, the web hosting server (Debian Linux 2.4), and the web server software (Apache). From that point on, whenever they upgraded a Cisco router in their network (they run a network with over 30 SDSL POPs and three housing locations), they upgraded flash memory and installed an IPv6-enabled IOS image whenever possible.

The Linux Kernel was already IPv6-ready when they needed it. Not so with the Apache 1.3 web server software they used for web hosting. Unfortunately, it was not possible to upgrade to Apache 2.0 because of module incompatibilities between Apache 1.3 and Apache 2.0. Only newer PHP versions (higher than 4) were running on Apache 2, and they still had customers running applications on PHP Version 3.0. So Apache 2.0 was set up in parallel to Version 1.3. With email and DNS over IPv6, cyberlink.ch was one of the first domains to have an IPv6-reachable nameserver registered.

The mail server is based on qmail (*http://www.qmail.org*) for SMTP, vpopmail (*http://www.inter7.com*) for POP, and courier-imap for IMAP (*http://www.courier-mta.org/imap*). Qmail installations use the tcpserver program to accept connections and forward the streams to the MTA, POP, or IMAP server, so to enable IPv6, it is sufficient to have an IPv6-capable tcpserver. To send email over IPv6, the basic qmail installation needs to be patched with qmail-send, another component of qmail.

Today, Cyberlink's LAN is fully dual stack, and they offer most of their services over IPv6, such as ADSL connectivity, SDSL on most of their POPs, Housing/Rack space with IPv6 upstream, and Web-/Mail-Hosting.

One of the problems they encountered is a lack of low-cost IPv6-enabled CPEs. They have learned that one needs to be persistent and keep asking software, hardware, or upstream suppliers again and again to provide support for IPv6. They found that the network layer is ready for IPv6, and many applications are ready to be used over IPv6.

Most problems they encountered were related to the IPv6 address format. Additionally, log parsers and management frontends for various software still ignore IPv6.

Their plans for the future include providing a 6to4 gateway as soon as customers request such services. When asked for their motivation to offer IPv6 services and a summary of their experience, Ueli Heuer from Cyberlink says:

> "We have taken the opportunity to build our internal expertise and our dual-stack backbone and service offering in the background when customers did not require it yet. This offered the possibility to integrate IPv6 step by step, without pressure. The only real extra cost we had was for the ugprade of router memory, but we would have needed to upgrade memory anyway. Today we can say that we have more than 5 years of experience with IPv6, and when customers start requesting IPv6 services, we are ready. We believe that this will become a business advantage in the near future."

Moonv6—The Largest IPv6 Test Network

Moonv6 is not a case study of a real-world deployment. But I have referred to it many times throughout this book, and it is one of the largest test beds with a broad participation of vendors. So I think it is appropriate to offer a more detailed description of the project.

Moonv6 is a collaboration between the New Hampshire InterOperability Laboratory (UNH-IOL), the U.S. Department of Defense (DoD), the North American IPv6 Task Force (NAv6TF), and Internet2. Moonv6 has established the most diverse and largest native IPv6 network in the world. It was created to advance the interoperability and deployment of the IPv6 protocol and to promote it throughout the industry. It is a platform for service providers, vendors, and equipment providers to work together in the design and testing of operative end-to-end solutions to address large pieces of the interoperability challenge. Moonv6 is an ongoing project and has so far gone through three main testing phases. Detailed information is available on the Moonv6 web site. This section includes a short summary taken from the information provided on the Moonv6 web site.

Phase I

Phase I took place in October 2003 and demonstrated that current IPv6 networking technology is stable, resilient, and ready for integration with today's Internet. More than 30 organizations pooled their products, technologies, and engineering resources in an industry showcase that confirmed the following:

- IPv6 is ready for widespread deployment throughout North America and the world.
- Numerous vendors have developed robust, stable, interoperable implementations of IPv6.
- Multiple interests (government, educational, and commercial) can act collectively to deploy IPv6.

Tests were conducted at nine locations across the United States. Common network applications were tested running natively over an IPv6 network connection. The applications used peer-to-peer or client-server models for communication and included HTTP and HTTPS, FTP and TFTP, Telnet and SSH, DNS, and DHCP. The compliance to the IPv6 base specification was tested. This included the verification of ICMPv6 Echo Request, Reply and Redirect, ICMP "hop limit exceeded," Neighbor Unreachability Detection, Path MTU Detection and Fragmentation/Reassembly, TCP/UDP interoperability, Address Autoconfiguration, Duplicate Address Detection, Multiple Prefixes, and Network Renumbering. As for routing protocols, only OSPF and BGP-4 were investigated during phase 1. Most of the testing took place in networks where IPv4 and IPv6 were running simultaneously and included scenarios where OSPFv2 was used for IPv4 and OSPFv3 was used for IPv6 at the same time. No interference between the two processes was observed. The testing included a verification of basic functionality and more advanced rerouting scenarios. Overall, the tests had a good rate of success; some minor issues were noted. Phase 1 also tested and proved several key areas of mobility. Basic Mobile Node to Correspondent Node and Mobile Node to Mobile Node communication tests worked without any issues. Various scenarios of Home Network Renumbering and Dynamic Home Agent Address Discovery were successfully tested. In the Security area, IPSec was proven to work with ICMP and TCP in the host-to-host scenarios. The most significant issues emerged in the user-unfriendliness of the key exchange. In the area of Transition scenarios, static tunnels, 6to4, ISATAP, Tunnel Broker, and Tunnel Setup Protocol were verified.

Phase II

Phase II ran from February to April 2004. It completed the initial testing by successfully demonstrating high-speed links, advanced routing functionality, firewalls, QoS, and other key features of IPv6. Phase II demonstrated that current IPv6 networking technology is stable and resilient in some of the scenarios tested, but more testing is necessary before it is ready for integration with today's Internet. More than two dozen vendors participated in the tests. The following technologies were tested: QoS forwarding, basic firewall functionality, transition techniques, Mobile IPv6, DNS, and IPv4/IPv6 routing protocols (such as OSPF, BGP, IS-IS) and applications (such as email and PKI). Testing results showed that while most applications run in a dual-stacked or tunneled environment, few applications support native IPv6 environments. Some interesting tests in phase II included operation of media players and web-enabled video cameras over native IPv6 networks. Several commercially available media conferencing applications were successfully tested. They turned PDAs equipped with a mini camera into mobile videophone devices. These applications were also tested to demonstrate IPv6 connectivity over IPv4 wireless networks. IPv6 prefix delegation was tested using a laptop as a mobile wireless router and an IPv6 camera as a remote device. The camera successfully autoconfigured itself and was reachable through the laptop. The camera remained available with short disruptions as the laptop was moving from one IPv4 network to another.

Phase III

The phase III test set, which ran in October and November 2004, used the same basic concept as earlier phases of testing. Applications such as VoIP and multicast streaming over the backbone were tested. More extensive testing of DNS and DHCPv6 was performed. There were some issues revealed in some implementations with DNS zone transfers and support for authentication. Testing also demonstrated that some popular clients cannot communicate with DNS servers in a native IPv6 network. Successful advanced DNS testing included ENUM-related queries and GSS-TSIG updates. The testing of Stateless DHCPv6 clients and server implementations generated positive results. Stateful DHCPv6 tests were not as successful due to a lack of server implementations with comprehensive support for Stateful DHCPv6. Note that these tests were performed in late 2004, so by the time this book is printed, the market situation will probably have changed quite a bit. Routing protocols and firewall functionality were tested extensively during phase III. Internet SCSI (iSCSI; see RFC 3720), a protocol that encapsulates SCSI commands and data for transport over a standard TCP/IP network to address a remote SCSI device as though it were attached via a local SCSI bus, was demonstrated to operate over native IPv6, even though the implementations tested were in alpha state. Further testing will be performed with products from a greater number of vendors. The largest hurdles to IPv6 deployment and adoption that Moonv6 has identified have been either specific device implementation or user configuration issues.

If you are interested in more details as to what was tested and more specific information about the testing results, please refer to the Moonv6 web site (*http://www.moonv6.com*). If you click on the Project button, you find detailed descriptions of the test phases, the items tested, and the white papers with descriptions of the results. When you get there, you may find more updated and recent test results than the ones described here. IPv6 is an evolving world.

The NAv6TF's vision for Moonv6 is to create a virtual Internet backbone with the ability to do preproduction IPv6 testing for security, multimedia, roaming devices, and other services as vendors and system integrators begin leveraging the innovative opportunities inherent in IPv6. It also offers participants who wish to test IPv6-capable technology the following opportunities:

- An operative interoperability setting designed to reduce time to market
- Compressed research, debugging, and development cycles, enabling faster and smoother creation of end-to-end networking solutions
- An ongoing platform for global IPv6 education and knowledge enhancement

What Is Missing?

The interest in IPv6 has grown a lot in the last year. Allocation of IPv6 address space has increased significantly. Many of the IPv6 deployments are experimental and research-based. Just like with IPv4, these institutions gathering early adopter experiences for the benefit of the whole market are universities, research networks, and government agencies.

This section outlines some of the missing pieces for broad IPv6 deployment. We hereby refer to a report created as part of the 6net project. The full report can be found at *http://www.6net.org/publications/deliverables*.

IPv6 Routing

IPv6 routing is robust and performs well. This has been proven in many different tests worldwide. The implementations in common router equipment are well-tested and optimized. It is important to verify that you are using router models that support hardware-based IPv6 routing.

The performance of IPv6 in the Internet will probably not be optimal in the early days because in the beginning, most of the Internet is IPv4-based and IPv6 tunneled. With the growing number of IPv6 Internet backbones, this situation will change. Check with your ISP to find out what kind of connection they have to the IPv6 Internet. When using tunnels, check the available options and choose your tunnel endpoints carefully.

Protocol Selection on Dual-Stack Nodes

As already mentioned in "DNS" in Chapter 9, a way will have to be found to optimize address selection on dual-stack nodes. The behavior of a dual-stack node largely depends on the implementation. If both protocols are available, a choice has to be made either by the application or by the protocol stack. The presence of A or AAAA records in DNS is no indicator to a dual-stack client which protocol would be the better choice and whether the service is reachable over both protocols. There are many situations and combinations possible here. The situation has to be analyzed and the best possible configuration chosen individually.

Multihoming with IPv6

Multihoming is when a host or a site is reachable over different IP addresses. A multihomed host has multiple global IP addresses. These addresses can come from one or more different providers, and they can be assigned to one or more different interfaces on the host. A multihomed site is connected to the Internet with multiple global IP addresses from one or different providers.

The main reasons to configure multihoming are the following:

Redundancy
    When a link fails, the connection can be maintained over the alternative link(s).

Load balancing

Provides more throughput because traffic is balanced over two or more links.

Cost

It may be desirable to have multiple providers—for instance, because one provider may have a better offering for certain types of services.

The autoconfiguration features of IPv6 support an easier maintenance of multihoming scenarios because devices are more flexible in recognizing network prefixes and can configure multiple IPv6 addresses based on Router Advertisements.

In the common IPv4 multihoming approach, a site's local prefixes are announced as distinct routing prefixes into the inter-domain routing system and propagated to the top-level hierarchy of the routing system. This approach works well if the address space of the site is provider-independent. But even though this approach covers most of the requirements for multihoming, it is not scalable. With the growing number of multihomed sites on the Internet, the number of prefixes in the global routing system increases linearly. The common opinion is that even modern routing hardware will eventually be overloaded in dealing with the number of entries in the global routing tables. Additionally, with IPv6, there is currently no such thing as provider-independent address space.

For these reasons, multihoming is an actively discussed topic in the working groups. The goal is to find solutions that provide multihoming without the scalability and transport issues. If you want to follow the discussions and upcoming specifications, go to the Multihoming Working group at *http://www.ietf.org/html.charters/multi6-charter.html* and *http://tools.ietf.org/wg/multi6*. They not only discuss the operations and known limitations of multihoming with IPv4, they provide lists of things to look at when designing multihoming, and discuss architectural approaches and possible threats for multihomed sites.

One of the proposals currently discussed is the Shim6 approach. The "Site Multihoming by IPv6 Intermediation" working group (*http://www.ietf.org/html.charters/shim6-charter.html*) will produce specifications for an IPv6-based site multihoming solution. It adds a new layer (shim) into the IP stack of end-system hosts. The approach enables hosts on multihomed sites to switch between a set of provider-dependent address prefixes and still allow applications to find alternate paths if one or more of the prefixes become unavailable. You can find the list of current drafts in the working group and at the end of this chapter.

 RFC 3582, "Goals for IPv6 Site-Multihoming Architectures," sets the goals for new multihoming architectures. Find a report on possible multihoming solutions called "Evaluation of Multihoming Solutions" at the 6net web site (*http://www.6net.org/publications/deliverables*).

DNS

Resolving DNS names over IPv6 is not implemented in all operating systems yet. With BSD and most Linux resolvers, this is not a problem. Windows XP does not support it. A client that cannot resolve DNS over IPv6 always needs to be dual-stacked and needs a DNS server that is accessible over IPv4.

Not all official registration agencies offer the registration of IPv6 DNS domains. This is important if you want to register IPv6-only services.

 By the way, did you know that five of the thirteen DNS root servers can be queried over IPv6? Find the complete list at *http://www.root-servers.org*.

Network Management

The most important standard for network management is SNMP (Simple Network Management Protocol). There aren't many implementations of SNMP over IPv6 yet. You can monitor your IPv6 network with SNMP over IPv4, though, so you only have a problem if you want to monitor an IPv6-only network.

The number of IPv6 MIBs (Management Information Base) is still limited, and there are no IPv6 Multicast MIBs yet. If you need an updated list of available MIBs, visit your RFC search engine and enter the search term "MIB".

A similar problem exists with the management of wireless access points. There is no problem running Wireless LANs with IPv6. But the configuration and administration of wireless access points is usually only possible over IPv4 or through the serial interface.

IPv4 Dependencies

Many issues with IPv6 arise because of the IP address format. For this reason, a huge effort has been made to analyze all existing RFCs for dependencies on IPv4 addresses. The results of this analysis have been published in a number of RFCs. In case you are interested in more details, here's the list of RFCs:

- RFC 3789, Introduction
- RFC 3790, Network protocols
- RFC 3791, Routing protocols
- RFC 3792, Security
- RFC 3793, Sub-IP
- RFC 3794, Transport protocols
- RFC 3795, Applications
- RFC 3796, Network Management

Security Aspects

Security issues with IPv6 and transition mechanisms are discussed in Chapter 5.

Applications

It will take some time until all applications support the transport over IPv6. There are applications that have no direct dependency on the IP layer. They run equally well without modification in IPv4 and IPv6 environments. But some applications have dependencies and need to be modified. And they should be modified to be protocol-independent if possible so that they can be used in IPv4 networks as well as in IPv6 networks. The results of different tests in the Moonv6 network have shown that most applications behave well in a dual-stacked or tunneled environment. More problems currently arise for applications in IPv6-only networks.

This section is not a guide to porting applications. The goal here is to make you aware of situations that you will face and what to look out for.

You will encounter the following situations:

- IPv4 applications on dual-stack nodes
- IPv6 applications on dual-stack nodes
- Applications supporting IPv4 and IPv6 on dual-stack nodes
- Applications supporting IPv4 and IPv6 on IPv4-only nodes
- Applications supporting IPv4 and IPv6 on IPv6-only nodes

The challenge for developers is to develop applications that work well in all situations. DNS names should be used whenever a service has to be called. But the DNS reply is not a reliable indicator of which protocol to use. For example, a host may be dual stack and have an A record with an IPv4 address and a AAAA record with an IPv6 address in DNS. But on this host, there may be an IPv4-only application. So even though resolving the host name returns an IPv6 address, the application is not reachable over IPv6. A workaround would be to enter services names with corresponding record types (A records for IPv4 services and AAAA records for IPv6 services) in DNS. But how this is handled depends on operational practice and is therefore not reliable. A node resolving a DNS name and getting multiple addresses in the reply should try them all until a connection can be established.

The following list shows the most important IP dependencies in applications:

- Format of the IP address (32-bit dotted decimal or 128-bit hexadecimal with colons)
- API functions for the establishment of connections and data exchange
- DNS, resolving host names to IP addresses and vice versa
- IP address selection, caching/storage of addresses

- Multicast applications, depending on situation; correspondence of IPv4 and IPv6 multicast addresses and selection of correct socket configuration options

The best way to go is to make applications independent of the IP version. This means that the source code should not have any IP dependencies. The communication library should provide APIs that have no dependencies on IP.

 Find a more detailed discussion of these issues in RFC 4038, "Application Aspects of IPv6 Transition."

The University of Tokyo and the Yokogawa Electric Corporation started the TAHI project in 1998. They develop tests that can be used by IPv6 developers to test their implementations for conformance to the standard and for interoperability. The tests can be used at no cost. This is their contribution to an efficient development and deployment of IPv6. The results of the tests are also provided to the developer community at no cost. On the TAHI web site (*http://www.tahi.org*), all tests are listed and documented.

The TAHI project works closely with other well-known projects: the WIDE project (*http://www.wide.ad.jp*), the KAME project (*http://www.kame.net*), and the USAGI project (*http://www.linux-ipv6.org*).

Cost of Introduction

Some people believe that the introduction of IPv6 is way too expensive, and they don't even start to think about it. Other people just want to know what it will cost. The next section contains aspects to consider and some thoughts on the business case for IPv6.

Hardware and Operating Systems

When planning ahead for IPv6, the cost for hardware upgrades is not extensive. In many cases, IPv6 is not part of the hardware and can be installed as part of the operating system or as a software upgrade. Most operating systems ship with IPv6 included at no extra cost as of a couple of years ago. If IP functions are implemented purely in hardware or if a system's software cannot be upgraded, the hardware must be replaced to support IPv6. If you plan ahead, though, this can usually be accomplished with the next upgrade in the regular lifecycle of the product and therefore generates no additional cost. As our case studies have shown, this is confirmed by organizations that have deployed IPv6.

Software

The time and effort needed to port applications to run over IPv6 depends on how the application is written and how it accesses the IP layer (if at all). If the application strictly separates the application layer from the communication layer, the porting is simple and quick. If the application uses complex middleware and customized APIs to communicate with the IP layer, the time and effort needed for porting is in direct relation to the complexity of the middleware. In this case, all dependencies on IP must be modified to support IPv6 (address length, header information, etc.).

It is to be expected that common applications already support IPv6 or will do so in their next major upgrade version. In this case, you can limit the cost for software by planning early and using the regular lifecycles of applications.

All proprietary and self-developed applications need to be tested for conformance and analyzed to find the best way to port them, or to find out whether they are too complex to be ported and need a rewrite to become IP independent. A simple porting of an application makes sure it runs equally well with IPv6 transport. A creative porting of an application may include using the advanced features of IPv6 and thereby extending the flexibility and functionality of the application. This can even be seen as cost associated with introducing advanced applications based on new technologies more than as cost of introducing IPv6.

Education

Every technology upgrade requires education: for developers, vendors, service providers, and the infrastructure and systems operators in organizations. For home users, it should be their ISP's job to make the transition simple.

A well-planned education program according to job responsibilities supports a smooth introduction of IPv6 substantially. For system operators, the time and effort needed for the learning is not higher than for maintaining the IPv4 infrastructure. We are used to integrating new technologies all the time to keep our networks state-of-the-art. We had to introduce DHCP, NAT, and VPNs in the past, and we mastered them. Now we are going to introduce IPv6 and the challenge is no bigger. And it is worth effort, time, and money because in the long term, the maintenance of an IPv6 network will be less costly than the maintenance of an IPv4 network. People that have a good understanding of IP and have mastered the previously mentioned technologies will have no problems mastering IPv6.

It is well worth it to take some time to learn about IPv6 before going into production. There are new concepts and possibilities in IPv6, and we need some time to become familiar with these, learn how to best make use of them, and then integrate the things we've learned into the planning.

Planning

The most important aspect of integration is the planning. The same rule applies here. Extending an infrastructure to keep it state-of-the-art always requires planning and should be seen as an investment. Instead of planning the next extension of IPv4, we will now plan the integration of IPv6.

The planning requires network architects and systems engineers with a good understanding of IPv4 and networking concepts. The first thing they need is a thorough IPv6 education and an IPv6 playground. The planning should not focus on how to make the same services available over IPv6. It should include understanding the new features of IPv6 and making use of them to create new concepts of architecture, security, mobility, and administration.

The introduction of IPv6 is smoother and cheaper the earlier you plan. A step-by-step integration is the best way to go, as it gives you time to integrate what you learn as you go. Step-by-step integration is possible thanks to the many available transition mechanisms.

Other Costs

Probably the highest costs arise when you wait too long. The longer you wait, the more investments you make into maintaining and extending your IPv4 infrastructure. This is money and effort you invest in an old technology. You may need to build band-aids for IPv4 (e.g., NAT) that later complicate the introduction of IPv6.

There are no reasons to tear down a performing network that fulfills all the requirements, but as soon as you have to invest in fixing or extending your IPv4 infrastructure, you should stop for a moment and consider IPv6 as an alternative. As mentioned earlier, putting IPv6 as an evaluation criterion on all your IT shopping lists for products that have more than two years' lifetime is a good idea. You may not want to turn IPv6 on tomorrow, but you may want to do so next year. If your equipment and software are ready, you can do it without additional cost when the right moment comes.

Another cost factor can be if a business-critical application comes out that is based on the advanced functionality of IPv6. If your infrastructure is IPv6-ready, you can introduce that application with moderate cost. If at the same time you have to master the transition to IPv6, this might create significant cost and put your current infrastructure at risk (plus create some headaches and sleepless nights).

Vendor Support

The first requirement is to have IPv6 support in host and router operating systems. In the last few years, there was a lot of activity in this area, and today we can say that most vendors support IPv6 on production level. The following sections provide an overview of the situation in 2005.

Operating Systems

Operating systems with IPv6 support include not only commercial operating systems such as Sun Solaris, HP-UX, IBM-AIX, Microsoft Windows (XP, .NET, and 2003 Server), Mac OS X, HP Tru64, HP OpenVMS, and SGI Irix, but also open source operating systems such as FreeBSD, KAME Stack, Linux, and NetBSD. Even some PDAs already have IPv6 support, such as Familiar Linux (on Compaq iPAQ), OpenZaurus (for Sharp Zaurus), and Windows CE. Embedded operating systems such as Elmic Systems, Embedded Linux, Symbian OSv7 (e.g., in Sony Ericsson P800 and P900), and Windriver have IPv6 support.

Many vendors have IPv6 information on their websites. Use the search option, a public search engine, or try the link *http://www.<vendor>.com/ipv6*.

Some links for embedded systems and PDAs:

- Elmic Systems, *http://www.treck.com*
- Embedded Linux, *http://www.embedded-linux.org*
- Symbian OS, *http://www.symbian.com*
- Windriver, *http://www.windriver.com*
- Familiar Linux, *http://familiar.handhelds.org*
- OpenZaurus, *http://www.openzaurus.org*
- Windows CE.NET, *http://msdn.microsoft.com/embedded*

The operating systems differ in the level of implementation. You have to ask specific questions, and vendors have to provide a list of which RFCs are supported in their implementation.

Router Support

The list of router vendors is large, with vendors such as Cisco, Juniper, Nortel, Hitachi, Ericsson, and 6WIND all well-represented. Most of them have been supporting IPv6 for almost a decade and continually upgraded and optimized their implementations. Again, be specific about the level of support offered. When evaluating a new router, compare the support on different models of the same vendor. Most router vendors have detailed lists available and roadmaps of what will be supported in the next release for each model.

When evaluating new router hardware, make sure to ask the following questions:

- Is IPv6 forwarding done on hardware or software level? (For backbone routers and ISP hardware, this is a critical factor.)

- Which transition mechanisms are implemented?
- Which routing protocols are supported?
- Which is the support level for VPN, packet filtering, and multicast?

Vendors offering Switches with layer 3 functionality and IPv6 support include Cisco, Foundry, Extreme, and Procket.

IP Address Management

Some DHCP implementations based on the RFC specification are already out there, one of them being the HP implementation plus some implementations based on open source operating systems. Cisco also has DHCPv6 functionality implemented. IP Management tools are in the queue, and the one with the broadest IPv6 support as of 2005 probably is INS's IPControl and NetControl. Lucent is working on the implementation of IPv6 address management in VitalQIP. More of these tools and better support will appear in the near future and may already be on the market when you read this book.

Firewalls

There is a lot of packet filtering software out there for IPv6, especially in the Linux and FreeBSD world, as well as for Mac OS Panther. Windows XP with Service Pack 2 includes a personal firewall called IPv6 Internet Connection Firewall. As IPv6 restores the end-to-end model, these personal firewalls will become increasingly more important. If you are looking for a Stateful firewall, Cisco supports it on IOS 12.3(7)T and above as well as in the PIX 7.0 series. CheckPoint's Firewall-1 has had Stateful IPv6 support for quite some time, and so do Juniper's NetScreen Firewalls and Internet Security Systems's Enterprise Protection Platform. This is not supposed to be a complete list. There may be other vendors of which I am not aware.

The next chapter introduces Mobile IPv6 and explains the concepts and how it works. Mobility may well become one of the drivers to deploy IPv6, because it greatly profits from the advanced features available with IPv6.

References

Here's a list of the most important RFCs and drafts mentioned in this chapter. Sometimes I include additional subject-related RFCs for your personal further study.

RFCs

- RFC 2185, "Routing Aspects Of IPv6 Transition," 1997
- RFC 2473, "Generic Packet Tunneling in IPv6 Specification," 1998

- RFC 2529, "Transmission of IPv6 over IPv4 Domains without Explicit Tunnels," 1999
- RFC 2553, "Basic Socket Interface Extensions for IPv6," March 1999
- RFC 2663, "IP Network Address Translator (NAT) Terminology and Considerations," 1999
- RFC 2765, "Stateless IP/ICMP Translation Algorithm (SIIT)," 2000
- RFC 2766, "Network Address Translation—Protocol Translation (NAT-PT)," 2000
- RFC 2767, "Dual Stack Hosts using the "Bump-In-the-Stack" Technique (BIS)," 2000
- RFC 2784, "Generic Routing Encapsulation (GRE)," 2000
- RFC 3022, "Traditional IP Network Address Translator (Traditional NAT)," 2001
- RFC 3053, "IPv6 Tunnel Broker," 2001
- RFC 3056, "Connection of IPv6 Domains via IPv4 Clouds," 2001
- RFC 3068, "An Anycast Prefix for 6to4 Relay Routers," 2001
- RFC 3142, "An IPv6-to-IPv4 Transport Relay Translator," 2001
- RFC 3162, "RADIUS and IPv6," 2001
- RFC 3338, "Dual Stack Hosts Using BIA," 2002
- RFC 3484, "Default Address Selection for Internet Protocol version 6 (IPv6)," 2003
- RFC 3489, "STUN - Simple Traversal of User Datagram Protocol (UDP) Through Network Address Translators (NATs)," 2003
- RFC 3493, "Basic Socket Interface Extensions for IPv6" 2003
- RFC 3542, "Advanced Sockets Application Program Interface (API) for IPv6," 2003
- RFC 3582, "Goals for IPv6 Site-Multihoming Architectures," 2003
- RFC 3715, "IPsec-Network Address Translation (NAT) Compatibility Requirements," 2004
- RFC 3789, "Introduction to the Survey of IPv4 Addresses in Currently Deployed IETF Standards Track and Experimental Documents," 2004
- RFC 3790, "Survey of IPv4 Addresses in Currently Deployed IETF Internet Area Standards Track and Experimental Documents," 2004
- RFC 3791, "Survey of IPv4 Addresses in Currently Deployed IETF Routing Area Standards Track and Experimental Documents," 2004
- RFC 3792, "Survey of IPv4 Addresses in Currently Deployed IETF Security Area Standards Track and Experimental Documents," 2004

- RFC 3793, "Survey of IPv4 Addresses in Currently Deployed IETF Sub-IP Area Standards Track and Experimental Documents," 2004

- RFC 3794, "Survey of IPv4 Addresses in Currently Deployed IETF Transport Area Standards Track and Experimental Documents," 2004

- RFC 3795, "Survey of IPv4 Addresses in Currently Deployed IETF Application Area Standards Track and Experimental Documents," 2004

- RFC 3796, "Survey of IPv4 Addresses in Currently Deployed IETF Operations & Management Area Standards Track and Experimental Documents," 2004

- RFC 3901, "DNS IPv6 Transport Operational Guidelines," 2004

- RFC 3964, "Security Considerations for 6to4," 2004

- RFC 3971, "SEcure Neighbor Discovery (SEND)," 2005

- RFC 3972, "Cryptographically Generated Addresses (CGA)," 2005

- RFC 4029, "Scenarios and Analysis for Introducing IPv6 into ISP Networks," 2005

- RFC 4038, "Application Aspects of IPv6 Transition," 2005

- RFC 4057, "IPv6 Enterprise Network Scenarios," 2005

- RFC 4159, "Deprecation of 'ip6.int'," 2005

- RFC 4177, "Architectural Approaches to Multi-homing for IPv6," 2005

- RFC 4191, "Default Router Preferences and More-Specific Routes," 2005

- RFC 4213, "Basic Transition Mechanisms for IPv6 Hosts and Routers," 2005

- RFC 4214, "Intra-Site Automatic Tunnel Addressing Protocol (ISATAP)," 2005

- RFC 4215, "Analysis on IPv6 Transition in Third Generation Partnership Project (3GPP) Networks," 2005

- RFC 4218, "Threats Relating to IPv6 Multihoming Solutions," 2005

- RFC 4219, "Things Multihoming in IPv6 (MULTI6) Developers Should Think About," 2005

- RFC 4241, "A Model of IPv6/IPv4 Dual Stack Internet Access Service," 2005

- RFC 4282, "The Network Access Identifier," 2005

- RFC 4380, "Teredo: Tunneling IPv6 over UDP through Network Address Translations (NATs)," 2006

Drafts

Drafts can be found at *http://www.ietf.org/ID.html*. To locate the latest version of a draft, refer to *https://datatracker.ietf.org/public/pidtracker.cgi*. You can enter the draft name without a version number, and the most current version will come up. If a draft does not show up, it was either deleted or published as an RFC. Alternatively, you can go to the new Internet drafts database interface at *https://datatracker.ietf.org/public/idindex.cgi*. *http://tools.ietf.org/wg* is also a very useful site. More information on the process of standardization, RFCs, and drafts can be found in Appendix A.

Here's a list of interesting drafts related to the topics or drafts to which I referred in this chapter:

- *draft-bound-dstm-exp-04.txt*, Dual Stack IPv6 Dominant Transition Mechanism (DSTM)
- *draft-blanchet-v6ops-tunnelbroker-tsp-03.txt*, IPv6 Tunnel Broker with the Tunnel Setup Protocol (TSP)
- *draft-ietf-v6ops-vlan-usage-01.txt*, Use of VLANs for IPv4-IPv6 Coexistence in Enterprise Networks
- *draft-ietf-dnsop-ipv6-dns-issues-12.txt*, Operational Considerations and Issues with IPv6 DNS (RFC queue)
- *draft-ietf-v6ops-bb-deployment-scenarios-04.txt*, ISP IPv6 Deployment Scenarios in Broadband Access Networks
- *draft-shin-v6ops-802-16-deployment-scenarios-00.txt*, ISP IPv6 Deployment Scenarios in Wireless Broadband Access Networks
- *draft-ietf-v6ops-natpt-to-exprmntl-03.txt*, Reasons to Move NAT-PT to Experimental
- *draft-ietf-v6ops-nap-02.txt*, IPv6 Network Architecture Protection
- *draft-ietf-shim6-proto-04.txt*, Level 3 multihoming shim protocol
- *draft-ietf-shim6-failure-detection-03.txt*, Failure Detection and Locator Pair Exploration Protocol for IPv6 Multihoming
- *draft-ietf-shim6-hba-01.txt*, Hash Based Addresses (HBA)
- *draft-ietf-shim6-reach-detect-01.txt*, Shim6 Reachability Detection
- *draft-vandevelde-v6ops-addcon-00.txt*, IPv6 Unicast Address Assignment Considerations

CHAPTER 11

Mobile IPv6

In the past, we were used to making phone calls from home or from the office. Public pay phones allowed us to make phone calls while on the road. Today, the use of mobile phones is common and we make phone calls from almost anywhere and in any life situation. The use of notebook computers, wireless networks, and portable devices is expanding, and we can imagine having smart devices and using them from wherever we are. If these devices are to use IP as a transport protocol, we need Mobile IP to make this work. We expect our device to remain connected when we move around and change our point of attachment to the network, just as we are used to roaming from one cell to the next with our mobile phones today. For example, suppose you have a PDA with an 802.11 (wireless) interface and a General Packet Radio Service (GPRS) interface. In your hotel room, you are connected to the network through your wireless interface; when you leave your room and go out to the street, you switch automatically to GPRS without losing your connection. All the applications running on your PDA stay up. Isn't this cool? This section about Mobile IP explores the mechanisms needed and shows how IPv6 is ready for this challenge.

With IPv4 and IPv6 alike, the prefix (subnet address) changes depending on the network to which we are attached. When a mobile node changes its point of access to the network, it needs to get a new IP address, which disrupts its TCP or UDP connections. RFC 3344, "IP Mobility Support for IPv4," describes Mobile IP concepts and specifications for IPv4. Using Mobile IP with IPv4 has certain limitations, though, which make it unsuitable for the requirements in a global network. One reason is the limited address space. If we even imagine only smart phones having an IP address, the number of addresses required globally to cover the number of devices far exceeds the IPv4 address space available. The other reason is that IPv6 and the use of Extension headers offers the possibility to optimize routing in a mobile world, and this is really needed if we talk about mobility for large masses of devices. The fact that IPv6 uses Neighbor Discovery (instead of ARP like IPv4) makes IPv6 more independent of the Link layer. Mobile IPv6 takes the experience from Mobile IPv4 and makes use of the advanced features of IPv6.

This chapter describes how Mobile IPv6 works and how it is suited to provide the foundation for mobile services of tomorrow. First I explain the most important terms that will be used throughout the chapter, then I provide an overview of the functionality, and after this I dive into the technical details of the protocol: the new headers, messages, options, processes, and communications. So take a deep breath and read on.

Overview

Mobile IPv6 is a protocol that allows a mobile node to move from one network to another without loosing its connections. It is specified in RFC 3775.

Most Internet traffic uses TCP connections. A TCP connection is defined by the combination of IP address and port number of both endpoints of the communication. If one of these four numbers changes, the communication is disrupted and has to be reestablished. If a mobile node connects to a different access point to the network, it needs a new IP address. Mobile IP addresses the challenge of moving a node to a different connection point without changing its IP address by assigning the mobile node two different IP addresses. One is the *home address*, which is static and does not change, and it is therefore used to identify the TCP connection. The second IP address is called the *care-of address*. It changes depending on the network to which the node is currently attached. So this works within homogeneous networks (if the node moves from an Ethernet segment to another Ethernet segment) but also in heterogeneous networks (if the node moves from an Ethernet segment to a wireless LAN).

In a wireless network, we are familiar with the *handover*, the event where a device moves from one access point to another. This is a handover on the Link layer. Mobile IPv6 solves the handover issue on the Network layer and maintains connections to applications and services if a device changes its temporary IP address.

Mobile IPv6 Terms

Here comes the definition of some terms that are used throughout the chapter.

Home address
> A global unicast address assigned to a mobile node. It is used as the permanent address for this node and is within the mobile node's home link. Regular routing mechanisms deliver packets to the home address of the mobile node.

Home subnet prefix
> The IP subnet prefix corresponding to a mobile node's home address.

Home link
> The link on which a mobile node's home subnet prefix is defined.

Mobile node
> A node that can change its point of attachment from one link to another while still being reachable via its home address.

Correspondent node
> A peer node with which a mobile node is communicating. The correspondent node may be either mobile or stationary.

Foreign subnet prefix
> Any IP subnet prefix other than the mobile node's home subnet prefix.

Foreign link
> Any link other than the mobile node's home link.

Care-of address
> A global unicast address for the mobile node while it is in a foreign network (away from home). The subnet prefix of the care-of address is the foreign subnet prefix. A mobile node may have multiple care-of addresses. The one being registered with its home agent is the primary care-of address.

Home agent
> A router on a mobile node's home link with which the mobile node has registered its current care-of address. While the mobile node is away from home, the home agent intercepts packets on the home link destined to the mobile node's home address, encapsulates them (IPv6 encapsulation), and tunnels them to the mobile node's registered care-of address.

Binding
> The association of the home address of a mobile node with a care-of address for that mobile node, along with the remaining lifetime of that association.

Registration
> The process during which a mobile node sends a Binding Update to its home agent or a correspondent node, causing a binding for the mobile node to be registered. The registration with the correspondent node is called Correspondent Registration.

Binding authorization
> A registration with a correspondent node needs to be authorized to allow the recipient to ensure that the sender has the right to specify a new binding.

Return routability procedure
> A procedure that authorizes registrations by the use of a cryptographic token exchange.

Keygen token
> A number supplied by a correspondent node in the return routability procedure to enable the mobile node to compute the necessary binding management key for authorizing a Binding Update.

Nonce

Random numbers used internally by the correspondent node in the creation of keygen tokens related to the return routability procedure. The nonces are not specific to a mobile node and are kept secret within the correspondent node.

Nonce index

Used to indicate which nonces have been used when creating keygen token values without revealing the nonces themselves.

How Mobile IPv6 Works

Figure 11-1 shows the components of Mobile IPv6 and how they interact.

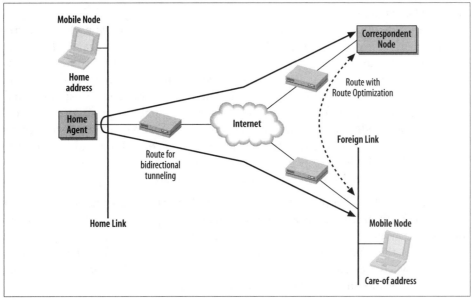

Figure 11-1. Overview Mobile IPv6

The home address is the IPv6 address within the home link prefix of a mobile node (MN). As long as the mobile node is at home, it receives packets through regular IP routing mechanisms and behaves like any other regular IP host. When the mobile node is away from home on a foreign link, it has an additional care-of address. It receives the care-of address through regular IPv6 mechanisms such as Stateless autoconfiguration or DHCPv6 when connecting to the new link.

The association of a home address and a care-of address is called a *binding*. While away from home, the mobile node registers its care-of address with a router on its home link, its *home agent* (HA). To register its care-of address, the mobile node sends a binding update message to the home agent. The home agent responds with a binding acknowledgement. Every node communicating with a mobile node is called a *correspondent node* (CN). Mobile nodes can also send registrations to the correspondent node directly (called a correspondent registration). A correspondent node can also be a mobile node.

There are two ways to communicate for a correspondent node and a mobile node:

Bidirectional Tunneling
Packets from the correspondent node are sent to the home agent, which encapsulates them in IPv6 and sends them to the care-of address of the mobile node. Packets from the mobile node are sent through the reverse tunnel to the home agent that forwards them to the correspondent node through regular routing mechanisms. This mode does not require any Mobile IPv6 support on the correspondent node and works without correspondent registration.

Route Optimization
With Route Optimization, the communication between mobile node and correspondent node can be direct without going through the home agent. This is one of the main advantages of Mobile IPv6 over Mobile IPv4, where route optimization is not possible. Route optimization requires that the mobile node registers its care-of address with the correspondent node (correspondent registration) and that this binding is authorized through the return routability procedure. The correspondent node uses a special routing header (type 2) when it sends packets to the mobile node directly. The mobile node uses the Home Address option (defined for Mobile IPv6) when sending packets to the correspondent node. The whole process is described in more detail later in the chapter.

The advantage of route optimization is that the shortest available path can be used between correspondent node and mobile node. The packets do not have to go through the home agent. This not only ensures shorter communication paths but also reduces the load on the home agent and the home link. This becomes very important when we talk about high numbers of mobile nodes constantly moving around, for instance in a VoIP (Voice over IP) scenario.

Mobile IPv6 also supports the option to have multiple home agents, and the mobile node can learn about reconfiguration of its home link or a change of IP address of its home agent through Dynamic Home Agent Address Discovery. If the prefix of its home link changes, the mobile node uses the Mobile Prefix Discovery mechanism to learn about the new prefix.

The following sections describe the protocol and new messages, options, and flags in more detail. After this, I dive into the communication flows that have just been described in an overview. Some people prefer to learn this way; other people prefer to learn about the processes and flows first and then about the technical details. Please read the sections in the order that best fits your preference.

The Mobile IPv6 Protocol

This section describes the components, messages, and options for Mobile IPv6.

Mobility Header and Mobility Messages

The Mobility Header (MH) has been defined for Mobile IPv6. It is an Extension header used by mobile node, correspondent node, and home agent. It is used in all messages that are related to establishing and maintaining bindings.

A Mobility Header is specified by the Next Header value 135 in the preceding header and has the format shown in Figure 11-2.

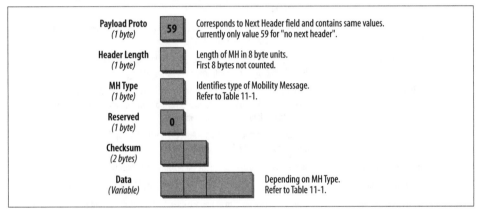

Figure 11-2. Format of the Mobility Header (MH)

The Payload Proto field corresponds to the Next Header field and identifies the following header. It can therefore contain the same values. The current specification sets the value in this field to 59 decimal, which means "no next header". It is designed to be used for future extensions. The Header Length field contains the length of the Mobility header in 8-byte units. The first 8 bytes are not counted. The length of the Mobility header is always a multiple of 8 bytes. The Checksum field contains the checksum for the Mobility header. It is calculated based on a pseudo-header and follows the rules defined in RFC 2460. The addresses used in the pseudo-header are the source and destination address in the IPv6 header. If the Mobility message contains a Home Address Destination option, the home address is used for the calculation of the checksum. The MH Type field identifies the type of Mobility message. The messages defined are listed in Table 11-1. The Data field is variable; it depends on the type of message.

Table 11-1 is an overview of the Mobility messages.

Table 11-1. Mobility message types

Value	Message type	Description
0	Binding Refresh Request	Sent by CN requesting the MN to update its binding.
1	Home Test Init	Sent by the MN to initiate the Return Routability Procedure and request a Home Keygen token from a CN. Sent to the CN through the tunnel via HA.
2	Care-of Test Init	Sent by the MN to initiate the Return Routability Procedure and request a Keygen token from a CN. Sent to the CN directly.
3	Home Test Message	Response to a Home Test Init message (type 1). Sent from the CN to MN. Contains a cookie and a Home Keygen token for the authorization in the Return Routability Process. Sent through the tunnel via HA.
4	Care-of Test Message	Response to Care-of Test Init message (type 2). Sent from CN to MN. Contains cookie and a Care-of Keygen token for the authorization in the Return Routability Procedure. Sent to the MN directly.
5	Binding Update	Sent by MN to notify a change of its care-of address. This message is explained in more detail later in the chapter.
6	Binding Ack	Sent as acknowledgement for receipt of a Binding Update message. This message is explained in more detail later in the chapter.
7	Binding Error	Sent by CN to signal an error related to mobility, such as an inappropriate attempt to use the Home Address destination option without an existing binding. The status field can have the following values: 1 = unkown binding for Home Address Destination option 2 = unrecognized MH type value
8	Fast Binding Update	Identical to binding update message, only with slightly different processing rules.
9	Fast Binding Ack	Sent as acknowledgement for receipt of a Fast Binding Update message.
10	Fast Neighbor Advertisement	Sent by mobile node to announce itself to its new access router.

Values 8, 9, and 10 have been assigned in RFC 4068, "Fast Handovers for Mobile IPv6." This RFC specifies a protocol to improve handover latency due to Mobile IPv6 procedures.

To help you understand the binding, the next section explores the Binding Update and the Binding Acknowledgement messages in more detail.

 You can find all message and option types as well as status codes at *http://www.iana.org/assignments/mobility-parameters*.

The Binding Update Message

The Binding Update message is used by the mobile node to inform the home agent or a correspondent node about a new care-of address. The message is also used to extend the lifetime of an existing binding.

The Binding Update message is of MH type 5 and has the format shown in Figure 11-3.

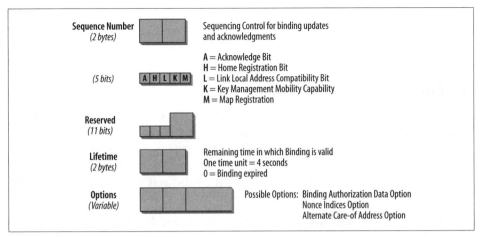

Figure 11-3. Format of the Binding Update message

The Sequence Number is used by the receiving node for sequencing Binding Updates. The sending node uses it to verify whether the Binding Acknowledgements received correspond to its Binding Updates. The Acknowledge bit (A-bit) is set by the mobile node if it expects an acknowledgement in answer to its Binding Update. The Home Registration bit (H-bit) is set by the mobile node to request the receiver to act as home agent for this node. This is possible only if the receiver is on the home link of the mobile node. The Link-Local Address Compatibility bit (L-bit) is set if the home address has the same Interface Identifier as the link-local address of the mobile node. The Key Management Mobility Capability bit (K-bit) is valid only in Binding Updates sent to the home agent. IPsec Security Associations should survive the move of the mobile node to another network. If that is the case, the K-bit is set. If that is not possible, the K-bit is set to 0. Correspondent nodes ignore the K-bit. The Lifetime shows in four-second units for how long the binding for the care-of address is valid. If the Lifetime is set to 0, the receiver must delete the entry in its Binding Cache. In this case, the mobile node must be on its home link, and the care-of address is the same as the home address.

The M-bit shown in Figure 11-3 has additionally been created to identify Local Binding Updates sent to a local Home Agent called a *Mobility Anchor Point* (MAP). This new node is used to improve Mobile IPv6 handover performance, to obtain efficient routing between the mobile node and correspondent nodes within the same geographical area, and to achieve location privacy. The mechanism is defined in RFC 4140, "Hierarchical Mobile IPv6 Mobility Management (HMIPv6)," and is explained in more detail at the end of this chapter. When the M-bit is set, the H-bit cannot be set and vice versa.

A Binding Update can have the following options:

- Binding Authorization Data option (this option is mandatory in Binding Updates sent to a correspondent node)
- Nonce Indices option
- Alternate Care-of Address option

The Binding Acknowledgement

The Binding Acknowledgement is sent to confirm receipt of a Binding Update. It has to be sent if the A-bit is set in the Binding Update. If the A-bit is not set (which means the sender of the Binding Update does not require an acknowledgment), the Binding Acknowledgement is sent only if there is a problem in the Binding Update. If the receiver accepts the Binding Update and the A-bit was not set, no acknowledgment is sent.

The Binding Acknowledgement is of MH type 6 and has the format shown in Figure 11-4.

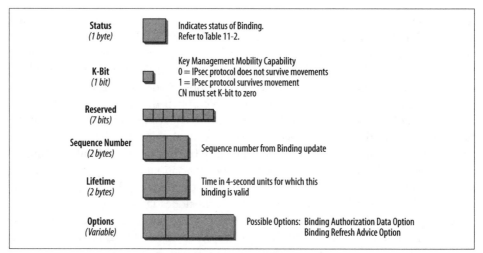

Figure 11-4. Format of the Binding Acknowledgement

The status field indicates the status of the Binding Update. Table 11-2 shows the status values. Values in the range of 0 to 127 indicate that the Binding Update has been accepted. Values above 128 indicate that the Binding Update has not been accepted.

Table 11-2. Status values in the Binding Acknowledgement

Value	Description	Defined in
0	Binding Update accepted	RFC 3775
1	Accepted but prefix discovery necessary	RFC 3775

Table 11-2. Status values in the Binding Acknowledgement (continued)

Value	Description	Defined in
128	Reason unspecified	RFC 3775
129	Administratively prohibited	RFC 3775
130	Insufficient resources	RFC 3775
131	Home Registration not supported	RFC 3775
132	Not home subnet	RFC 3775
133	Not home agent for this mobile node	RFC 3775
134	Duplicate Address Detection failed	RFC 3775
135	Sequence number out of window	RFC 3775
136	Expired home nonce index	RFC 3775
137	Expired care-of nonce index	RFC 3775
138	Expired nonces	RFC 3775
139	Registration type change disallowed	RFC 3775
140	Mobile Router Operation not permitted	RFC 3963
141	Invalid Prefix	RFC 3963
142	Not Authorized for Prefix	RFC 3963
143	Forwarding Setup failed	RFC 3963
144	MIPV6-ID-MISMATCH	RFC 4285
145	MIPV6-MESG-ID-REQD	RFC 4285
146	MIPV6-AUTH-FAIL	RFC 4285

The K-bit is the Key Management Mobility Capability bit (see the description earlier in "The Binding Update Message"). This bit is of importance only in bindings between mobile node and home agent. Correspondent nodes ignore this bit. The Sequence Number in the Binding Acknowledgement is copied from the Sequence Number field in the Binding Update. It is used by the mobile node in matching this Binding Acknowledgement with an outstanding Binding Update. The Lifetime shows in 4-second units for how long the binding for the care-of address is valid. During the time indicated here, either the home agent or the correspondent node keeps the entry for this binding in its Binding Cache. In a Binding Acknowledgement that indicates that the Binding has not been accepted (value of 128 or higher), the Lifetime is not specified.

A Binding Acknowledgement can have the following options:

- Binding Authorization Data option (this option is mandatory in Binding Acknowledgements sent by a correspondent node)
- Binding Refresh Advice option

Mobility Options

A mobility message can contain zero, one, or more options. These options are included in the variable data field of the mobility header. This architecture is very flexible, as options are inserted only if needed and additional options can easily be defined in the future.

The presence of options is indicated in the header length field of the mobility header. They have the known TLV format (Type 1 Byte, Length 1 Byte, Value variable).

Table 11-3 contains an overview of the currently defined options for mobility messages.

Table 11-3. Mobility options

Value Length	Name	Description	Defined in
Type 0	Pad1	Used to insert one padding Byte. This option has a special format; it contains only a type field, and no fields for length and data.	RFC 3775
Type 1	PadN	Used to insert two or more padding Bytes.	RFC 3775
Type 2 Length 2	Binding Refresh Advice	Indicates the remaining time until the MN should send a new home registration to HA. Only valid in Binding Acks sent from the HA in response to a home registration. The interval must be shorter than the lifetime value in the Binding Acknowledgement. A time unit is four seconds.	RFC 3775
Type 3 Length 16	Alternate Care-of address	Contains an address to use as the care-of address for the binding rather than using the Source address of the packet as the care-of address. Only in Binding Update messages.	RFC 3775
Type 4 Length 4	Nonce Indices	Has two additional fields besides the Type and Length field. The Home Nonce Index field tells the CN which nonce value to use when producing the Home Keygen Token. The Care-of Nonce field indicates the value for generating the Care-of Keygen Token. Valid only in the Binding Update message sent to a CN, and only when present together with a Binding Authorization Data option.	RFC 3775
Type 5 Length variable	Binding Authorization Data	Contains a cryptographic value that can be used to determine that the message in question comes from the right authority. Rules for calculating this value depend on the authorization procedure used. Must always be the last option in the MH. Only valid in Binding Update and Binding Acknowledgement. Used for the Return Routability process. In this case, the calculation of the Authenticator value is based on care-of address of MN, IPv6 address of CN, and data from the MH.	RFC 3775
Type 6	Mobile Network Prefix Option	Included in the Binding Update to indicate the prefix information for the Mobile Network to the HA.	RFC 3963
Type 7	Mobility Header Link-Layer Address option	Link-layer address option carried in an MH; used for Fast Handovers.	RFC 4068
Type 8	MN-ID-OPTION-TYPE	Optional suboption in the MH to specify the type of identifier used to identify the MN.	RFC 4283

Table 11-3. Mobility options (continued)

Value Length	Name	Description	Defined in
Type 9	AUTH-OPTION-TYPE	When receiving a binding update, the HA must check the timestamp field. If it is invalid, it replies with a binding acknowledgment including this status code.	RFC 4285
Type 10	MESG-ID-OPTION-TYPE	Defines the type of mobility option.	RFC 4285
Type 201 Length 16	Home Address	Contains the home address of MN. Sent by MN when away from home to indicate its home address to the receiver. Carried in a Destination Options header. Must be inserted after Routing header and before Fragment, AH, or ESP header (if present).	RFC 3775

With the exception of the Binding Authorization Data option, these options can appear in arbitrary order. The Home Address option is an exception, as it is carried in a Destination Options header and not in the Mobility Header (MH).

RFC 4283, "Mobile Node Identifier Option for Mobile IPv6 (MIPv6)," extends the original specification to allow MIPv6 nodes (HA, CN, MN) to use identifiers other than an IP address. It defines an option with a subtype number to specify the identifier type. The identifier type can be a Network Access Identifier (NAI; see RFC 4282), an International Mobile Station Identifier (IMSI), or an application/deployment specific opaque identifier. Additional identifier types will be specified in the future.

Routing Header Type 2

A new Routing header has been defined for Mobile IPv6. This Extension header allows the data exchange between the care-of address of a mobile node and a correspondent node without being routed through the home agent. In other words, it is used when communication is performed with route optimization after a successful return routability procedure.

In addition to the Type 0 Routing Extension header described in Chapter 2, RFC 3775 defines the Type 2 Routing header. It allows, among other things, the configuration of specific rules for Mobile IPv6 packets on firewalls.

When a correspondent node sends an IPv6 datagram to a mobile node using route optimization, the Destination Address field in the IPv6 header contains the care-of address of the mobile node. The Routing Header Type 2 inserted contains the home address of the mobile node. The Routing Header Type 2 can only contain one unicast address. IPv6 nodes that process these Routing headers must verify that the IPv6 address contained corresponds to the home address of the mobile node.

The format of the Routing Header Type 2 corresponds to the Routing Header Type 0 shown in Chapter 2 (Figure 2-5). The Header Extension Length field has the value 2; this header does not have a variable length, as it only contains one address. In the

Routing Type field, the value 2 is indicated, and the Segments Left field is set to 1 for one address. The Home Address field carries the home address of the mobile node.

If an IPv6 datagram carries two Routing Headers, the Type 0 routing header must be first, followed by the Type 2 routing header. How this Routing Header Type 2 is used and processed is described later in this chapter.

ICMPv6 and Mobile IPv6

This section describes two new ICMPv6 message pairs and some modifications to Neighbor Discovery (ND).

Home Agent Address Discovery

The Home Agent Address Discovery mechanism is used by the mobile node to determine the address of its home agent on its home link. There are two ICMPv6 message pairs and the home agents list, which is a list to be maintained by each home agent.

ICMPv6 Home Agent Address Discovery messages

This message pair consists of a Home Agent Address Discovery Request and Reply message. As the name implies, the mobile node uses these messages to find its home agent on the home link dynamically. Normally mobile nodes are configured statically with a home agent address. In the case where a home agent is renumbered or goes down and is replaced by another home agent with a different IP address, dynamic discovery of the home agent address may be a useful mechanism.

The mobile node sends a Discovery message to the Home Agent Anycast address (Anycast ID decimal 126, hexadecimal 0x7E; see Chapter 3) on its home link. The Source address field in the IPv6 header carries the care-of address of the mobile node.

The home agents on the home link that are configured for the Home Agent Anycast address respond with a Home Agent Address Discovery Reply message.

The Discovery message has a type value of 150; the Reply message has a type value of 151. The Code field is always set to 0. The Identifier field is inserted by the mobile node and copied over by the home agent for the Reply. This allows to identify corresponding messages. The Reply carries a Home Address field, which can carry one or more home agent addresses. This address or list of addresses is generated from the home agents list (described next).

 For a detailed description of the header fields in an ICMPv6 message, please refer to Chapter 4.

Home agents list

Every home agent needs to maintain a home agents list. In this list, every router must be listed that sits on the same link and provides home agent services. A router advertises itself as a home agent by setting the H-bit in the Router Advertisement. A router maintains a home agents list for each link on which it acts as a home agent. The list is updated through Router Advertisements and contains the following information:

- Link-local address of the HAs on the link. This address is learned from the Source address field in the IPv6 header of Router Advertisements.

- One or more global IPv6 unicast addresses for these HAs. These addresses are learned from the Prefix Option in the Router Advertisements.

- Remaining lifetime for this HA entry. When the lifetime expires, the HA has to be deleted from the list.

- Preference for this HA. Higher values means higher preference. This value is learned from the Home Agent Preference field in the Home Agent Information option in a Router Advertisement (if present). If not present, this value is set to 0. A HA uses this preference to sort the HA list when sending out an Home Agent Address Discovery Reply message.

The HA sending out a Home Agent Address Discovery Reply must list all HAs on the link, sorted by preference. Only the global IPv6 unicast addresses of the home agents are contained in the home agent address field of the home agent address discovery reply message. The reply must not be larger than 1280 bytes. Sorting by preference ensures that HAs with a high priority are listed in this packet.

Mobile Prefix Solicitation

The Mobile Prefix Solicitation message is sent by a mobile node away from home to determine changes in the prefix configuration of its home link (i.e., home network renumbering). The HA answers the Solicitation message with a Prefix Advertisement. Based on this reply, the mobile node can adjust its home address.

The mobile node sends an ICMPv6 Mobile Prefix Solicitation message to its HA. The IPv6 header carries the care-of address as Source address. A Home Address Destination option is inserted. IPsec headers are supported and should be used. The Mobile Prefix Solicitation can carry options that have to follow the format described in Chapter 4 (RFC 2461). Currently, there are no specific options defined. The type value field of an Mobile Prefix Solicitation message is set to 152; the Code field is set to 0.

The HA replies with an ICMPv6 Mobile Prefix Advertisement message to the care-of address of the mobile node. The HA can also send out unsolicited Advertisements at regular intervals. The Advertisement carries a Routing header type 2. The reply is sent to the Source address of the Solicitation message. If the Advertisement is unsolicited, it is sent to the care-of address of registered mobile nodes. The type value for the Advertisement is set to 153. If it is the answer to a Solicitation, the Identifier is copied over from the Solicitation. The Advertisement contains the Prefix option described in Chapter 4. It carries all prefixes that should be used by the mobile node to configure its home addresses.

Changes in Neighbor Discovery (ND)

Some changes and new options have been defined in ND for the use with Mobile IPv6.

Modified Router Advertisement format

As already mentioned in Chapter 4, there is a new flag in the Router Advertisement. The M-flag and the O-flag are followed by the H-flag, which allows a router to advertise that it acts as a home agent on this link.

Modified Prefix option

In order to build an updated HA list based on Router Advertisements, a mobile node must know the global unicast address of the routers. A regular Router Advertisement lists only the link-local address of the router. For this purpose, the Prefix Option has been modified. The Prefix option now carries an additional flag, the R-flag (Router Address). When this flag is set, it indicates that the Prefix option field does not contain a Prefix, but rather a global IPv6 unicast address for the router.

New Advertisement Interval option

The Advertisement Interval option is used in Router Advertisements. It indicates the interval at which the router will send unsolicited multicast Router Advertisements. The option follows the TLV format (Time, Length, Value) and has a type value of 7. The Advertisement Interval field has 4 bytes and carries the time in milliseconds between unsolicited Router Advertisements. The mobile node uses this information in its Movement Detection Algorithm (described later in this chapter).

New Home Agent Information option

The Home Agent Information option is used in Router Advertisements and follows the TLV format. The type value is 8.

The HA Preference field has a length of 2 bytes. In a Router Advertisement, the HA can use this field to indicate which level of preference should be associated to it. A higher value means a higher preference. When this option is not set, the HA has a preference of 0. This field can be used by the HA to dynamically adjust to different situations, e.g., to the number of mobile nodes currently connected or based on how many ressources are available to serve additional mobile nodes. Alternatively, the preference can be configured manually.

The Home Agent Lifetime field also has a length of 2 bytes. It indicates the lifetime for this HA in seconds. The default value corresponds to the value in the basic Router Advertisement header. The maximum possible value is 18.2 hours. A value of 0 is not accepted. The HA Lifetime field only relates to the HA service of this router, so it can be present only in a Router Advertisement with the H-bit (home agent) set.

Changes in the Router Advertisement Interval

The Neighbor Discovery specification specifies a minimum interval of three seconds for unsolicited multicast Router Advertisements. Mobile nodes are dependent on learning as fast as possible when moving to a new network to create new care-of addresses accordingly and send out Binding Updates. They detect their movement to a new network based on Router Advertisements from routers they don't know yet. As a consequence, routers supporting Mobile IPv6 must be configurable with a shorter Router Advertisement Interval. Alternatively mobility information from lower layers (i.e., layer 2) can be used to aid the mobile node in achieving faster movement detection.

Mobile IPv6 Communication

This section discusses Mobile IPv6 terms and goes into more details on the communication processes.

Binding Cache

Every correspondent node and home agent maintains a Binding Cache for each of its global IPv6 addresses. It lists all mobile nodes for which it has a binding. If it wants to send data to a certain destination, it first searches its Binding Cache, and after this, the Destination Cache for an address.

A Binding Cache entry carries the following information:

- Home address of the mobile node for the entry. This field is the key to determining the destination address when sending a packet.
- Care-of address for the mobile node indicated by the Home Address field in this binding cache entry.
- Lifetime value for the binding.
- A flag indicating whether this entry is a home registration entry. Present only on a node that acts as a home agent.
- Maximum value of the Sequence Number field of all previous Binding Updates received for this home address.
- Information on the use of this entry.

Binding Update List

Every mobile node maintains a Binding Update List. The list has an entry for each Binding Update the mobile node has sent to its home agent(s) and to correspondent nodes for which the lifetime has not expired. If it has sent more than one Binding Update, only the last message with the highest Sequence number is listed.

A Binding Update List carries the following information:

- IPv6 address of the node to which the Binding Update has been sent
- Home address for which the Binding Update has been sent
- Care-of address that was indicated in this Binding Update
- Lifetime that was indicated in the Binding Update
- Remaining lifetime for the Binding
- Highest used Sequence number for this Binding
- Time when Binding Update was sent
- State of any retransmissions needed
- A flag indicating whether further Binding Updates have to be sent to this destination

Return Routability Procedure

The Return Routability Procedure is designed to allow a correspondent node to detect whether the mobile node is reachable at its care-of address as well as at its home address. Only when this has been successfully proven can route optimization (i.e., direct communication between correspondent node and mobile node) be used. The fact that the mobile node can be reached at both addresses indicates that it really is on the foreign link and has a valid registration for the home address. This reduces (but does not eliminate) the risk that this Binding Update is a security attack. Only after a successful Return Routability test does the correspondent node accept Binding Updates from the mobile node and send datagrams to the care-of address of the mobile node directly.

The message flow for the Return Routability Procedure consists of the following steps (for MH types, refer to Table 11-1):

1. MN sends a Home Test Init message (MH type 1) via HA to the CN. This message carries a Home Init Cookie. This way the CN learns the Home Address of the MN.
2. MN sends a Care-of Test Init message (MH type 2) to the CN. This message carries a Care-of Init Cookie. It is sent to the CN directly (not through HA). This way, the CN learns the care-of address of the MN.
3. CN replies to the Home Test Init message with a Home Test message (MH type 3) sent via HA. It carries the Home Init Cookie, the Home Keygen Token, and the Home Nonce Index. The MN can now generate a Home Keygen Token.

4. CN replies to the Care-of Test Init message with a Care-of Test message (MH type 4) sent to the MN's care-of address. It carries the Care-of Init Cookie, the Care-of Keygen Token, and the Care-of Nonce Index. The MN can now generate a Care-of Keygen Token.

Once the mobile node has received the Home Test and the Care-of Test messages, the Return Routability Procedure has been accomplished. The mobile node hashes the two tokens and creates a 20-byte Management Key, which is obviously also known to the correspondent node that generated the two tokens in the first place. This key will be used by the mobile node to secure the Binding Update to the correspondent node. Upon a successful security check, the correspondent node can accept the Binding Update since the mobile node has proven that it is reachable on the home and care-of addresses contained in the Binding Update.

RFC 4225, "Mobile IP Version 6 Route Optimization Security Design Background," outlines the security considerations and choices that were made when the Return Routability Procedure was defined. The goal of this informational document is to help implementors of MIPv6 understand the design choices and to help people who design mobility of multihoming solutions to avoid some common security pitfalls. The security problems and possible countermeasures are discussed in detail.

Home Agent Operation

When the mobile node is away from home, the HA must intercept all packets destined to the mobile node and tunnel them to the care-of address of the mobile node. It uses Proxy Neighbor Discovery to do so.

Proxy Neighbor Discovery

In order to intercept packets destined to the mobile node on the home link, the HA must pretend to be the mobile node. The HA sends Neighbor Advertisements to the All-nodes Multicast address, providing its own link-layer address as link-layer address for the home address of the mobile node. The ND message has the following information:

- The Source address in the IPv6 header of the Neighbor Advertisement is the address of the HA.
- The Target Address field in the ND message carries the IPv6 address of the mobile node.
- The ND Advertisement contains a Target Link-layer Address option carrying the link-layer address of the HA.
- The Router Flag (R-flag) must be set to 0.
- The Override Flag (O-flag) must be set. All nodes on the link will update their Neighbor Caches and store the link-layer address.

Now the HA receives all packets on this link that are destined to the IPv6 address of the mobile node. The HA acts as a proxy for the mobile node. It must inspect all Neighbor Solicitations it receives and verify whether the Target Address field corresponds to a Home Registration entry in its Binding Cache. If so, it replies with a Neighbor Advertisement indicating its own link-layer address as the link-layer address for the mobile node. This procedure also defends the mobile node's home address from other home link nodes trying to configure that same address (i.e., Duplicate Address Detection, as explained in Chapter 4).

Bidirectional Tunneling

To forward packets destined to the home address of the mobile node, the HA uses an IPv6 tunnel. It inserts an additional IPv6 header called the Tunnel header. The Source address in the Tunnel header is the IPv6 address of the HA. The destination address is the primary care-of address of the mobile node. The mobile node processes the Tunnel header and forwards the decapsulated packet internally to the upper-layer protocols and applications.

In order to receive multicast packets when away from home, the mobile node must register for these group memberships. There are two ways to accomplish this:

- The mobile node can register with local routers on the Home Link using its care-of address. In this case, it can receive multicast packets directly. These memberships will not survive if the mobile node moves to another foreign network.

- The mobile node can register for multicast group memberships on its Home Link by sending MLD registrations to its HA, which in turn will forward multicast packets to the mobile node using the tunnel. This will always work no matter how many times the mobile node changes the network.

The following packets are not forwarded to the mobile node:

- Packets sent to the link-layer address of the mobile node. These packets are answered with an ICMPv6 Destination Unreachable message.

- Packets sent to the site-local address of the mobile node. (Site-local addresses have been deprecated after the publication of the Mobile IPv6 specification; this will be changed in a future version of this RFC.)

- Multicast packets sent to a link-local, site-local, or organization-local scope.

Packets sent through the Reverse Tunnel from the mobile node to the HA are decapsulated by the HA and forwarded to their destinations through regular routing mechanisms.

When the HA itself sends data to the mobile node, it behaves like a regular correspondent node, which means it does not use the tunnel, but inserts a Routing Header type 2, which carries the Home Address of the mobile node.

Mobile Node Operation

As long as the MN is at home, no Mobile IPv6 mechanisms are necessary. If the MN is away from home, it uses its home address as well as its care-of address. For each communication, it must choose which address to use. Applications and processes above the IP layer usually communicate using the home address of the MN.

If a communication has to survive a move of the MN to another network, the home address must be used. As soon as the MN has a communication with a correspondent node for which there is a Binding, the communication can be routed directly. If there is no Binding, all data will be tunneled through the home agent. For certain communications, the MN can also choose to use its care-of address without Mobile IPv6 functionality, just as a regular unicast address. When the MN communicates with local nodes in a foreign network—e.g., for Neighbor Discovery—it should communicate directly and not use the Home Address Destination option.

The choice of the best communication path and the corresponding address depends on the requirements of the application, and that is where the choice has to be made. This definition is not part of the Mobile IPv6 specification.

Route Optimization in detail

When a mobile node away from home communicates with a correspondent node for which it has a Binding, it uses the process called Route Optimization.

The MN goes through the following steps: it checks its Binding Update List for an entry of its home address for this correspondent node. This verifies whether the correspondent node can process the Home Address Destination Option. Then, it checks the Binding Update List for the following:

- Whether the Source Address it wants to use corresponds to the Home Address in the entry.
- Whether the Destination address it wants to use corresponds to the address of the correspondent node in the entry.
- Whether its current care-of address is listed as care-of address in this entry.
- Whether the Binding is valid and the lifetime greater than zero.

If all these requirements are met, the mobile node knows that the correspondent node has a valid Binding Cache entry. A packet sent from the MN to this correspondent node contains the following information:

- The Source address field in the IPv6 header contains the care-of address.
- The packet carries a Destination Options header with a Home Address option containing the Home Address of the mobile node.

The correspondent node receiving this packet copies the home address from the Destinations Options header into the Source address field of the IPv6 header before processing the packet to upper layer protocols and applications. To the upper layers and the application, it looks as though the packet was sent from the home address of the mobile node. When the correspondent node wants to send data to a MN, it checks its Binding Cache for an entry for the destination. If there is such an entry, it inserts a Routing Header type 2.

When the correspondent node replies, address management looks as follows:

- The Destination address in the IPv6 header contains the care-of address of the mobile node.

- The packet contains a Routing Header type 2. The address field in the Routing Header contains the home address of the mobile node.

- The mobile node exchanges the address in the Destination address field of the IPv6 header with the home address copied from the Routing Header, reduces the Segments Left field in the Routing Header by one to zero, and processes the packet internally to upper-layer protocols and applications. Again, to the upper layers, it looks as though the packet had been sent to the home address of the mobile node.

Figure 11-5 shows the communication between MN and the correspondent node, as well as the specific headers associated with Route Optimization.

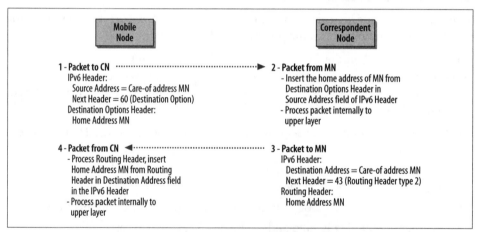

Figure 11-5. Header information with Route Optimization

This figure illustrates the processes described previously. The main goal of Mobile IPv6 is for an MN to keep connectivity to services and applications while moving from one network to another. The goal of Route Optimization is to allow for direct routing between MN and the correspondent node. With the use of Destination options and Routing type 2 header, both nodes can process the packets internally as though they were in direct communication with the MN on its home link. So to the application, it looks as though the mobile node is on its home link.

This explains why Mobility with IPv6 is much more scalable and well-suited for widespread mobility. The Extension header architecture allows for Route Optimization.

Imagine millions of mobile nodes communicating through their home agents to reach their correspondent nodes. The home agent would be a bottleneck, a single point of failure, and the home link unnecessarily overloaded. In many cases, the route from the mobile node to the correspondent node is much shorter than the route going through the home agent.

Communication with Bidirectional Tunneling

If the MN wants to communicate with a correspondent node for which it does not have a Binding, it uses the Reverse Tunneling mechanism. In this case, the packet is sent through the tunnel via the home agent. The Source address in the original packet carries the home address of the MN and the correspondent node's address as a destination address. This packet is encapsulated in another IPv6 header carrying the care-of address of the MN in the Source address field and the IPv6 address of the home agent in the Destination address field. The home agent processes the first header and forwards the original packet to the correspondent node. Figure 11-6 illustrates the header information.

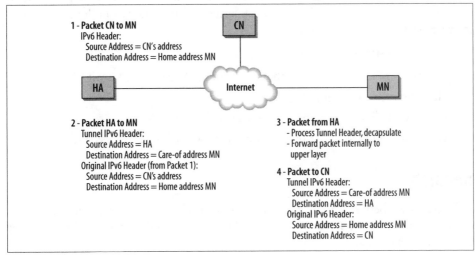

Figure 11-6. Header information with Bidirectional Tunneling

Movement Detection

How does the MN detect that it has moved to another network? Movement Detection is based on the process of Neighbor Unreachability Detection (NUD; for details, see Chapter 4). Using NUD, the MN detects when its default router is no longer available. In this case, the MN tries to find a new default router. It performs Duplicate Address Detection (DAD) for its link-local addresses, chooses a new default router based on the Router Advertisements, and builds new care-of addresses based on the Router prefixes advertised. When the new addresses are initialized, it performs a Binding Update with its home agent first and then with all correspondent nodes for which it has Bindings.

The fact that new routers advertise new prefixes is not necessarily a sign that the MN is in a new network. There may be a new router or a prefix change in the current network. Procedures have to be defined to prevent an MN from unnecessarily updating all Bindings when it has not moved to another network. The following procedures have been defined so far:

- If the MN receives RAs from new routers with new prefixes but its default router is still reachable, it will not perform any Binding Updates. It uses NUD to detect whether its default router is still available.

- RAs can carry an Advertisement Interval Option. This allows the MN to detect whether this router is still available based on the comparison of the interval in different RAs.

- If the default router does not reply to a Neighbor Solicitation, the MN should perform a Multicast Router Solicitation.

Returning home

When the MN detects that it is back on its home link, it sends a Binding Update to the home agent to inform it that it is back home and that the HA no longer needs to forward packets through the tunnel.

This Home Registration looks as follows:

- The A-bit (Acknowledge) and the H-bit (Home Registration) must be set.
- The Lifetime field is set to 0.
- The care-of address must be the same as the home address.
- The Source address in the IPv6 header must be the home address of the MN.

Security

If the data flow between home agent and mobile node is not secured, there are many possibilities for attacks—for example, Man-in-the-Middle attacks, Hijacking, or Denial of Service attacks.

To secure the tunnel between home agent and mobile node, an IPsec tunnel is configured. IPsec ESP is required for Mobile IPv6 messages. The Mobile IPv6 specification details this.

The following data flows have to be secured:

- Binding Update and Binding Ack between MN and HA
- Home Test Init and Home Test messages sent via HA during the Return Routability procedure
- ICMPv6 messages between MN and HA used for prefix discovery

All control messages between mobile node and home agent need authentication, integrity, proper sequencing, and anti-replay protection. This protection requires a Security Association between home agent and mobile node. IPsec does not provide any means to control the sequence of messages. A correct sequence is given by the Sequence number in Binding Update and Acknowledgement messages. Higher protection from replay attacks can be provided only when Internet Key Exchange (IKE) is used.

 For a description of security terms and concepts, refer to Chapter 5.

Binding Updates between the mobile node and correspondent node are protected by the SA established during the Return Routability procedure. Binding Updates between the mobile node and correspondent node must also be protected by the Binding Authorization Data option. This option includes a Binding Management Key, which is generated during the Return Routability procedure.

A more detailed discussion of Security aspects and mechanisms with Mobile IPv6 can be found in RFC 3775 ("Mobility Support in IPv6") and RFC 3776 ("Using IPsec to Protect Mobile IPv6 Signaling between mobile nodes and home agents"), as well as in general security RFCs.

RFC 4285, "Authentication Protocol for Mobile IPv6," specifies an alternate mechanism to secure MIPv6 messages in 3GPP2 networks. It is an informational RFC not reviewed by the IETF and consists of a MIPv6-specific mobility message authentication option that can be added to MIPv6 signaling messages.

Extensions to Mobile IPv6

A number of extensions have already been defined for Mobile IPv6 to make it more flexible and scalable. The following sections describe them.

NEMO

An extension to Mobile IPv6 called Network Mobility (NEMO) has been specified in RFC 3963. The NEMO Basic Support protocol enables Mobile Networks to attach to different points in the Internet. It allows session continuity for every node in the Mobile Network even as the Mobile Router changes its point of attachment to the Internet. It also allows every node in the Mobile Network to be reachable while moving around. The solution supports both mobile nodes and hosts that do not support mobility in the Mobile Network.

The processes and messages are basically the same as in Mobile IPv6, except that in this case, the mobile node is a *Mobile router*. In the current NEMO specification, communication between nodes in the mobile network and correspondent nodes always goes through the home agent. Route Optimization has not been defined yet. Theoretically, nested mobility can be configured where a Mobile router allows another Mobile router to attach to its Mobile network. This opens ways for many scenarios with high mobility. The future will show how we use these technologies, and the developments in the past couple years show that sometimes unexpected applications spring up overnight and are used en masse.

Hierarchical Mobile IPv6

With RFC 4140, "Hierarchical Mobile IPv6 Mobility Management," the scalability of Mobile IPv6 is further extended. It is designed to significantly enhance performance of Mobile IPv6 and to reduce the number of messages a mobile node sends over a link in order to update its bindings with the home agent and the correspondent node. It also allows mobile nodes to hide their location from correspondent nodes and home agents when using route optimization.

Hierarchical Mobile IPv6 introduces a new node type, the *Mobility Anchor Point* (MAP). The MAP can be located anywhere in the hierarchical network of routers. It is essentially a local home agent in the geographical region of the mobile node. The mobile node now sends binding updates to the local MAP rather than to the home agent and correspondent nodes. By sending one binding update message to the MAP, all further traffic from the home agent and the correspondent nodes is rerouted to the new location of the mobile node. The correspondent node and home agent operation are not affected by this and therefore need no changes. Figure 11-7 illustrates the concept.

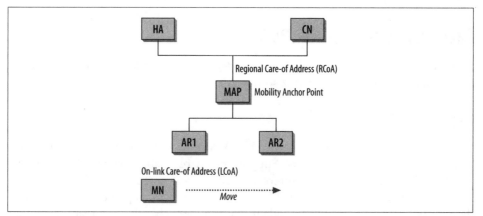

Figure 11-7. Hierarchical Mobile IPv6

When the mobile node enters a MAP domain, it receives Router Advertisements containing information on one or more local MAPs (MAP option). The *Regional Care-of Address* (RCoA) of the MAP corresponds to the care-of address in the base MIPv6 specification. After registering with a MAP, the mobile node registers its RCoA with its home agent and eventually with its current correspondent nodes. The RCoA is now used as the mobile node's care-of address. It is the address used by the home agent and correspondent nodes to communicate with the mobile node away from home. When the mobile node moves from one network to another within a MAP domain, it registers its new *On-link Care-of Address* (LCoA) with the MAP. The MAP, acting like a local home agent, receives all packets on behalf of the mobile node and will encapsulate and forward them to the mobile node's current address. The boundaries of a MAP domain are defined by the Access Routers (AR1 and AR2 in Figure 11-7). This obviously greatly enhances performance of Mobile IPv6, because binding updates do not have to be sent to the home agent and the correspondent nodes every time the mobile node moves to another network within the MAP domain.

As mentioned in the section on the Binding Update message, a new bit has been added to the Binding Update message, the M-bit, which indicates that this is a MAP registration and not a Binding Update with a home agent. There is also an extension to Neighbor Discovery specified to include the MAP's global IPv6 address.

A MAP can exist anywhere in the hierarchical network. Several MAPs can be located within the same domain independently. In addition, overlapping MAP domains are allowed and recommended. Both static and dynamic hierarchies are supported.

Fast Handover

In RFC 4068, a protocol is specified to reduce the mobile node's handover latency when moving from one network to another. It is called "Fast Handover for Mobile IPv6." The handover operationally consists of movement detection, address configuration, and address update. The combined handover latency is often sufficient to affect real-time applications (e.g., VoIP). This specification describes a set of protocols and procedures to significantly reduce the handover latency. All throughput-sensitive applications can benefit from the Fast Handover.

RFC 4260, "Mobile IPv6 Fast Handovers for 802.11 Networks," discusses and gives some deployment examples for Mobile IPv6 Fast Handovers on 802.11 networks.

Now that you have worked through all aspects of IPv6, the next chapter invites you to get your hands dirty. Experience comes from using technology. Enjoy IPv6!

References

Here's a list of the most important RFCs and drafts mentioned in this chapter. Sometimes I include additional subject-related RFCs for your personal further study.

RFCs

- RFC 2406, "IP Encapsulating Security Payload (ESP)," 1998
- RFC 2409, "The Internet Key Exchange (IKE)," 1998

- RFC 2710, "Multicast Listener Discovery (MLD) for IPv6," 1999
- RFC 3344, "IP Mobility Support for IPv4," 2002
- RFC 3775, "Mobility Support in IPv6," 2004
- RFC 3776, "Using IPsec to Protect Mobile IPv6 Signaling Between Mobile Nodes and Home Agents," 2004
- RFC 3963, " Network Mobility (NEMO) Basic Support Protocol," 2005
- RFC 4065, "Instructions for Seamoby and Experimental Mobility Protocol IANA Allocations," 2005
- RFC 4068, "Fast Handovers for Mobile IPv6," 2005
- RFC 4140, "Hierarchical Mobile IPv6 Mobility Management (HMIPv6)," 2005
- RFC 4225, "Mobile IP Version 6 Route Optimization Security Design Background," 2005
- RFC 4260, "Mobile IPv6 Fast Handovers for 802.11 Networks," 2005
- RFC 4282, "The Network Access Identifier," 2005
- RFC 4283, "Mobile Node Identifier Option for Mobile IPv6 (MIPv6)," 2005
- RFC 4285, "Authentication Protocol for Mobile IPv6," 2006

Drafts

Drafts can be found at *http://www.ietf.org/ID.html*. To locate the latest version of a draft, refer to *https://datatracker.ietf.org/public/pidtracker.cgi*. You can enter the draft name without a version number, and the most current version will come up. If a draft does not show up, it was either deleted or published as an RFC. Alternatively, you can go to the new Internet drafts database interface at *https://datatracker.ietf.org/public/idindex.cgi*. *http://tools.ietf.org/wg* is also a very useful site. More information on the process of standardization, RFCs, and drafts can be found in Appendix A.

Here's a list of interesting drafts related to the topics or drafts to which I referred in this chapter:

- *draft-ietf-mip6-ikev2-ipsec-05.txt*, Mobile IPv6 Operation with IKEv2 and the revised IPsec
- *draft-ietf-mip6-cn-ipsec-02.txt*, Using IPsec between Mobile and Correspondent IPv6 Nodes
- *draft-ietf-mip6-aaa-ha-goals-01.txt*, Goals for AAA-HA interface
- *draft-ietf-mip6-firewalls-04.txt*, Mobile IPv6 and Firewalls: Problem statement
- *draft-ietf-mip6-mipv6-mib-07.txt*, Mobile IPv6 Management Information Base
- *draft-ietf-mobike-protocol-08.txt*, IKEv2 Mobility and Multihoming Protocol (MOBIKE)
- *draft-ietf-mobike-design-08.txt*, Design of the MOBIKE Protocol

CHAPTER 12

Get Your Hands Dirty

This chapter is your quick-start guide to using different IPv6 stacks. Mastering technology is not done by reading about it, so get your hands dirty and play with it. You have plenty of options.

This chapter offers an overview of some common stacks that can be used. It is not a complete list. I decided to focus on Microsoft Windows, Macintosh, Sun Solaris, BSD, and a Linux implementation in the beginning. This chapter describes where to get the stacks and how to install them, and lists the most common utilities for configuring and troubleshooting IPv6. Once you are familiar with one of the stacks, you will have no problems applying your know-how to other stacks.

Linux

There are a number of different Linux distributions on the market, all based on the same kernel and identified by its version number. The Linux kernel has supported IPv6 since version 2.2.x.

> For the most actual kernel consult the homepage of your distributor or have a look at *http://www.kernel.org*.

Where to Get Linux

Most of the common Linux distributions can be downloaded from the Internet, but they can also be purchased from the sales channels of their respective makers, including CDs and manuals. It is usually advisable to buy a distribution because you will have the manual in printed form, and if you download it, the files are rather big (about 200 MB–2.5 GB).

Find more information about the Linux standard and the different available implementations at *http://www.linuxbase.org*. For a complete list of different distributions, consult *http://www.linux.org/dist/ list.html*. For an IPv6-specific Linux site, refer to *http://www.linux-ipv6.org*.

Installation

I used SuSE Linux Version 9. SuSE Linux 9.1 ships with kernel Version 2.6. The installation is very easy, and an assistant will guide you through all the steps. The IPv6 protocol stack will automatically be enabled in addition to the IPv4 stack. The current *inet* daemon supports IPv6 and is responsible for all networking tasks, such as FTP, telnet, or finger. If you install the web server Apache2, it will communicate both IPv6 and IPv4 without any further configuration.

After the base installation, I had a Linux host communicating over IPv4 and IPv6.

Utilities

There are two packages that you need to download and install to get the cool utilities for Linux. One of them is *net-tools*. This package contains utilities such as *ifconfig*, *netstat*, *route*, and *hostname*. Another package you'll need is called *iputils*, which can usually be found on your distribution CD. It contains *ping6*, *tracepath6*, and *traceroute6*. If you can't find these tools on your system, use *YaST* on SuSE or *apt* in the Debian Distribution.

For further information on how to install the utilities, configure your IPv6 stack, or compile source code, go to *http://www.bieringer.de/ linux/IPv6*. This is a great site where you also find a lot of useful information about Linux and protocols. If you need the most current packages for net-tools, go to *http://freshmeat.net*.

Following is a short description of some of the utilities that can be helpful when working with IPv6. As you probably know, the online help for all Linux utilities is very detailed, and there are two ways you can access it:

Manpages
  The manpages can be accessed by entering man `utilityname`, where `utilityname` is the name of the utility about which you want information. The manpages contain all information about available options and detailed descriptions.

Help screens
  Help screens can be accessed by entering the utility name with the parameter `--help`. To get the information for ifconfig, enter `ifconfig --help`. This screen is like a short version of the manpages.

The following utilities are interesting and new for IPv6:

ifconfig
>   This tool is used for general network configuration of the Linux box. If you are using SuSE 9, the installed inetd supports IPv6. Using the address flag [address family] lets you switch between IPv4 (inet) and IPv6 (inet6) address families. You can use *ifconfig* to start and stop the interface and to view many different kinds of statistics.

netstat
>   The *netstat* version on your Linux box after the installation supports IPv6. However, by installing *net-tools*, you get the most current version. The *netstat* tool provides a lot of useful options and statistics, such as port information, routing table, and interface table. For all IPv6-related information, you need the --inet6 flag. As an example, use netstat -lnptu | grep "httpd2\W*$" to find out on which ports and addresses Apache2 is listening.

route
>   If you enter route without any parameters, it displays the routing table for IPv4. For viewing the IPv6 routing table, add the flag --inet6.

ping6, traceroute6, tracepath6, hostname
>   Most of the utilities for IPv6 are similar to the utilities that we know from IPv4. Instead of using *ping* or *traceroute*, I now use *ping6* or *traceroute6*. Refer to the manpages for details. Instead of using *traceroute6*, try *tracepath6*. It not only displays the path, but also includes MTU information.

ip
>   If you want to have more functionality related to IPv6, install the iproute2 package. It includes the command ip. With ip, you can display and change the neighbor cache, set static IPv6 addresses, configure routes and tunnels, and much more. To perform IPv6 commands, use the flag -6 or -family inet6. As an example, use ip -6 neigh show to locate your IPv6 neighbors or ip -6 addr add 2001: DB8::202:B3FF:FE1E:8329/64 dev eth0 to assign a static IPv6 address.

tcpdump
>   This is a well-known and advanced console tool for packet analysis. For IPv6 filtering, use the flags proto ip6, or if you want to trace only IPv6 hosts, try ip6 host *hostname*. Check the manpages to learn more about this powerful tool.

BSD

Berkeley Software Distribution (BSD) began in 1977 from the efforts of the Computer Systems Research Group (CSRG) of the University of California at Berkeley. It began as a supplement to Sixth Edition Unix, which was developed by Bell Telephone Laboratories.

In 1978, the Department of Defense Advanced Research Project Agency (DARPA) turned its attention to Unix due to its portability across multiple hardware platforms. Seeking a common baseline, they decided to contract Berkeley to release 4BSD with the requested performance enhancements incorporated. They also wanted a faster filesystem and TCP/IP networking to be incorporated. Berkley Fast Filesystem (FFS) and TCP/IP networking, along with a reliable signal model, were incorporated into 4.2BSD in 1983.

In June of 1993, 4.4BSD was released and included support for the Intel i386 architecture. It was released as two versions: one required a UNIX Software license, and the other was without any licensed source code. This was the first open source release.

One of the projects based on the original BSD is OpenBSD. The OpenBSD project then became the root of other interesting projects, such as OpenSSH (Secure Shell), OpenNTPD (Network Time Protocol Daemon), and OpenCVS (Concurrent Versions System).

But that is enough history for the moment. Because of its IPv6 implementation and security features, which are counted among the best, I've decided to give you a short introduction to the BSD distribution OpenBSD. In my lab, I currently use the latest release of OpenBSD, Version 3.7. As an aside, OpenBSD has supported IPv6 since Version 2.7.

Find more information about OpenBSD at *http://www.openbsd.org*. For all other available BSD implementations, go to *http://www.bsd.org*.

Installation

After a basic setup of OpenBSD, IPv6 already works as expected without any special tweaks, stack configuration, or kernel patches.

If you are new to OpenBSD, you will find an easy install guide at *http://www.openbsd.org/faq/faq4.html*.

Because OpenBSD is intended to work as a router, it does not accept Router Advertisements by default. If you check ifconfig *interface*, you notice that only a link-local address is assigned to the interface. You can now do a static configuration of your interface(s) or configure the system to accept Router Advertisements. To configure the system to accept Router Advertisements, edit */etc/sysctl.conf*. Change the line net.inet6.ip6.accept_rtadv=0 to net.inet6.ip6.accept_rtadv=1. To tell the router solicitation daemon to request Router Advertisements only for a desired interface, edit rtsold_flags="*interface*" in */etc/rc.conf*. Restart *rtsold* or reboot your system, and you have a fully functional and secure IPv6 OpenBSD host.

Figure 12-1 shows the output of ifconfig with IPv6 configured.

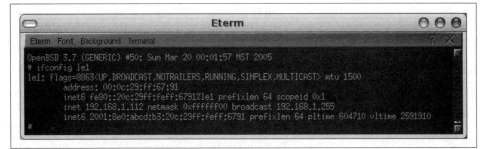

Figure 12-1. ifconfig on OpenBSD configured for IPv6

The first address line shows the MAC address of the interface le1. The second address line shows the link-local address using the interface identifier based on the MAC address (refer to Chapter 3 for the explanation of how this interface identifier is built). The %le1 string at the end of the address is used to identify the interface on the host. The prefix length is set to /64, and the scope ID is set to 1. The third address line shows the IPv4 information for this interface. Finally, the last address line shows the global unicast address assigned to this interface.

Utilities

Each of the following tools is available for IPv6 after a basic installation of Open-BSD. The online documentation includes manuals for each console command and its parameters. Try also man *command*.

ifconfig
New parameters are available to show or configure IPv6 interfaces. Use the manual to see all options.

netstat
In addition to IPv4 information, the command may now display IPv6-related information. Use netstat -f inet6. As an example, to display the routing table for IPv6 and IPv4, use netstat -rn. Find more options in the manual.

route
If you enter route show, it displays the routing table for IPv4 and IPv6. For viewing only the IPv6 routing table, add the flag -inet6.

ping6, traceroute6, tracepath6, hostname
Most of the utilities for IPv6 are similar to the utilities that we know from IPv4. Instead of using *ping* or *traceroute*, I now use *ping6* or *traceroute6*. Refer to the

manpages for details. Instead of using *traceroute6*, try *tracepath6*. It not only displays the path, but also includes MTU information.

ndp

The *ndp* command displays and modifies the IPv6 neighbor cache as specified in the IPv6 Neighbor Discovery (ND) protocol. To display the entire neighbor cache, use ndp -a -n; to completely flush all remote entries, use ndp -F.

KAME Project

The KAME Project was a joint effort to create a single solid software set especially targeting IPv6/IPsec. Talented researchers from several Japanese organizations such as Fujitsu, Hitachi, NEC, IIJ (Internet Initiative Japan), and Toshiba joined the project. This joint effort aimed to avoid unnecessary duplicated development in the same areas and to effectively provide a high-quality, advanced, featured package.

The goal of the KAME Project was to make free implementations of IPv6, IPsec (IPv4 and IPv6), and Advanced Internetworking functions such as Advanced Packet Queueing, ATM, Mobility, and much more available for all BSD variants.

The KAME project began as a two-year project (April 1998–March 2000). There were several two-year deadline extensions, and the project was concluded in March 2006. This decision was based on the observation that the project has achieved its development and deployment mission. To conclude the KAME project, the focus is on integrating all remaining KAME functionality into all variants of BSD operating systems.

Some advanced features developed and distributed by the KAME project are not ready to be implemented into BSD systems yet. They include SCTP/DCCP, Mobile IPv6, NEMO, and IKEv2. The research and development activities on these features will continue in other working groups in the WIDE (*http://www.wide.ad.jp*) project.

> For more information about the KAME Project itself, visit *http://www.kame.net*; for ported applications, visit *http://www.kame.net/apps*. FreeBSD users can find IPv6 software to play with at *http://www.freebsd.org/ports/ipv6.html*.

The KAME site has the famous KAME, which dances when you access the site with IPv6.

Other IPv6-related activities, such as the USAGI project (*http://www.linux-ipv6.org*, IPv6 code for Linux) and the TAHI project (*http://www.tahi.org*, IPv6 testing and evaluation), will be continued.

Sun Solaris

IPv6 support is available since Solaris 8. The Solaris software is downloadable from Sun Microsystem's homepage, or you can buy the CD.

The current release is Solaris 10. It brings some new features, including IPv6 support for both BIND 8.4.2 and BIND 9.2.3. Solaris 10 includes support for the Basic and Advanced Socket Interface Extensions for IPv6 (RFCs 3493 and 3542). Default Address Selection (RFC 3484) is also fully supported. IPsec/IKE with IPv6 and configured and automatic IPv6-over-IPv4 tunnels are supported, too. Java Runtime Version 1.4.0 supports IPv6 in a transparent manner. Applications using Java Runtime do not need any modifications to work over IPv6.

Enable IPv6 and Get Started

IPv6 is enabled during the OS installation. For the configuration of the IPv6 address, a choice between static or automatic address definition is possible. Automatic means that the system will use Neighbor Discovery to obtain an IPv6 address; static means that the administrator configures the IPv6 address manually. All IPv6-specific adapter configurations are stored in */etc/hostname6.<interface>*.

Utilities

All utilities described in the following list are available after the Solaris installation and have IPv6 support. The online documentation contains a good description of the command-line utilities and possible parameters.

If you want to display IPv6-related information by default when using the tools *ifconfig* and *netstat*, you need to change the file */etc/default/inet_type* and add the entry DEFAULT_IP=BOTH.

ifconfig
> There are new parameters available to get IPv6-related adapter information. The manpages show all the options.

netstat
> In addition to IPv4 information, it is possible to display IPv6 information. Use the following switch: netstat -f inet6. If you changed the default inet type, netstat -p displays the ARP table for IPv4 and the neighbor cache for IPv6. netstat -rn displays the routing table for IPv4 and IPv6.

route
> *route* can be used for both IPv4 and IPv6 routes. Use the option -inet6 to perform operations on IPv6 routes or to change the default inet type.

ping, traceroute

> *ping* and *traceroute* used with IPv6 addresses or IPv6 DNS record entries display IPv6-related information.

snoop

> *snoop* is a well-known network analysis tool included with Solaris. The latest version has IPv6 support. IPv6 traffic can be viewed by using `snoop ip6`.

 A lot of good information about Solaris system administration is available at *http://www.sun.com/bigadmin*.

Macintosh

Mac OS X is the latest version of the Mac OS, the operating system software for Macintosh computers. Mac OS X was first commercially released in 2001. It consists of two main parts: Darwin, an open source Unix-like environment based on the Berkley Software Distribution (BSD) and the Mach microkernel, adapted and further developed by Apple Computer with involvement from independent developers, and a proprietary GUI named Aqua developed by Apple.

Mac OS X versions are named after large felines. Currently, there are five versions released (the newest release, called Leopard, is announced for the end of 2006 or early 2007):

- OS X v10.0, "Cheetah"
- OS X v10.1, "Puma"
- OS X v10.2, "Jaguar"
- OS X v10.3, "Panther"
- OS X v10.4, "Tiger"

Network services are based on the standard TCP/IP implementation of FreeBSD. The IPv6 and IPsec implementation is based on the basic principles of the KAME project (*http://www.kame.net*), briefly described earlier in the section on BSD.

OS X currently comes with the following services with IPv6 support:

- DNS (BIND)
- IP Firewall
- Mail (POP, IMAP, SMTP)
- SMB
- HTTP (Apache 2)

Basically, all command-line tools from FreeBSD, such as *traceroute6*, *ping6*, and *netstat* may be used in Mac OS X without any problems. See the manpages for all parameters.

The GUI tool for network configuration supports IPv6 configuration since version 10.3. Figure 12-2 shows the network configuration wizard in 10.4.

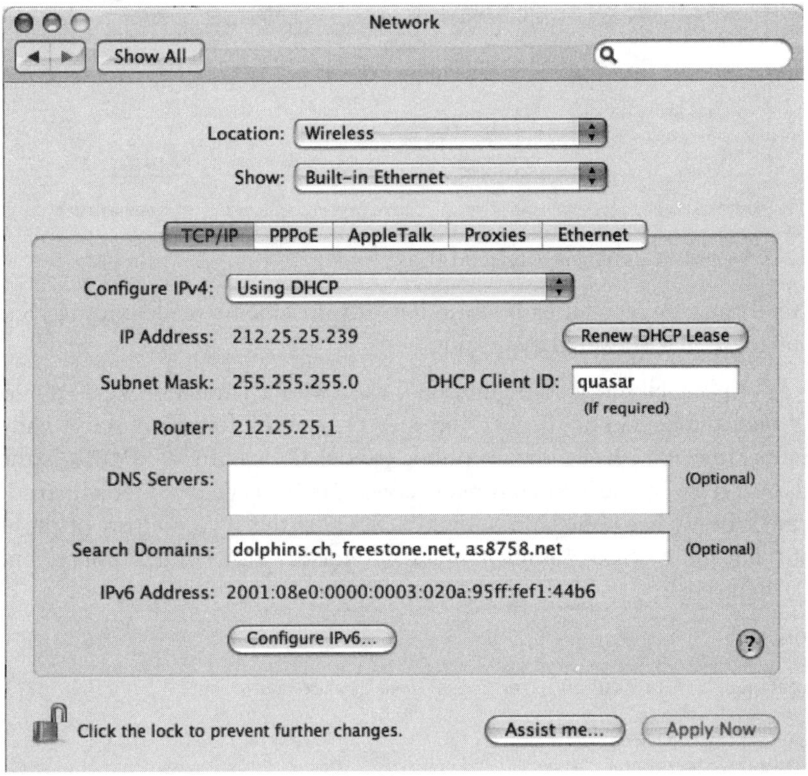

Figure 12-2. Network configuration in MAC OS X

This screenshot shows the part of the network dialog where you find the IPv4 configuration options—in this case, of the built-in wireless interface. At the bottom of the screenshot, the IPv6 address and the Configure IPv6... button used to access the IPv6 configuration are displayed.

What you see in Figure 12-3 is displayed when you press the Configure IPv6 button. In this case, it shows the configuration options in manual mode.

In the first option, you can choose between Stateless autoconfiguration and manual configuration. If you choose Stateless autoconfiguration, the interface will configure itself following the rules for Stateless autoconfiguration. In this case, no options can be configured (they will be grayed out). If you choose static configuration, the mode called Manually, you must enter your own IPv6 address, your Default Router's link-local IPv6 address, and the prefix length.

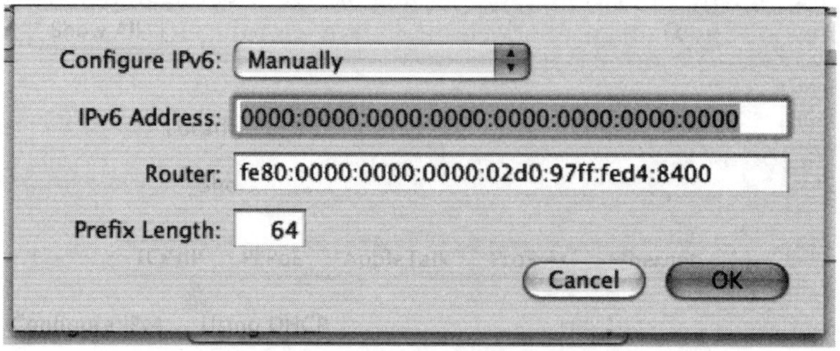

Figure 12-3. IPv6 manual configuration in MAC OS X

If OS X's IPv6 stack recognizes IPv6 Router Advertisements while booting, Stateless autoconfiguration is activated by default.

Here is a sample shell script configuration for use with a Tunnel Broker. You need an account on a public Tunnel Broker and may change the following script with your personal parameters. LOCAL4 is your public (static) IPv4 address; REMOTE4 is the tunnel endpoint given by the Tunnel Broker service. LOCAL6 is your router's IPv6 address, which must be within your IPv6 subnet. REMOTE6 is the IPv6 address of the tunnel endpoint. For more detailed information on tunneling and Tunnel Broker concepts, refer to Chapter 10.

```
#!/bin/sh
#
# configuration in case of using swiss tunnelbroker.as8758.net

LOCAL4=213.160.42.62
REMOTE4=212.25.25.23
LOCAL6=2001:08e0:abcd::2ce/126
REMOTE6=2001:08e0:abcd::2cd/126

ifconfig gif0 create
ifconfig gif0 tunnel ${LOCAL4} ${REMOTE4}
ifconfig gif0 inet6 alias ${LOCAL6}
route add -inet6 default -interface gif0
```

Microsoft

Microsoft released the first research IPv6 stack in 1998. It runs on Windows NT 4.0 and Windows 2000. Since Windows XP with Service Pack 1, a fully functional and productive IPv6 stack is implemented. The .NET and Windows 2003 Server Family also come with good IPv6 support. The research stack on Windows NT and Windows 2000 will never reach production status; there is no further development. Other IPv6-capable platforms are Windows CE, Windows XP Embedded, and Windows Mobile for SmartPhones.

Windows .NET Server 2003

The IPv6 protocol for the Windows .NET 2003 Server Family in the current version includes the following features:

- Basic IPv6 Support
- 6to4
- ISATAP
- Teredo
- 6over4
- PortProxy
- Privacy Option (randomly generated interface IDs)
- DNS
- IPsec (with some limitations)
- RPC support
- Static router support
- IPv6 firewall functionality (SP1 required)
- Application support (DCOM, DFS, FTP, Winsock, file and print sharing)
- Site prefixes in Router Advertisements

The Basic IPv6 Support also includes Mobility Support for correspondent nodes. In DNS, you can add AAAA Records, send DNS requests over IPv6, or use the dynamic DNS registering function, which gives you the possibility to resolve hosts with dynamic IPv6 addresses.

The following utilities and components come with IPv6 Support: Internet Explorer, FTP Client, Telnet Client, Internet Information Services (IIS) Version 6, file and print sharing (CIFS, SMB), Windows Media Services, Network Monitor, and SNMP MIB Support.

The configuration of the IPv6 Stack is usually done via *netsh*, a console command. Here are some examples:

Enable Routing Interface
```
netsh interface ipv6 set interface <interfacename> forwarding=enabled
```

Configure static routes
```
netsh interface ipv6 add route
```

Enable Router Advertisements
```
netsh interface ipv6 set interface interface=<interface> advertise=enabled
```

 Microsoft's official IPv6 web site can be found at *http://www.microsoft. com/ipv6*.

Windows XP

Microsoft Windows XP (prior to SP1) included a developer-release version of the IPv6 protocol. Microsoft Windows XP SP1 includes a production-quality version of the IPv6 protocol. In order to use IPv6 on Windows XP with full functionality, you have to install the Advanced Networking Pack in addition to SP1. With Service Pack 2, the Advanced Networking Pack isn't required anymore, because it's already included.

The IPv6 stack for Windows XP in the current version (SP2) includes the following features:

- 6to4
- ISATAP
- Teredo
- 6over4
- Privacy option (randomly generated interface ID)
- Site prefixes in Router Advertisements
- Limited DNS support (see below)
- IPsec support (with some limitations)
- RPC support
- Static router support
- IPv6 firewall functionality

The IPv6 protocol for all versions of Windows XP does not include IPv6 support for file and print sharing or IPv6 support for the WinInet, IPHelper, and DCOM APIs. The Windows XP DNS resolver can request AAAA records but only communicates over IPv4.

Installation and configuration

To install IPv6 on Windows XP, simply open a command prompt and enter `ipv6 install`. If you want to verify that IPv6 is installed on an XP host, type `netsh interface ipv6 show interface` at the command line. You may also use `ipconfig /all` to display interface information. Alternatively, since SP2 you can install IPv6 via the GUI, where you configure other interfaces or protocols; IPv6 appears in the list of available protocols to be installed and, after installation, shows up in the list of installed protocols.

Utilities

The *netsh* command can be used to configure IPv6. It is designed to replace *ipv6.exe*, the utility that was included in the Windows NT IPv6 research stack. *ipv6.exe* is indeed still integrated in Windows XP, but it should not be used anymore. Like *ipv6.exe*, *netsh* can be used to change or view your network configuration or to display all sorts of statistics. Interesting for network administration is the scripting possibility in *netsh*, which allows you to run a set of commands in batch mode to automate your network setup. *netsh* runs only on the command line. For each task, a special context has to be specified to use or analyze functions in it. It can be compared to specifying the actual directory path for file access, e.g., *c:\windows\system32*. Use help to show a list of subcontexts and commands of the actual context. Available contexts and commands depend on installed network components. Figure 12-4 shows the output of the help command in the IPv6 context.

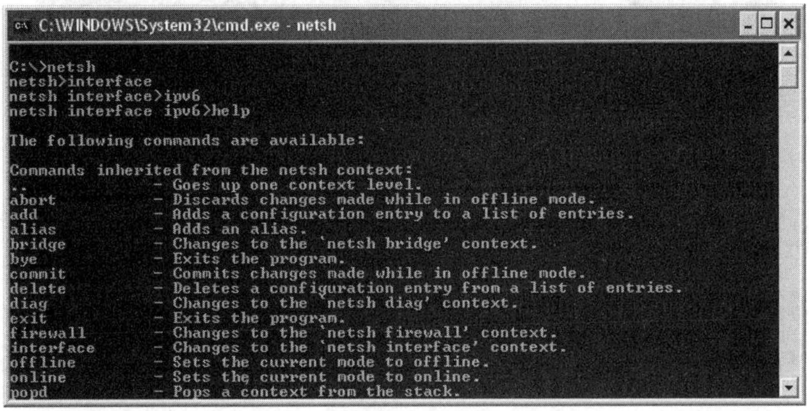

Figure 12-4. The netsh command

In the command prompt, enter netsh to start the utility. Now change to the desired context. You can do that step-by-step by first entering interface to change the context to interface; after that, enter ipv6. You can also change directly to the desired context by entering interface ipv6. Use help to show context-specific commands. By the way, analogous to the filesystem, you can use .. to change to the parent context.

Figure 12-5 shows the output of two options that might be helpful when troubleshooting.

The show global command shows the standard configuration parameters; show interface lists all interfaces and their options, such as MTU size, connection name, etc., as well as pseudointerfaces (Teredo, 6to4, ISATAP).

Besides *netsh*, there are a set of IPv6 tools such as *ipv6.exe*, *ping6.exe*, *tracert6.exe*, *ipsec6.exe*. I do not discuss them in detail here, because the online documentation in Windows XP is well done and shows all possible options for every command. On the command prompt, you can also enter any command with the /? parameter. This lists all options available for the command. More great information can be found by searching for "IPv6" in Windows XP help. There you get any relevant information, such as an overview of IPv6 utilities and configuration possibilities regarding *netsh*. The help topics include detailed manuals about the different transition mechanisms

```
C:\WINDOWS\System32\cmd.exe - netsh                              _ □ ×

netsh interface ipv6>show global
Querying active state...

General Global Parameters
----------------------------------------
Default Hop Limit                    : 128 hops
Neighbor Cache Limit                 : 256 entries per interface
Route Cache Limit                    : 32 entries
Reassembly Limit                     : 8383936 bytes

netsh interface ipv6>show interface
Querying active state...

Idx  Met  MTU   State         Name
---  ---  ----  ------------  -----------------------------------
  8    0  1374  Connected     LAN
  5    2  1280  Disconnected  Teredo Tunneling Pseudo-Interface
  4    0  1284  Connected     {09BC1846-441C-4EF2-802E-91FD65BD00E7}
  3    1  1280  Connected     6to4 Pseudo-Interface
  2    1  1280  Connected     Automatic Tunneling Pseudo-Interface
  1    0  1500  Connected     Loopback Pseudo-Interface

netsh interface ipv6>
```

Figure 12-5. Using netsh for IP and interface information

such as Teredo, ISATAP, and 6to4. By default, all mechanisms are enabled as soon as the IPv6 stack is activated.

> For a FAQ about IPv6 with Windows XP, see *http://www.microsoft.com/ technet/prodtechnol/winxppro/plan/faqipv6.mspx*.

Microsoft's Roadmap

Microsoft plans to continue to deliver significant enhancements to IPv6 in future releases of their products. The next release of the Windows operating system, named Windows Vista, and Windows Server "Longhorn" will both natively support IPv6. A single networking stack for both protocols, IPv4 and IPv6, will replace the current dual-stack architecture. IPv6 will be installed and enabled by default and will be the preferred protocol. The entire suite of networking services, including DNS, DHCP, Point-to-Point Protocol (PPP), and Internet Protocol security (IPsec), will be IPv6-capable.

Microsoft is also currently conducting Technology Previews for Mobile IPv6 and Teredo Server Relay. Additionally, they are working on delivering IPv6 support in their enterprise applications and services along with Longhorn. Products such as SQL Server, Microsoft Office, and others will have IPv6 support in the Longhorn time frame.

Cisco Router

This section contains a short description of how to configure a Cisco router for IPv6. Configuration of other routers might be fairly similar. If you are familiar with your routing hardware, you will figure out how to do it, or your vendor can provide the necessary information.

Cisco's IPv6 support begins with the Cisco IOS 12.2(2) Technology release. Make sure you are using the latest release because new features will be supported with every update.

 Cisco's official IPv6 homepage can be found at *http://www.cisco.com/ ipv6*. There you find, among other things, a detailed roadmap with information about which RFCs are supported in the different IOS release versions, as well as interesting whitepapers and manuals.

Figure 12-6 shows the interface configuration options.

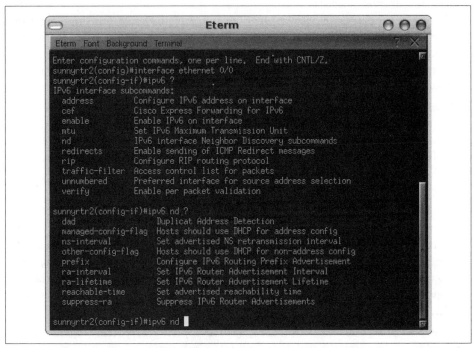

Figure 12-6. Cisco Interface configuration options

First, I needed to enable IPv6 packet forwarding. This is not enabled by default (different from IPv4). It is done with the global command `ipv6 unicast-routing` (not shown on the screenshot). Next, I configured the interface Ethernet 0/0. By typing `ipv6 ?`, I received a list of available commands. From this screen, the IPv6 address can be configured, as well as options for linking MTU, Neighbor Discovery, routing, and filters. The command `ipv6 nd ?` displays the options available for the configuration of Neighbor Discovery. From this screen, you can configure flags to specify whether hosts on this link should use DHCP for address-related or non-address-related information and different intervals, such as the router advertisement interval. The subnet prefix and the lifetime advertised in Router Advertisement messages are also configured here. I made the first configuration steps and set this router up as a 6to4 tunnel with the Microsoft 6to4 relay router as tunnel destination.

Here are some interesting ND commands that you can use on your Cisco router. This is not a complete list, but it should help you get started and give an idea of how you can configure your routers:

`ipv6 nd dad attempts` *number*

Configures the number of Duplicate Address Detection (DAD) and Neighbor Solicitation messages to send before considering an address unique. DAD can be disabled by specifying `ipv6 nd dad attempts 0`.

`ipv6 nd ra-interval` *seconds*

Configures the interval between IPv6 Router Advertisement transmissions from this interface. The value for this should be less than or equal to the IPv6 Router Lifetime if this is a default router. The default is 200 seconds. To prevent synchronization with other IPv6 nodes, the actual value used is randomly adjusted to within plus or minus 20 percent of the specified value.

`ipv6 nd ra-lifetime` *seconds*

Configures the lifetime of a Router Advertisement. This value is included in all IPv6 Router Advertisements sent out from this interface. If the router is not a default router, this will have a value of zero. If the router is a default router, this value will be nonzero and should not be less than the minimum Router Advertisement interval. The default value is 1,800 seconds.

`[no] ipv6 nd suppress-ra`

Controls transmission of IPv6 Router Advertisements on the interface. The default is to send Router Advertisments (RAs) on Ethernet, FDDI, or Token Ring interfaces if IPv6 unicast routing is enabled. Use the command `ipv6 nd supress-ra` to turn off RAs on LAN interfaces. On other types of interfaces, the default is never to send an RA. Use the command `no ipv6 nd suppress-ra` to send RAs on interfaces such as serial or tunnel interfaces.

`[no] ipv6 nd prefix` *prefix* | `default` [[*valid-lifetime preferred-lifetime*] | [`at` *valid-date preferred-date*] [`off-link`] [`no-autoconfig`]]

By default, all prefixes configured as addresses on the interface are advertised in Router Advertisements. This command allows control over the individual parameters per prefix, including whether the prefix should be advertised. The `default` keyword can be used to set default parameters for all prefixes. A date can be set for prefix expiration. The valid and preferred lifetimes are counted down in real time. When the expiration date is reached, the prefix is no longer advertised.

`[no] ipv6 nd managed-config-flag`

Defaults to OFF. When OFF, Router Advertisements sent from this interface have the Managed Address Configuration Flag turned off. Hosts are thus permitted to use IPv6 Stateless autoconfiguration to create global unicast addresses for themselves.

For a complete list of router configuration commands, refer to your Cisco documentation. For a discussion of routing protocols, refer to Chapter 8.

The next step I performed was to verify my interface configuration. Figure 12-7 shows the output.

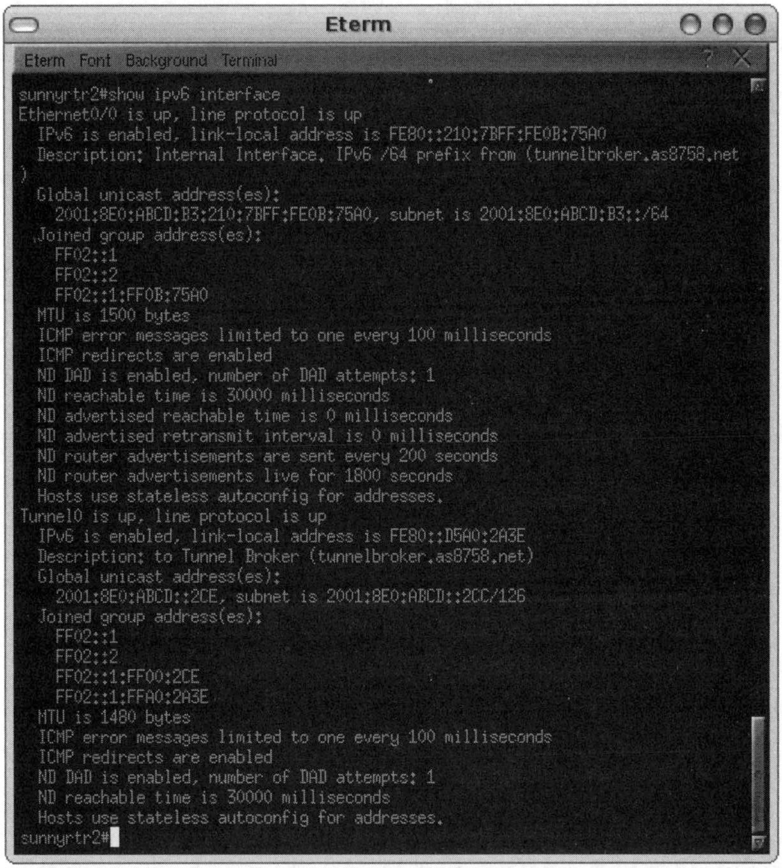

```
sunnyrtr2#show ipv6 interface
Ethernet0/0 is up, line protocol is up
  IPv6 is enabled, link-local address is FE80::210:7BFF:FE0B:75A0
  Description: Internal Interface, IPv6 /64 prefix from (tunnelbroker.as8758.net
)
  Global unicast address(es):
    2001:8E0:ABCD:B3:210:7BFF:FE0B:75A0, subnet is 2001:8E0:ABCD:B3::/64
  Joined group address(es):
    FF02::1
    FF02::2
    FF02::1:FF0B:75A0
  MTU is 1500 bytes
  ICMP error messages limited to one every 100 milliseconds
  ICMP redirects are enabled
  ND DAD is enabled, number of DAD attempts: 1
  ND reachable time is 30000 milliseconds
  ND advertised reachable time is 0 milliseconds
  ND advertised retransmit interval is 0 milliseconds
  ND router advertisements are sent every 200 seconds
  ND router advertisements live for 1800 seconds
  Hosts use stateless autoconfig for addresses.
Tunnel0 is up, line protocol is up
  IPv6 is enabled, link-local address is FE80::D5A0:2A3E
  Description: to Tunnel Broker (tunnelbroker.as8758.net)
  Global unicast address(es):
    2001:8E0:ABCD::2CE, subnet is 2001:8E0:ABCD::2CC/126
  Joined group address(es):
    FF02::1
    FF02::2
    FF02::1:FF00:2CE
    FF02::1:FFA0:2A3E
  MTU is 1480 bytes
  ICMP error messages limited to one every 100 milliseconds
  ICMP redirects are enabled
  ND DAD is enabled, number of DAD attempts: 1
  ND reachable time is 30000 milliseconds
  Hosts use stateless autoconfig for addresses.
sunnyrtr2#
```

Figure 12-7. Verifying the interface configuration

The output shows that I have a link-local address with the prefix FE80 and a global unicast address with the prefix 2001. Both addresses have the same interface identifier of 210:7BFF:FE0B:75A0. The multicast group addresses joined are FF02::1 (all nodes), FF02::2 (all routers), and FF02::1:FF0B:75A0 (solicited-node multicast address). A list with all the configuration options follows, stating timers, intervals, and address configuration options. As you can see on this screenshot, there is also an interface called tunnel0. It shows the current configuration of our tunnel to the as8758 Tunnel Broker. The tunnel entry point on our side has the global unicast address of 2001:08E0:ABCD:: 2CE. This address must be known to the tunnel exit point—in this situation, by as8758.

Other tools that can be used on Cisco's current IOS are *ping*, *traceroute*, and a DNS client, all operational in IPv6.

Figure 12-8 shows the Router Advertisement in the trace file.

```
No. St Source Address                    Dest Address        Summary
  1  M fe80::210:7bff:fe0b:75a0          ff02::1             ICMPv6:  Router Advertisement Code=0

⊞■💾 DLC: Ethertype=86DD, size=110 bytes
⊞★ IPv6: Flow=0x000000
⊟👊 ICMPv6: ----- ICMPv6 Header -----
    📄 ICMPv6:
    ☑ ICMPv6: Type                       = 134 (Router Advertisement)
    📄 ICMPv6: Code                       = 0
    📄 ICMPv6: Checksum                   = 982B (correct)
    📄 ICMPv6: Current Hop Limit          = 32
    📄 ICMPv6: M/O/H/Reserved bits        = 40
    📄 ICMPv6:          0... ....         = administered protocol not used (address)
    📄 ICMPv6:          .1.. ....         = administered protocol used (non-address)
    📄 ICMPv6:          ..0. ....         = Home Agent bit
    📄 ICMPv6:          ...0 0000         = Reserved            = 0x00
    📄 ICMPv6: Router Lifetime            = 1800 s
    📄 ICMPv6: Reachable Time             = 0 ms (unspecified)
    📄 ICMPv6: Retrans Timer              = 0 ms (unspecified)
    📄 ICMPv6:
    📄 ICMPv6: Options follow
    📄 ICMPv6: Type                       = 1 (Source Link-Layer Address)
    📄 ICMPv6: Length                     = 1 (units of 8 octets)
    📄 ICMPv6: Link Layer Address         = Station Cisco 0B75A0
    📄 ICMPv6: Type                       = 3 (Prefix Information)
    📄 ICMPv6: Length                     = 4 (units of 8 octets)
    📄 ICMPv6: Prefix Length              = 64
    📄 ICMPv6: L/A/R bits                 = C0
    📄 ICMPv6:          1... ....         = on-link determination
    📄 ICMPv6:          .1.. ....         = autonomous address configuration
    📄 ICMPv6:          ..0. ....         = Router Address bit
    📄 ICMPv6:          ...0 0000         = Reserved            = 0x00
    📄 ICMPv6: Valid Lifetime             = 4294967295 s (infinity)
    📄 ICMPv6: Preferred Lifetime         = 4294967295 s (infinity)
    📄 ICMPv6: Reserved                   = 0x00000000
    📄 ICMPv6: Prefix                     = caff:ca01:0:56::
    📄 ICMPv6:
```

Figure 12-8. Router Advertisement in the trace file

The router sends the advertisement to the all-nodes multicast address FF02::1, so all nodes on the link receive it. Looking at this packet in the detail window, we can see how the router is configured. The hop limit is set to 32. DHCP (administered protocol) is not used for address information, but is to be used by the hosts to get non-address-related information through DHCP. The lifetime is configured for 1,800 seconds. The first option of type 1 contains the router's link-layer address. The Type field of the second option is set to 3 for prefix information. The prefix length is 64 bits, and the lifetime is set to infinite. The prefix advertised in this case is CAFF:CA01: 0:56::/64. This is what I had configured on the router prior to taking this trace file. All hosts that boot on this link send out a Router Solicitation message and receive this Router Advertisement. They learn all the parameters, including the prefix information from the router and autoconfigure for one or more IPv6 address(es).

Applications

Use your lab, install your favorite applications, test the IPv6 support, and make your own experiences. You can find actual information about IPv6 applications on the JOIN home page of the University of Münster at *http://www.join.uni-muenster.de/Implementationen/Software.php?lang=en*. There you find links to server applications such as HTTP-, FTP-, DNS-, Mail-, Fileserver, firewalls, or client applications such as email, chat, or conferencing software. Another reference for an overview of IPv6 applications is *http://www.ipv6.org*.

Description of the Tests

This next section has a description of some tests that I created and analyzed in trace files.

 Some interesting IPv6 online tools such as DNS Lookup, *traceroute*, *ping*, etc., can be found at *http://www.ipv6tools.com*. Because the remote server performs the queries for you, you don't need an IPv6 connection to the Internet.

Pinging with IPv6

On the command prompt of host Marvin, I entered the following command:

```
ping6 fe80::202:b3ff:fe1e:8329%4
```

The %4 at the end of the address is not a typo; it is mandatory when pinging an IPv6 link-local address. It identifies the source interface from which the ICMPv6 packet should be sent. In this case, the interface number for the local area connection is 4. To find the interface number on a Windows host, use the command netsh interface ipv6 show interface. On a Linux host, set the parameter -I *interface name* instead of the %*interface number*.

The result in the trace file is shown in Figure 12-9.

Frame 1 is the Echo Request sent out by Marvin; Frame 2 is the Echo Reply from the other host, Ford. In the DLC header, we see the link-layer addresses of the source and the destination interface. The Ethertype is set to 86DD for IPv6. In the Source and Destination address fields in the IPv6 header, you can see how the MAC address is used to build the link-local IPv6 address with the prefix FE80. Between the third and fourth byte of the MAC address, FFFE is inserted. The Payload Length field tells us the length of the data carried after the header. The Next Header field is the same field as the Protocol Type field in IPv4. Protocol number 58 specifies ICMPv6. The ICMPv6 header shows what type of ICMPv6 message this is. Message type 128 is an Echo Request, and 129 is an Echo Reply. The identifier and sequence number are

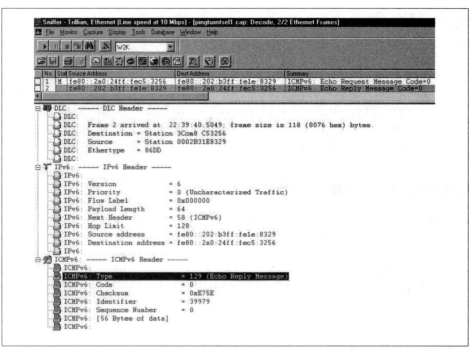

Figure 12-9. Tracefile with an IPv6 ping

used to match requests and replies. All these fields are important when you need to troubleshoot.

 To understand ICMPv6 and become familiar with the whole range of functionality, refer to Chapter 4 on ICMPv6. There you can also find tables with Protocol Numbers and Next Header values.

Pinging the 6Bone over the IPv4 Infrastructure

The trace file in Figure 12-10 shows a ping to a remote host on the Internet. Because our ISP does not offer native IPv6, I've configured a 6to4 Gateway internally, so we have the possibility to tunnel our IPv6 data over an IPv4 route. In the IPv4 header (marked gray) you see the public IPv4 address of the 6to4 relay (131.107.152.32), which receives and decapsulates the IPv4 packet and forwards the IPv6 packet to an IPv6 host. The IPv4 sender address (62.2.84.115) is the address of our 6to4 gateway.

The IPv6 address of the remote host is 2002:836B:9820::836B:9820. The summary line shows the Echo Request, the Echo Reply, and the two beautiful IPv6 addresses. The Protocol field in the IPv4 header, which cannot be seen in this screenshot, has the value 41 for IPv6.

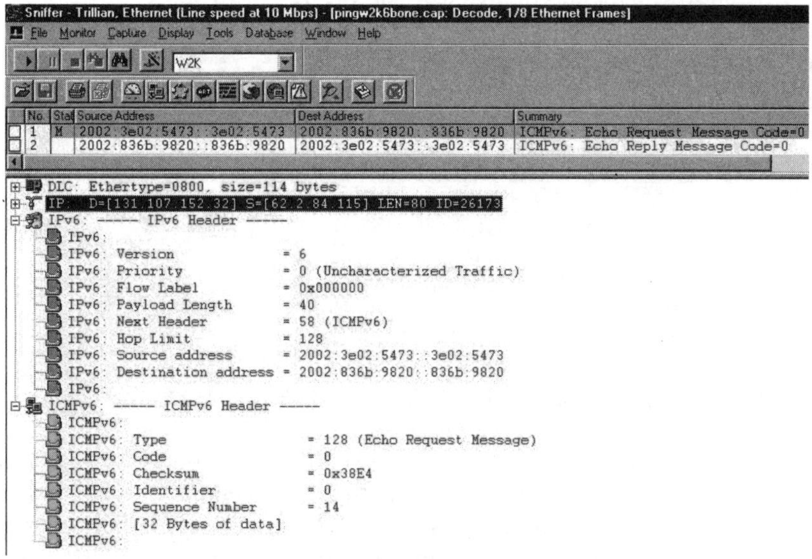
Sniffer - Trillian, Ethernet (Line speed at 10 Mbps) - [pingw2k6bone.cap: Decode, 1/8 Ethernet Frames]
File Monitor Capture Display Tools Database Window Help
W2K
No. Stat Source Address Dest Address Summary
1 M 2002:3e02:5473::3e02:5473 2002:836b:9820::836b:9820 ICMPv6: Echo Request Message Code=0
2 2002:836b:9820::836b:9820 2002:3e02:5473::3e02:5473 ICMPv6: Echo Reply Message Code=0
DLC: Ethertype=0800, size=114 bytes
IP: D=[131.107.152.32] S=[62.2.84.115] LEN=80 ID=26173
IPv6: ----- IPv6 Header -----
IPv6:
IPv6: Version = 6
IPv6: Priority = 0 (Uncharacterized Traffic)
IPv6: Flow Label = 0x000000
IPv6: Payload Length = 40
IPv6: Next Header = 58 (ICMPv6)
IPv6: Hop Limit = 128
IPv6: Source address = 2002:3e02:5473::3e02:5473
IPv6: Destination address = 2002:836b:9820::836b:9820
IPv6:
ICMPv6: ----- ICMPv6 Header -----
ICMPv6:
ICMPv6: Type = 128 (Echo Request Message)
ICMPv6: Code = 0
ICMPv6: Checksum = 0x38E4
ICMPv6: Identifier = 0
ICMPv6: Sequence Number = 14
ICMPv6: [32 Bytes of data]
ICMPv6:

Figure 12-10. Pinging the 6bone through an IPv4 infrastructure

Traceroute with IPv6

The screenshot in Figure 12-11 shows the output of a *traceroute* command. As described in Chapter 4, *traceroute* uses the Echo Request and Reply messages. By raising the hop limit by one for every packet, *traceroute* forces all routers on the path to a given destination to send back an ICMP Time Exceeded message. This way, the source host gets a list of all routers along the path.

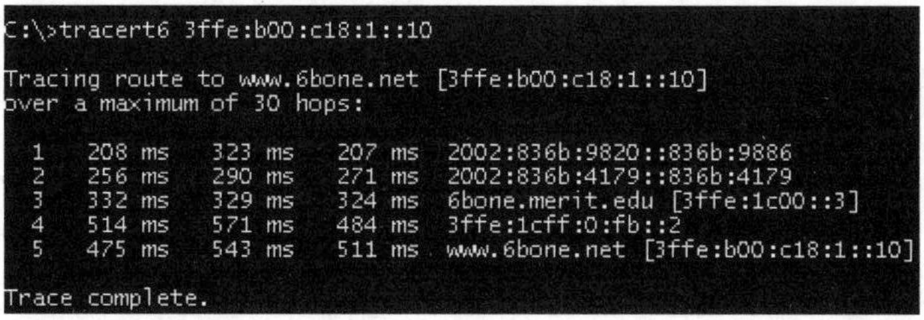
C:\>tracert6 3ffe:b00:c18:1::10
Tracing route to www.6bone.net [3ffe:b00:c18:1::10]
over a maximum of 30 hops:
1 208 ms 323 ms 207 ms 2002:836b:9820::836b:9886
2 256 ms 290 ms 271 ms 2002:836b:4179::836b:4179
3 332 ms 329 ms 324 ms 6bone.merit.edu [3ffe:1c00::3]
4 514 ms 571 ms 484 ms 3ffe:1cff:0:fb::2
5 475 ms 543 ms 511 ms www.6bone.net [3ffe:b00:c18:1::10]
Trace complete.

Figure 12-11. tracert6 to www.6bone.net

I issued *tracert6.exe* for `3FFE:B00:C18:1::10`, the IPv6 address of *www.6bone.net*. The first hop, `2002:836B:9820::836B:9886`, is the endpoint of the tunnel. To get there, any number of IPv4 hops is possible. *tracert6* cannot provide any information about the tunnel. Only the hops from the endpoint of the tunnel to the final destination are displayed.

Figure 12-12 shows this same command when tracing it with Sniffer.

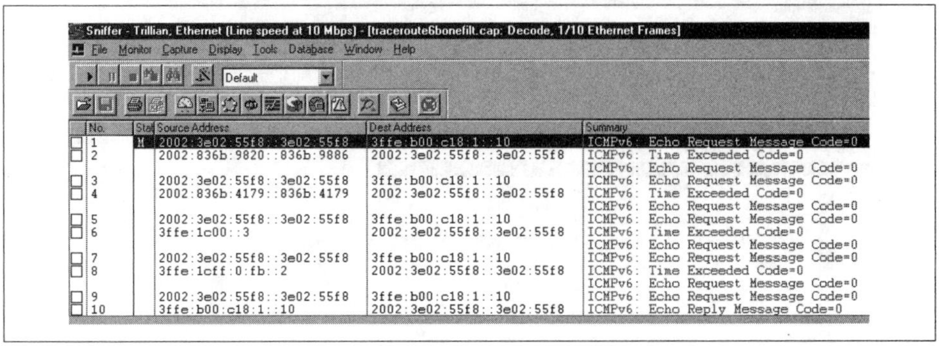

Figure 12-12. tracert6 to the 6Bone in the trace file

The first frame shows the first Echo Request sent to the final destination. This packet has a hop limit of 1. The first router in the path, 2002:836B:9820::836B:9886, replies with a Time Exceeded message. Frames 2, 4, 6, 8, and 10 are the replies from the routers along the path to the destination. Compare the source address of these replies with the *tracert6* output in Figure 12-11, and hey, do they match?

Browsing with IPv6

There are many IPv6-accessible web sites in the World Wide Web. For a list of IPv6-accessible web sites, go to *http://www.ipv6.org/v6-www.html*. To test your IPv6 connectivity, you can also try our web site, *http://ipv6.sunny.ch*. It's accessible only over IPv6. Current browser implementations on IPv6-capable and -enabled operating systems are usually able to display IPv6 web sites. If you have a proxy server configured in your browser configuration, make sure it's also IPv6-compatible. If not, you need to disable the proxy server for IPv6 surfing.

Figure 12-13 shows a Firefox screenshot of an interesting web site that is accessible only over IPv6.

As a test, I chose Peter Bieringer's IPv6 web site at *http://www.ipv6.bieringer.de*. The screenshot shows interesting details about my IPv6 connection. It was taken on a Debian Linux host with the IPv6-capable browser Mozilla Firefox.

This should be enough to whet your appetite. I hope this chapter gives you some ideas to start playing with IPv6. Have fun! And remember: "Experience is what you get if you don't get what you wanted."

Welcome to

www.ipv6.bieringer.de

(access via native IPv6 only)

Your client		
EUI48	EUI-48 identifier (MAC address)	00:0b:cd:32:4a:e8
EUI48_SCOPE	EUI-48 scope	global
EUI48_TYPE	EUI-48 address type	unicast
IID	Interface identifier	020b:cdff:fe32:4ae8
IPV6	IPv6 address	2001:08e0:abcd:00b3:020b:cdff:fe32:4ae8
IPV6_REGISTRY	Registry of IPv6 address	RIPENCC
OUI	Vendor identification of network interface card	"Compaq (HP)"
SLA	Site Level Aggregator (subnet)	00b3
TYPE	Address type	unicast,global-unicast,productive
USERAGENT	User agent identification	Mozilla/5.0 (X11; U; Linux i686; en-US; rv:1.7.8) Gecko/20050610 Firefox/1.0.4 (Debian package 1.0.4-3)
This server		
EUI64_SCOPE	EUI-64 scope	local
IID	Interface identifier	0000:0000:0147:0006
IPV6	IPv6 address	2001:07b0:1101:0002:0000:0000:0147:0006
IPV6_REGISTRY	Registry of IPv6 address	RIPENCC
NAME	Reverse DNS resolution	www.ipv6.bieringer.de
SLA	Site Level Aggregator (subnet)	0002
TYPE	Address type	unicast,global-unicast,productive

Generated by ipv6calcweb.cgi 0.46, (P) & (C) 2002-2003 by Peter Bieringer
Powered by ipv6calc 0.48, (P) & (C) 2001-2004 by Peter Bieringer

Figure 12-13. Browsing over IPv6 with Mozilla Firefox

RFCs

If you want to learn more about IPv6 or any other standardized protocol, you need to read RFCs. They are the most accurate source of information, but yes, I do agree, not always a fun reading (except if you read the ones published on April 1). This appendix provides a short overview of the standards and the RFC process. It also includes a list of IPv6-relevant RFCs.

General RFC Information

The Internet Engineering Task Force (IETF) and the Internet Engineering Steering Group (IESG) are the organizations that define the official specification documents of the Internet Protocol suite. These documents are recorded and published as standards track Request for Comment (RFC). If you want to understand the role of the IETF and the standardization process, if you need a list of all the organizations involved in the process and a description of what they do, or if you wish to attend an IETF meeting, there is an interesting and humorous RFC that describes the background, processes, and rules: RFC 3160, titled "The Tao of IETF—A Novice's Guide to the Internet Engineering Task Force."

RFCs are written reports describing most of the information regarding TCP/IP and the architecture, protocols, and history of the Internet. There are many sites on the Internet where RFCs are electronically accessible. The sites are very different, but most of them support some form of search mechanism. Find the site that best suits your preferences.

A good starting point is *http://www.rfc-editor.org*. There is a tribute to Jon Postel, one of the fathers of the Internet, who died in October 1998. He was *the* RFC editor. Besides this information, there is also an overview of the RFC series and process.

On the search and retrieve page of this site, there are many ways to access the wealth of information. RFCs can be viewed by number or in an index; they can be in forward or reverse chronological order; and they can be searched by author, title, number, or keyword. Of course, there is also a link to alternative RFC repositories.

RFC 2555 is an interesting overview of 30 years of RFC history and a good description of the contribution of Jon Postel's services to the Internet community. There is even more information about Jon Postel at *http://www.postel.org/postel.html*.

The first RFC, RFC 0001, was published by Steve Crocker on April 7, 1969. Today, the number of RFCs continues to rise quickly and has exceeded 4,000. RFCs can have different statuses, such as standard, informational, experimental, and historic. A good overview of the different statuses and current level of standardization can be found at *http://www.rfc-editor.org*. Here's a short list of some important basic RFCs of which you should be aware:

RFC 3700, "Official Protocol Standard"
> Known as the Internet Official Protocol Standard, this RFC lists only official RFC protocol standards and is therefore not a complete index. It contains the state of standardization as of July 2004. Find the most updated version by searching for the title of the document or go to *http://www.rfc-editor.org/rfcxx00.html*.

RFC 3232, "Assigned Numbers Document" (obsoletes RFC 1700)
> RFC 1700 used to be the number one reference for the assignment of all protocol parameters for the Internet protocol suite. The Internet Assigned Numbers Authority (IANA) is the central coordinator for the assignment of these parameters. RFC 1700 has been deprecated in RFC 3232 and replaced by an online database at *http://www.iana.org/numbers.html*.

RFCs 1122 and 1123, Host Requirements Documents
> These two RFCs are known as Host Requirements Documents and cover the requirements for Internet host software. RFC 1122 covers the communications protocol layers such as link layer, IP layer, and transport layer. RFC 1123 covers the application and support protocols. Many terms widely used throughout all RFCs are defined in these two documents. These two documents are not IPv6-specific, but they are a good read for general understanding.

RFC 1812, "Requirements for IPv4 Routers"
> This RFC covers the requirements for IPv4 Routers and is very informative. RFC 4294, "IPv6 Node Requirements," covers the requirements for IPv6 nodes. The term "node" includes host and routers.

The RFCs ending in 99 are usually a summary of the previous 99 RFCs and their status. For instance, if you need a summary about the RFCs from 3000 to 3098, refer to RFC 3099.

Drafts

I refer to drafts often throughout this book. Drafts always have version numbers in their names, and this number often increases frequently during the process. So let us have a closer look at the draft process:

During the standardization process, the drafts are published on the Internet. Drafts may eventually become RFCs. At the IETF web site at *http://www.ietf.org*, click on Internet Drafts to find all documents. To use the search engine and find the most updated status of any document, refer to *https://datatracker.ietf.org/public/pidtracker.cgi*. You can also click on "IETF Working Group" to find all groups sorted by areas (application, operation, routing, security, etc). Within the groups, you find all relevant RFCs and drafts. This is the best place to find out what is in the queue and what groups are working on. The goal of this process is to make a specification under development accessible to a large audience in order to get reviews and comments. Another good link to get an overview of RFCs and active drafts with regard to specific working groups is *http://tools.ietf.org*.

So let us understand the draft version numbers. As you have noted, it can change frequently. When you enter a draft name in the search engine, it will always show you the latest version. The rules for draft numbers are as follows:

Every time a draft is updated, it receives a new version number. At some point, a draft may be published as an RFC and then be removed from the draft directory. A draft with a specific version number has a lifetime of 6 months at a maximum. After this, if it has not been updated or become an RFC, it is removed from the draft directory. As this book is going to be on the market for some time, some drafts mentioned in here might not be active when you try to find them. They may have been removed or published as RFCs.

Drafts are not standards and should not be implemented in commercial products, because they are going to change for sure in the case they ever become an RFC. This can also lead to incompatibility issues, such as when vendors implement drafts at different maturity levels of development or if one implementation is based on draft and another on RFC. In practice, you will find draft implementations in commercial products, but now you know to be careful when using them.

RFC Index for IPv6

This is a list of all RFCs relevant to IPv6 and RFCs regarding related technologies published as of September 2005. It is sorted by RFC number.

General IPv6 RFCs

- RFC 791, "Internet Protocol," 1981
- RFC 854, "TELNET PROTOCOL SPECIFICATION," 1983
- RFC 855, "TELNET OPTION SPECIFICATIONS," 1983
- RFC 959, "FILE TRANSFER PROTOCOL (FTP)," 1985
- RFC 1058, "Routing Information Protocol," 1988
- RFC 1191, "Path MTU Discovery," 1991
- RFC 1195, "Use of OSI IS-IS for Routing in TCP/IP and Dual Environments," 1990
- RFC 1321, "The MD5 Message Digest Algorithm," 1992
- RFC 1546, "Host Anycasting Service," 1993
- RFC 1584, "Multicast Extensions to OSPF," 1994
- RFC 1587, "The OSPF NSSA Option," 1994
- RFC 1700, "Assigned Numbers," 1994
- RFC 1745, "BGP4/IDRP for IP—OSPF Interaction," 1994
- RFC 1771, "A Border Gateway Protocol 4 (BGP-4)," 1995
- RFC 1793, "Extending OSPF to Support Demand Circuits," 1995
- RFC 1812, "Requirements for IP Version 4 Routers," 1995
- RFC 1819, "Internet Stream Protocol Version 2," 1995
- RFC 1828, "IP Authentication using Keyed MD5," 1995
- RFC 1829, "The ESP DES-CBC Transform," 1995
- RFC 1918, "Address Allocation for Private Internets," 1996
- RFC 1981, "Path MTU Discovery for IP version 6," 1996
- RFC 1997, "BGP Communities Attribute," 1996
- RFC 2003, "IP Encapsulation within IP" (October, 1996)
- RFC 2080, "RIPng for IPv6," 1997
- RFC 2085, "HMAC-MD5 IP Authentication with Replay Prevention," 1997
- RFC 2101, "IPv4 Address Behaviour Today," 1997
- RFC 2104, "HMAC: Keyed-Hashing for Message Authentication," 1997
- RFC 2136, "Dynamic Updates in the Domain Name System," 1997
- RFC 2149, "Multicast Server Architectures for MARS-based ATM multicasting," 1997
- RFC 2185, "Routing Aspects Of IPv6 Transition," 1997
- RFC 2205, "Resource ReSerVation Protocol (RSVP)—Version 1 Functional Specification," 1997

- RFC 2207, "RSVP Extensions for IPSEC Data Flows," 1997
- RFC 2210, "The Use of RSVP with IETF Integrated Services," 1997
- RFC 2233, "The Interfaces Group MIB using SMIv2," 1997
- RFC 2236, "Internet Group Management Protocol, Version 2," 1997
- RFC 2324, "Hyper Text Coffee Pot Control Protocol (HTCPCP/1.0)," 1998
- RFC 2328, "OSPF Version 2," 1998
- RFC 2362, "Protocol Independent Multicast-Sparse Mode (PIM-SM): Protocol Specification," 1998
- RFC 2365, "Administratively Scoped IP Multicast," 1998
- RFC 2375, "IPv6 Multicast Address Assignments," 1998
- RFC 2401, "Security Architecture for the Internet Protocol," 1998
- RFC 2402, "IP Authentication Header," 1998
- RFC 2403, "The Use of HMAC-MD5-96 within ESP and AH," 1998
- RFC 2404, "The Use of HMAC-SHA-1-96 within ESP and AH," 1998
- RFC 2405, "The ESP DES-CBC Cipher Algorithm With Explicit IV," 1998
- RFC 2406, "IP Encapsulating Security Payload (ESP)," 1998
- RFC 2407, "The Internet IP Security Domain of Interpretation for ISAKMP," 1998
- RFC 2408, "Internet Security Association and Key Management Protocol (ISAKMP)," 1998
- RFC 2409, "The Internet Key Exchange (IKE)," 1998
- RFC 2410, "The NULL Encryption Algorithm and Its Use With IPsec ," 1998
- RFC 2411, "IP Security Document Roadmap," 1998
- RFC 2412, "The OAKLEY Key Determination Protocol," 1998
- RFC 2428, "FTP Extensions for IPv6 and NATs," 1998
- RFC 2430, "A Provider Architecture for Differentiated Services and Traffic Engineering (PASTE)," 1998
- RFC 2450, "Proposed TLA and NLA Assignment Rules," 1998
- RFC 2451, "The ESP CBC-Mode Cipher Algorithms," 1998
- RFC 2453, "RIP Version 2," 1998
- RFC 2460, "Internet Protocol, Version 6 (IPv6) Specification," 1998
- RFC 2461, "Neighbor Discovery for IP Version 6," 1998
- RFC 2462, "IPv6 Stateless Address Autoconfiguration," 1998
- RFC 2463, "Internet Control Message Protocol (ICMPv6)," 1998
- RFC 2464, "Transmission of IPv6 Packets over Ethernet Networks," 1998

- RFC 2465, "Management Information Base for IP Version 6: Textual Conventions and General Group," 1998
- RFC 2466, "Management Information Base for IP Version 6: ICMPv6 Group," 1998
- RFC 2471, "IPv6 Testing Address Allocation" (6Bone), 1998
- RFC 2473, "Generic Packet Tunneling in IPv6 Specification," 1998
- RFC 2474, "Definition of the Differentiated Services Field (DS Field) in the IPv4 and IPv6 Headers," 1998
- RFC 2475, "An Architecture for Differentiated Services," 1998
- RFC 2507, "IP Header Compression," 1999
- RFC 2526, "Reserved IPv6 Subnet Anycast Addresses," 1999
- RFC 2529, "Transmission of IPv6 over IPv4 Domains without Explicit Tunnels," 1999
- RFC 2545, "Use of BGP-4 Multiprotocol Extensions for IPv6 Inter-Domain Routing," 1999
- RFC 2553, "Basic Socket Interface Extensions for IPv6," March 1999
- RFC 2597, "Assured Forwarding PHB Group," 1999
- RFC 2608, "Service Location Protocol, Version 2," 1999
- RFC 2663, "IP Network Address Translator (NAT) Terminology and Considerations," 1999
- RFC 2675, "IPv6 Jumbograms," 1999
- RFC 2710, "Multicast Listener Discovery (MLD) for IPv6," 1999
- RFC 2711, "IPv6 Router Alert Option," 1999
- RFC 2715, "Interoperability Rules for Multicast Routing Protocols," 1999
- RFC 2740, "OSPF for IPv6," 1999
- RFC 2765, "Stateless IP/ICMP Translation Algorithm (SIIT)," 2000
- RFC 2766, "Network Address Translation, Protocol Translation (NAT-PT)," 2000
- RFC 2767, "Dual Stack Hosts using the "Bump-In-the-Stack" Technique (BIS)," 2000
- RFC 2772, "6Bone Backbone Routing Guidelines," 2000
- RFC 2784, "Generic Routing Encapsulation (GRE)," 2000
- RFC 2796, "BGP Route Reflection," 2000
- RFC 2842, "Capabilities Advertisement with BGP-4," 2000
- RFC 2845, "Secret Key Transaction Authentication for DNS (TSIG)," 2000
- RFC 2858, "Multiprotocol Extensions for BGP-4," 2000

- RFC 2874, "DNS Extensions to Support IPv6 Address Aggregation and Renumbering," 2000
- RFC 2884, "Performance Evaluation of Explicit Congestion Notification (ECN) in IP Networks," 2000
- RFC 2894, "Router Renumbering for IPv6," 2000
- RFC 2908, "The Internet Multicast Address Allocation Architecture," 2000
- RFC 2914, "Congestion Control Principles," 2000
- RFC 2921, "6BONE pTLA and pNLA Formats (pTLA)," 2000
- RFC 2925, "Definitions of Managed Objects for Remote Ping, Traceroute, and Lookup Operations," 2000
- RFC 2928, "Initial IPv6 Sub-TLA ID Assignments," 2000
- RFC 2963, "A Rate Adaptive Shaper for Differentiated Services," 2000
- RFC 2983, "Differentiated Services and Tunnels," 2000
- RFC 2993, "Architectural Implications of NAT," 2000
- RFC 2998, "A Framework for Integrated Services Operation over Diffserv Networks," 2000
- RFC 3006, "Integrated Services in the Presence of Compressible Flows," 2000
- RFC 3007, "Secure Domain Name System (DNS) Dynamic Update," 2000
- RFC 3008, "Domain Name System Security (DNSSEC) Signing Authority," 2000
- RFC 3019, "IP Version 6 Management Information Base for The Multicast Listener Discovery Protocol," 2001
- RFC 3022, "Traditional IP Network Address Translator (Traditional NAT)," 2001
- RFC 3027, "Protocol Complications with the IP Network Address Translator," 2001
- RFC 3041, "Privacy Extensions for Stateless Address Autoconfiguration in IPv6," 2001
- RFC 3053, "IPv6 Tunnel Broker," 2001
- RFC 3056, "Connection of IPv6 Domains via IPv4 Clouds," 2001
- RFC 3065, "Autonomous System Confederations for BGP," 2001
- RFC 3068, "An Anycast Prefix for 6to4 Relay Routers," 2001
- RFC 3086, "Definition of Differentiated Services Per Domain Behaviors and Rules for their Specification," 2001
- RFC 3111, "Service Location Protocol Modifications for IPv6," 2001
- RFC 3118, "Authentication for DHCP Messages," 2001
- RFC 3122, "Extensions to IPv6 Neighbor Discovery for Inverse Discovery Specification," 2001

- RFC 3124, "The Congestion Manager," 2001
- RFC 3140, "Per Hop Behavior Identification Codes," 2001
- RFC 3142, "An IPv6-to-IPv4 Transport Relay Translator," 2001
- RFC 3162, "RADIUS and IPv6," 2001
- RFC 3168, "The Addition of Explicit Congestion Notification (ECN) to IP," 2001
- RFC 3175, "Aggregation of RSVP for IPv4 and IPv6 Reservations," 2001
- RFC 3177, "IAB/IESG Recommendations on IPv6 Address Allocations to Sites," 2001
- RFC 3178, "IPv6 Multihoming Support at Site Exit Routers," 2001
- RFC 3226, "DNSSEC and IPv6 A6 aware server/resolver message size requirements," 2001
- RFC 3246, "An Expedited Forwarding PHB," 2002
- RFC 3247, "Supplemental Information for the New Definition of the EF PHB (Expedited Forwarding Per-Hop Behavior)," 2002
- RFC 3260, "New Terminology and Clarifications for Diffserv," 2002
- RFC 3289, "Management Information Base for the Differentiated Services Architecture," 2002
- RFC 3290, "An Informal Management Model for Diffserv Routers," 2002
- RFC 3306, "Unicast-Prefix-based IPv6 Multicast," 2002
- RFC 3307, "Allocation Guidelines for IPv6 Multicast Addresses," 2002
- RFC 3315, "Dynamic Host Configuration Protocol for IPv6 (DHCPv6)," 2003
- RFC 3317, "Differentiated Services Quality of Service Policy Information Base," 2003
- RFC 3319, "Dynamic Host Configuration Protocol (DHCPv6) Options for Session Initiation Protocol (SIP) Servers," 2003
- RFC 3338, "Dual Stack Hosts Using BIA," 2002
- RFC 3344, "IP Mobility Support for IPv4," 2002
- RFC 3353, "Overview of IP Multicast in a Multi-Protocol Label Switching (MPLS) Environment," 2002
- RFC 3376, "Internet Group Management Protocol, Version 3," 2002
- RFC 3392, "Capabilities Advertisement with BGP-4," 2002
- RFC 3484, "Default Address Selection for Internet Protocol version 6 (IPv6)," 2003
- RFC 3489, "STUN, Simple Traversal of User Datagram Protocol (UDP) Through Network Address Translators (NATs)," 2003
- RFC 3493, "Basic Socket Interface Extensions for IPv6" 2003

- RFC 3513, "Internet Protocol Version 6 (IPv6) Addressing Architecture," 2003
- RFC 3514, "The Security Flag in the IPv4 Header," April 1, 2003
- RFC 3526, "More Modular Exponential (MODP) Diffie-Hellman groups for Internet Key Exchange (IKE)," 2003
- RFC 3542, "Advanced Sockets Application Program Interface (API) for IPv6," 2003
- RFC 3569, "An Overview of Source-Specific Multicast (SSM)," 2003
- RFC 3582, "Goals for IPv6 Site-Multihoming Architectures," 2003
- RFC 3587, "IPv6 Global Unicast Address Format," 2003
- RFC 3590, "Source Address Selection for the Multicast Listener Discovery (MLD) Protocol," 2003
- RFC 3596, "DNS Extensions to Support IP Version 6," 2003
- RFC 3602, "The AES-CBC Cipher Algorithm and Its Use with IPsec," 2003
- RFC 3631, "Security Mechanisms for the Internet," 2003
- RFC 3633, "IPv6 Prefix Options for Dynamic Host Configuration Protocol (DHCP) version 6," 2003
- RFC 3646, "DNS Configuration options for Dynamic Host Configuration Protocol for IPv6 (DHCPv6)," 2003
- RFC 3697, "IPv6 Flow Label Specification," 2004
- RFC 3715, "IPsec-Network Address Translation (NAT) Compatibility Requirements," 2004
- RFC 3717, "IP over Optical Networks: A Framework ," 2004
- RFC 3736, "Stateless Dynamic Host Configuration Protocol (DHCP) Service for IPv6," 2004
- RFC 3739, "Internet X.509 Public Key Infrastructure: Qualified Certificates Profile," 2004
- RFC 3740, "The Multicast Group Security Architecture," 2004
- RFC 3748, "Extensible Authentication Protocol (EAP)," 2004
- RFC 3754, "IP Multicast in Differentiated Services (DS) Networks," 2004
- RFC 3756, "IPv6 Neighbor Discovery (ND) Trust Models and Threats," 2004
- RFC 3765, "NOPEER Community for Border Gateway Protocol (BGP) Route Scope Control," 2004
- RFC 3769, "Requirements for IPv6 Prefix Delegation," 2004
- RFC 3775, "Mobility Support in IPv6," 2004
- RFC 3776, "Using IPsec to Protect Mobile IPv6 Signaling Between Mobile Nodes and Home Agents," 2004

- RFC 3789, "Introduction to the Survey of IPv4 Addresses in Currently Deployed IETF Standards Track and Experimental Documents," 2004

- RFC 3790, "Survey of IPv4 Addresses in Currently Deployed IETF Internet Area Standards Track and Experimental Documents," 2004

- RFC 3791, "Survey of IPv4 Addresses in Currently Deployed IETF Routing Area Standards Track and Experimental Documents," 2004

- RFC 3792, "Survey of IPv4 Addresses in Currently Deployed IETF Security Area Standards Track and Experimental Documents," 2004

- RFC 3793, "Survey of IPv4 Addresses in Currently Deployed IETF Sub-IP Area Standards Track and Experimental Documents," 2004

- RFC 3794, "Survey of IPv4 Addresses in Currently Deployed IETF Transport Area Standards Track and Experimental Documents," 2004

- RFC 3795, "Survey of IPv4 Addresses in Currently Deployed IETF Application Area Standards Track and Experimental Documents," 2004

- RFC 3796, "Survey of IPv4 Addresses in Currently Deployed IETF Operations & Management Area Standards Track and Experimental Documents," 2004

- RFC 3810, "Multicast Listener Discovery Version 2 (MLDv2) for IPv6," 2004

- RFC 3849, "IPv6 Documentation Address," 2004

- RFC 3879, "Deprecating Site Local Addresses," 2004

- RFC 3898, "Network Information Service (NIS) Configuration Options for Dynamic Host Configuration Protocol for IPv6 (DHCPv6)," 2004

- RFC 3901, "DNS IPv6 Transport Operational Guidelines," 2004

- RFC 3936, "Procedures for Modifying the Resource reSerVation Protocol (RSVP)," 2004

- RFC 3947, "Negotiation of NAT-Traversal in the IKE," 2005

- RFC 3948, "UDP Encapsulation of IPsec ESP Packets," 2005

- RFC 3956, "Embedding the Rendezvous Point (RP) Address in an IPv6 Multicast Address," 2004

- RFC 3963, " Network Mobility (NEMO) Basic Support Protocol," 2005

- RFC 3964, "Security Considerations for 6to4," 2004

- RFC 3971, "SEcure Neighbor Discovery (SEND)," 2005

- RFC 3972, "Cryptographically Generated Addresses (CGA)," 2005

- RFC 3973, "Protocol Independent Multicast, Dense Mode (PIM-DM): Protocol Specification (Revised)," 2005

- RFC 3986, "Uniform Resource Identifier (URI): Generic Syntax," 2005

- RFC 4007, "IPv6 Scoped Address Architecture," 2005

- RFC 4022, "Management Information Base for the Transmission Control Protocol," 2005
- RFC 4029, "Scenarios and Analysis for Introducing IPv6 into ISP Networks," 2005
- RFC 4033, "DNS Security Introduction and Requirements," 2005
- RFC 4035, "Protocol Modifications for the DNS Security Extensions," 2005
- RFC 4038, "Application Aspects of IPv6 Transition," 2005
- RFC 4057, "IPv6 Enterprise Network Scenarios," 2005
- RFC 4065, "Instructions for Seamoby and Experimental Mobility Protocol IANA Allocations," 2005
- RFC 4068, "Fast Handovers for Mobile IPv6," 2005
- RFC 4074, "Common Misbehavior Against DNS Queries for IPv6 Addresses," 2005
- RFC 4075, "Simple Network Time Protocol (SNTP) Configuration Option for DHCPv6," 2005
- RFC 4076, "Renumbering Requirements for Stateless Dynamic Host Configuration Protocol for IPv6 (DHCPv6)," 2005
- RFC 4094, "Analysis of Existing Quality-of-Service Signaling Protocols," 2005
- RFC 4106, "The Use of Galois/Counter Mode (GCM) in IPsec Encapsulating Security Payload (ESP)," 2005
- RFC 4107, "Guidelines for Cryptographic Key Management," 2005
- RFC 4109, "Algorithms for Internet Key Exchange version 1 (IKEv1)," 2005
- RFC 4113, "Management Information Base for the User Datagram Protocol," 2005
- RFC 4135, "Goals of Detecting Network Attachment in IPv6," 2005
- RFC 4140, "Hierarchical Mobile IPv6 Mobility Management (HMIPv6)," 2005
- RFC 4159, "Deprecation of 'ip6.int,'" 2005
- RFC 4177, "Architectural Approaches to Multi-homing for IPv6," 2005
- RFC 4191, "Default Router Preferences and More-Specific Routes," 2005
- RFC 4192, "Procedures for Renumbering an IPv6 Network without a Flag Day," 2005
- RFC 4193, "Unique Local IPv6 Unicast Addresses," 2005
- RFC 4213, "Basic Transition Mechanisms for IPv6 Hosts and Routers," 2005
- RFC 4214, "Intra-Site Automatic Tunnel Addressing Protocol (ISATAP)," 2005
- RFC 4215, "Analysis on IPv6 Transition in Third Generation Partnership Project (3GPP) Networks," 2005
- RFC 4218, "Threats Relating to IPv6 Multihoming Solutions," 2005

- RFC 4219, "Things Multihoming in IPv6 (MULTI6) Developers Should Think About," 2005
- RFC 4225, "Mobile IP Version 6 Route Optimization Security Design Background," 2005
- RFC 4241, "A Model of IPv6/IPv4 Dual Stack Internet Access Service," 2005
- RFC 4242, "Information Refresh Time Option for Dynamic Host Configuration Protocol for IPv6 (DHCPv6)," 2005
- RFC 4243, "Vendor-Specific Information Suboption for the Dynamic Host Configuration Protocol (DHCP) Relay Agent Option," 2005
- RFC 4260, "Mobile IPv6 Fast Handovers for 802.11 Networks," 2005
- RFC 4280, "Dynamic Host Configuration Protocol (DHCP) Options for Broadcast and Multicast Control Servers," 2005
- RFC 4282, "The Network Access Identifier," 2005
- RFC 4283, "Mobile Node Identifier Option for Mobile IPv6 (MIPv6)," 2005
- RFC 4285, "Authentication Protocol for Mobile IPv6," 2006
- RFC 4286, "Multicast Router Discovery," 2005
- RFC 4291, "IP Version 6 Addressing Architecture," 2006
- RFC 4294, "IPv6 Node Requirements," 2006
- RFC 4301, "Security Architecture for the Internet Protocol," 2005
- RFC 4302, "IP Authentication Header," 2005
- RFC 4303, "IP Encapsulating Security Payload (ESP)," 2005
- RFC 4305, "Cryptographic Algorithm Implementation Requirements for Encapsulating Security Payload (ESP) and Authentication Header (AH)," 2005
- RFC 4306, "Internet Key Exchange (IKEv2) Protocol," 2005
- RFC 4307, "Cryptographic Algorithms for Use in the Internet Key Exchange Version 2 (IKEv2)," 2005
- RFC 4308, "Cryptographic Suites for IPsec," 2005
- RFC 4309, "Using Advanced Encryption Standard (AES) CCM Mode with IPsec Encapsulating Security Payload (ESP)," 2005
- RFC 4339, "IPv6 Host Configuration of DNS Server Information Approaches" 2006
- RFC 4359, "The Use of RSA/SHA-1 Signatures within Encapsulating Security Payload (ESP) and Authentication Header (AH)," 2006
- RFC 4380, "Teredo: Tunneling IPv6 over UDP through Network Address Translations (NATs)," 2006
- ·RFC 4443, "Internet Control Message Protocol (ICMPv6) for the Internet Protocol Version 6 (IPv6) Specification," 2006

RFCs Referring to Topologies

- RFC 2464, "Transmission of IPv6 Packets over Ethernet Networks," 1998
- RFC 2467, "Transmission of IPv6 Packets over FDDI Networks," 1998
- RFC 2470, "Transmission of IPv6 Packets over Token Ring Networks," 1998
- RFC 2472, "IP Version 6 over PPP," 1998
- RFC 2491, "IPv6 over Non-Broadcast Multiple Access (NBMA) networks," 1999
- RFC 2492, "IPv6 over ATM Networks," January, 1999
- RFC 2497, "Transmission of IPv6 Packets over ARCnet Networks," 1999
- RFC 2590, "Transmission of IPv6 Packets over Frame Relay Networks Specification," 1999
- RFC 3146, "Transmission of IPv6 Packets over IEEE 1394 Networks," 2001
- RFC 3162, "Radius and IPv6," 2001
- RFC 4338, "Transmission of IPv6, IPv4, and Address Resolution Protocol (ARP) Packets over Fibre Channel," 2006
- RFC 4472, "Operational Considerations and Issues with IPv6 DNS," 2006

IPv6 Resources

For easy reference, this appendix contains all the resources that I mention in the book.

Ethertype Field

Table B-1 lists possible values for the Ethertype number. You can find the complete list at *http://www.iana.org/assignments/ethernet-numbers*. Transmission of IP datagrams over Ethernet is defined in RFCs 894 and 895. The Ethertype for IPv6 is, as Table B-1 shows, 86DD.

Table B-1. Ethertype numbers

Ethertype (hex)	Description
0000–05DC	IEEE802.3 Length field
0101–01FF	Experimental
0200	XEROX PUP (see 0A00)
0201	PUP Addr Trans (see 0A01)
0400	Nixdorf
0600	XEROX NS IDP
0660	DLOG
0661	DLOG
0800	Internet IP (IPv4)
0801	X.75 Internet
0802	NBS Internet
0803	ECMA Internet
0804	Chaosnet
0805	X.25 Level 3
0806	ARP

Ethertype (hex)	Description
0807	XNS Compatability
0808	Frame Relay ARP
081C	Symbolics Private
0888–088A	Xyplex
0900	Ungermann-Bass net debugr
0A00	Xerox IEEE802.3 PUP
0A01	PUP Addr Trans
0BAD	Banyan VINES
0BAE	VINES Loopback
0BAF	VINES Echo
1000	Berkeley Trailer nego
1001–100F	Berkeley Trailer encap/IP
1600	Valid Systems
4242	PCS Basic Block Protocol
5208	BBN Simnet
6000	DEC Unassigned (Exp.)
6001	DEC MOP Dump/Load
6002	DEC MOP Remote Console
6003	DEC DECNET Phase IV Route
6004	DEC LAT
6005	DEC Diagnostic Protocol
6006	DEC Customer Protocol
6007	DEC LAVC, SCA
6008–6009	DEC Unassigned
6010–6014	3Com Corporation
6558	Trans Ether Bridging
6559	Raw Frame Relay
7000	Ungermann-Bass download
7002	Ungermann-Bass dia/loop
7020–7029	LRT
7030	Proteon
7034	Cabletron
8003	Cronus VLN
8004	Cronus Direct
8005	HP Probe
8006	Nestar

Table B-1. Ethertype numbers (continued)

Ethertype (hex)	Description
8008	AT&T
8010	Excelan
8013	SGI diagnostics
8014	SGI network games
8015	SGI reserved
8016	SGI bounce server
8019	Apollo Domain
802E	Tymshare
802F	Tigan, Inc.
8035	Reverse ARP
8036	Aeonic Systems
8038	DEC LANBridge
8039–803C	DEC Unassigned
803D	DEC Ethernet Encryption
803E	DEC Unassigned
803F	DEC LAN Traffic Monitor
8040–8042	DEC Unassigned
8044	Planning Research Corp.
8046	AT&T
8047	AT&T
8049	ExperData
805B	Stanford V Kernel exp.
805C	Stanford V Kernel prod.
805D	Evans & Sutherland
8060	Little Machines
8062	Counterpoint Computers
8065	Univ. of Mass., Amherst
8066	Univ. of Mass., Amherst
8067	Veeco Integrated Auto.
8068	General Dynamics
8069	AT&T
806A	Autophon
806C	ComDesign
806D	Computgraphic Corp.
806E–8077	Landmark Graphics Corp.
807A	Matra

Table B-1. Ethertype numbers (continued)

Ethertype (hex)	Description
807B	Dansk Data Elektronik
807C	Merit Internodal
807D–807F	Vitalink Communications
8080	Vitalink TransLAN III
8081–8083	Counterpoint Computers
809B	Appletalk
809C–809E	Datability
809F	Spider Systems Ltd.
80A3	Nixdorf Computers
80A4–80B3	Siemens Gammasonics Inc.
80C0–80C3	DCA Data Exchange Cluster
80C4	Banyan Systems
80C5	Banyan Systems
80C6	Pacer Software
80C7	Applitek Corporation
80C8–80CC	Intergraph Corporation
80CD–80CE	Harris Corporation
80CF–80D2	Taylor Instrument
80D3–80D4	Rosemount Corporation
80D5	IBM SNA Service on Ether
80DD	Varian Associates
80DE–80DF	Integrated Solutions TRFS
80E0–80E3	Allen-Bradley
80E4–80F0	Datability
80F2	Retix
80F3	AppleTalk AARP (Kinetics)
80F4–80F5	Kinetics
80F7	Apollo Computer
80FF–8103	Wellfleet Communications
8107–8109	Symbolics Private
8130	Hayes Microcomputers
8131	VG Laboratory Systems
8132–8136	Bridge Communications
8137–8138	Novell, Inc.
8139–813D	KTI
8148	Logicraft

Table B-1. Ethertype numbers (continued)

Ethertype (hex)	Description
8149	Network Computing Devices
814A	Alpha Micro
814C	SNMP
814D	BIIN
814E	BIIN
814F	Technically Elite Concept
8150	Rational Corp
8151–8153	Qualcomm
815C–815E	Computer Protocol Pty Ltd
8164–8166	Charles River Data Systems
817D	XTP
817E	SGI/Time Warner prop.
8180	HIPPI-FP encapsulation
8181	STP, HIPPI-ST
8182	Reserved for HIPPI-6400
8183	Reserved for HIPPI-6400
8184–818C	Silicon Graphics prop.
818D	Motorola Computer
819A–81A3	Qualcomm
81A4	ARAI Bunkichi
81A5–81AE	RAD Network Devices
81B7–81B9	Xyplex
81CC–81D5	Apricot Computers
81D6–81DD	Artisoft
81E6–81EF	Polygon
81F0–81F2	Comsat Labs
81F3–81F5	SAIC
81F6–81F8	VG Analytical
8203–8205	Quantum Software
8221–8222	Ascom Banking Systems
823E–8240	Advanced Encryption Systems
827F–8282	Athena Programming
8263–826A	Charles River Data Systems
829A–829B	Inst Ind Info Tech
829C–82AB	Taurus Controls
82AC–8693	Walker Richer & Quinn

Table B-1. Ethertype numbers (continued)

Ethertype (hex)	Description
8694–869D	Idea Courier
869E–86A1	Computer Network Tech
86A3–86AC	Gateway Communications
86DB	SECTRA
86DE	Delta Controls
86DD	IPv6
86DF	ATOMIC
86E0–86EF	Landis & Gyr Powers
8700–8710	Motorola
876B	TCP/IP Compression
876C	IP Autonomous Systems
876D	Secure Data
880B	PPP
8847	MPLS Unicast
8848	MPLS Multicast
8A96–8A97	Invisible Software
9000	Loopback
9001	3Com(Bridge) XNS Sys Mgmt
9002	3Com(Bridge) TCP-IP Sys
9003	3Com(Bridge) loop detect
FF00	BBN VITAL-LanBridge cache
FF00–FF0F	ISC Bunker Ramo
FFFF	Reserved

Next Header Field Values (Chapter 2)

Table B-2 lists the possible values for the Next Header field in the IPv6 Header (see the explanation in Chapter 2). You can also find the complete list at *http://www.iana. org/assignments/protocol-numbers*.

Table B-2. Next Header field values

Decimal	Protocol	Reference
0	IPv6 Hop-by-Hop Option	RFC 1883
1	Internet Control Message	RFC 792
2	Internet Group Management	RFC 1112
3	Gateway-to-Gateway	RFC 823
4	IP in IP (encapsulation)	RFC 2003

Table B-2. Next Header field values (continued)

Decimal	Protocol	Reference
5	Stream	RFC 1190, RFC 1819
6	Transmission Control	RFC 793
7	CBT	Ballardie
8	Exterior Gateway Protocol	RFC 888, DLM1
9	Any private interior gateway (used by Cisco for their IGRP)	IANA
10	BBN RCC Monitoring	SGC
11	Network Voice Protocol	RFC 741, SC3
12	PUP	PUP, Xerox
13	ARGUS	RWS4
14	EMCON	BN7
15	XNET, Cross Net Debugger	IEN158, JFH2
16	CHAOS	NC3
17	UDP	RFC 768, JBP
18	Multiplexing (MUX)	IEN90, JBP
19	DCN Measurement Subsystems	DLM1
20	Host Monitoring (HMP)	RFC 869, RH6
21	Packet Radio Measurement (PRM)	ZSU
22	XEROX NS IDP	ETHERNET, XEROX
23	Trunk-1	BWB6
24	Trunk-2	BWB6
25	Leaf-1	BWB6
26	Leaf-2	BWB6
27	Reliable Data Protocol (RDP)	RFC 908, RH6
28	Internet Reliable Transaction (IRTP)	RFC 938, TXM
29	ISO Transport Protocol Class 4	RFC 905, RC77
30	Bulk Data Transfer Protocol	RFC 969, DDC1
31	MFE Network Services Protocol	MFENET, BCH2
32	MERIT Internodal Protocol	HWB
33	Datagram Congestion Control Protocol (DCCP)	*draft-ietf-dccp-spec-11*
34	Third Party Connect Protocol	SAF3
35	Inter-Domain Policy Routing Protocol	MXS1
36	XTP	GXC
37	Datagram Delivery Protocol (DDP)	WXC
38	IDPR Control Message Transport Protocol	MXS1
39	TP++ Transport Protocol	DXF

Table B-2. Next Header field values (continued)

Decimal	Protocol	Reference
40	IL Transport Protocol	Presotto
41	IPv6	Deering
42	Source Demand Routing Protocol (SDRP)	DXE1
43	Routing Header for IPv6	Deering
44	Fragment Header for IPv6	Deering
45	Inter-Domain Routing Protocol (IDRP)	Sue Hares
46	Reservation Protocol (RSVP)	Bob Braden
47	General Routing Encapsulation (GRE)	Tony Li
48	Mobile Host Routing Protocol (MHRP)	David Johnson
49	BNA	Gary Salamon
50	Encapsulated Security Payload	RFC 2406
51	Authentication Header	RFC 2402
52	Integrated Net Layer Security TUBA	GLENN
53	IP with Encryption (SWIPE)	JI6
54	NBMA Address Resolution Protocol (NARP)	RFC 1735
55	IP Mobility	Perkins
56	Transport Layer Security Protocol (TLSP)	Oberg
57	SKIP	Markson
58	ICMP for IPv6 (IPv6-ICMP)	RFC 1883
59	No Next Header for IPv6 (IPv6-NoNxt)	RFC 1883
60	Destination Options for IPv6 (IPv6-Opts)	RFC 1883
61	Any host internal protocol	IANA
62	CFTP	CFTP, HCF2
63	Any local network	IANA
64	SATNET and Backroom EXPAK	SHB
65	Kryptolan	PXL1
66	Remote Virtual Disk Protocol (RVD)	MBG
67	Internet Pluribus Packet Core (IPPC)	SHB
68	Any distributed file system	IANA
69	SATNET Monitoring	SHB
70	VISA Protocol	GXT1
71	Internet Packet Core Utility (IPCU)	SHB
72	Computer Protocol Network Executive (CPNX)	DXM2
73	Computer Protocol Heart Beat (CPHB)	DXM2
74	Wang Span Network (WSN)	VXD
75	Packet Video Protocol (PVP)	SC3

Table B-2. Next Header field values (continued)

Decimal	Protocol	Reference
76	Backroom SATNET Monitoring	SHB
77	SUN ND PROTOCOL-Temporary	WM3
78	WIDEBAND Monitoring	SHB
79	WIDEBAND EXPAK	SHB
80	ISO Internet Protocol	MTR
81	VMTP	DRC3
82	SECURE-VMTP	DRC3
83	VINES	BXH
84	TTP	JXS
85	NSFNET-IGP	HWB
86	Dissimilar Gateway Protocol (DGP)	DGP, ML109
87	TCF	GAL5
88	EIGRP	CISCO, GXS
89	OSPFIGP	RFC 1583, JTM4
90	Sprite RPC Protocol	SPRITE, BXW
91	Locus Address Resolution Protocol (LARP)	BXH
92	Multicast Transport Protocol (MTP)	SXA
93	AX.25 Frames	BK29
94	IP-within-IP Encapsulation Protocol	JI6
95	Mobile Internetworking Control Protocol (MICP)	JI6
96	Semaphore Communications Sec. Protocol	HXH
97	Ethernet-within-IP Encapsulation	RFC 3378
98	Encapsulation Header	RFC 1241, RXB3
99	Any private encryption scheme	IANA
100	GMTP	RXB5
101	Ipsilon Flow Management Protocol (IFMP)	Hinden
102	PNNI over IP	Callon
103	Protocol Independent Multicast (PIM)	Farinacci
104	ARIS	Feldman
105	SCPS	Durst
106	QNX	Hunter
107	Active Networks	Braden
108	IP Payload Compression Protocol	RFC 2393
109	Sitara Networks Protocol (SNP)	Sridhar
110	Compaq Peer Protocol	Volpe

Table B-2. Next Header field values (continued)

Decimal	Protocol	Reference
111	IPX in IP	Lee
112	Virtual Router Redundancy Protocol (VRRP)	RFC 3768
113	Reliable Transport Protocol (PGM)	Speakman
114	Any zero-hop protocol	IANA
115	Layer Two Tunneling Protocol	Aboba
116	Data Exchange (DDX)	Worley
117	Interactive Agent Transfer Protocol (IATP)	Murphy
118	Schedule Transfer Protocol (STP)	JMP
119	SpectraLink Radio Protocol (SRP)	Hamilton
120	UTI	Lothberg
121	Simple Message Protocol (SMP)	Ekblad
122	SM	Crowcroft
123	Performance Transparency Protocol (PTP)	Welzl
124	ISIS over IPv4	Przygienda
125	FIRE	Partridge
126	Combat Radio Transport Protocol (CRTP)	Sautter
127	Combat Radio User Datagram (CRUDP)	Sautter
128	SSCOPMCE	Waber
129	IPLT	Hollbach
130	Secure Packet Shield (SPS)	McIntosh
131	Private IP Encapsulation within IP (PIPE)	Petri
132	Stream Control Transmission Protocol (SCTP)	Stewart
133	Fibre Channel (FC)	Rajagopal
134	RSVP-E2E-IGNORE	RFC 3175
135	Mobility Header	RFC 3775
136	UDPLite	RFC 3828
137	MPLS-in-IP	RFC 4023
138-252	Unassigned	IANA
253	Use for experimentation and testing	RFC 3692
254	Use for experimentation and testing	RFC 3692
255	Reserved	IANA

Reserved Anycast IDs (Chapter 3, RFC 2526)

Table B-3 lists the anycast IDs that have been assigned so far.

Table B-3. Reserved anycast IDs

Decimal	Hexadecimal	Description
127	7F	Reserved
126	7E	Mobile IPv6 Home-Agents anycast
0-125	00-7D	Reserved

Values for the Multicast Scope Field (Chapter 3, RFC 4291)

The values listed in Table B-4 have been defined in RFC 4291 for the Multicast Scope field.

Table B-4. Values for the Multicast Scope field

Value	Description
0	Reserved
1	Interface-local scope (used to be called Node-local scope in earlier specs)
2	Link-local scope
3	Reserved
4	Admin-local scope
5	Site-local scope
6, 7	Unassigned
8	Organization-local scope
9, A, B, C, D	Unassigned
E	Global scope
F	Reserved

Well-Known Multicast Group Addresses (Chapter 3, RFC 2375)

RFC 2375 defines the initial assignment of IPv6 multicast addresses that are permanently assigned. Some assignments are made for fixed scopes; other assignments are valid in different scopes. Table B-5 lists them.

Table B-5. Well-known multicast addresses with fixed scope

Address	Description
(Interface-local) or Node-local scope	
FF01:0:0:0:0:0:0:1	All-nodes address
FF01:0:0:0:0:0:0:2	All-routers address

Table B-5. Well-known multicast addresses with fixed scope (continued)

Address	Description
Link-local scope	
FF02:0:0:0:0:0:0:1	All-nodes address
FF02:0:0:0:0:0:0:2	All-routers address
FF02:0:0:0:0:0:0:3	Unassigned
FF02:0:0:0:0:0:0:4	DVMRP routers
FF02:0:0:0:0:0:0:5	OSPFIGP
FF02:0:0:0:0:0:0:6	OSPFIGP designated routers
FF02:0:0:0:0:0:0:7	ST routers
FF02:0:0:0:0:0:0:8	ST hosts
FF02:0:0:0:0:0:0:9	RIP routers
FF02:0:0:0:0:0:0:A	EIGRP routers
FF02:0:0:0:0:0:0:B	Mobile agents
FF02:0:0:0:0:0:0:D	All PIM routers
FF02:0:0:0:0:0:0:E	RSVP encapsulation
FF02:0:0:0:0:0:0:16	All MLDv2-capable routers
FF02:0:0:0:0:0:0:6A	All snoopers
FF02:0:0:0:0:0:1:1	Link name
FF02:0:0:0:0:0:1:2	All DHCP agents
FF02:0:0:0:0:0:1:3	Link-local Multicast Name Resolution
FF02:0:0:0:0:0:1:4	DTCP Announcement
FF02:0:0:0:0:1:FFXX:XXXX	Solicited-node address
Site-local scope	
FF05:0:0:0:0:0:0:2	All-routers address
FF05:0:0:0:0:0:1:3	All DHCP servers
FF05:0:0:0:0:0:1:4	Deprecated
FF05:0:0:0:0:0:1:1000 to FF05:0:0:0:0:0:01:13FF	Service location (SLP) Version 2

Table B-6 lists the currently assigned multicast group addresses with variable scope. The addresses are noted beginning with FF0X, X being the placeholder for a variable scope value. Find an updated list at *http://www.iana.org/assignments/ipv6-multicast-addresses*.

Table B-6. Assigned IPv6 multicast group addresses with variable scope

Address	Group
FF0X:0:0:0:0:0:0:0	Reserved Multicast Address
FF0X:0:0:0:0:0:0:C	SSDP
FF0X:0:0:0:0:0:0:100	VMTP Managers Group

Table B-6. Assigned IPv6 multicast group addresses with variable scope (continued)

Address	Group
FF0X:0:0:0:0:0:0:101	Network Time Protocol (NTP)
FF0X:0:0:0:0:0:0:102	SGI-Dogfight
FF0X:0:0:0:0:0:0:103	Rwhod
FF0X:0:0:0:0:0:0:104	VNP
FF0X:0:0:0:0:0:0:105	Artificial Horizons - Aviator
FF0X:0:0:0:0:0:0:106	NSS - Name Service Server
FF0X:0:0:0:0:0:0:107	AUDIONEWS - Audio News Multicast
FF0X:0:0:0:0:0:0:108	SUN NIS+ Information Service
FF0X:0:0:0:0:0:0:109	MTP Multicast Transport Protocol
FF0X:0:0:0:0:0:0:10A	IETF-1-LOW-AUDIO
FF0X:0:0:0:0:0:0:10B	IETF-1-AUDIO
FF0X:0:0:0:0:0:0:10C	IETF-1-VIDEO
FF0X:0:0:0:0:0:0:10D	IETF-2-LOW-AUDIO
FF0X:0:0:0:0:0:0:10E	IETF-2-AUDIO
FF0X:0:0:0:0:0:0:10F	IETF-2-VIDEO
FF0X:0:0:0:0:0:0:110	MUSIC-SERVICE
FF0X:0:0:0:0:0:0:111	SEANET-TELEMETRY
FF0X:0:0:0:0:0:0:112	SEANET-IMAGE
FF0X:0:0:0:0:0:0:113	MLOADD
FF0X:0:0:0:0:0:0:114	any private experiment
FF0X:0:0:0:0:0:0:115	DVMRP on MOSPF
FF0X:0:0:0:0:0:0:116	SVRLOC
FF0X:0:0:0:0:0:0:117	XINGTV
FF0X:0:0:0:0:0:0:118	microsoft-ds
FF0X:0:0:0:0:0:0:119	nbc-pro
FF0X:0:0:0:0:0:0:11A	nbc-pfn
FF0X:0:0:0:0:0:0:11B	lmsc-calren-1
FF0X:0:0:0:0:0:0:11C	lmsc-calren-2
FF0X:0:0:0:0:0:0:11D	lmsc-calren-3
FF0X:0:0:0:0:0:0:11E	lmsc-calren-4
FF0X:0:0:0:0:0:0:11F	ampr-info
FF0X:0:0:0:0:0:0:120	mtrace
FF0X:0:0:0:0:0:0:121	RSVP-encap-1
FF0X:0:0:0:0:0:0:122	RSVP-encap-2
FF0X:0:0:0:0:0:0:123	SVRLOC-DA
FF0X:0:0:0:0:0:0:124	rln-server

Table B-6. Assigned IPv6 multicast group addresses with variable scope (continued)

Address	Group
FF0X:0:0:0:0:0:0:125	proshare-mc
FF0X:0:0:0:0:0:0:126	dantz
FF0X:0:0:0:0:0:0:127	cisco-rp-announce
FF0X:0:0:0:0:0:0:128	cisco-rp-discovery
FF0X:0:0:0:0:0:0:129	gatekeeper
FF0X:0:0:0:0:0:0:12A	iberiagames
FF0X:0:0:0:0:0:0:12B	X Display
FF0X:0:0:0:0:0:0:12C	emware-moap
FF0X:0:0:0:0:0:0:12D	DvbServDisc
FF0X:0:0:0:0:0:0:201	"rwho" Group (BSD) (unofficial)
FF0X:0:0:0:0:0:0:202	SUN RPC PMAPPROC_CALLIT
FF0X:0:0:0:0:0:0:300	Mbus/Ipv6
FF0X:0:0:0:0:0:2:0000 to FF0X:0:0:0:0:0:2:7FFD	Multimedia Conference Calls
FF0X:0:0:0:0:0:2:7FFE	SAPv1 Announcements
FF0X:0:0:0:0:0:2:7FFF	SAPv0 Announcements (deprecated)
FF0X:0:0:0:0:0:2:8000 to FF0X:0:0:0:0:0:2:FFFF	SAP Dynamic Assignments

ICMPv6 Message Types and Code Values (Chapter 4, RFC 2463)

Table B-7 provides an overview of the ICMPv6 error message types, along with the additional code information, which depends on the message type.

Table B-7. ICMPv6 error messages and code type

Message number	Message type	Code field
1	Destination Unreachable	0 = no route to destination 1 = communication with destination administratively prohibited 2 = beyond scope of Source address 3 = address unreachable 4 = port unreachable 5 = Source address failed ingress/egress policy 6 = reject route to destination
2	Packet Too Big	Code field set to 0 by the sender and ignored by the receiver
3	Time Exceeded	0 = hop limit exceeded in transit 1 = fragment reassembly time exceeded

Table B-7. ICMPv6 error messages and code type (continued)

Message number	Message type	Code field
4	Parameter Problem	0 = erroneous header field encountered 1 = unrecognized next header type encountered 2 = unrecognized IPv6 option encountered The pointer field identifies the octet offset within the invoking packet where the error was detected. The pointer points beyond the end of the ICMPv6 packet if the field in error is beyond what can fit in the maximum size of an ICMPv6 error message.
100 and 101	Private experimentation	RFC 4443
127	Reserved for expansion of ICMPv6 error messages	RFC 4443

Table B-8 provides an overview of the ICMPv6 informational messages.

Table B-8. ICMPv6 informational messages

Message number	Message type	Description
128	Echo Request	RFC 4443. Used for the ping command.
129	Echo Reply	
130	Multicast Listener Query	RFC 2710. Used for multicast goup management.
131	Multicast Listener Report	
132	Multicast Listener Done	
133	Router Solicitation	RFC 2461. Used for neighbor discovery and autoconfiguration.
134	Router Advertisement	
135	Neighbor Solicitation	
136	Neighbor Advertisement	
137	Redirect Message	
138	Router Renumbering	RFC 2894 Codes: 0 = Router renumbering command 1 = Router renumbering result 255 = Sequence number reset
139	ICMP Node Information Query	*draft-ietf-ipngwg-icmp-name-lookups-15.txt*
140	ICMP Node Information Response	
141	Inverse ND Solicitation	RFC 3122
142	Inverse ND Adv Message	RFC 3122
143	Version 2 Multicast Listener Report	RFC 3810

Table B-8. ICMPv6 informational messages (continued)

Message number	Message type	Description
144	ICMP Home Agent Address Discovery Request Message	RFC 3775 ICMPv6 Messages for Mobile IPv6
145	ICMP Home Agent Address Discovery Reply Message	
146	ICMP Mobile Prefix Solicitation Message	
147	ICMP Mobile Prefix Advertisement Message	
148	Certification Path Solicitation Message	RFC 3971 ICMPv6 Messages for SEcure Neighbor Discovery
149	Certification Path Advertisement Message	
151	Multicast Router Advertisement	RFC 4286
152	Multicast Router Solicitation	
153	Multicast Router Termination	
200	Private experimentation	RFC 4443
201		
255	Reserved for expansion of ICMPv6 informational messages	RFC 4443

Table B-9 lists the possible code values of the Destination Unreachable message (type 1).

Table B-9. Code values of the Destination Unreachable message (type 1)

Code	Description
0	"No route to destination."
	This code is used if a router cannot forward a packet because it does not have a route in its table for a destination network. This can happen only if the router does not have an entry for a default route.
1	"Communication with destination administratively prohibited."
	This type of message can, for example, be sent by a firewall that cannot forward a packet to a host inside the firewall because of a packet filter. It might also be sent if a node is configured not to accept unauthenticated Echo Requests.
2	"Beyond scope of Source address."
	This code is used if the Destination address is beyond the scope of the Source address, e.g., if a packet has a link-local Source address and a global Destination address.
3	"Address unreachable."
	This code is used if a Destination address cannot be resolved into a corresponding network address or if there is a data-link layer problem preventing the node from reaching the destination network.

Table B-9. Code values of the Destination Unreachable message (type 1) (continued)

Code	Description
4	"Port unreachable."
	This code is used if the transport protocol (e.g., UDP) has no listener and there is no other means to inform the sender. For example, if a Domain Name System (DNS) query is sent to a host and the DNS server is not running, this type of message is generated.
5	"Source address failed ingress/egress policy."
	This code is used if a packet with this Source address is not allowed due to ingress or egress filtering policies.
6	"Reject route to destination."
	This code is used if the route to the destination is a reject route.

Table B-10 shows the Code fields for the Time Exceeded message.

Table B-10. Code values for Time Exceeded message (type 3)

Code	Description
0	"Hop limit exceeded in transit."
	Possible causes: the initial hop limit value is too low; there are routing loops; or use of the *traceroute* utility.
1	"Fragment reassembly time exceeded."
	If a fragmented packet is sent by using a fragment header (refer to Chapter 2 for more details) and the receiving host cannot reassemble all packets within a certain time, it notifies the sender by issuing this ICMP message.

Table B-11 shows the Code fields for the Parameter Problem message.

Table B-11. Code values for Parameter Problem (type 4)

Code	Description
0	Erroneous header field encountered
1	Unrecognized next header type encountered
2	Unrecognized IPv6 option encountered

Table B-12 shows an overview of the different Neighbor Discovery options and the message types in which they are used.

Table B-12. Overview of ND options

Option type	Used in
Type 1 Source link-layer address	Neighbor solicitation Router solicitation Router advertisement IND solicitation/advertisement
Type 2 Target link layer address	Neighbor advertisement Redirect IND solicitation/advertisement

Table B-12. Overview of ND options (continued)

Option type	Used in
Type 3 Prefix	Router advertisement
Type 4 Redirected header	Redirect
Type 5 MTU	Router advertisement IND solicitation/advertisement
Type 7 Advertisement interval	Router advertisement (defined in Mobile IPv6 specification)
Type 8 Home Agent information	Router advertisement (defined in Mobile IPv6 specification)
Type 9 Source address list	IND Solicitation
Type 10 Target address list	IND Advertisement

A Neighbor Cache entry can be in one of five states according to RFC 2461. The five states are explained in Table B-13.

Table B-13. States of Neighbor Cache entries

State	Description
Incomplete	Address resolution is currently being performed and awaiting either a response or a timeout. Specifically, a Neighbor Solicitation has been sent to the solicited-node multicast address of the target, but the corresponding Neighbor Advertisement has not yet been received.
Reachable	This neighbor is currently reachable, which means positive confirmation was received within the last ReachableTime milliseconds that the neighbor was functioning properly.
Stale	More than ReachableTime milliseconds have elapsed since the last positive confirmation that the forward path was functioning properly was received. No action will take place regarding this neighbor until a packet is sent.
Delay	This neighbor's Reachable Time has expired, and a packet was sent within the last DelayFirstProbeTime seconds. If no confirmation is received within the DelayFirstProbeTime seconds, send a Neighbor Solicitation and change the neighbor state to Probe state. The use of Delay allows upper-layer protocols additional time to provide reachability confirmation. Without this extra time, possible redundant traffic would be generated.
Probe	A reachability confirmation is being actively attempted by sending Neighbor Solicitations every RetransTimer milliseconds until reachability is confirmed.

QoS in IPv6 (Chapter 6)

Table B-14 shows the division of the DSCP-Pools defined in RFC 2474. You can also refer to *http://www.iana.org/assignments/dscp-registry*.

Table B-14. The codepoint pools

Pool	Codepoint space	Assignment policy
1	xxxxx0	Standard use
2	xxxx11	Experimental/local use
3	xxxx01	Experimental/local use; potential standard use in the future

Table B-15 shows currently defined router types. Find an updated list at *http://www.iana.org/assignments/ipv6-routeralert-values*.

Table B-15. Currently defined router types

Value	Description
0	IP packet contains a Multicast Listener Discovery message.
1	IP packet contains an RSVP message.
2	IP packet contains an Active Networks message—the sender is attempting to load a program into the router for executing customized functions.
3–35	IP packet contains an Aggregated Reservation Nesting Level (RFC 3175, RSVP)
36–65,535	Reserved to IANA for future use.

Multicast Group Addresses and Token Ring Functional Addresses (Chapter 7)

Table B-16 shows how IPv6 multicast addresses are mapped to Token Ring functional addresses.

Table B-16. Mapping IPv6 multicast addresses to Token Ring Functional Addresses

MAC Functional Address (canonical)	Multicast addresses
03-00-80-00-00-00	All-nodes (FF01::1 and FF02::1) Solicited-node (FF02:0:0:0:0.1:FFxx:xxxx)
03-00-40-00-00-00	All-routers (FF0X::2)
03-00-00-80-00-00	Any other multicast address with three least significant bits = 000
03-00-00-40-00-00	Any other multicast address with three least significant bits = 001
03-00-00-20-00-00	Any other multicast address with three least significant bits = 010
03-00-00-10-00-00	Any other multicast address with three least significant bits = 011
03-00-00-08-00-00	Any other multicast address with three least significant bits = 100
03-00-00-04-00-00	Any other multicast address with three least significant bits = 101
03-00-00-02-00-00	Any other multicast address with three least significant bits = 110
03-00-00-01-00-00	Any other multicast address with three least significant bits = 111

OSPFv3 Messages and the Link State Database (Chapter 8)

Table B-17 lists all possible OSPF for IPv6 packet types.

Table B-17. OSPF for IPv6 packet types

Packet type	Name	Description
1	Hello	Initializes and maintains adjacencies. Also used to elect DR and BDR. See the section "Forming Adjacencies."
2	Database Description	Exchanges database description during the formation of adjacencies. See the section "Forming Adjacencies."
3	Link State Request	Requests missing or changed LSAs. See the section "Forming Adjacencies."
4	Link State Update	Transmits LSAs either responding to requests when forming adjacencies or during LSA flooding. See the sections "Forming Adjacencies" and "LSA Flooding."
5	Link State Acknowledgment	Acknowledges the reception of an LSA. Every LSA must be acknowledged. See the sections "Forming Adjacencies" and "LSA Flooding."

The Options field describes the optional capabilities of the router. Table B-18 explains the bits used in the Options field.

Table B-18. The Options field

Bit	Name	Description
0–17	Not used	Reserved for future use.
18	DC	Handling of Demand Circuits, as described in RFC 1793.
19	R	Indicates that the originator of the Hello packet is an active router. If this bit is set to 0, the originator will not forward packets: for example, a multihomed host that wants to build an OSPF routing table without actually routing packets.
20	N	All routers within an NSSA must set this bit. In addition, the E bit must be set to 0 (see RFC 3101).
21	MC	Multicast capability, as defined in RFC 1584.
22	E	External-routes capability of the router. All members of an area must agree on the external capability. In a stub area, all routers must set this bit to 0 to achieve adjacency. The E bit is meaningful only in Hello packets (similar to the N bit).
23	V6	Indicates that the router supports OSPF for IPv6. If set to 0, this router/link should be excluded from IPv6 routing calculation.

Table B-19 shows possible link state types. The LS type is represented in hexadecimal notation to reflect the flooding scope.

Table B-19. Link state (LS) types

LS type	Name	Flooding scope	Advertised by	Link State ID
0x2001	Router-LSA	Area	Each router	Router ID
0x2002	Network-LSA	Area	DR	DR's Interface ID of the transit link

Table B-19. Link state (LS) types (continued)

LS type	Name	Flooding scope	Advertised by	Link State ID
0x2003	Inter-Area-Prefix-LSA	Area	ABR	A locally unique ID set by ABR
0x2004	Inter-Area-Router-LSA	Area	ABR	A locally unique ID set by ABR
0x4005	AS-External-LSA	AS	ASBR	A locally unique ID set by ASBR
0x2006	Group-Membership-LSA	Area	See RFC 1584	See RFC 1584
0x2007	Type-7-LSA	Area	See RFC 3101	See RFC 3101
0x0008	Link-LSA	Link	Each router for each link	Locally unique Interface ID
0x2009	Intra-Area-Prefix-LSA	Area	Each router	A locally unique ID set by router

The Flags field indicates the special function of the router originating the LSA. Table B-20 shows the possible values and their corresponding functions

Table B-20. Flags in Router-LSA

Bit	Name
W bit	The router is a wildcard multicast receiver. See RFC 1584 for more information.
V bit	The router is the endpoint of a virtual link using this area as a transit area.
E bit	The router is an ASBR.
B bit	The router is an ABR.

The link types shown in Table B-21 describe the possible link types of an interface in a Router-LSA.

Table B-21. Link type supported in a Router-LSA

Link type	Name	Neighbor Interface ID	Neighbor Router ID
1	Point-to-point	Interface ID of the neighbor on the other end of the point-to-point link	Router-ID of the neighbor on the other end of the point-to-point link
2	Transit	Interface ID of the DR on this link	Router ID of the DR on this link
3	Reserved	N/A	N/A
4	Virtual	Interface ID of the neighbor on the other end of the virtual link	Router ID of the neighbor on the other end of the virtual link

Table 2-22 explains the prefix options starting with the leftmost bit in an Inter-Area-Prefix-LSA.

Table 2-22. Prefix options starting with the leftmost bit

Bit	Name	Description
0–3	Reserved	N/A
4	P bit	Propagate bit: if set, the NSSA ABR readvertises the prefix into the backbone. Used only in Type-7-LSA.

Table 2-22. Prefix options starting with the leftmost bit (continued)

Bit	Name	Description
5	MC bit	Multicast bit: if set, the prefix should be included in IPv6 multicast routing calculations.
6	LA bit	Local address bit: if set, the prefix is actually a local IPv6 address of the originating router.
7	NU bit	No unicast bit: if set, the prefix should be excluded from IPv6 unicast calculation.

BGP-4 Message Types and Parameters (Chapter 8)

Table B-23 explains the possible BGP message types in BGP message Header.

Table B-23. BGP message types

Type	Name	Description
1	OPEN	Initializes BGP connection and negotiates session parameters
2	UPDATE	Exchanges feasible and withdrawn BGP routes
3	NOTIFICATION	Reports errors or terminates BGP connections
4	KEEPALIVE	Keeps the BGP connection from expiring

At the moment, two optional parameters are specified in an OPEN message, as explained in Table B-24. The optional parameter BGP Capability is very important for IPv6 support.

Table B-24. Optional parameters

Type	Name	Description
1	Authentication	The parameter consists of two fields: Authentication Code and Authentication Data. The Authentication Code defines the authentication mechanism used and how the marker and authentication data fields are to be computed.
2	BGP Capability	The parameter consists of one or more <Code, Length, Value> triplets identifying different BGP Capabilities. It is defined in RFC 3392. The capability parameter may appear more than once in the OPEN message. The Capability Code set to 1 indicates the Multiprotocol Extension Capability as defined in RFC 2858.

Table B-25 lists and explains some of the most common attributes. Detailed explanations should be taken directly from RFC 1771 or any RFC extending BGP (e.g., BGP Route Reflection defines attribute types 9 and 10).

Table B-25. BGP attributes

Type	Name/flags	Description
1	ORIGIN (well-known)	Defines the original source of this route. 0=IGP, 1=EGP, 2=Incomplete
2	AS_PATH (well-known)	A sequence of AS numbers that this route has crossed during its update. The rightmost AS number defines the originating AS. Each AS crossed is prepended. Prevents loops and can be used for policies.

Type	Name/flags	Description
3	NEXT_HOP (well-known)	Specifies the next hop's IPv4 address. Cannot be used for IPv6.
4	MED (optional nontransitive)	The MULTI_EXIT_DISC (MED) indicates a desired preference (4-byte) of the route to the peer—the lower the better. Designed for multiple EBGP connections between two ASes to load-share inbound traffic.
5	LOCAL_PREF (well-known)	Defines a local preference (4 byte) of the route. The higher the better. It is usually calculated on routes arriving from external peers and preserved to internal peers. Designed for multiple EBGP connections to any AS to manage outbound traffic.
6	ATOMIC_AGGREGATE (well-known)	Specifies that one of the routers has selected the less-specific route over a more-specific route.
7	AGGREGATOR (optional transitive)	The BGP Identifier of the router that aggregated routes into this route.
8	COMMUNITY (optional transitive)	Carries a 4-byte informational tag. Can be used by the route selection process. Defined in RFC 1997.
14	MP_REACH_NLRI (optional nontransitive)	Advertises multiprotocol NLRI. Used for IPv6 prefixes. See "BGP Multiprotocol Extension for IPv6."
15	MP_UNREACH_NLRI (optional nontransitive)	Withdraws multiprotocol NLRI. Used for IPv6 prefixes. See "BGP Multiprotocol Extension for IPv6."

DHCPv6 and Multicast Addresses for SLP over IPv6 (Chapter 9)

The DHCPv6 messages types shown in Table B-26 have been specified in RFC 3315.

Table B-26. DHCPv6 message types

Message type	Description
SOLICIT (1)	Used by clients to locate DHCP servers.
ADVERTISE (2)	Used by servers as a response to Solicit.
REQUEST (3)	Used by clients to get information from servers.
CONFIRM (4)	Used by clients to verify that their address and configuration parameters are still valid for their link.
RENEW (5)	Used by clients to extend the lifetime of their IP address and renew their configuration parameters with their original DHCP server when their lease is about to expire.
REBIND (6)	Used by clients to extend the lifetime of their address(es) and renew their configuration parameters with any DHCP server when their lease is about to expire and they have not received a reply to their Renew message.
REPLY (7)	Used by DHCP servers to respond to Solicit messages with a Rapid Commit Option, as well as to Request, Renew, and Rebind messages. A Reply to an Information Request message contains only configuration parameters, but no IP address. A Reply to a Confirm message contains a confirmation that the client's IP address(es) are still valid for the link (or a decline). A server sends a Reply as an acknowledgment for a Release or Decline message.

Table B-26. DHCPv6 message types (continued)

Message type	Description
RELEASE (8)	Used by clients to release their IP address. The message is sent to the server, from which the address was received.
DECLINE (9)	Used by clients to indicate to the server that one or more addresses assigned to them are already in use on the link. This is determined by the client through Duplicate Address Detection (DAD).
RECONFIGURE (10)	Used by DHCP servers to inform clients that the server has new or updated configuration information. The clients then must initiate a Renew or Information Request message in order to obtain the updated information.
INFORMATION REQUEST (11)	Sent by clients to request additional configuration parameters (without IP address information).
RELAY-FORW (12)	Used by DHCP relays to forward client messages to servers. The relay encapsulates the client message in an option in the Relay Forward message. The message can be sent directly to a DHCP server or via other relay agents. If a DHCP message is relayed multiple times, it is encapsulated multiple times.
RELAY-REPL (13)	Used by DHCP servers to send messages to clients through a relay. The client message is encapsulated as an option in the Relay Reply message. The relay decapsulates the message and forwards it to the client. The Relay Reply message takes the same path back through which the Relay Forward message traveled and may therefore also be encapsulated multiple times if there is more than one relay agent on the path.

Table 2-27 shows an overview of possible DHCP options defined in RFC 3315.

Table 2-27. DHCP options

Option	Value	Description
Client Identifier	1	Used for the client DUID. A DUID is a unique identifier (described later in this chapter).
Server Identifier	2	Used for the server DUID.
Identity Association for Nontemporary Addresses (IA_NA)	3	Used to indicate the IA_NA, the parameters, and the nontemporary addresses associated with it.
Identity Association for Temporary Adresses (IA_TA)	4	Used to indicate the IA_TA, the parameters, and the temporary addresses associated to it. All addresses contained in this option are used as temporary addresses by the client (according to RFC 3041 on Privacy Extensions for Stateless Address Autoconfiguration).
IA Address	5	Used to indicate the addresses associated with an IA_NA or IA_TA.
Option Request	6	Used in a message between client and server to identify a list of options. Can be contained in a Request, Renew, Rebind, Confirm, or Information Request message. The server can use this option in a Reconfigure message to indicate which options have been changed or added.
Preference	7	Sent by the server to influence the choice of a client for a DHCP server.
Elapsed Time	8	Contains the time when the client started the DHCP transaction. Indicated in hundredths of a second. In the first message sent by a client it is set to 0. Can be used by a secondary DHCP server to detect whether a primary server responds in time.
Relay Message	9	Contains the original message in a Relay Forward or Relay Reply message (remember that the original message is encapsulated in a Relay Forward or Reply message).

Table 2-27. DHCP options (continued)

Option	Value	Description
Authentication	11	Contains information to authenticate the identity and the content of DHCP messages.
Server Unicast	12	The server sends this option to the client to indicate that unicast can be used for communication. The option contains the IP address of the DHCP server, which is to be used by the client.

Table B-28 lists the multicast addresses that have been defined for SLP over IPv6.

Table B-28. Multicast addresses for SLP over IPv6

Multicast address	Description
FF0X:0:0:0:0:0:0:116	Service Agent (SA), used for Service Type and Attribute Request Messages.
FF0X:0:0:0:0:0:0:123	Directory Agent (DA), used by User Agents (UAs) and SAs to discover DAs. Also used by DA for sending unsolicited DA Advertisement messages.
FF0X:0:0:0:0:0:1:1000 to FF0X:0:0:0:0:0:1:13FF	Service Location, used by SAs to join the groups that correspond to the Service Types of the services they advertise. The Service Type string is used to determine the corresponding value in the 1000 to 13FF range, which has been assigned by IANA for this purpose. For an explanation of the algorithm used to calculate the group ID, refer to RFC 3111.

The X in FF0X is the placeholder for the multicast scope to be used for this group ID. For instance, 2 is link-local scope and 5 is site-local scope.

Mobile IPv6 (Chapter 11, RFC 3775)

The Mobility Header Type field identifies the type of Mobility message. Table B-29 is an overview of the Mobility messages.

Table B-29. Mobility message types

Value	Message type	Description
0	Binding Refresh Request	Sent by CN requesting the MN to update its binding.
1	Home Test Init	Sent by the MN to initiate the Return Routability Procedure and request a Home Keygen token from a CN. Sent to the CN through the tunnel via HA.
2	Care-of Test Init	Sent by the MN to initiate the Return Routability Procedure and request a Keygen token from a CN. Sent to the CN directly.
3	Home Test Message	Response to a Home Test Init message (type 1). Sent from the CN to MN. Contains a cookie and a Home Keygen token for the authorization in the Return Routability Process. Sent through the tunnel via HA.
4	Care-of Test Message	Response to Care-of Test Init message (type 2). Sent from CN to MN. Contains cookie and a Care-of Keygen token for the authorization in the Return Routability Procedure. Sent to the MN directly.
5	Binding Update	Sent by MN to notify a change of its care-of address. This message is explained in more detail later in the chapter.

Table B-29. Mobility message types (continued)

Value	Message type	Description
6	Binding Ack	Sent as acknowledgement for receipt of a Binding Update message. This message is explained in more detail later in the chapter.
7	Binding Error	Sent by CN to signal an error related to mobility, such as an inappropriate attempt to use the Home Address destination option without an existing binding. The status field can have the following values: 1 = unkown binding for Home Address Destination option 2 = unrecognized MH type value
8	Fast Binding Update	Identical to binding update message, only with slightly different processing rules.
9	Fast Binding Ack	Sent as acknowledgement for receipt of a Fast Binding Update message.
10	Fast Neighbor Advertisement	Sent by mobile node to announce itself to its new access router.

Values 8, 9, and 10 have been assigned in RFC 4068 "Fast Handovers for Mobile IPv6." Find all message and option types as well as status codes at *http://www.iana. org/assignments/mobility-parameters*.

Table B-30 shows the status values of the Binding Update. Values in the range of 0 to 127 indicate that the Binding Update has been accepted. Values above 128 indicate that the Binding Update has not been accepted.

Table B-30. Status values in the Binding Acknowledgement

Value	Description	Defined in
0	Binding Update accepted	RFC 3775
1	Accepted but prefix discovery necessary	RFC 3775
128	Reason unspecified	RFC 3775
129	Administratively prohibited	RFC 3775
130	Insufficient resources	RFC 3775
131	Home Registration not supported	RFC 3775
132	Not home subnet	RFC 3775
133	Not home agent for this mobile node	RFC 3775
134	Duplicate Address Detection failed	RFC 3775
135	Sequence number out of window	RFC 3775
136	Expired home nonce index	RFC 3775
137	Expired care-of nonce index	RFC 3775
138	Expired nonces	RFC 3775
139	Registration type change disallowed	RFC 3775
140	Mobile Router Operation not permitted	RFC 3963
141	Invalid Prefix	RFC 3963
142	Not Authorized for Prefix	RFC 3963

Table B-30. Status values in the Binding Acknowledgement (continued)

Value	Description	Defined in
143	Forwarding Setup failed	RFC 3963
144	MIPV6-ID-MISMATCH	RFC 4285
145	MIPV6-MESG-ID-REQD	RFC 4285
146	MIPV6-AUTH-FAIL	RFC 4285

Table B-31 shows an overview of the currently defined options for mobility messages.

Table B-31. Mobility options

Value Length	Name	Description	Defined in
Type 0	Pad1	Used to insert one padding Byte. This option has a special format; it contains only a type field, and no fields for length and data.	RFC 3775
Type 1	PadN	Used to insert two or more padding Bytes.	RFC 3775
Type 2 Length 2	Binding Refresh Advice	Indicates the remaining time until the MN should send a new home registration to HA. Only valid in Binding Acks sent from the HA in response to a home registration. The interval must be shorter than the lifetime value in the Binding Acknowledgement. A time unit is four seconds.	RFC 3775
Type 3 Length 16	Alternate Care-of address	Contains an address to use as the care-of address for the binding rather than using the Source address of the packet as the care-of address. Only in Binding Update messages.	RFC 3775
Type 4 Length 4	Nonce Indices	Has two additional fields besides the Type and Length field. The Home Nonce Index field tells the CN which nonce value to use when producing the Home Keygen Token. The Care-of Nonce field indicates the value for generating the Care-of Keygen Token. Valid only in the Binding Update message sent to a CN, and only when present together with a Binding Authorization Data option.	RFC 3775
Type 5 Length variable	Binding Authorization Data	Contains a cryptographic value that can be used to determine that the message in question comes from the right authority. Rules for calculating this value depend on the authorization procedure used. Must always be the last option in the MH. Only valid in Binding Update and Binding Acknowledgement. Used for the Return Routability process. In this case, the calculation of the Authenticator value is based on care-of address of MN, IPv6 address of CN, and data from the MH.	RFC 3775
Type 6	Mobile Network Prefix Option	Included in the Binding Update to indicate the prefix information for the Mobile Network to the HA.	RFC 3963
Type 7	Mobility Header Link-Layer Address option	Link-layer address option carried in an MH; used for Fast Handovers.	RFC 4068
Type 8	MN-ID-OPTION-TYPE	Optional suboption in the MH to specify the type of identifier used to identify the MN.	RFC 4283

Table B-31. Mobility options (continued)

Value Length	Name	Description	Defined in
Type 9	AUTH-OPTION-TYPE	When receiving a binding update, the HA must check the timestamp field. If it is invalid, it replies with a binding acknowledgment including this status code.	RFC 4285
Type 10	MESG-ID-OPTION-TYPE	Defines the type of mobility option.	RFC 4285
Type 201 Length 16	Home Address	Contains the home address of MN. Sent by MN when away from home to indicate its home address to the receiver. Carried in a Destination Options header. Must be inserted after Routing header and before Fragment, AH, or ESP header (if present).	RFC 3775

APPENDIX C
Recommended Reading

This appendix provides a list of books that I recommend.

- *Mobile IPv6*, by Hesham Soliman (Addison Wesley)
- *IPv6 Network Administration,* by David Malone and Niall Richard Murphy (O'Reilly)
- *DNS and BIND*, by Paul Albitz and Cricket Liu (O'Reilly)
- *Novell's Guide to Troubleshooting TCP/IP*, by Silvia Hagen and Stephanie Lewis (John Wiley & Sons)
- *SSH—The Secure Shell: The Definitive Guide*, Second Edition, by Daniel J. Barrett, Richard E. Silverman and Robert G. Byrnes (O'Reilly)
- *Ethernet: The Definitive Guide*, by Charles E. Spurgeon (O'Reilly)
- *Guide to Service Location Protocol*, by Silvia Hagen (*podbooks.com*)
- *Internetworking with TCP/IP: Principles, Protocols and Architectures*, by Douglas E. Comer (Prentice Hall)
- *Novell's Guide to LAN/WAN Analysis*, by Laura A. Chappell (Wiley)
- *Routing in the Internet*, by Christian Huitema (Prentice Hall)
- *The Biology of Transcendence: A Blueprint of the Human Spirit*, by Joseph Chilton Pearce (Park Street Press)

Index

We'd like to hear your suggestions for improving our indexes. Send email to *index@oreilly.com*.

About the Author

Silvia Hagen has been in the networking industry since 1990. She began her career as a successful instructor, and has trained hundreds of system engineers. Today she is CEO of Sunny Connection AG in Switzerland and works as a professional consultant and analyst for many mid- and large-sized companies. Her expertise is in identity management and protocol analysis. She loves technologies that create frameworks for collaboration. She is the author of a number of successful books, develops workshops, and presents internationally on various networking topics for Cisco Conferences, Burton Catalyst Conferences, Novell's Brainshare, and NetWare Users International Conferences. She also offers customized corporate presentations. She is a founding member of the Swiss IPv6 Task Force.

Colophon

The animal on the cover of *IPv6 Essentials*, Second Edition, is a rigatella snail. The rigatella snail (*Eobania vermiculata*) is native to the Mediterranean region, especially to Turkey and Crete. The snail lives in gardens, hedges, and dunes, where it feeds on vegetation. The snail got its scientific name because the rings on its shell resemble vermicelli (a type of pasta). It is also sometimes called the "noodle snail."

Rigatella snails commonly have about five brown rings on their cream-colored shells. Their eyes sit on stalks, or tentacles, which protrude from their heads. The snails are 17 to 21 millimeters high and 20 to 25 millimeters wide. They move by rhythmically contracting their muscular base, or foot. As they move, the snails secrete a colorless discharge that creates a type of carpet, which protects them from the surfaces on which they travel. This discharge is so effective that a snail could crawl along the blade of a razor and not be cut.

Rigatella snails are edible. They are one of the most popular types of snail used to make the European delicacy, escargot.

The cover image is a 19th-century engraving from *Cuvier's Animals*. The cover font is Adobe ITC Garamond. The text font is Linotype Birka; the heading font is Adobe Myriad Condensed; and the code font is LucasFont's TheSans Mono Condensed.

Better than e-books

Buy *IPv6 Essentials*, 2nd Edition, and access
the digital edition FREE on Safari for 45 days.

Go to www.oreilly.com/go/safarienabled
and type in coupon code NNGK-26PF-YV3A-5FF3-RXN1

Search
thousands of
top tech books

Download
whole chapters

Cut and Paste
code examples

Find
answers fast

Search Safari! The premier electronic reference
library for programmers and IT professionals.

Related Titles from O'Reilly

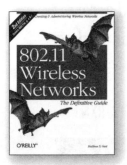

Networking

802.11 Wireless Networks: The Definitive Guide, *2nd Edition*

Asterisk: The Future of Telephony

Cisco Cookbook

Cisco IOS Access Lists

Cisco IOS in a Nutshell, *2nd Edition*

DNS & BIND Cookbook

DNS & BIND, 4th Edition

Essential SNMP, *2nd Edition*

Exchange Server Cookbook

IP Routing

IPv6 Essentials

IPv6 Network Administration

LDAP System Administration

Managing NFS and NIS, *2nd Edition*

Network Troubleshooting Tools

RADIUS

sendmail, *3rd Edition*

sendmail Cookbook

SpamAssassin

Switching to VoIP

TCP/IP Network Administration, *3rd Edition*

Unix Backup and Recovery

Using Samba, *2nd Edition*

Using SANs and NAS

VoIP Hacks

Time Management for System Administrators

Windows Server 2003 Network Administration

Wireless Hacks, *2nd Edition*

Zero Configuration Networking: The Definitive Guide